COPYRIGHT AND THE COURT OF JUSTICE
OF THE EUROPEAN UNION

Copyright and the Court of Justice of the European Union

ELEONORA ROSATI

OXFORD
UNIVERSITY PRESS

OXFORD
UNIVERSITY PRESS

Great Clarendon Street, Oxford, OX2 6DP,
United Kingdom

Oxford University Press is a department of the University of Oxford.
It furthers the University's objective of excellence in research, scholarship,
and education by publishing worldwide. Oxford is a registered trade mark of
Oxford University Press in the UK and in certain other countries

© Eleonora Rosati 2019

First Edition published in 2019

Published in the United States of America by Oxford University Press
198 Madison Avenue, New York, NY 10016, United States of America

British Library Cataloguing in Publication Data
Data available

Library of Congress Control Number: 2018957196

ISBN 978–0–19–883717–6

With a foreword by Maciej Szpunar, First Advocate General at the Court of Justice of the European Union

Foreword by Maciej Szpunar (First Advocate General at the Court of Justice of the European Union)

The field of copyright law has witnessed important developments in recent years, emerging from the advent of Internet services and digital media. While the need to ensure a high level of protection for copyright and related rights has guided EU harmonization efforts, defining the scope of those rights has become an increasingly complex endeavour.

As the title of this book suggests, the Court of Justice has played an active role in shaping the discourse of copyright law at the EU level. Professor Rosati thoughtfully examines the current framework of relevant EU Directives (e.g., the InfoSoc Directive and Enforcement Directive) and international instruments (e.g., the Berne Convention) through the lens of Court of Justice judgments and AG opinions.

The European judiciary has in recent years been tasked with deciding a number of interesting copyright-related questions perhaps not contemplated by the EU legislature at the time of drafting, from cloud-based recording platforms and linking to peer-to-peer ('P2P') networks and file-sharing. Through thought-provoking discussions of landmark decisions, Professor Rosati aptly underscores how technological advancements are, in a number of areas, outpacing the legislative process. Judicial interpretations of legal acts must therefore adapt and respond to new markets and behaviours, a phenomenon Professor Rosati refers to as 'dynamism.'

The Court of Justice applied this evolutionary approach in interpreting the EU Directive on Rental and Lending Rights in *Vereniging Openbare Bibliotheken*. In that decision, the Court found that the concept of 'lending' provided for in the Directive covers temporary digital copies of electronic books made accessible to the public by libraries. This is just one of the many examples Professor Rosati introduces to illustrate the importance of considering the underlying context and objectives sought by certain provisions in EU copyright law.

I should note that there are a number of novel copyright issues beyond the technology sphere, but certainly of no less importance from a legal and cultural standpoint. Professor Rosati's discussion of *Levola Hengelo* and the Opinion of my esteemed colleague AG Wathelet are a fine example. Through a referral for a preliminary ruling from the Netherlands, the Court of Justice was presented with the question of whether EU law should be interpreted to extend 'sensory copyright' protection to the taste of a particular cheese. At the time this book is headed to print, the question of whether or not the taste of a cheese is entitled to copyright protection as a 'work' within the meaning of the InfoSoc Directive has yet to be decided. Nonetheless, it is clear that much remains to be done in terms of harmonising the EU notion of 'protectable work' and the varied protections provided for under differing national systems.

As Professor Rosati correctly points out, the need to strike a fair balance between the competing interests of rights holders, third parties, and the public at large will continue to present great challenges to copyright protection at the EU level. In recent decisions, the Court of Justice has assessed the scope of copyright protection in light of the fundamental rights enshrined in the EU Charter of Fundamental Rights and the principle of proportionality. As the decisions in *UPC Telekabel, SENA,* and *Promusicae* demonstrate, Member States bear the obligation of transposing and interpreting Directives in a manner consistent with fundamental rights such as the freedom of information and expression, though the fair balance assessment is rarely a straightforward one. Several cases concerning the same issue are currently pending before the Court, which I believe will provide further guidelines concerning the fair balance between fundamental rights and copyright protection.

This extremely profound analysis by Professor Rosati of EU copyright protection and relevant Court of Justice decisions constitutes uncharted territory, unveiling new information, perhaps never considered, even by members of the Court like myself. Professor Rosati's book addresses, from an original and forward-thinking perspective, some of the most complex, challenging, and pressing aspects of the EU copyright framework. I am certain that the book will contribute to an awareness of the many challenges facing copyright protection, both on the EU and global level, as well as the importance of EU law and the Court of Justice.

Maciej Szpunar
First Advocate General at the Court of Justice of the European Union

Acknowledgements

I discovered copyright by pure chance, when I was an undergraduate law student at the University of Florence (Italy).

It was love at first sight.

Since then, I have had the privilege of meeting and working with some of the most brilliant academics and professionals in the field of copyright. Above all, I am grateful for the opportunities that they have afforded me to learn, as well as their friendship over the years. I will never be able to thank enough Sir Richard Arnold, Lionel Bently, Bill Patry, and Jeremy Phillips for all their help, support, and guidance.

Now, this book. EU copyright law has been my main interest for some time. I have tried to follow closely the cases referred to and decided by the Court of Justice of the European Union (CJEU). As I shall explain in more detail, this is not a book about EU copyright, but it is rather about the CJEU *and* EU copyright.

I wish to thank my brother, Carlo Maria Rosati, MD, currently a cardiothoracic surgery fellow at the University of Michigan in Ann Arbor, MI (USA), for working with me on the idea of applying the statistical methods used in medical research to copyright law. Together, we developed a Data-Based Case Law (DBCL, to be pronounced like 'debacle': /deɪˈbɑːk(ə)l/ … *nomen omen*?). I enjoyed developing this project, and am thankful to Carlo for his dedication, patience, and time.

The book obviously builds upon a few years of conversations and exchanges. I would like to thank the following in particular for the discussions held and for their input, feedback, and criticisms: Alberto Bellan, Elena Blobel, Patrick Charnley, Jonathan Griffiths, Hugh Hansen, Sir Robin Jacob, Lenard Koschwitz, Tim Kuik, Ros Lynch, Cédric Manara, Probir Mehta, Simon Morrison, Massimiliano Mostardini, Lauri Rechardt, Julia Reda, Nicholas Saunders QC, Daniel Segoin, Jule Sigall, Sophie Stalla-Bourdillon, Robin Stout, and Kiaron Whitehead. I am also indebted to the students I have had the privilege of teaching and for whom I developed some of the study aid materials that I have also reproduced in the book. Huge thanks also go to the contributors and readers of The IPKat, without whom several of my ideas would have not been developed.

Last but not least, I would like to thank Advocate General Maciej Szpunar for accepting to write a foreword to this book. After reading his thought-provoking copyright Opinions, I first met him in person when he kindly accepted my invitation to speak at a copyright event I organized in London in early 2017, and even agreed to take a selfie together. We met again in Luxembourg, and on that occasion the selfie also included the Advocate General's *référendaires*, whose enthusiasm and work are very much appreciated.

There is no need to say that this work has been possible, not just because of the growing activity of the CJEU in the copyright field, but also and especially thanks to the constant, indefatigable, and enthusiastic support of my family, without which all this would have been much more difficult. The book is dedicated to them.

Eleonora Rosati
London, August 2018

Email: eleonora@e-lawnora.com
Website: http://www.elawnora.com/

Table of Contents

II. BEYOND THE LAW? A CJEU-MADE COPYRIGHT SYSTEM

List of Figures and Tables

List of Figures

List of Tables

Table of Case Law

Opinions of Advocates General of the Court of Justice of the European Union

EUROPEAN COURT OF HUMAN RIGHTS (ECtHR)

NATIONAL CASE LAW

Austria

Czech Republic

France

Germany

Greece

Italy

Table of International and EU Legislation

List of Abbreviations

1988 Green Paper	**Commission of the European Communities, *Green Paper on copyright and the challenge of technology—Copyright issues requiring immediate action*, COM (88) 172 final**
1991 Software Directive	Council Directive 91/250/EEC of 14 May 1991 on the legal protection of computer programs, OJ L 122, 17.05.1991, 42–46
1992 Rental and Lending Rights Directive	Council Directive 92/100/EEC of 19 November 1992 on rental right and lending right and on certain rights related to copyright in the field of intellectual property, OJ L 346, 27.11.1992, 61–66
1993 White Paper	European Commission, *White Paper on Growth, competitiveness, employment. The challenges and ways forward into the 21st century*, COM (93) 700
1995 Green Paper	European Commission, *Green Paper of 27 July 1995 on Copyright and Related Rights in the Information Society*, COM (95) 382 final
1996 Internet Treaties	WIPO Copyright Treaty and WIPO Performances and Phonograms Treaty
2008 Green Paper	Commission of the European Communities, *Green Paper on Copyright in the knowledge economy*, COM (2008) 466/3
AG/AGs	Advocate General/Advocates General
Berne Convention	Berne Convention for the Protection of Literary and Artistic Works, as last amended on 28 September 1979
Brussels I Regulation	Council Regulation (EC) No 44/2001 of 22 December 2000 on jurisdiction and the recognition and enforcement of judgments in civil and commercial matters, OJ L 12, 16.01.2001, 1-23
Brussels I Regulation recast	Regulation (EU) No 1215/2012 of the European Parliament and of the Council of 12 December 2012 on jurisdiction and the recognition and enforcement of judgments in civil and commercial matters, OJ L 351, 20.12.2012, 1-32
CDPA	Copyright, Designs and Patents Act 1988 (UK)
CJEU	Court of Justice of the European Union
Collective Rights Management Directive	Directive 2014/26/EU of the European Parliament and of the Council of 26 February 2014 on collective management of copyright and related rights and multi-territorial licensing of rights in musical works for online use in the internal market, OJ L 84, 20.03.2014, 72–98
Coreper	Comité des représentants permanents (Committee of permanent representatives)
CPI	Code de la propriété intellectuelle (France)
Database Directive	Directive 96/9/EC of the European Parliament and of the Council of 11 March 1996 on the legal protection of databases, OJ L 77, 27.03.1996, 20-28

DBCL	Data-Based Case Law
Design Directive	Directive 98/71/EC of the European Parliament and of the Council of 13 October 1998 on the legal protection of designs, OJ L 289, 28.10.1998, 28–35
Directive implementing the Marrakesh Treaty in the EU	Directive (EU) 2017/1564 of the European Parliament and of the Council of 13 September 2017 on certain permitted uses of certain works and other subject matter protected by copyright and related rights for the benefit of persons who are blind, visually impaired or otherwise print-disabled and amending Directive 2001/29/EC on the harmonisation of certain aspects of copyright and related rights in the information society, OJ L 242, 20.09.2017, 6-13
Directive on privacy and electronic communications	Directive 2002/58/EC of the European Parliament and of the Council of 12 July 2002 concerning the processing of personal data and the protection of privacy in the electronic communications sector, OJ L 201, 31.07.2002, 37-47
(Draft/Proposed) DSM Directive	Proposal for a Directive of the European Parliament and of the Council on copyright in the Digital Single Market, COM/2016/0593 final—2016/0280 (COD).
DSM	Digital Single Market
DSMS	Communication from the Commission to the European Parliament, the Council, the European Economic and Social Committee and the Committee of the Regions, A Digital Single Market Strategy for Europe, /* COM/2015/0192 final */
EC	European Community
EC Treaty	Treaty establishing the European Community (Consolidated version 2002), OJ C 325, 24.12.2002, 33–184
ECHR	European Convention for the Protection of Human Rights and Fundamental Freedoms
ECJ	European Court of Justice
E-commerce Directive	Directive 2000/31/EC of the European Parliament and of the Council of 8 June 2000 on certain legal aspects of information society services, in particular electronic commerce, in the Internal Market, OJ L 178, 17.07.2000, 1-16
ECtHR	European Court of Human Rights
EEA	European Economic Area
Enforcement Directive	Corrigendum to Directive 2004/48/EC of the European Parliament and of the Council of 29 April 2004 on the enforcement of intellectual property rights (OJ L 157, 30.04.2004), OJ L 195, 02.06.2004, 16-25
EU	European Union
EU Charter	Charter of Fundamental Rights of the European Union, C 364, 18.12.2000, 1-22
InfoSoc Directive	Directive 2001/29/EC of the European Parliament and of the Council of 22 May 2001 on the harmonisation of certain aspects of copyright and related rights in the information society, OJ L 167, 22.06.2001, 10–19

IPRED	Corrigendum to Directive 2004/48/EC of the European Parliament and of the Council of 29 April 2004 on the enforcement of intellectual property rights (OJ L 157, 30.04.2004), OJ L 195, 02.06.2004, 16–25
ISP/ISPs	Internet Service Provider/Internet Service Providers
Marrakesh Treaty	Marrakesh Treaty to Facilitate Access to Published Works for Persons Who Are Blind, Visually Impaired or Otherwise Print Disabled
Monti Report	M Monti, *A new strategy for the single market at the service of Europe's economy and society. Report to the President of the European Commission José Manuel Barroso*, 09.05.2010
OCSSP/OCSSPs	Online Content Sharing Service Provider/Online Content Sharing Service Providers
Orphan Works Directive	Directive 2012/28/EU of the European Parliament and of the Council of 25 October 2012 on certain permitted uses of orphan works, OJ L 299, 27.10.2012, 5-12
P2P	Peer-to-Peer
Performers and Sounds Recordings Term Directive	Directive 2011/77/EU of the European Parliament and of the Council of 27 September 2011 amending Directive 2006/116/EC on the term of protection of copyright and certain related rights, OJ L 265, 11.10.2011, 1-5
Portability Regulation	Regulation (EU) 2017/1128 of the European Parliament and of the Council of 14 June 2017 on cross-border portability of online content services in the internal market, OJ L 168, 30.06.2017, 1–11
Regulation implementing the Marrakesh Treaty in the EU	Regulation on the cross-border exchange between the Union and third countries of accessible format copies of certain works and other subject matter protected by copyright and related rights for the benefit of persons who are blind, visually impaired or otherwise print-disabled, OJ L 242, 20.09.2017, 1–5
Rental and Lending Rights Directive	Directive 2006/115/EC of the European Parliament and of the Council of 12 December 2006 on rental right and lending right and on certain rights related to copyright in the field of intellectual property (codified version), OJ L 376, 27.12.2006, 28–35
Resale Right Directive	Directive 2001/84/EC of the European Parliament and of the Council of 27 September 2001 on the resale right for the benefit of the author of an original work of art, OJ L 272, 13.10.2001, 32–36
Rome II Regulation	Regulation (EC) No 864/2007 of the European Parliament and of the Council of 11 July 2007 on the law applicable to non-contractual obligations (Rome II), OJ L 199, 31.07.2007, 40-49
Rules of Procedure	Rules of Procedure of the Court of Justice, OJ L 265, 29.09.2012, 1–42
Satellite and Cable Directive	Council Directive 93/83/EEC of 27 September 1993 on the coordination of certain rules concerning copyright and rights related to copyright applicable to satellite broadcasting and cable retransmission, OJ L 248, 06.10.1993, 15–21

SCA	Senior Courts Act 1981 (UK)
Services Directive	Directive 2006/123/EC of the European Parliament and of the Council of 12 December 2006 on services in the internal market, OJ L 376, 27.12.2006, 36–68
Single Market Act	Communication from the Commission to the European Parliament, the Council, the Economic and Social Committee and the Committee of the Regions, *Single Market Act—Twelve levers to boost growth and strengthen confidence—'Working together to create new growth'*, COM (2011) 206 final
Software Directive	Directive 2009/24/EC of the European Parliament and of the Council of 23 April 2009 on the legal protection of computer programs (codified version), OJ L 111, 05.05.2009, 16–22
Statute	TFEU, Protocol (No 3) on the Statute of the Court of Justice of the European Union
Term Directive	Directive 2006/116/EC of the European Parliament and of the Council of 12 December 2006 on the term of protection of copyright and certain related rights, OJ L 372, 27.12.2006, 12–18
TEU	Consolidated version of the Treaty on European Union, OJ C 326, 26.10.2012, 13–390
TFEU	Consolidated version of the Treaty on the Functioning of the European Union, OJ C 326, 26.10.2012, 47–390
Treaty of Lisbon	Treaty of Lisbon amending the Treaty on European Union and the Treaty establishing the European Community, signed at Lisbon, 13 December 2007, OJ C 306, 17.12.2007, 1–271
TRIPS	Agreement on Trade-Related Aspects of Intellectual Property Rights
UK	United Kingdom
UrhG	Urheberrechtsgesetz (Germany)
UUC	User-Uploaded Content
VAT Directive	Council Directive 2006/112/EC of 28 November 2006 on the common system of value added tax, OJ L 347, 1–118
WIPO	World Intellectual Property Organization

Introduction

Compared to other areas of intervention at the European Union (EU) level, copyright harmonization is a relatively recent phenomenon. Compared to other areas of intellectual property law, copyright harmonization has not been as complete as with other rights.

Yet, two phenomena may be observed: one the one hand, copyright policy and legislative initiatives have intensified over the past few years; on the other hand, the large number of references to the Court of Justice of the European Union (CJEU) has substantially shaped the EU copyright framework and, with it, also the copyright framework of individual EU Member States.

This contribution focuses on the CJEU, and seeks to understand its *role* and *action* in the area of copyright, also outlining whether the latter has been informed by any particular vision of what EU copyright should be like, and what the *legacy* of all this might be. To this end, the book contains an exclusive survey that covers twenty years of and nearly one hundred CJEU judgments in the area of copyright.

1. What This Book Is Not about

In order to achieve this objective, it is perhaps necessary to start by saying what this book is *not* about. As it will be promptly apparent to anyone who takes a quick look at the table of contents or goes through the various pages, this contribution is not meant to be a comprehensive guide to EU copyright law. In this sense, there are significant limitations to the scope of the analysis conducted. For instance, the book neither substantially tackles areas such as databases, software or collective rights management, nor does it significantly engage with the content of EU copyright directives other than Directive 2001/29[1] (InfoSoc Directive) and a few others. The book does not even contain a complete analysis of the legislation it is mostly focused on. For instance, there is no substantial discussion of technological protection measures (despite these being regulated in the InfoSoc Directive), nor is there a review of all the enforcement tools subject to Directive 2004/48[2] (Enforcement Directive).

Reasons for limitations—There are three reasons why this book has such notable gaps and why I embarked on this project. First, there are already excellent books on the market that provide a comprehensive guide to EU legislation in the field of copyright.[3] Second, over the past few years several authors have worked on specific

---

[1] Directive 2001/29/EC of the European Parliament and of the Council of 22 May 2001 on the harmonisation of certain aspects of copyright and related rights in the information society, OJ L 167, 22 June 2001, 10–19.

[2] Corrigendum to Directive 2004/48/EC of the European Parliament and of the Council of 29 April 2004 on the enforcement of intellectual property rights (OJ L 157, 30 April 2004), OJ L 195, 2 June 2004, 16–25.

[3] A compact, yet exhaustive, example is T Dreier and PB Hugenholtz (eds), *Concise European Copyright Law* (Wolters Kluwer:2016), 2nd edn.

areas of copyright, and have managed to make sense of legislation that is at times confusing and case law that has not always clarified things. In this sense, those seeking responses to particular aspects within specific areas of copyright would find what they are looking for in those works. The third reason is linked to consideration that the role of the CJEU in the area of copyright has become increasingly central over the past few years.

Such centrality is not just due to the increased workload, but also to the fact rulings have grown in their significance. The Court has pushed the boundaries of EU harmonization beyond the literal wording of provisions and—at times—even beyond the original intention of EU legislature. All this has happened fast. And when things happen fast, it is not always easy to make sense of them.

2. What This Book Is about

This book, despite all its limitations, seeks indeed to find a *fil rouge*, some sort of rationale, underlying CJEU action in the area of copyright. The goal is providing readers with a sense of direction of EU copyright case law. In order to achieve this, an attempt to 'tidy up' and rationalize the rulings issued so far is carried out.

It is essentially in light of this objective that the book is structured in three parts. The first part is about the *role* of the CJEU (well, everything in this book is about the CJEU, but this part is rather more about the CJEU as an EU institution). Following a discussion of the impact of CJEU interpretation of certain EU copyright provisions (notably their preemptive force on individual EU Member States' freedom), the second part is concerned with CJEU *action* (and *vision*) in respect of three key areas of copyright: the construction of economic rights, exceptions and limitations, and enforcement. The final part focuses on CJEU *legacy* as broadly intended.

Chapter 1—Following an overview of legislative harmonization, Chapter 1 discusses the composition, role, and functioning of the Court before moving on to provide some numbers regarding specific activity in the field of copyright. In relation to this, it presents data on: the composition of the Court in copyright cases with particular regard to the appointment of Judges-Rapporteur and Advocates General (AGs), the relationship between the Court and its Judges-Rapporteur, areas in which national courts have sought guidance from the CJEU, and data on EU Member States from which the relevant referrals have been made, interventions of individual EU Member States in copyright cases. Employment of statistical analysis has allowed consideration of a number of questions, including whether the Court tends to agree with the (non-binding) Opinion of the AG appointed in a certain case more or less often when the interpretation provided of a certain copyright provision is expansive or not (it does), and whether the background of the AG, in particular whether academic or non-academic, has had any relevance from a statistical standpoint (it has not).

Chapter 2—Chapter 2 proceeds to the identification of eleven key standards that the Court has consistently employed in its copyright case law, and the discussion of their nature and content. These standards include: high level of protection, autonomous concepts of EU law, effectiveness, proportionality, fair balance of different rights and interests, interpretation in light of international instruments, interpretation in light of wording and context of provisions, interpretation in light of objectives pursued by legislation at issue, interpretation in light of fundamental rights as granted by the

Charter of Fundamental Rights of the European Union[4] (EU Charter), preventive nature of economic rights, and strict interpretation of exceptions and limitations.

This chapter also conducts a statistical analysis of the selected rulings, with the aim of identifying relationships between these standards (considered in pairs), both in general and with particular regard to selected areas (economic rights, exceptions and limitations, and enforcement). The goal is to provide readers with an understanding of how different standards interact with each other.

Chapter 3—Part II begins with a chapter devoted to outlining a trend that, with increasing clarity, has been emerging at the level of CJEU case law: on the one hand, the harmonizing force of EU copyright law—especially as interpreted by the Court—is greater than what individual Member States' practices have suggested; on the other hand, and as a result of this, the freedom left to the various national legislatures (and courts) in areas harmonized by EU legislation is more limited than has been believed in the past. A discussion and application of the emerging doctrine of EU preemption is provided in relation to selected areas (economic rights and exceptions and limitations).

Chapter 4—Turning specifically to the discussion of economic rights, Chapter 4 attempts to show how the Court's application of certain standards discussed in Chapter 2 has resulted in common approaches—and overall broad scope—of the economic rights harmonized by the InfoSoc Directive, these being the rights of reproduction, communication/making available to the public, and distribution. This chapter also contains a discussion of the de facto harmonization of the originality requirement at the EU level and the understanding of 'work' under the InfoSoc Directive. With regard to the right of distribution, its exhaustion—especially with regard to the first lawful sale copies in digital format (digital exhaustion)—is also discussed.

Chapter 5—The analysis moves on to consider exceptions and limitations under the InfoSoc Directive. In particular, attention focuses on three areas—parody, quotation, and private copying—which serve to outline how the application of certain key standards—notably the one according to which concepts in EU directives that make no reference to the laws of individual EU Member States should be intended as autonomous concepts of EU law that must be given uniform application throughout the EU, strict interpretation of exceptions and limitations, but also effectiveness of exceptions and limitations and achieving a fair balance in the protection of contrasting rights—have allowed the creation of an EU system of exceptions and limitations. In this sense, the role of the Court has been pivotal in strengthening, at least in part, the admittedly weak harmonizing force of the InfoSoc Directive. This chapter also discusses the nature and function of the three-step test as found in Article 5(5) of that directive.

Chapter 6—Chapter 6 considers enforcement, showing how the legislative framework alone has limited relevance. What has been key to the creation of an EU enforcement framework has been—instead—the role of the Court, which is particularly visible in respect of injunctions against intermediaries, costs and damages, and international jurisdiction. Again, reliance on certain of the standards discussed in Chapter 2 has been decisive.

Chapter 7—Part III is devoted to assessing the legacy of CJEU case law. Chapter 7 discusses the impact on national copyright regimes, even beyond the wording of EU directives transposed into national legal systems. To this end, it focuses on the United

---

[4] Charter of Fundamental Rights of the European Union, C 364, 18 December 2000, 1–22.

Kingdom and, following a discussion of what immediate—default—changes the departure from the EU and the European Economic Area (EEA) would have (also with regard to issues of exhaustion), it explores to what extent CJEU case law has changed UK copyright law. EU decisions have had an impact in areas such as: copyright subsistence, subject matter categorization, primary/accessory liability, standard of infringement, exceptions and limitations, and enforcement (with particular regard to website-blocking jurisprudence). Overall, this chapter shows the legacy of CJEU case law, and how pervasive the impact of such case law is.

Chapter 8—The final chapter tackles recent initiatives for a reform of the EU copyright *acquis*. In particular, it focuses on a number of selected areas in the proposed Directive on copyright in the Digital Single Market[5] (draft DSM Directive), which need to be considered in light, not just of existing legislation, but also—and perhaps most importantly—existing case law of the CJEU. These areas are: the 'value gap' ('transfer of value') proposal, the press publishers' right, fair compensation for private copying, and licensing of out-of-commerce works. This part discusses whether and to what extent these initiatives may be regarded as a 'codification' of existing case law, or rather as a departure from it. Either way, the centrality of judicial interpretation of existing legislation is apparent also in the context of policy discourse.

3. Approach and Aim

Given the focus of this contribution, CJEU case law takes centre stage. As explained earlier, the selection of areas of discussion too has been undertaken based on the presence and relevance of CJEU decisions. The way in which case law has been selected is explained further in Chapter 1, Section 4. The selection is up-to-date as of the time when the manuscript was sent to print, ie August 2018.

Inclusion of national perspectives has occurred on a functional basis, without any ambition or expectation of completeness. They serve to illustrate how certain concepts included by the CJEU in its rulings have been interpreted and applied, and with what results, at the level of individual EU Member States. Discussion of UK copyright law has been included because of the forthcoming departure of this Member State from the EU and, possibly, also the EEA. However, some of the considerations explored in Chapter 7 are applicable *mutatis mutandis* to other EU Member States in order to consider the default effects that leaving the EU and EEA would have on their own copyright regimes.

Given the significantly fast pace at which EU copyright has been developing, any attempt to provide a 'still' image of what EU copyright law 'looks like' proves challenging. However, the hope is that readers will find this contribution helpful in pinpointing at least some of the dots that compose the increasingly crowded and complex picture that EU copyright law has been becoming.

---

[5] Proposal for a Directive of the European Parliament and of the Council on copyright in the Digital Single Market, COM/2016/0593 final—2016/0280 (COD).

PART I

EU HARMONIZATION AND THE FUNCTIONING OF THE CJEU

CJEU activity in the area of copyright has increased over time and, in parallel to it, so has the activism of the Court. Yet, the role of EU judiciary in the construction of the EU copyright architecture could not be understood if we did not frame it within the policy and legislative process of increasing EU harmonization in this field, which has occurred through the adoption of a number of directives and, to a more limited extent, regulations that have reduced the differences across the copyright laws of the various EU Member States.

Chapter 1, 'EU Copyright Harmonization and CJEU Role and Action', starts with an overview of the process of EU harmonization and then explains the structure, composition, and work of the Court, as well as the mechanism—references for a preliminary ruling—through which the CJEU has mostly been asked to consider copyright legislation. It concludes by providing data on selected aspects of CJEU activity, including areas of the cases referred to the Court, Member States of referring courts, intervention of EU Member States, Judges-Rapporteur, and AGs who have worked on copyright cases. It concludes with a statistical analysis aimed at determining whether and to what extent the Court has agreed with the relevant AGs in relation to expansive or non-expansive interpretations of relevant copyright provisions, the goal being to determine whether copyright case law shows a tendency towards an expansive approach to the scope of copyright protection.

Chapter 2, 'Standards Employed in Relevant Copyright Case Law', focuses on the standards that the Court has applied in its case law. It seeks to select and illustrate the content of the policies and principles that the CJEU has used to develop its own understanding of EU copyright directives. The analysis thus considers general and special standards, the former being standards that the Court has applied transversally to different areas of copyright and the latter being relevant to specific areas, for example, economic rights or exceptions and limitations. General standards include: the guarantee of a high level of protection; the need to interpret certain concepts as autonomous concepts of EU law; effectiveness; proportionality; the need for a fair balance of different rights and interests; the requirement to interpret provisions in relevant directives in light of their wording and context, as well as the objectives pursued by the directive in question; and the increasing reliance on an interpretation of relevant provisions in light of fundamental rights as also protected in the EU Charter. Special standards include the requirement of interpreting economic rights as having a preventive nature and exceptions and limitations strictly. The second part of this chapter contains a novel statistical analysis, that Carlo Maria Rosati, MD and I have called 'data-based case law' (DBCL) and serves to illustrate relations and correlations between the various standards employed in CJEU case law.

1

EU Copyright Harmonization and CJEU Role and Action

Introduction

The 'pillars' of the EU harmonization project—Over the past thirty years or so, copyright reform in Europe has been based on two 'pillars': harmonization at the EU level and modernization at the EU and national levels. Harmonization has been prompted by internal market concerns, but also by concerns regarding the overall competitiveness and appropriateness of the EU copyright regime. Similarly, individual EU Member States have undertaken copyright reforms that would render their systems better suited to accommodate technological change and also make them more attractive to investments.

The 1988 Green Paper—Policy discourse around EC harmonization of copyright laws began in the late 1970s.[1] Before any policy initiative was undertaken, it became apparent—also through litigation reaching the then European Court of Justice (ECJ)[2]—that copyright protection and differences in the laws of individual Member States had an internal market relevance. In its decision in *EMI Electrola*, C-341/87, for instance, the ECJ stressed how—problematically—EC law at the time was characterized by lack of harmonization or approximation of copyright legislations.[3]

The 1988 *Green Paper on copyright and the challenge of technology—Copyright issues requiring immediate action*[4] (1988 Green Paper) by the then Commission of the European Communities (now EU Commission) signals the start of a more concrete discourse around the role of copyright harmonization in light of the internal market objective. In that document the Commission noted how intervention at the then EC level should address four distinct 'general concerns'. The first concern was an internal market one: 'creators and providers of copyright goods and services should be able to treat the Community as a single internal market. This requires the elimination of obstacles and legal differences that substantially disrupt the functioning of the market by obstructing or distorting cross-frontier trade in those goods and services as well as distorting competition.'[5] The second concern related to the overall competitiveness of the EC economy in relation to its trading partners, notably in areas of potential growth at that time like media and information, and how such competitiveness could

---

[1] For instance, in 1978 Adolf Dietz published a study on copyright harmonization which he had prepared at the request of the then Commission of the European Communities: A Dietz, *Copyright Law in the European Community* (Sijthoff & Noordhoff:1978).

[2] *Coditel*, C-62/79, EU:C:1980:84; *Gema*, C-55/80, EU:C:1981:10; *Polydor*, C-270/80, EU:C:1982:43; *Cinéthèque*, C-60/84, EU:C:1985:329; *EMI Electrola*, C-341/87, EU:C:1989:30; *Warner Brothers and Metronome Video*, C-158/86, EU:C:1988:242; *Tournier*, C-395/87, EU:C:1989:319; *Phil Collins*, C-92/92, EU:C:1993:847.

[3] *EMI Electrola*, C-341/87, EU:C:1989:30, para 11.

[4] Commission of the European Communities, *Green Paper on copyright and the challenge of technology—Copyright issues requiring immediate action*, COM (88) 172 final.

[5] Ibid, §1.3.2.

be enhanced.[6] The third concern was linked to the need for effective enforcement of copyright: 'intellectual property resulting from creative effort and substantial investment within the Community should not be misappropriated by others outside its external frontiers. It should enjoy a fair return when exploited in non-Member States. This is frequently not the case.'[7] Finally, the Commission highlighted how any action at the EC level should strike a fair balance between different interests: not just those of the rightholders, but also those of third parties and the public at large.[8]

The EU copyright *acquis*—Since then, the EC first and, now, the EU have adopted a number of directives aimed at reducing or removing certain differences in the copyright laws of EU Member States, as well as a limited number of regulations that touch upon specific aspects of copyright law. Besides directives that are relevant to copyright and its enforcement—of which the Directive on certain legal aspects of information society services, in particular electronic commerce, in the Internal Market (E-commerce Directive)[9] deserves particular mention—the EU copyright *acquis* is composed of the following:

- Directive on the coordination of certain rules concerning copyright and rights related to copyright applicable to satellite broadcasting and cable retransmission[10] (Satellite and Cable Directive);

- Directive on the legal protection of databases[11] (Database Directive);

- Directive on the harmonisation of certain aspects of copyright and related rights in the information society (InfoSoc Directive);

- Directive on rental right and lending right and on certain rights related to copyright in the field of intellectual property[12] (Rental and Lending Rights Directive);

---

[6] Ibid, §1.3.3.   [7] Ibid, §1.3.4.   [8] Ibid, §§1.3.5–1.3.6.

[9] Directive 2000/31/EC of the European Parliament and of the Council of 8 June 2000 on certain legal aspects of information society services, in particular electronic commerce, in the Internal Market, OJ L 178, 17 July 2000, 1–16. Other relevant directives are: Council Directive 87/54/EEC of 16 December 1986 on the legal protection of topographies of semiconductor products, OJ L 24, 27 January 1987, 36–40; and Directive 98/84/EC of the European Parliament and of the Council of 20 November 1998 on the legal protection of services based on, or consisting of, conditional access, OJ L 320, 28 November 1998, 54–7.

[10] Council Directive 93/83/EEC of 27 September 1993 on the coordination of certain rules concerning copyright and rights related to copyright applicable to satellite broadcasting and cable retransmission, OJ L 248, 6 October 1993, 15–21. The directive is currently under review under the framework of the Digital Single Market Strategy (on which see further Chapter 8): Proposal for a Regulation of the European Parliament and of the Council laying down rules on the exercise of copyright and related rights applicable to certain online transmissions of broadcasting organisations and retransmissions of television and radio programmes, COM/2016/0594 final—2016/0284 (COD).

[11] Directive 96/9/EC of the European Parliament and of the Council of 11 March 1996 on the legal protection of databases, OJ L 77, 27 March 1996, 20–8. Over time, this directive has been subject to a series of evaluations by the EU Commission itself: see Commission of the European Communities, *DG Internal Market and Services Working Paper—First evaluation of Directive 96/9/EC on the legal protection of databases*, 12 December 2005; and European Commission, *Commission Staff Working Document—Evaluation of Directive 96/9 on the legal protection of databases*, SWD(2018) 146 final.

[12] Directive 2006/115/EC of the European Parliament and of the Council of 12 December 2006 on rental right and lending right and on certain rights related to copyright in the field of intellectual property (codified version), OJ L 376, 27 December 2006, 28–35. This directive repealed and replaced Council Directive 92/100/EEC of 19 November 1992 on rental right and lending right and on certain rights related to copyright in the field of intellectual property, OJ L 346, 27 November 1992, 61–6 (1992 Rental and Lending Rights Directive).

- Directive on the term of protection of copyright and certain related rights[13] (Term Directive);
- Directive on the resale right for the benefit of the author of an original work of art[14] (Resale Right Directive);
- Directive on the enforcement of intellectual property rights (Enforcement Directive or IPRED);
- Directive on the legal protection of computer programs[15] (Software Directive);
- Directive on the term of protection of copyright and certain related rights amending the previous 2006 Directive[16] (Performers and Sounds Recordings Term Directive);
- Directive on certain permitted uses of orphan works[17] (Orphan Works Directive);
- Directive on collective management of copyright and related rights and multi-territorial licensing of rights in musical works for online use in the internal market[18] (Collective Rights Management Directive);
- Directive on certain permitted uses of certain works and other subject matter protected by copyright and related rights for the benefit of persons who are blind, visually impaired or otherwise print-disabled[19] (Directive implementing the Marrakesh Treaty in the EU);
- Regulation on the cross-border exchange between the Union and third countries of accessible format copies of certain works and other subject matter protected by copyright and related rights for the benefit of persons who are blind, visually impaired or otherwise print-disabled[20] (Regulation implementing the Marrakesh Treaty in the EU);

---

[13] Directive 2006/116/EC of the European Parliament and of the Council of 12 December 2006 on the term of protection of copyright and certain related rights, OJ L 372, 27 December 2006, 12–18. This directive repealed and replaced Council Directive 93/98/EEC of 29 October 1993 harmonizing the term of protection of copyright and certain related rights, OJ L 290, 24 November 1993, 9–13.

[14] Directive 2001/84/EC of the European Parliament and of the Council of 27 September 2001 on the resale right for the benefit of the author of an original work of art, OJ L 272, 13 October 2001, 32–6.

[15] Directive 2009/24/EC of the European Parliament and of the Council of 23 April 2009 on the legal protection of computer programs (codified version), OJ L 111, 5 May 2009, 16–22. This directive repealed and replaced Council Directive 91/250/EEC of 14 May 1991 on the legal protection of computer programs, OJ L 122, 17 May 1991, 42–6 (1991 Software Directive).

[16] Directive 2011/77/EU of the European Parliament and of the Council of 27 September 2011 amending Directive 2006/116/EC on the term of protection of copyright and certain related rights, OJ L 265, 11 October 2011, 1–5.

[17] Directive 2012/28/EU of the European Parliament and of the Council of 25 October 2012 on certain permitted uses of orphan works, OJ L 299, 27 October 2012, 5–12.

[18] Directive 2014/26/EU of the European Parliament and of the Council of 26 February 2014 on collective management of copyright and related rights and multi-territorial licensing of rights in musical works for online use in the internal market, OJ L 84, 20 March 2014, 72–98.

[19] Directive (EU) 2017/1564 of the European Parliament and of the Council of 13 September 2017 on certain permitted uses of certain works and other subject matter protected by copyright and related rights for the benefit of persons who are blind, visually impaired or otherwise print-disabled and amending Directive 2001/29/EC on the harmonisation of certain aspects of copyright and related rights in the information society, OJ L 242, 20 September 2017, 6–13.

[20] Regulation (EU) 2017/1563 of the European Parliament and of the Council of 13 September 2017 on the cross-border exchange between the Union and third countries of accessible format copies of certain works and other subject matter protected by copyright and related rights for the benefit of persons who are blind, visually impaired or otherwise print-disabled, OJ L 242, 20 September 2017, 1–5.

- Regulation on cross-border portability of online content services in the internal market[21] (Portability Regulation).

Currently, the EU is working towards the adoption of a number of legislative instruments, proposed by the Commission under the umbrella of its 2015 Digital Single Market Strategy, including the draft DSM Directive, discussed more in detail in Chapter 8).

Europeanization of copyright laws—Overall, in the field of copyright the process of Europeanization of national laws has resulted in their rapprochement to and convergence with EU law:

This process has placed national courts and authorities in a novel situation. The 'law' they are obliged to apply in many fields is no longer purely national, but a mix of EU law and national law. The same has occurred in academic commentaries. Describing the valid law of the Member States, for example, in fields as diverse as competition, copyright, environment, VAT, immigration and asylum, and family law is no longer a purely domestic affair.[22]

1. The Legislative Basis

Copyright harmonization in an internal market perspective—EC/EU intervention in the area of copyright has been traditionally linked mostly—though not exclusively[23]—to internal market concerns, in the belief that certain differences in the laws of EU Member States would raise barriers to the free movement of goods and services based on or incorporating copyright works and other protected subject matter. The legislative basis for initiatives in this area of the law has thus been mostly what are currently the provisions contained in Articles 26 and 114 of the Treaty on the Functioning of the European Union[24] (TFEU).

Articles 26 and 114 TFEU—The former clarifies EU competence to adopt measures with the aim of establishing or ensuring the functioning of the internal market (which is defined at paragraph 2 thereof as comprising an area without internal frontiers in which the free movement of goods, persons, services, and capital is ensured), in accordance with the relevant provisions of the EU Treaties. The first paragraph of the latter stipulates that the European Parliament and the Council shall, acting in accordance with the ordinary legislative procedure and after consulting the Economic and Social Committee, adopt the measures for the approximation of the provisions laid

---

[21] Regulation (EU) 2017/1128 of the European Parliament and of the Council of 14 June 2017 on cross-border portability of online content services in the internal market, OJ L 168, 30 June 2017, 1–11. In 2018 the EU Commission sent a letter to competent national authorities expressing concerns that a number of service providers across the EU had applied portability in certain ways which might be contrary to the Regulation, and which might prevent consumers from enjoying this right (European Commission, *Letter to the attention of the competent national authorities on the application of Regulation (EU) 2017/1128*, 1 June 2018, available at <https://ec.europa.eu/digital-single-market/en/news/portability-regulation-letter-sent-competent-national-authorities> (last accessed 15 August 2018)).

[22] N Jääskinen, 'Europeanisation of national law: a legal-theoretical analysis' (2015) 40(5) EL Rev 667, 668.

[23] See A Kur and T Dreier, *European Intellectual Property Law— Text, Cases & Materials* (Edward Elgar:2013), 246–9; and the interesting study conducted by A Ramalho, 'Copyright law-making in the EU: what lies under the "internal market" mask?' (2014) 9(3) JIPLP 208.

[24] Consolidated version of the Treaty on the Functioning of the European Union, OJ C 326, 26 October 2012, 47–390.

down by law, regulation, or administrative action in Member States which have as their object the establishment and functioning of the internal market.

As has been correctly observed,[25] rooting EC/EU competence in the area of copyright within the internal market-building process has had the effect of not posing any particular limitations to the types of issues upon which the EC/EU could intervene. The result has been a heterogeneous set of initiatives supported by the overarching goal of ensuring the free movement of goods and services based on, or incorporating, copyright or other protected content. Overall, EU competence in the field of copyright based on Article 114 TFEU does not say much about how such competence is to be exercised, in that such provision has no specific normative content. Some commentators have stressed how all this might have the effect of making any harmonization programme greatly dependent on the discretion that Article 114 TFEU confers.[26] The picture would however be incomplete if one omitted to, at least, mention four additional aspects.

Considerations beyond internal market-building—The first is that realization of the internal market is not a goal per se and that the TFEU allows derogations from free movement rules. Article 36 TFEU, in fact, allows EU Member States to set prohibitions or restrictions on imports, exports, or goods in transit justified, inter alia, to protect industrial and commercial property, insofar as such prohibitions or restrictions do not constitute a means of arbitrary discrimination or a disguised restriction on trade between Member States. In addition, at the level of secondary sources, the freedom to provide services within Article 16 of the Directive on services in the internal market (Services Directive)[27] does not apply, among other things, to copyright and related rights. Striking an appropriate balance between the need to respect national property rules, on the one hand, and internal market and undistorted competition goals, on the other, has not always been easy. In any case, it is a task undertaken also by the ECJ/CJEU, at least since the seminal decision in *Deutsche Grammophon*, C-78/70.[28]

Other objectives underlying EU intervention—Besides internal market building objectives, other objectives have also supported EC/EU intervention in the area of copyright, including ensuring a high level of protection (this has been the case, inter alia, of the InfoSoc and Enforcement Directives) or favouring competitiveness of the EC/EU as a whole. The latter has been, for instance, the case of the Orphan Works Directive. An EU initiative in the area of orphan works was rooted within the idea that the need for it—especially in the print sector—followed consideration that while, in the USA, by virtue of the settlement achieved in 2008 with the Association of American Publishers (AAP) and the Authors Guild,[29] Google would have not required prior permission to make text-based orphan works available, in Europe it would have been difficult for it to develop its sophisticated fully indexed and searchable online library. This would have resulted in US universities, cultural institutions, and researchers having a competitive edge over their European counterparts in terms of access to

---

[25] T Georgopoulos, 'The legal foundation of European copyright law', in TE Synodinou (ed), *Codification of European Copyright Law. Challenges and Perspectives* (Kluwer Law International:2012), 34.

[26] A Ramalho, 'Conceptualising the European Union's competence in copyright—what can the EU do?' (2014) 45(2) IIC 178, 182.

[27] Directive 2006/123/EC of the European Parliament and of the Council of 12 December 2006 on services in the internal market, OJ L 376, 27 December 2006, 36–68.

[28] *Deutsche Grammophon*, C-78/70, EU:C:1971:59, para 11.

[29] Although the proposed settlement was preliminarily approved, the US District Court for the Southern District of New York rejected it in 2011 (*The Authors Guild et al v Google Inc*, 05 Civ 8136 (DC)).

information.[30] More recently, certain EU proposals have been rooted within fairness considerations: this has been, notably, the case of the proposed press publishers' right within Article 11 and the so-called 'value gap' proposal within Article 13 of the proposed DSM Directive (see further Chapter 8).

Subsidiarity and proportionality of EU action—As in all cases of shared competence, such as copyright and—more generally—intellectual property, legislative intervention must comply with the requirements of subsidiarity (Article 2(2) TFEU) and proportionality (Article 5 of the Treaty on European Union,[31] TEU). EU Member States may exercise their competence to the extent that the Union has not exercised its competence. The Member States shall exercise their competence again to the extent that the Union has decided to cease exercising its competence (the principle of EU preemption is discussed further in Chapter 3). In any case, action by the EU should not go beyond what is necessary to achieve the objectives of the EU Treaties.

The role of the EU Charter—There are other primary sources that inform copyright law-making, aside from those mentioned above. Yet these have not always been visible in the language of legislative proposals, but have been relied upon by the CJEU in its copyright case law with increasing frequency. Examples in this sense are the provisions of the EU Charter which, since the 2007 Treaty of Lisbon,[32] has had the status of primary source of EU law. Of particular relevance are the provisions concerning copyright protection within the right to property (Article 17(2)), freedom of expression/information (Article 11), and freedom to conduct a business (Article 16).

Article 118(1) TFEU and an EU copyright title—As a final point, it should be recalled that the Treaty of Lisbon introduced a provision, Article 118(1) TFEU, which could provide—though not necessarily without problems—the legal basis for a more ambitious harmonization than has been the case so far, including the establishment of an EU-wide copyright title.[33] This provision vests the European Parliament and the Council, when acting in accordance with the ordinary legislative procedure, with the power to establish measures for the creation of EU intellectual property rights to provide uniform protection of intellectual property rights throughout the EU and for the setting up of centralized Union-wide authorization, coordination, and supervision arrangements.

The creation of an EU-wide copyright title has been discussed for a long time. As early as 1998, in the context of the 1997 proposal of what would eventually become the InfoSoc Directive, Dietz wondered:

whether sooner or later we must arrive at a point where we should leave the process of step by step harmonisation behind and begin to start a more systematic approach, which would

---

[30] European Commission, *Commission Staff Working Paper Impact Assessment on the cross-border online access to orphan works accompanying the document 'Proposal for a directive of the European Parliament and of the Council on certain permitted uses of orphan works'* (24 May 2011) SEC(2011) 615 final, 7.

[31] Consolidated version of the Treaty on European Union, OJ C 326, 26 October 2012, 13–390.

[32] Article 6(1) of the Treaty of Lisbon amending the Treaty on European Union and the Treaty establishing the European Community, signed at Lisbon, 13 December 2007, OJ C 306, 17 December 2007, 1–271 states: 'The Union recognises the rights, freedoms and principles set out in the Charter of Fundamental Rights of the European Union of 7 December 2000, as adapted at Strasbourg, on 12 December 2007, which shall have the same legal value as the Treaties.'

[33] T Cook and E Derclaye, 'An EU Copyright Code: what and how, if ever?' (2011) 2011/3 IPQ 259, 261; F Gotzen, 'The European legislator's strategy in the field of copyright', in Synodinou (ed), *Codification of European Copyright Law* 51–2. See also A Strowel, 'Towards a European copyright law: four issues to consider', in I Stamatoudi and P Torremans (eds), *EU Copyright Law – A Commentary* (Edward Elgar:2014), §§21.04–21.08, outlining the obstacles to copyright unification.

eventually result in a *community copyright* in the same way as such a community right exists already in the trademark field and—*mutatis mutandis*—at least in draft form also in the patent field.[34]

Overall, greater harmonization, or even unification, of Member States' laws has been also linked to the objective of establishing a more modern framework. In his Opinion in *Amazon.com International Sales and Others*, C-521/11, AG Mengozzi noted that:

a large number of problems relating to the application of Directive 2001/29 arise from the insufficient level of harmonisation of copyright law within the Union ... [T]his demonstrates that although it is important to respect the ... legal traditions and views which exist in that regard in the Member States, for the purpose of developing a modern legal framework for copyright in Europe which, having regard to the various interests at stake, makes it possible to safeguard the existence of a genuine single market in that sector, by promoting creativity, innovation and the emergence of new business models, it is necessary to move towards pursuing a much greater level of harmonisation of national law than that attained by Directive 2001/29.[35]

For the moment, despite full harmonization having been considered at different levels (see further in Section 2) and also the attempt of the Wittem Group of academics to propose a model for an EU copyright code,[36] the creation of an EU-wide title (whether optional or not) is not a concrete option. In 2015 the EU Commission called unification of copyright laws a long-term target, but also highlighted the difficulties that such a project would face:

[t]he full harmonisation of copyright in the EU, in the form of a single copyright code and a single copyright title, would require substantial changes in the way our rules work today. Areas that have so far been left to the discretion of national legislators would have to be harmonised. Uniform application of the rules would call for a single copyright jurisdiction with its own tribunal, so that inconsistent case law does not lead to more fragmentation.

These complexities cannot be a reason to relinquish this vision as a long-term target. Notwithstanding the particularities of copyright and its link with national cultures, difficulties and long lead-times have also accompanied the creation of single titles and single rule-books in other areas of intellectual property, notably trademarks and patents, where they are now a reality.

The EU should pursue this vision for the very same reason it has given itself common copyright legislation: to build the EU's single market, a thriving European economy and a space where the diverse cultural, intellectual and scientific production of Europe travel across the EU as freely as possible.[37]

---

[34] A Dietz, 'The protection of intellectual property in the information age—the draft E.U. Copyright Directive of November 1997' (1998) 1998/4 IPQ 335, 336 (emphasis in the original).

[35] Opinion of Advocate General Paolo Mengozzi in *Amazon.com International Sales and Others*, C-521/11, EU:C:2013:145, para 6.

[36] Wittem Group, *The Wittem Project—European Copyright Code* (2010), available at <https://www.ivir.nl/publicaties/download/Wittem_European_copyright_code_21_april_2010.pdf> (last accessed 15 August 2018). For a discussion of a potential EU copyright code, see also T Chiou, 'Lifting the (dogmatic) barriers in intellectual property law: fragmentation v integration and the practicability of a European Copyright Code' (2015) 37(3) EIPR 138, 141–6.

[37] European Commission, Communication from the Commission to the European Parliament, the Council, the European Economic and Social Committee and the Committee of the Regions, *Towards a modern, more European copyright framework*, COM(2015) 626 final, §6.

2. EU Copyright Policy: From the Early Days to the Revamped Agenda of the Late 2010s

The first copyright directives—Following the release of the free movement-rooted 1988 Green Paper,[38] harmonization initiatives that would follow up on the agenda set forth therein were adopted. The first EC directives touched upon specific areas of copyright, by harmonizing the conditions of protection and resulting scope of protection for software (1991 Software Directive), rental right (1992 Rental and Lending Rights Directive), term (Council Directive 93/98), satellite and cable (Satellite and Cable Directive), and databases (Database Directive). In parallel with these ad hoc initiatives, the policy agenda gradually became more ambitious and increasingly stressed the relationship between copyright and the competitiveness of the then EC economic system as a whole.[39]

The policy discourse in the 1990s and the adoption of the InfoSoc Directive—In its 1995 *Green Paper on Copyright and Related Rights in the Information Society* (1995 Green Paper), which—rather than setting out an overall policy and approach to copyright harmonization—tackled specific issues,[40] the Commission referred to the need to deepen harmonization of Member States' copyright laws, considering that a wide variation in the level of protection of copyright works and other subject matter would likely create obstacles to the development of the information society (a term which was first used in the 1993 White Paper[41]) and negatively affect the functioning of the internal market.[42]

It was in the follow-up activity to the 1995 Green Paper that the seeds that would eventually lead to the adoption of the InfoSoc Directive in 2001 were sown. In its 1996 Communication,[43] in fact, the Commission identified four areas of priority for legislative action: the rights of reproduction, communication to the public, and distribution, and the legal protection of anti-copying systems. In that document the Commission also noted how an intervention of the then EC alone in these areas would be insufficient, and that impetus at the international level would be also necessary.

It was indeed in that year that the World Intellectual Property Organization (WIPO) Copyright Treaty and Performances and Phonograms Treaty were adopted (1996 Internet Treaties). These were signed by the EU Member States, as well as by the EC, which became thus committed to implementing the new international instruments

---

[38] See the analysis in H Cohen Jehoram, 'European copyright law—ever more horizontal' (2001) 32(5) IIC 532, 535–6.

[39] European Commission, *White Paper on Growth, competitiveness, employment. The challenges and ways forward into the 21st century*, COM (93) 700, Bulletin of the European Communities, Supplement 6/93, 100; European Commission, *Growth, competitiveness and employment. White Paper follow-up, Europe and the global information society. Recommendations of the high-level group on the information society to the Corfu European Council* (Bangemann Group), Bulletin of the European Union, Supplement 2/94, 21.

[40] The Green Paper was criticized for such an approach, with some considering it akin to a 'glorified questionnaire': see M Pullen, 'The Green Paper on copyright and related rights in the information society (is it all a question of binary numbers?)' (1996) 7(2) Ent L Rev 80, 80.

[41] European Commission, *White Paper on Growth, competitiveness, employment. The challenges and ways forward into the 21st century*, COM (93) 700, Bulletin of the European Communities, Supplement 6/93, 13.

[42] European Commission, *Green Paper of 27 July 1995 on Copyright and Related Rights in the Information Society*, COM (95) 382 final, 4.

[43] European Commission, Communication from the Commission, *Follow-up to the Green Paper on copyright and related rights in the information society*, COM (1996) 568 final.

and ensuring harmonized transpositions into EU Member States' laws. The proposal of what would eventually be the InfoSoc Directive was first issued in 1997.[44] The directive, however, only saw the light in 2001. This instrument remains the most ambitious EC/EU intervention in the area of copyright as of today, in that it sought to achieve a horizontal harmonization of economic rights, and related exceptions and limitations (the latter being an area that was not present in the Commission's documents issued prior to the proposal for and adoption of the InfoSoc Directive).

EU action *post* adoption of the InfoSoc Directive—After the InfoSoc Directive, the EU harmonization agenda lost momentum.[45] With the exception of the Enforcement Directive (which was adopted in 2004) and a Communication on collective rights management,[46] not much happened until the late 2000s. The 2004 Commission Staff Working Paper[47] was modest in both scope and result: it only recommended a minor adjustment to the definition of reproduction and an extension in the application of the exception for certain temporary acts of reproduction under Article 5(1) of the InfoSoc Directive to cover computer programs and databases. In 2004 the Commission was of the opinion that no further harmonization measures were necessary besides those already included in the *acquis*. This was, among other things, the case of the originality requirement and ownership of copyright, the definition of the term 'public', exhaustion, and moral rights.[48]

The 2008 *Green Paper on Copyright in the knowledge economy* [49] (2008 Green Paper), which sought to commence a debate on how knowledge for research, science, and education would be best disseminated in the online environment, was equally unambitious. While focusing, among other things, on exceptions and limitations that are most relevant for the dissemination of knowledge, including those for libraries and archives, teaching and research purposes, for the benefit of people with a disability, and discussing the possibility of introducing a specific user-generated content exception, this document did not lead to any substantial follow-up initiatives. This is apparent from the 2009 *Communication on Copyright in the knowledge economy*,[50]

---

[44] Proposal for a European Parliament and Council Directive on the harmonization of certain aspects of copyright and related rights in the Information Society, /* COM/97/0628 final—COD 97/0359 */. See also Amended proposal for a European Parliament and Council Directive on the harmonisation of certain aspects of copyright and related rights in the Information Society, /* COM/99/0250 final—COD 97/0359 */.

[45] For a discussion of the reasons, see PB Hugenholtz, 'Is harmonization a good thing? The case of the copyright *acquis*', in A Ohly and J Pila (eds), *The Europeanization of Intellectual Property Law—Towards a European Legal Methodology* (OUP:2013), 61–2.

[46] European Commission, Communication from the Commission to the Council, the European Parliament and the European Economic and Social Committee, *The management of copyright and related rights in the internal market*, COM (2004) 261 final.

[47] European Commission, *Commission Staff Working Paper on the review of the EC legal framework in the field of copyright and related rights* (2004), 995.

[48] With regard to the latter, see MC Janssens, 'Invitation for a 'Europeanification' of moral rights', in P Torremans (ed), *Research Handbook on Copyright Law* (Edward Elgar:2017), 2nd edn, 209–21, advocating EU harmonization of moral rights. See also L Bently and A Radauer, 'European intellectual property law: what lies ahead' in Directorate General for Internal Policies—Policy Department C: Citizens' Rights and Constitutional Affairs, *Upcoming Issues of EU law—Compilation of In-depth Analyses* (2014), available at <http://www.europarl.europa.eu/RegData/etudes/IDAN/2014/509987/IPOL_IDA(2014)509987_EN.pdf?utm_content=buffer3f39b&utm_medium=social&utm_source=twitter.com&utm_campaign=buffer> (last accessed 15 August 2018), 152, noting how moral rights are among those thorny issues that have long divided the approaches of countries such as the United Kingdom from those of France and Germany.

[49] Commission of the European Communities, *Green Paper on Copyright in the knowledge economy*, COM (2008) 466/3.

[50] Commission of the European Communities, Communication from the Commission—*Copyright in the knowledge economy*, COM (2009) 532 final.

which recommended a structured dialogue between relevant stakeholders, facilitated by services of the European Commission, to help tackle the issues raised in the 2008 Green Paper.

Unification of copyright laws?—In 2009 the EU Commission also issued a cautious[51] Reflection Document[52] aimed at *initiating* a discussion of possible responses of the EU to the challenges facing dematerialization of content, in particular by considering a framework that would accommodate user creativity and issues facing rights management. The Reflection Document nonetheless contains the first mention in a Commission document of a project of full harmonization of EU copyright laws. Article 118(1) TFEU could be the legislative basis for issuing an EU regulation to establish a 'European Copyright Law'.[53] Although the introduction of an EU-wide copyright title is discussed alongside other options (including alternative forms of remuneration), the Reflection Document deems it advantageous from an internal market perspective in that it would also overcome issues of territoriality. As of today, territoriality of copyright laws remains one of the major obstacles to the establishment of a fully functioning internal market for copyright works and other protected subject matter,[54] especially if one considers that the copyright internal market has become increasingly a services market with cross-border reach, rather than just a 'goods' market.[55] The choice of the EU legislature to proceed through 'a mixed process of partial and full harmonisation'[56] has failed to remove the fragmentation that is inherent in a territorial approach to copyright protection in the EU.

Unification of copyright at the EU level would enhance legal security and transparency for rightholders and users alike, reducing transaction and licensing costs, and facilitating effective rights management. It could also restore the balance between rights and exceptions, by creating a level playing field for exclusive rights and relevant exceptions and limitations (the latter would lose the optional character that they have in certain directives, most notably the InfoSoc Directive). An EU-wide copyright title could be construed as taking precedence over national titles, thus removing territoriality with respect to applicable national copyright rules, or could be an option for rightholders which would not replace, but rather exist together with, national copyright titles.[57]

The revamped EU copyright agenda in the late 2000s and 2010s—In parallel with growing activity and activism of the CJEU, policy attention towards copyright also increased over the course of 2000s–2010s. In 2010 Mario Monti prepared a report (Monti Report) at the request of the then President of the EU Commission,

---

[51] I previously referred to it as taking a 'Pontius Pilates-like' approach to copyright reform in E Rosati, 'Towards an EU-wide copyright? (Judicial) pride and (legislative) prejudice' (2013) 2013/1 IPQ 47, 49.

[52] European Commission, Reflection Document of DG INFSO and DG MARKT on *Creative Content in a European digital single market: challenges for the future*, 22 October 2009.

[53] Ibid, 18.

[54] M van Eechoud, PB Hugenholtz, S van Gompel, L Guibault, and N Helberger, *Harmonizing European Copyright Law—The Challenges of Better Lawmaking* (Wolters Kluwer:2009), 308. See also P Jougleux, 'The plurality of legal systems in copyright law: an obstacle to a European codification?', in Synodinou (ed), *Codification of European Copyright Law* 61–3.

[55] M Martin-Prat, 'An introduction—The EU copyright agenda', in IA Stamatoudi (ed), *New Developments in EU and International Copyright Law* (Wolters Kluwer:2016), 184–5.

[56] Opinion of Advocate General Niilo Jääskinen in *Donner*, C-5/11, EU:C:2012:195, para 25.

[57] European Commission, Reflection Document of DG INFSO and DG MARKT on *Creative Content in a European digital single market: challenges for the future*, 22 October 2009, 18–19. Further harmonization or even unification of EU Member States' copyright laws has been however regarded as undesirable by A Rahmatian, 'European copyright inside or outside the European Union: pluralism of copyright laws and the "Herderian paradox"' (2016) 47(8) IIC 912.

José Manuel Barroso, in which he made a number of recommendations to re-launch the internal market project. Among other things, he expressly referred to copyright, highlighting the need for a reform of rights clearance and management mechanisms. Overall, Monti stressed the need for EU-wide copyright rules, including a framework for digital rights management and cross-border online transactions that take place at the location of supply and extended collective licensing.[58]

Following the Monti Report and a set of fifty proposals that were the subject of a public consultation,[59] in 2011 the EU Commission issued its Single Market Act.[60] Among other things, this highlighted the lack of an EU-wide framework for the efficient management of copyright across the EU, and noted that this would negatively affect the dissemination of knowledge, notably in the online context. The blueprint issued that same year highlighted the functional role that the intellectual property framework has in the internal market, and anticipated that initiatives would be taken in areas like copyright governance and management, user-generated content, private copying levies, access to Europe's cultural heritage, media plurality, performers' rights, audiovisual works, and artists' resale right.[61] The blueprint also referred to the possibility of harmonizing copyright fully at the EU level, indicating how this objective might be achieved. In particular, the Commission explained that full harmonization might be realized through two distinct and alternative routes: either a codification of the current *acquis*, or the adoption of an ad hoc regulation that would establish an optional EU copyright title.[62]

Despite the ambitious tone of the blueprint, follow-up initiatives were not particularly remarkable. Besides areas in which no real reform has ever occurred (examples being private copying levies[63] or a re-opening of the InfoSoc Directive), other initiatives also failed to develop successfully, an example being the stakeholder-led dialogue on licensing under the umbrella of Licences for Europe.[64] For projects that have eventually materialized, including the adoption of an Orphan Works Directive,[65] the resulting breadth and ambition are limited.[66] Following the adoption of the Orphan Works

---

[58] M Monti, *A new strategy for the single market at the service of Europe's economy and society. Report to the President of the European Commission José Manuel Barroso*, 9 May 2010, §2.3.

[59] European Commission, Communication from the Commission to the European Parliament, the Council, the Economic and Social Committee and the Committee of the Regions, *Towards a Single Market Act for a highly competitive social market economy—50 proposals for improving our work, business and exchanges with one another*, COM (2010) 608 final.

[60] European Commission, Communication from the Commission to the European Parliament, the Council, the Economic and Social Committee and the Committee of the Regions, *Single Market Act—Twelve levers to boost growth and strengthen confidence—'Working together to create new growth'*, COM (2011) 206 final.

[61] European Commission, Communication from the Commission to the European Parliament, the Council, the European Economic and Social Committee and the Committee of the Regions, *A Single Market for Intellectual Property Rights boosting creativity and innovation to provide economic growth, high quality jobs and first class products and services in Europe*, COM(2011) 287 final, §3.3.

[62] Ibid, 11.

[63] See also A Vitorino, *Recommendations resulting from the Mediation on Private Copying and Reprography Levies* (2013), available at <http://ec.europa.eu/internal_market/copyright/docs/levy_reform/130131_levies-vitorino-recommendations_en.pdf> (last accessed 15 August 2018).

[64] European Commission, Communication from the Commission *On content in the Digital Single Market*, /* COM/2012/0789 final */. See also the *Licences for Europe* website at <https://ec.europa.eu/licences-for-europe-dialogue/> (last accessed 15 August 2018).

[65] Directive 2012/28/EU of the European Parliament and of the Council of 25 October 2012 on certain permitted uses of orphan works, see n 17.

[66] See my criticisms in E Rosati, 'The Orphan Works Directive, or throwing a stone and hiding the hand' (2013) 8(4) JIPLP 303, 308–10.

Directive in 2012 and the (also limited) Collective Rights Management Directive[67] in 2014, it would be necessary to wait until 2015 before a renewed policy impetus around copyright would occur, in the context of the Digital Single Market Strategy[68] (DSMS) of the EU Commission led by Jean-Claude Juncker (see further Chapter 8).

3. The CJEU

In parallel to the EU policy and legislative agenda, the construction of the EU copyright framework owes a great deal to the role undertaken by the CJEU. By hearing references for a preliminary ruling from national courts, the Court has—as of today (August 2018)—decided several cases (see further Section 4) by means of which it has provided its own interpretation of relevant provisions and standards. All this has resulted, on the one hand, in a reduction of the perceived divide between *droit d'auteur* continental copyright traditions and common law copyright regimes[69] and, on the other hand, in the development and establishment of an EU copyright system.[70]

3.1 Composition of the Court

Members of the Court: Judges and Advocates General—The CJEU—referred to in the EU Treaties as 'Court of Justice'—is composed of one judge from each Member State (Article 19(2) TEU) and is assisted by eight AGs (Article 252 TFEU), who are chosen in accordance with Article 253 TFEU 'from persons whose independence is beyond doubt and who possess the qualifications required for appointment to the highest judicial offices in their respective countries or who are jurisconsults of recognised competence'. The appointment is by common accord of EU Member States' governments. AGs are in office for a term of six years.

Article 253 TFEU provides that every three years there shall be a partial replacement of the judges and AGs, in accordance with the conditions laid down in the Statute of the Court of Justice of the European Union (Statute).[71] When, every three years, the judges are partially replaced, fourteen and thirteen judges shall be replaced alternately. When, every three years, the AGs are partially replaced, four AGs shall be replaced on each occasion (Article 9 of the Statute).

The CJEU usually sits in chambers of three or five judges, but may also sit as a Grand Chamber (fifteen judges). The former consists of the President of the relevant Chamber, the Judge-Rapporteur, and the number of judges required to attain the number of three and five judges respectively. Composition as a Grand Chamber includes the President and the Vice-President of the Court, three Presidents of Chambers of five judges, the Judge-Rapporteur and the number of judges necessary to reach

---

[67] Directive 2014/26/EU of the European Parliament and of the Council of 26 February 2014 on collective management of copyright and related rights and multi-territorial licensing of rights in musical works for online use in the internal market, see n 18.

[68] European Commission, Communication from the Commission to the European Parliament, the Council, the European Economic and Social Committee and the Committee of the Regions, *A Digital Single Market Strategy for Europe*, /* COM/2015/0192 final */.

[69] In this sense, see G Davies, 'The convergence of copyright and authors' rights—reality or chimera?' (1995) 26(6) IIC 964, 985.

[70] J Pila, 'A constitutionalized doctrine of precedent and the *Marleasing* principle as bases for a European legal methodology' in Ohly and Pila (eds), *The Europeanization of Intellectual Property Law* 230–2 also speaks of a European legal methodology.

[71] TFEU, Protocol (No 3) on the Statute of the Court of Justice of the European Union.

fifteen, as per Article 27 of the Rules of Procedure of the Court of Justice[72] (Rules of Procedure). The default rule is that a case shall be heard and decided by a Chamber of three or five judges. Assignment to the Grand Chamber is possible on consideration of the difficulty or importance of the case or particular circumstances at issue (Article 60 of the Rules of Procedure).

Autonomy of EU law and the role of the Court—Since the landmark decision in *Van Gend & Loos*, C-26/62, the EU legal order has been characterized as 'a new legal order of international law for the benefit of which the states have limited their sovereign rights, albeit within limited fields, and the subjects of which comprise not only Member States but also their nationals'.[73] EU law thus imposes obligations and confers rights on Member States and citizens alike and, although it forms part of national law, retains its special and autonomous character. This means that the validity and applicability of EU law, as well as its interpretation, are derived explicitly from EU law without being determined by national law. To secure this autonomous character of EU law, 'the CJEU has the sole jurisdiction to interpret EU law, while it lacks jurisdiction to apply or interpret the (purely) national law of the Member States. The relationship between EU law and national law is thus *asymmetrical*.'[74]

References for a preliminary ruling—The role of the CJEU is to 'ensure that in the interpretation and application of the Treaties the law is observed' (Article 19(1) TEU). The CJEU may be involved in different types of action, including preliminary rulings, infringement proceedings, actions for annulment, actions for failure to act, and actions for damages. For the sake of the present analysis, attention will focus solely on preliminary rulings. The system of references for a preliminary rulings is a fundamental mechanism of EU law and is meant to ensure the uniform interpretation and application of EU law, by offering courts and tribunals of the Member States a means of bringing before the CJEU for a preliminary ruling questions concerning the interpretation of EU law or the validity of acts adopted by the institutions, bodies, offices, or agencies of the EU.[75]

3.2 References for a preliminary ruling: content, submissions, and the role of AGs

The referral mechanism—Article 267 TFEU vests the CJEU with jurisdiction to give preliminary rulings concerning both the interpretation of the EU Treaties (early copyright cases focused especially on free movement provisions under what was at that time the EC Treaty[76]) and the validity and interpretation of acts of the institutions, bodies, offices, or agencies of the EU, including EU directives. A court in a Member State has the discretion to raise questions of interpretation of EU law, and hence make a reference for a preliminary ruling, if it considers that a decision on the question is necessary to enable it to give judgment. If, however, the court or tribunal

---

[72] Rules of Procedure of the Court of Justice, OJ L 265, 29 September 2012, 1–42.

[73] *Van Gend & Loos*, C-26/62, EU:C:1963:1, 12.

[74] Jääskinen, 'Europeanisation of national law' 668 (emphasis in the original).

[75] Recommendations to national courts and tribunals, in relation to the initiation of preliminary ruling proceedings, OJ C 439, 25 November 2016, 1–8, in 'Introduction'.

[76] Treaty establishing the European Community (Consolidated version 2002), OJ C 325, 24 December 2002, 33–184. Examples include: *Deutsche Grammophon*, C-78/70, EU:C:1971:59; *Gema*, C-55/80, EU:C:1981:10; *Polydor*, C-270/80, EU:C:1982:43; *Cinéthèque*, C-60/84, EU:C:1985:329; *Warner Brothers and Metronome Video*, C-158/86, EU:C:1988:242; *EMI Electrola*, C-341/87, EU:C:1989:30; *Phil Collins*, C-92/92 and C-326/92, EU:C:1993:847.

in question is one against whose decisions there is no judicial remedy under national law, then that court or tribunal is under an obligation to bring the matter before the CJEU.[77]

As clarified by the Rules of Procedure (Article 94), when referring a case to the CJEU, the national court shall provide: the text of the questions referred to the Court for a preliminary ruling; a summary of the subject matter of the dispute and the relevant findings of fact as determined by the referring court or tribunal, or, at least, an account of the facts on which the questions are based; the tenor of any national provisions applicable in the case and, where appropriate, the relevant national case law; a statement explaining why the referring court or tribunal is to inquire about the interpretation or validity of certain provisions of EU law, and the relationship between those provisions and the national legislation applicable to the main proceedings.

Designation of the Judge-Rapporteur and the Advocate General—As soon as possible after the document initiating proceedings has been lodged, the President of the Court shall designate a judge to act as Rapporteur (Article 15 of the Rules of Procedure), while the First Advocate General of the Court (chosen by the Court, after hearing the AGs, for a period of one year as per Article 14 of the Rules of Procedure) shall assign the relevant case to an AG (Article 16 of the Rules of Procedure). In case of exceptional importance, the Court may also sit as a full Court.

Participation in the proceedings—Besides the parties to the main proceedings, Article 19 of the Statute also allows participation of the Member States, the EU Commission, the institution which adopted the act the validity or interpretation of which is in dispute, the states other than the Member States, which are parties to the EEA Agreement,[78] and also the EFTA Surveillance Authority (this is possible where a question concerning one of the fields of application of that Agreement is referred to the Court for a preliminary ruling).

Procedure—The procedure before the Court consists of a written and an oral part (Article 20 of the Statute). The former consists of the communication to the parties to the national proceedings and the EU institutions whose decisions are in dispute, of any applications, statements of case, defences and observations, replies, as well as of all papers and documents in support or of certified copies of them. The latter envisages the reading of the report prepared by the Judge-Rapporteur, the hearing by the Court of agents, advisers, and lawyers and of the submissions of the AG (who shall act with complete impartiality and independence), as well as the hearing, if any, of witnesses and experts. During this phase, the Court may decide not to seek an Opinion of the appointed AG if, after hearing him/her, it concludes that the case at issue raises no new point of law. In such cases, as will be discussed further in Section 3.3, the Court decides by means of an order, rather than a judgment. If the Court, instead, requests the appointed AG to submit an Opinion, this will address the substance of the questions referred by the national court and will conclude with recommendations to the Court on how the questions referred should be answered. The Opinion of an AG is in any case not binding on the Court.

---

[77] For practical considerations regarding the referral mechanism from the perspective of an intellectual property judge, see R Jacob, 'The relationship between European and national courts in intellectual property law' in Ohly and Pila (eds), *The Europeanization of Intellectual Property Law* 196–8.

[78] Agreement on the European Economic Area, OJ L 1, 3 January 1994, 3-570.

3.3 How the Court decides

Judgments and orders—There are two possible outcomes of a reference for a preliminary ruling: the Court may decide by means of an order or a judgment. The former is issued when, as mentioned, the questions referred raise no new points of law. This might be the case where (Article 99 of the Rules of Procedure):

- A question referred to the Court for a preliminary ruling is identical to a question on which the Court has already ruled;
- The reply to such a question may be clearly deduced from existing case law; or
- The answer to the question referred for a preliminary ruling admits of no reasonable doubt.

The Court may decide to issue a reasoned order at any time, on a proposal from the Judge-Rapporteur having heard the appointed AG. In these cases, the order must be reasoned and, besides the operative part, must contain a summary of the facts and the grounds for the decision (Article 89 of the Rules of Procedure). Somewhat similarly (at least structure-wise) to a reasoned order, following a summary of the facts, judgments too contain the grounds for the decision and the operative part, including, where appropriate, a decision as to costs (Article 87 of the Rules of Procedure).

Secrecy of deliberations—A characteristic of the procedure before the CJEU is that its deliberations 'shall be and shall remain secret' (Article 32 of the Rules of Procedure). Following the relevant hearing, only the judges who participated in that hearing shall take part in the deliberative procedure. Each and every judge taking part in the deliberations shall state their reasoned opinion and that the conclusion reached by the majority of the judges after final discussion shall be the decision of the Court (Article 32 of the Rules of Procedure). In the CJEU system there is no room for dissenting opinions/judgments.

Lack of *stare decisis*—Another feature is that there is no *formal* system of binding precedent. The reason underlying this choice was the view that a system of *stare decisis* would be inappropriate for an institution acting as court of first and last resort. Envisaging binding precedent would mean that, to challenge a certain decision, a review of the Treaties would be necessary.[79] However, the very fact that the Court would issue an order, in lieu of a judgment, in cases that contain questions identical to those on which the Court has already ruled or the reply to which may be clearly deduced from existing case law is indicative that earlier decisions have in fact a value which, if not akin to that of a binding precedent, is at least one in which earlier decisions matter. In addition, the Court often refers to earlier decisions as 'settled case law' and it is rare that the CJEU departs from its previous decisions. What is likely to happen, and as indeed happened (eg, with regard to the construction of the right of communication to the public, on which see Chapter 4, Section 2) is for the Court to employ a technique of incremental development: by means of a dialogue with national courts (through the instrument of referrals for a preliminary ruling), the Court progressively refines its analysis of relevant provisions in the EU *acquis*. Overall, the approach of the CJEU, which is now codified but was first initiated by the Court in its seminal decision in *Da Costa*, C-28 to 30/62,[80] may indeed be regarded as *substantially* akin to a system of precedent under EU law.[81]

---

[79] A Arnull, *The European Union and its Court of Justice* (OUP: 1999), 529.
[80] *Da Costa*, C-28/62, C-29/62 and C-30/62, EU:C:1963:6.
[81] P Craig and G de Búrca, *EU Law. Text, Cases and Materials* (OUP:2015), 6th edn, 472.

As already mentioned, the objective underlying the system of references for a preliminary ruling is ensuring the uniform interpretation and application of EU law across the Member States. However, following a certain decision of the CJEU, it shall be for the national courts or tribunals to assess whether they consider that sufficient guidance is given by a preliminary ruling, or whether it appears to them that a further reference to the Court is required (Article 104 of the Rules of Procedure.)

4. The Copyright Cases: CJEU Activity at a Glance

Case law considered—Early case law in the area of copyright tackled issues from a free movement perspective: in this sense national courts sought clarification on the compatibility of certain national rules with relevant EC Treaty provisions.[82] Overall, this contribution focuses on understanding how the Court has interpreted relevant copyright legislation, what standards have guided its action, and whether it is possible to discern any unifying lens(es) in resulting case law. For this reason, the CJEU judgments covered are those issued between 1998 (when the first decisions concerning interpretation of the 1992 Rental and Lending Rights Directive were issued) and August 2018 (when this monograph was sent to print).

Table 1.1 includes ninety-eight decisions, displayed in reverse chronological order.[83] They have been selected according to the following criteria:

- The decisions interpret provisions *within* the EU copyright *acquis* (as defined in Section 1) or relevant provisions within Regulation 1215/2012[84] (Brussels I Regulation recast), formerly Regulation 44/2001[85] (Brussels I Regulation);

- The decisions *directly* concern copyright provisions. This means that, although relevant to certain aspects of copyright, notably enforcement and remedies, cases concerning, for example, the interpretation of provisions in directives like the Enforcement Directive, which is part of the EU *acquis*, that do not directly and specifically apply also to copyright (an example being the third sentence in Article 11) have been left outside the scope of the analysis, although they are tackled elsewhere in the book[86]). Thus, the analysis takes into account judgments that, albeit related to subject matter other than copyright (eg, trade marks or even patents) in the background national proceedings, concern the interpretation of provisions applicable also in copyright cases;

---

[82] Examples include: *Deutsche Grammophon*, C-78/70, EU:C:1971:59; *Gema*, C-55/80, EU:C:1981:10; *Polydor*, C-270/80; *Cinéthèque*, C-60/84, EU:C:1985:329; *EMI Electrola*, C-341/87, EU:C:1989:30; *Warner Brothers and Metronome Video*, C-158/86, EU:C:1988:242; *Phil Collins*, C-92/92, EU:C:1993:847.

[83] The cases are referenced according to the method used on the Curia website: <https://curia.europa.eu/jcms/jcms/j_6/en/> (last accessed 15 August 2018).

[84] Regulation (EU) No 1215/2012 of the European Parliament and of the Council of 12 December 2012 on jurisdiction and the recognition and enforcement of judgments in civil and commercial matters, OJ L 351, 20 December 2012, 1–32.

[85] Council Regulation (EC) No 44/2001 of 22 December 2000 on jurisdiction and the recognition and enforcement of judgments in civil and commercial matters, OJ L 12, 16 January 2001, 1–23.

[86] This has been, for instance, the case of the seminal decision in *L'Oréal and Others*, C-324/09, EU:C:2011:474. In that case the Court focused on intermediary injunctions within the meaning of the third sentence in Article 11 of the Enforcement Directive. While the principles expressed by the Court are also applicable to copyright injunctions (see further the discussion in Chapter 6, Sections 1 and 1.1, and Chapter 8, Section 1.2), that provision expressly relates to intellectual property rights other than copyright.

- Pending cases as of the time when this monograph was submitted have not been included (this means that cases for which an AG Opinion was issued but not also the CJEU decision were also excluded).[87]

Overall, of the ninety-eight cases reported here, thirteen have been decided by the Court in a Grand Chamber composition. These cases are indicated in Table 1.1, by use of the sign '•' before the case details.

Table 1.1 CJEU copyright decisions

Judgment	Date
SNB-REACT, C-521/17, EU:C:2018:639	07.08.2018
Renckhoff, C-161/17, EU:C:2018:634	07.08.2018
VCAST, C-265/16, EU:C:2017:913	29.11.2017
Stichting Brein, C-610/15, EU:C:2017:456	14.06.2017
Stichting Brein, C-527/15, EU:C:2017:300	26.04.2017
AKM, C-138/16, EU:C:2017:218	16.03.2017
ITV Broadcasting, C-275/15, EU:C:2017:144	01.03.2017
Verwertungsgesellschaft Rundfunk, C-641/15, EU:C:2017:131	16.02.2017
Stowarzyszenie Oławska Telewizja Kablowa, C-367/15, EU:C:2017:36	25.01.2017
NEW WAVE CZ, C-427/15, EU:C:2017:18	18.01.2017
Tommy Hilfiger, C-494/15, EU:C:2016:528	07.06.2016
Soulier and Doke, C-301/15, EU:C:2016:878	16.11.2016
Vereniging Openbare Bibliotheken, C-174/15, EU:C:2016:856	10.11.2016
Montis Design, C-169/15, EU:C:2016:790	20.10.2016
Ranks and Vasiļevičs, C-166/15, EU:C:2016:762	12.10.2016
Microsoft Mobile Sales International and Others, C-110/15, EU:C:2016:717	22.09.2016
Mc Fadden, C-484/14, EU:C:2016:689	15.09.2016
GS Media, C-160/15, EU:C:2016:644	08.09.2016
	(continued)

---

[87] At the time of writing (August 2018), the following cases (in alphabetical order) have been referred to the CJEU and are awaiting a decision:

- *Bastei Lübbe*, C-149/17, on which AG Szpunar issued his Opinion in mid-2018 (Opinion of Advocate General Maciej Szpunar in *Bastei Lübbe*, C-149/17, EU:C:2018:400—see E Rosati, 'Respect of family life cannot be abused to trump copyright protection, says AG Szpunar' (6 June 2018) The IPKat, available at <http://ipkitten.blogspot.com/2018/06/respect-of-family-life-cannot-be-abused.html> (last accessed 15 August 2018));
- *Cofemel*, C-683/17, on which see further Chapter 4, Section 1.2;
- *Dacom*, C-313/18;
- *Funke Medien NRW*, C-469/17;
- *Levola Hengelo*, C-310/17, on which AG Melchior Wathelet issued his Opinion in mid-2018 (Opinion of Advocate General Melchior Wathelet in *Levola Hengelo*, C-310/17, EU:C:2018:618: see further Chapter 3, Section 1 and Chapter 4, Section 1.2);
- *Nederlands Uitgeversverbond and Groep Algemene Uitgevers*, C-263/18, on which see further Chapter 4, Section 3.5;
- *Pelham and Others*, C-476/17, on which see further Chapter 4, Section 1.3;
- *Spiegel Online*, C-516/17;
- *Syed*, C-572/17;
- *VG Media*, C-299/17.

Further references for a preliminary ruling may be found at <https://ipcuria.eu/all_referrals.php> and <https://www.gov.uk/government/publications/references-to-the-court-of-justice-of-the-european-union> (both last accessed 15 August 2018).

Table 1.1 Continued

Judgment	Date
United Video Properties, C-57/15, EU:C:2016:611	28.07.2016
EGEDA and Others, C-470/14, EU:C:2016:418	09.06.2016
• *Reha Training*, C-117/15, EU:C:2016:379	31.05.2016
Austro-Mechana, C-572/14, EU:C:2016:286	21.04.2016
Liffers, C-99/15, EU:C:2016:173	17.03.2016
SBS Belgium, C-325/14, EU:C:2015:764	19.11.2015
Hewlett-Packard Belgium, C-572/13, EU:C:2015:750	12.11.2015
Verlag Esterbauer, C-490/14, EU:C:2015:735	29.10.2015
Coty Germany, C-580/13, EU:C:2015:485	16.07.2015
Diageo Brands, C-681/13, EU:C:2015:471	16.07.2015
Sociedade Portuguesa de Autores CRL, C-151/15, EU:C:2015:468	14.07.2015
Dimensione Direct Sales and Labianca, C-516/13, EU:C:2015:315	13.05.2015
C More Entertainment, C-279/13, EU:C:2015:199	26.03.2015
Copydan Båndkopi, C-463/12, EU:C:2015:144	05.03.2015
Christie's France, C-41/14, EU:C:2015:119	26.02.2015
Hejduk, C-441/13, EU:C:2015:28	22.01.2015
Art & Allposters International, C-419/13, EU:C:2015:27	22.01.2015
Ryanair, C-30/14, EU:C:2015:10	15.01.2015
BestWater, C-348/13, EU:C:2014:2315	21.10.2014
Eugen Ulmer, C-117/13, EU:C:2014:2196	11.09.2014
•*Deckmyn and Vrijheidsfonds*, C-201/13, EU:C:2014:2132	03.09.2014
Public Relations Consultants Association, C-360/13, EU:C:2014:1195	05.06.2014
ACI Adam and Others, C-435/12, EU:C:2014:254	10.04.2014
Hi Hotel HCF, C-387/12, EU:C:2014:215	03.04.2014
UPC Telekabel Wien, C-314/12, EU:C:2014:192	27.03.2014
OSA, C-351/12, EU:C:2014:110	27.02.2014
Svensson and Others, C-466/12, EU:C:2014:76	13.02.2014
Blomqvist, C-98/13, EU:C:2014:55	06.02.2014
Nintendo and Others, C-355/12, EU:C:2014:25	23.01.2014
Innoweb, C-202/12, EU:C:2013:850	19.12.2013
Pinckney, C-170/12, EU:C:2013:635	03.10.2013
Amazon.com International Sales and Others, C-521/11, EU:C:2013:515	11.07.2013
VG Wort, C-457/11, EU:C:2013:426	27.06.2013
ITV Broadcasting, C-607/11, EU:C:2013:147	07.03.2013
Football Dataco and Others, C-173/11, EU:C:2012:642	18.10.2012
•*UsedSoft*, C-128/11, EU:C:2012:407	03.07.2012
Donner, C-5/11, EU:C:2012:370	21.06.2012
•*SAS Institute*, C-406/10, EU:C:2012:259	02.05.2012
DR and TV2 Danmark, C-510/10, EU:C:2012:244	26.04.2012
Bonnier Audio and Others, C-461/10, EU:C:2012:219	19.04.2012
Phonographic Performance (Ireland), C-162/10, EU:C:2012:141	15.03.2012

Table 1.1 Continued

Judgment	Date
SCF, C-135/10, EU:C:2012:140	15.03.2012
Football Dataco and Others, C-604/10, EU:C:2012:115	01.03.2012
SABAM, C-360/10, EU:C:2012:85	16.02.2012
Luksan, C-277/10, EU:C:2012:65	09.02.2012
Infopaq International, C-302/10, EU:C:2012:16	17.01.2012
Painer, C-145/10, EU:C:2011:798	01.12.2011
Circul Globus București, C-283/10, EU:C:2011:772	24.11.2011
Scarlet Extended, C-70/10, EU:C:2011:771	24.11.2011
Airfield and Canal Digitaal, C-431/09, EU:C:2011:648	13.10.2011
• *Football Association Premier League and Others*, C-403/08 and C-429/08, EU:C:2011:631	04.10.2011
Cassina, C-198/10, EU:C:2011:570	09.09.2011
VEWA, C-271/10, EU:C:2011:442	30.06.2011
Stichting de Thuiskopie, C-462/09, EU:C:2011:397	16.06.2011
Flos, C-168/09, EU:C:2011:29	27.01.2011
Bezpečnostní softwarová asociace, C-393/09, EU:C:2010:816	22.12.2010
Padawan, C-467/08, EU:C:2010:620	21.10.2010
Fundación Gala-Salvador Dalí and VEGAP, C-518/08, EU:C:2010:191	15.04.2010
Organismos Sillogikis Diacheirisis Dimiourgon Theatrikon kai Optikoakoustikon Ergon, C-136/09, EU:C:2010:151	18.03.2010
Infopaq International, C-5/08, EU:C:2009:465	16.07.2009
Apis-Hristovich, C-545/07, EU:C:2009:132	05.03.2009
LSG-Gesellschaft zur Wahrnehmung von Leistungsschutzrechten, C-557/07, EU:C:2009:107	19.02.2009
• *Sony Music Entertainment*, C-240/07, EU:C:2009:19	20.01.2009
Directmedia Publishing, C-304/07, EU:C:2008:552	09.10.2008
Peek & Cloppenburg, C-456/06, EU:C:2008:232	17.04.2008
• *Promusicae*, C-275/06, EU:C:2008:54	29.01.2008
SGAE, C-306/05, EU:C:2006:764	07.12.2006
• *Laserdisken*, C-479/04, EU:C:2006:549	12.09.2006
Uradex, C-169/05, EU:C:2006:365	01.06.2006
Lagardère Active Broadcast, C-192/04, EU:C:2005:475	14.07.2005
• *Fixtures Marketing*, C-444/02, EU:C:2004:697	09.11.2004
• *Fixtures Marketing*, C-338/02, EU:C:2004:696	09.11.2004
• *The British Horseracing Board and Others*, C-203/02, EU:C:2004:695	09.11.2004
• *Fixtures Marketing*, C-46/02, EU:C:2004:694	09.11.2004
SENA, C-245/00, EU:C:2003:68	06.02.2003
Ricordi, C-360/00, EU:C:2002:346	06.06.2002
EGEDA, C-293/98, EU:C:2000:66	03.02.2000
Butterfly Music, C-60/98, EU:C:1999:333	29.06.1999
• *FDV*, C-61/97, EU:C:1998:422	22.09.1998
Metronome Musik, C-200/96, EU:C:1998:172	28.04.1998

4.1 CJEU copyright decisions

Areas of preliminary rulings over time—As mentioned in Sections 1–2, in the context of discussion around the legislative process of harmonization, the types of areas affected by EU intervention have been heterogeneous. In terms of case law resulting from references for a preliminary ruling made by national courts, the following trends may be detected. During the late 1990s and over the 2000s a significant number of cases concerned related rights (including broadcasting rights), databases, and economic rights (the first decision on the right of communication to the public, *SGAE*, C-306/05, was issued in 2006); over the 2010s the Court has remained focused on certain subject matter (particularly databases and computer programs), but the most significant contribution has been to the construction of economic rights (notably, the right of communication to the public), exceptions and limitations (the decision in *Padawan*, C-275/06, was issued in 2010), and remedies (notably with regard to the role of intermediaries and injunctions against them).

Referrals and preliminary rulings in numbers, and relevant areas—Figures 1.1 and 1.2 below show how the activity of the Court has increased over time, with more and more references for a preliminary ruling being made by national courts. Figure 1.1[88] displays the number of references made over time, and Figure 1.2[89] displays the number of preliminary rulings issued over time. With regard to the areas in which the relevant references were made, the numbers shown in Figure 1.3 may be observed.[90]

4.2 Referring courts

EU enlargements—The number of Member States of, first, the EC and, now, the EU has grown over time.[91] Through progressive enlargements (the last one in 2014), Member States have passed from the original six (Belgium, France, Germany, Italy, Luxembourg, and the Netherlands) in 1958 to twenty-eight as of 2018 (Austria, Belgium, Bulgaria, Croatia, Cyprus, Czech Republic, Denmark, Estonia, Finland, France, Germany, Greece, Hungary, Ireland, Italy, Latvia, Lithuania, Luxembourg, Malta, the Netherlands, Poland, Portugal, Romania, Slovakia, Slovenia, Spain, Sweden, and the United Kingdom).

Referring courts in numbers—The different times of joining the EC/EU are of course to be borne in mind when considering the geographic origin of the references for a preliminary ruling in the field of copyright. So far, courts and tribunals in certain, newer Member States have not referred any of the copyright cases listed in Table 1.1 in Section 4.1. While it may not be surprising to see that Germany (a Member State since 1958) is where the highest number of references has been made, followed by the Netherlands (also a founding Member State), courts and tribunals in a relatively new Member State, Austria, have referred the third highest number of copyright cases to the CJEU. Figure 1.4 provides an illustration of the number of cases referred by courts and tribunals in relevant Member States, which have been considered for the present analysis.[92] The date in parenthesis next to each Member State indicates the year of EU accession.

---

[88] Up-to-date as of August 2018. For 2017 referrals, data includes both cases decided and cases pending before the CJEU as of August 2018.

[89] Up-to-date as of August 2018. Pending cases were excluded from the analysis.

[90] Ibid.   [91] Ibid.

[92] Up-to-date as of August 2018. For 2017 referrals, data includes both cases decided and cases pending before the CJEU as of August 2018.

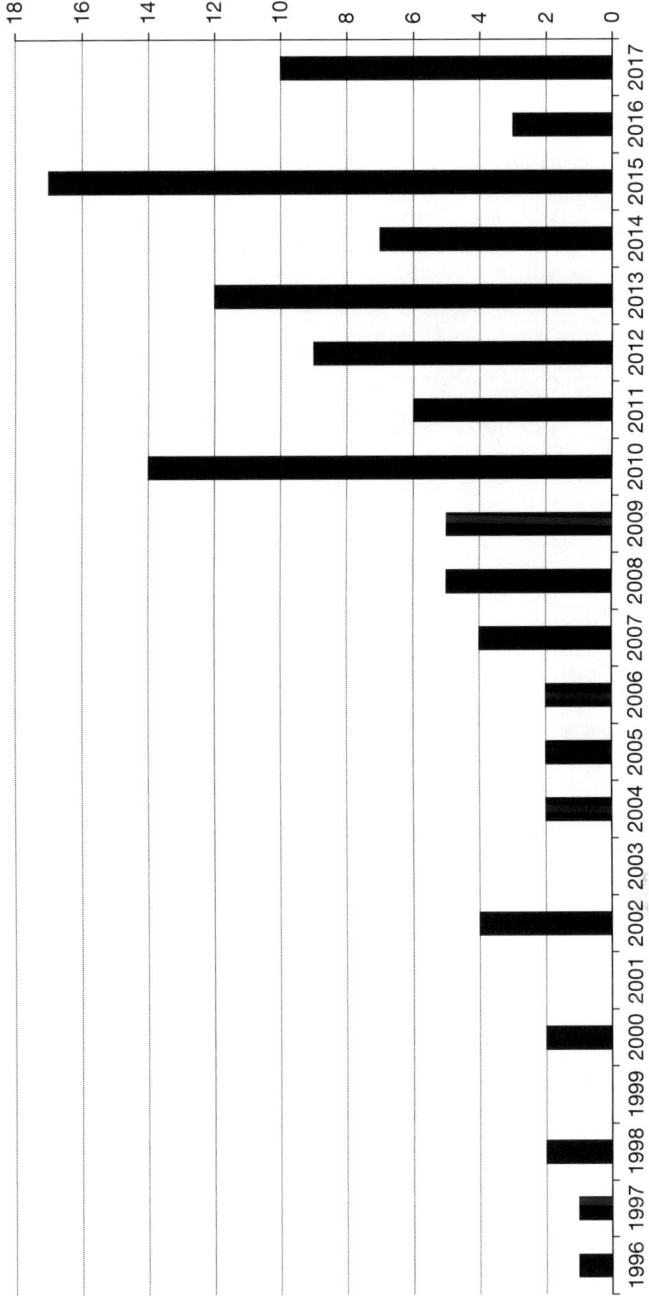

Figure 1.1 References for a preliminary ruling made over time (1998–2017)

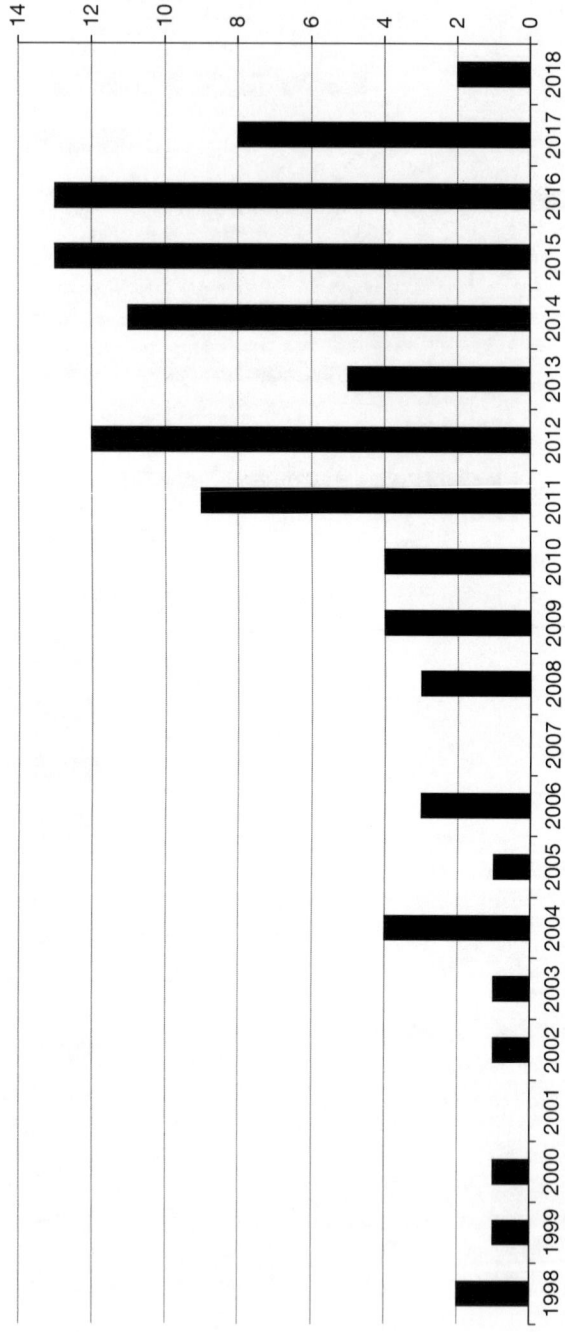

Figure 1.2 Preliminary rulings over time (1998–2018)

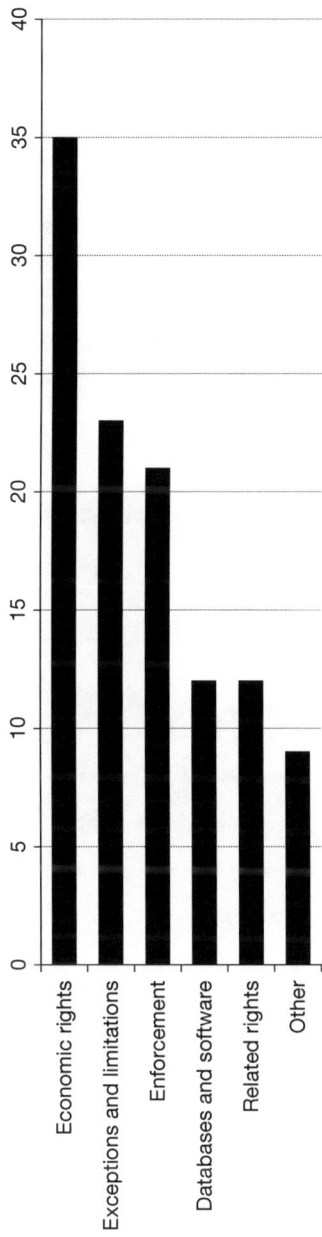

Figure 1.3 Areas of preliminary rulings (1998–2018)

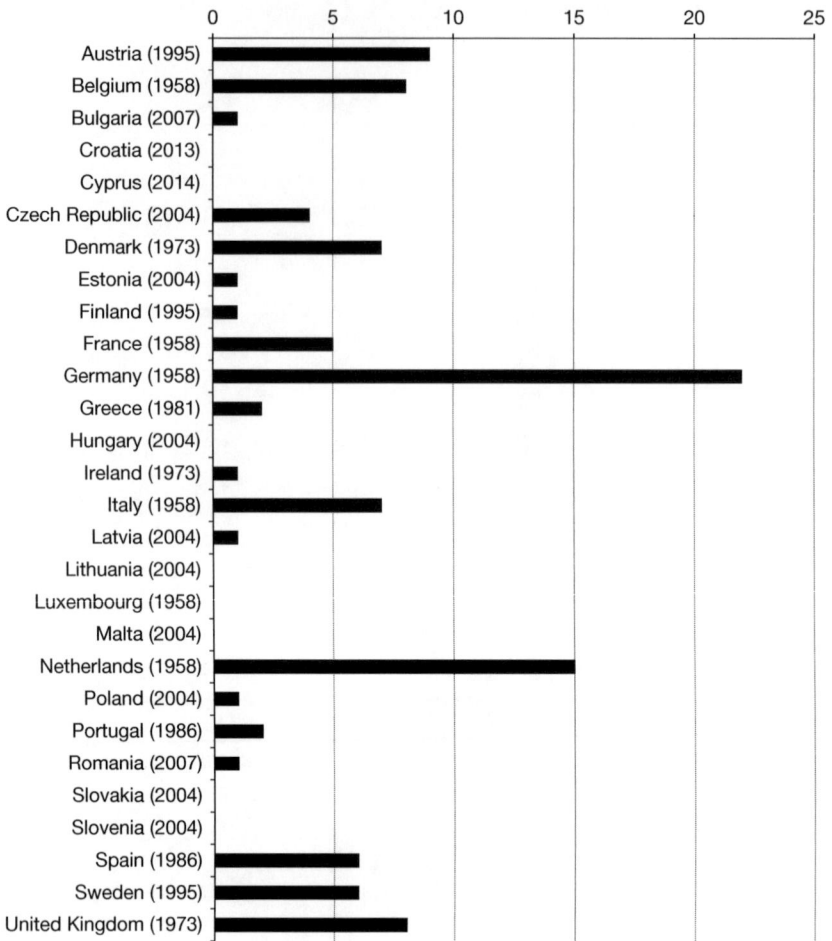

Figure 1.4 Member States of referring courts (1998–2018)

4.3 Member States' interventions

Interventions[93] **in numbers**—Similarly to what has been observed in Section 4.2, different timings of joining the EC/EU are to be borne in mind when considering the submission of observations by individual Member States in the context of references for a preliminary ruling. Besides noting that certain Member States have refrained from intervening in any of the preliminary rulings considered in the present analysis, the Member States that have intervened the most before the CJEU are France and Italy. This is not surprising, not only considering the longstanding status of these countries as Member States (since 1958), but also the traditional emphasis that protection of *droit d'auteur/diritto d'autore* has received at several levels, including at the governmental one. Following Italy and France, the most active Member State has been Poland, which only joined the EU in 2004.

---

[93] Up-to-date as of August 2018. Pending cases were excluded from the analysis.

Figure 1.5 shows Member States' interventions in the copyright cases selected according to the criteria indicated in Section 4.1, and already decided (pending cases were omitted). The date in parenthesis next to each Member State indicates the year of initial EC/EU membership.

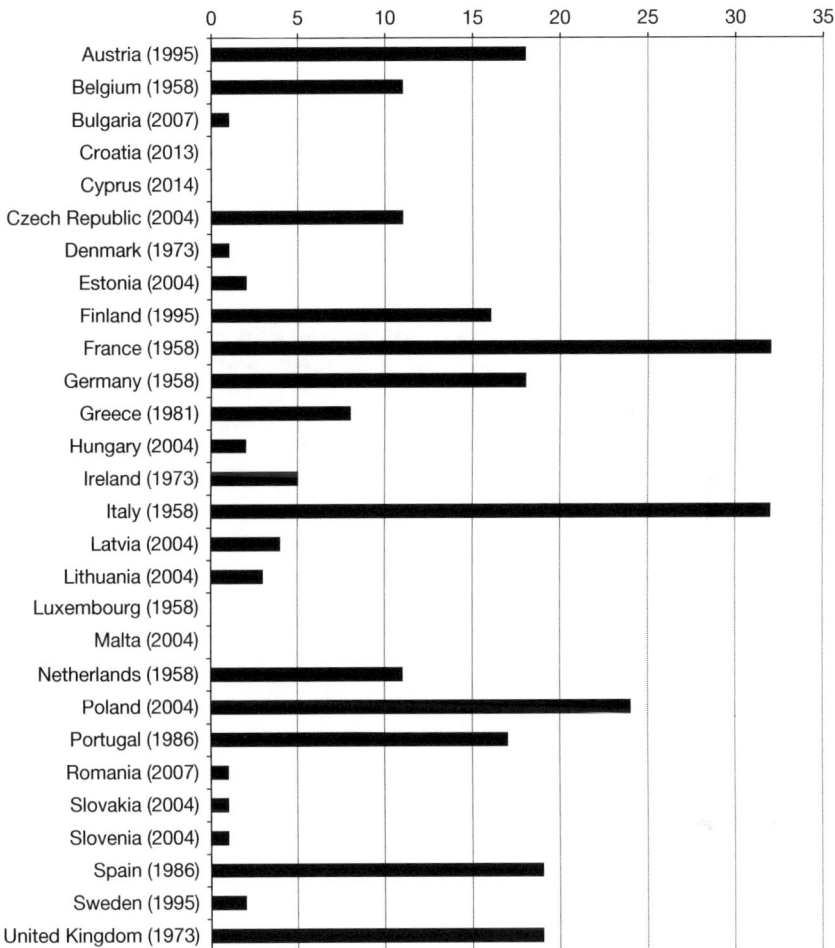

Figure 1.5 Member States intervened in preliminary rulings (1998–2018)

4.4 Judges-Rapporteur and AGs

De facto copyright specialization of Judges-Rapporteur—A decisive role in the construction of CJEU copyright architecture is likely to be attributed to the fact that, although the Court does not have specialist sections for specific areas or specialist intellectual property expertise, as a matter of fact specialization may be discerned in respect of copyright cases.[94] This has been possible both through the appointment, each

---

[94] In this sense, see also the interesting study conducted by M Favale, M Kretschmer, and P Torremans, 'Is there a EU copyright jurisprudence? An empirical analysis of the workings of the European Court of Justice' (2016) 79(1) MLR 31.

time, of a Judge-Rapporteur from a narrow pool (with Jiří Malenovský acting as Judge-Rapporteur in over 50 per cent of the cases) and that for certain issues (for example, AG Yves Bot in cases concerning interpretation of the Software Directive) the same AG has been also appointed. This has allowed the Court to develop its understanding of the EU copyright architecture in a fairly coherent (though not problem-free) fashion, discussed more extensively in Chapter 2. Figure 1.6 shows the allocation of preliminary referrals by Judge-Rapporteur.[95]

Advocates General appointed in copyright cases—Figure 1.7 shows the AGs appointed in the various references for a preliminary ruling, Eleanor Sharpston being the AG appointed the highest number of times.[96]

4.5 AG Opinions and CJEU rulings: statistical analysis suggests that the Court has a tendency towards favouring expansive approaches to the scope of copyright protection

Cases decided with and without a prior Opinion of an Advocate General—As mentioned earlier, the Court may decide to rule in a case without seeking the Opinion of the appointed AG and—even if an Opinion is provided—this is not binding on the Court. Figure 1.8 shows how often, in respect of the copyright cases discussed in this book, the CJEU has eventually ruled with or without the Opinion of an AG.[97]

A tendency of the Court to agree with expansive AG Opinions—With regard to the relationship between AG Opinions and resulting CJEU rulings, analysis of data extracted from case law shows that the Court has shown a greater tendency towards disagreeing with the AG Opinion when this has proposed a non-expansive interpretation of copyright provisions. In other words, the Court tends to substantially agree with its AGs when they adopt a broad interpretation of copyright provisions, although the reasoning of the appointed AG and the resulting judgment may differ. By 'expansive' (and 'non-expansive') is hereby intended a reading of relevant provisions in copyright directives that eventually results in broader protection for authors and copyright holders and, as a result, greater control on how their subject matter may be used.[98] This has followed from a tendency to favour a broad reading of the scope of economic rights and/or a narrow interpretation of the scope of available exceptions and limitations, and/or a broad interpretation of enforcement tools, including identification of competent courts and remedies available for the enforcement of copyright. The question, as a result, is whether what appears to be the case at an empirical level is also statistically relevant.

Does the background of the AG matter?—An additional question is whether the background of the appointed AG, in particular whether the AG appointed in a certain case may or may not be regarded as having a background as an academic (by 'academic' is meant an AG who, prior to their appointment at the Court, was linked to a university institution[99]), has any statistical relevance in determining whether the Court would prefer to agree with the Opinion of AGs with an academic background

---

[95] Up-to-date as of August 2018. Pending cases were excluded from the analysis.
[96] Ibid.   [97] Ibid.
[98] T Rendas, 'Copyright, technology and the CJEU: an empirical study' (2018) 49(2) IIC 153, 168–70, suggests however that the CJEU tends to safeguard the lawfulness of technologically enabled uses of copyright works.
[99] Relevant information has been extracted from <https://curia.europa.eu/jcms/jcms/Jo2_7026/en/> (last accessed 15 August 2018).

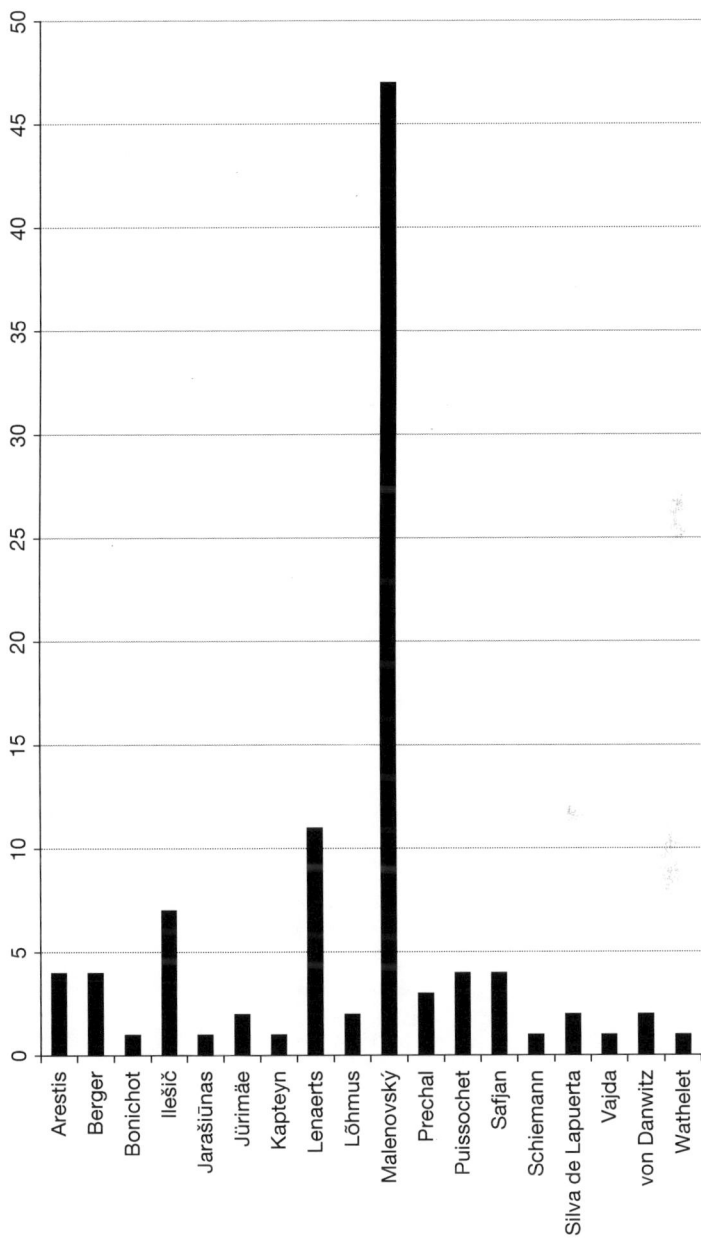

Figure 1.6 Judges-Rapporteur in preliminary rulings (1998–2018)

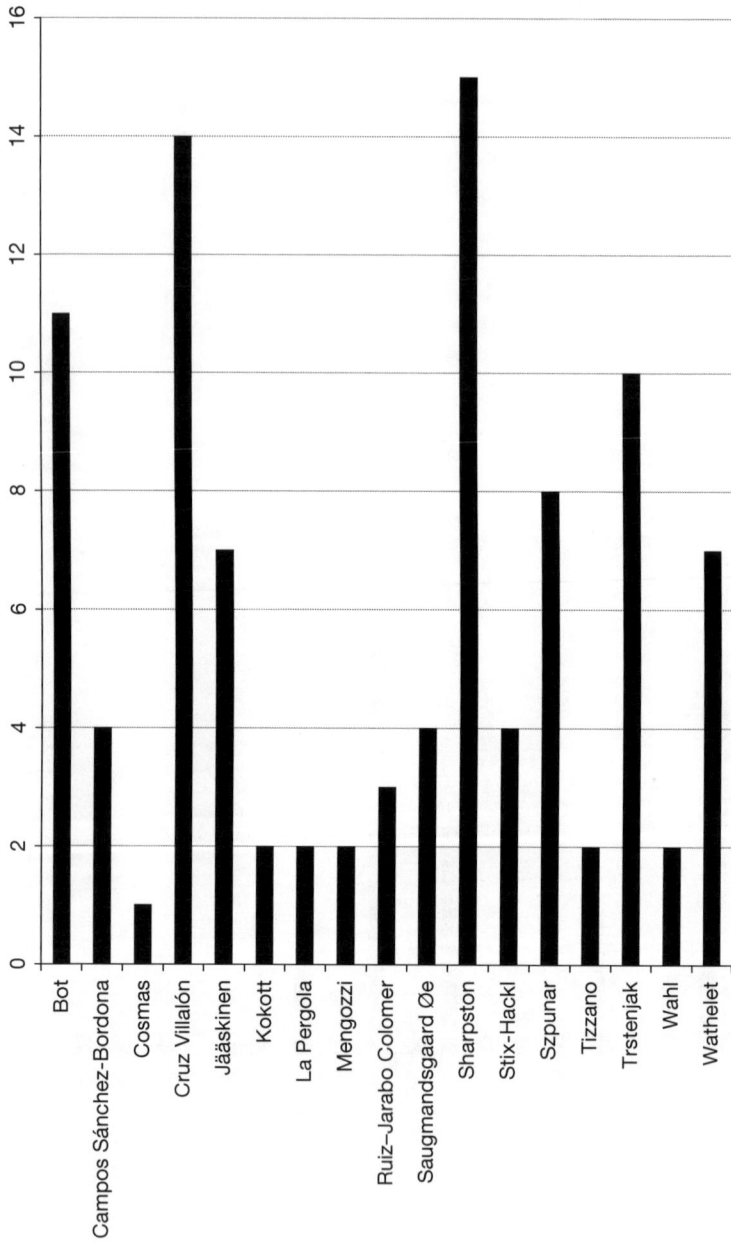

Figure 1.7 Advocates General in preliminary rulings (1998–2018)

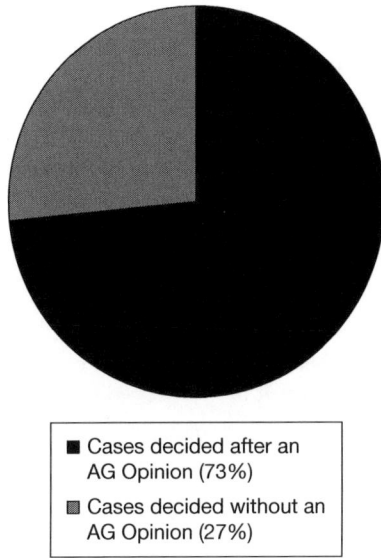

Figure 1.8 Preliminary rulings and AG Opinions (1998–2018)

or rather AGs with different types of background, for example, experience in national judiciary or government.

Results (with Carlo Maria Rosati, MD*)—Excluding two decisions for which the Opinion of the AG was neutral, for the remaining seventy decisions, the Court agreed with the AG Opinion in forty-four out of forty-seven cases (93.6 per cent) and in thirteen out of twenty-three cases (56.5 per cent) when such Opinion was expansive vs non-expansive, respectively. Such a difference was statistically significant (Fisher exact test; p value < 0.001).

		Did the Court follow the AG Opinion?	
		Yes	No
AG Opinion	Expansive	44	3
	Non-expansive	13	10

As shown in the table below, the Court agreed with the AG Opinion in twenty-nine out of thirty-five cases (82.9 per cent) and in thirty out of thirty-seven cases (81.1 per cent) when the AG had an academic vs non-academic background, respectively. Such difference was not statistically significant (chi square test; p value = 1).

		Did the Court follow the AG Opinion?	
		Yes	No
AG's background	Academic	29	6
	Non-academic	30	7

* University of Michigan, Ann Arbor (MI, USA). Email: carlo.m.rosati@gmail.com.

In conclusion:

- The CJEU has had a tendency to agree with the AG Opinion when this proposed an expansive interpretation of copyright provisions. This means that an expansive AG Opinion is more likely to be accepted by the Court than a non-expansive one.
- The background of the AG was not statistically relevant when considering whether the CJEU has or has not departed from the relevant AG Opinion.

Conclusion

The process of EU copyright harmonization saw its official start with the adoption of the 1991 Software Directive, and has progressed over time with further directives and—more recently—tightly targeted regulations that have tackled different areas of copyright. In parallel to this, the EU judiciary has acquired an increasingly central role, with the Court ruling on nearly a hundred preliminary references over a timeframe of twenty years. Statistical analysis has also shown that the CJEU tends to favour an expansive approach to copyright protection. This is signalled by the fact that the Court tends to agree with the Opinion of the AG appointed in a certain case when this proposed an interpretation of EU copyright provisions that favours authors and copyright holders, whether in construing the scope of economic rights and exceptions and limitations or when defining the type and limits of available enforcement tools and remedies.

The next chapter will focus on the standards employed in CJEU case law, and will conduct a statistical analysis intended to show relations between them. This will serve as a basis for understanding what forces and patterns have contributed to orienting the approaches and work of the Court which, in relation to selected areas, will be discussed in Part II.

2

Standards Applied in Relevant Copyright Rulings

A Data-Based Case Law Analysis

Introduction

This chapter seeks to achieve three principal objectives. The first is identifying the policies and principles (cumulatively, standards) that the CJEU has relied upon in its copyright cases and exploring the relevant content thereof. The second is indicating the statistical relevance of relying on certain standards. The third is performing a statistical analysis using open source software for statistical computing and graphics R (<https://www.r-project.org/>), using Fisher exact test and chi square test for categorical data (analysis of contingency tables), as appropriate. This will serve to examine how certain standards are used in combination with others, and what the statistical relevance thereof is. It will be shown that the Court has relied consistently on certain standards in relation to specific areas, and that trends similar to those occurred in the past may also be expected in the future. In this sense, reliance on certain standards has been of assistance to the Court in building its own framework for EU copyright rules.

Policies and principles—As already mentioned, I am referring to what follows as *policies* and *principles*. According to Dworkin, the former are standards that set out a goal to be reached, while the latter are standards that are to be observed, not because they will advance or secure an economic, political, or social situation deemed desirable, but because it is a requirement of justice or fairness or some other dimension of morality.[1] Reliance on such standards has helped the Court define the content of the *rules* included in relevant EU legislation.[2]

1. Standards Employed in CJEU Copyright Case Law

Origin of the standards employed by the CJEU—In its case law the CJEU has employed several policies and principles that have helped it shape the EU framework, by creating an actual EU approach to copyright,[3] which goes beyond the traditional dichotomy between continental-style *droit d'auteur* and common law

---

[1] RM Dworkin, 'The model of rules' (1967) 35(1) U Chi L Rev 14, 23.   [2] Ibid, 27–9.
[3] Also noting that the CJEU has crafted 'a truly *communautaire* copyright', see E Derclaye, 'The Court of Justice copyright case law: quo vadis?' (2014) 36(11) EIPR 716, 722–3.

copyright.[4] Some of the standards relied upon by the CJEU have been derived from the language of EU copyright legislation, while others may be regarded as general principles of EU law, standards derived from fundamental rights as enshrined in the EU Charter, or standards developed by the CJEU itself.

Standards considered by the CJEU—The analysis of CJEU case law has resulted in the detection and extraction of the following standards, which are analyzed (for mere convenience) in an order that lists, first, generally applicable standards (G) and, secondly, standards that have been applied more frequently (though not necessarily exclusively) in specific areas of copyright (S), for example, economic rights or exceptions and limitations.

- High level of protection (G);
- Autonomous concepts of EU law (G);
- Effectiveness (G);
- Proportionality (G);
- Fair balance of different rights and interests (G);
- Interpretation in light of international instruments (G);
- Interpretation in light of wording and context of provisions (G);
- Interpretation in light of objectives pursued by legislation at issue (G);
- Interpretation in light of fundamental rights as granted by the EU Charter of Fundamental Rights (G);
- Preventive nature of economic rights (S);
- Strict interpretation of exceptions and limitations (S).

Other standards—The list above is not exhaustive, as the CJEU has also referred to other standards in its decisions, including:

- The need for an evolutionary interpretation of relevant legislation;
- Consideration of *travaux préparatoires*;
- Review of different language versions of a certain piece of legislation;
- Need to attribute the same meaning to the same concepts in different pieces of legislation;
- Interpretation in light of general EU law principles.

An overview of the standards the Court has relied upon—By means of a necessary simplification, Figure 2.1[5] displays what principles the CJEU has referred to or relied upon in the decisions listed in Chapter 1, Section 4.1.

[4] According to some commentators, reliance on such principles has also allowed the Court to inject some flexibility into the system: R Xalabarder, 'The role of the CJEU in harmonizing EU copyright law' (2016) 47(6) IIC 635, 635.
[5] Up-to-date as of August 2018. Pending cases were excluded from the analysis.

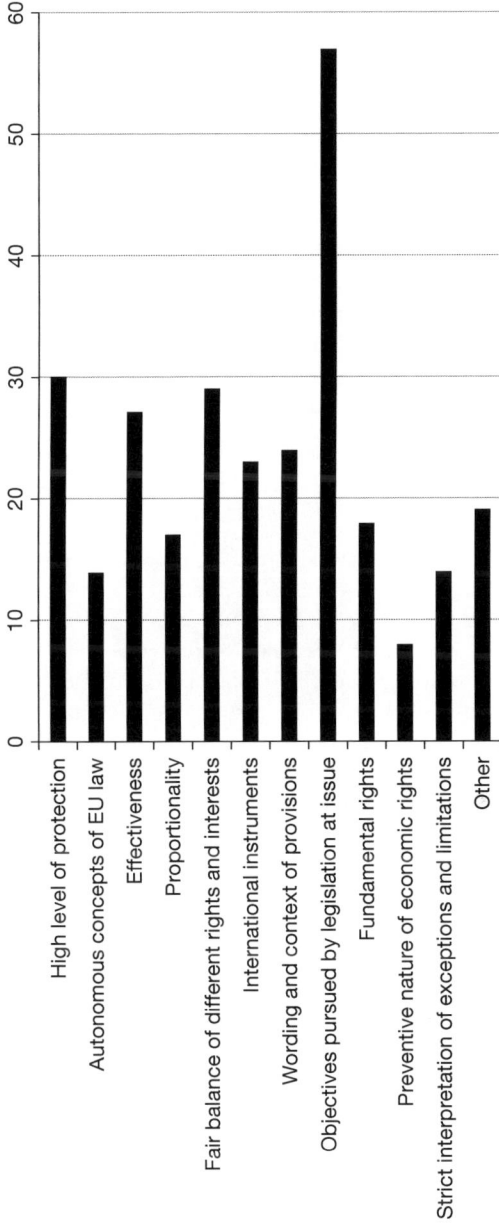

Figure 2.1 Standards employed by the CJEU in its copyright case law (1998–2018)

2. The Meaning and Content of the Standards Employed by the CJEU

What is the content of the standards employed by the CJEU?—The Court has relied upon different standards that have allowed certain interpretations of relevant provisions in EU directives. The following sections will discuss the content and meaning of the following standards: need to guarantee a 'high level of protection'; interpretation of concepts in relevant directives that do not refer to the law of individual EU Member States as 'autonomous concepts' of EU law; effectiveness; proportionality; need to guarantee a fair balance of different rights and interests; need to interpret relevant provisions in light of international instruments that the EU directives at issue have implemented into the EU legal order and are meant to comply with; consideration of the wording and context of relevant provisions also taking into account, if necessary, different language versions of the same piece of legislation or referring to identical concepts found in other EU legislation; need to interpret relevant provisions in light of the objectives pursued by the piece of legislation at issue, also considering at times the *travaux préparatoires* or adopting an evolutionary interpretation of relevant legislation; interpretation in light of fundamental rights as granted by the EU Charter; preventive nature of economic rights; and strict interpretation of exceptions and limitations.

2.1 Guarantee of a 'high level of protection'

Occurrence—This is a standard that the CJEU has relied upon almost invariably every time when deciding a case concerning economic rights and enforcement/remedies, with the result that the outcome of the relevant case would favour an expansive approach to the scope of copyright protection. The principle that protection must be at a high level is stated explicitly in both the InfoSoc Directive (Recitals 4 and 9) and the Enforcement Directive (Recital 10), while it is only implied in Recital 5 of the Rental and Lending Rights Directive.[6] The Enforcement Directive (Recital 32) links the duty of guaranteeing the full respect of intellectual property to the obligation of protecting it as stemming from Article 17(2) of the EU Charter. This 'maximalist' understanding of intellectual property, according to some commentators, would result from the ambiguous language of Article 17(2) of the EU Charter itself, including its different language versions.[7] For others, envisaging a high level of protection for copyright would only be justified if the standard for protection (originality) were also high.[8]

An expansive view of copyright protection—From the analysis of relevant CJEU case law, as mentioned, what appears is that each and every time that the Court has referred to this standard, the resulting decision has favoured a broad understanding of economic rights and remedies.

---

[6] In this sense, *Vereniging Openbare Bibliotheken*, C-174/15, EU:C:2016:856, para 47. According to A Peukert, 'Intellectual property as an end in itself?' (2011) 33(2) EIPR 67, 67–8, statements in EU directives regarding the need to ensure a 'high level of protection' show a certain tendency towards a self-sufficient property logic.

[7] C Geiger, 'Intellectual property shall be protected!? Article 17(2) of the Charter of Fundamental Rights of the European Union: a mysterious provision with an unclear scope' (2009) 31(3) EIPR 113, 114–15.

[8] C Handig, 'The copyright term "work"—European harmonisation at an unknown level' (2009) 40(6) IIC 665, 680.

Laserdisken—The first case in which the Court referred to it is *Laserdisken*, C-479/
04. In interpreting the content of relevant EC Treaty provisions concerning Member
States' cultural policy and educational policy, the CJEU considered that the content
thereof is reflected—expressly or in essence—in a number of recitals in the preamble to
the InfoSoc Directive.[9] In particular, as is apparent from Recitals 9 and 11:

> any harmonisation of copyright and related rights must take as a basis a high level of protection,
> since such rights are crucial to intellectual creation and a rigorous, effective system for their
> protection is one of the main ways of ensuring that European cultural creativity and produc-
> tion receive the necessary resources and of safeguarding the independence and dignity of artistic
> creators and performers.[10]

This, together with consideration that adequate protection by means of copyright and
related rights is 'of great importance from a cultural standpoint'[11] and that the InfoSoc
Directive—through its system of exceptions and limitations—allows Member States to
exercise their powers, inter alia, in the fields of education and teaching,[12] led the CJEU
to conclude that the cultural and educational aspects specific to EU Member States have
been taken into account fully by the EU legislature when adopting the InfoSoc Directive.[13]

High level of protection ... of what/whom?—Although in *Laserdisken*, C-479/04,
the 'high level of protection' that needs to be guaranteed was referred to copyright and
related rights,[14] case law on this point has not always been consistent. There are in fact
decisions that link the 'high level of protection' to copyright and related rights (Recitals
4 and 9 in the preamble to the InfoSoc Directive refer, respectively, to 'intellectual
property' and 'copyright and related rights'), while another group of decisions refers to
rightholders,[15] and a third group to authors.[16]

In relation to the InfoSoc Directive, this lack of consistency is likely attributable
to the very language of Recitals 9, 10, and 11 in the preamble thereof, which refer to
a heterogeneous group, by mentioning authors, performers, producers, and culture
industry alike, as well as consumers and the public at large, while also affirming that
intellectual property has been recognized as an integral part of property. In relation to
enforcement of copyright under the umbrella of the Enforcement Directive, what is
deserving of a high level of protection is intellectual property.[17] The objective of that
piece of legislation is in fact to approximate the legislative systems of the EU Member

---

[9] *Laserdisken*, C-479/04, EU:C:2006:549, para 74.
[10] Ibid, para 75.   [11] Ibid, para 76.   [12] Ibid, para 78.   [13] Ibid, para 80.
[14] In this sense, see also *Peek & Cloppenburg*, C-456/06, EU:C:2008:232, para 37; *Stichting de
Thuiskopie*, C-462/09, EU:C:2011:397, para 32; *Dimensione Direct Sales and Labianca*, C-516/13,
EU:C:2015:315, para 34; *Stichting Brein*, C-610/15, EU:C:2017:456, para 32.
[15] *Svensson and Others*, C-466/12, EU:C:2014:76, para 17; *UPC Telekabel Wien*, C-314/12,
EU:C:2014:192, para 31.
[16] *SGAE*, C-306/05, EU:C:2006:764, para 36; *Peek & Cloppenburg*, C-456/06, EU:C:2008:232,
para 37; *Infopaq International*, C-5/08, EU:C:2009:465, para 40; *Bezpečnostní softwarová asociace*,
C-393/09, EU:C:2010:816, para 54; *Football Association Premier League and Others*, C-403/08 and
C-429/08, EU:C:2011:631, para 186; *Painer*, C-145/10, EU:C:2011:798, para 107; *Luksan*, C-
277/10, EU:C:2012:65, para 66; *ITV Broadcasting*, C-607/11, EU:C:2013:147, para 20; *Nintendo
and Others*, C-355/12, EU:C:2014:25, para 27; *OSA*, C-351/12, EU:C:2014:110, para 23; *Art &
Allposters International*, C-419/13, EU:C:2015:27, para 47; *Sociedade Portuguesa de Autores CRL*, C-
151/15, EU:C:2015:468, para 12; *SBS Belgium*, C-325/14, EU:C:2015:764, para 14; *GS Media*, C-
160/15, EU:C:2016:644, para 30; *Soulier and Doke*, C-301/15, EU:C:2016:878, para 30 (implicitly);
ITV Broadcasting, C-275/15, EU:C:2017:144, para 22; *Stichting Brein*, C-527/15, EU:C:2017:300,
para 27; *Stichting Brein*, C-610/15, EU:C:2017:456, para 22; *Renckhoff*, C-161/17, EU:C:2018:634,
para 18.
[17] *NEW WAVE CZ*, C-427/15, EU:C:2017:18, para 24; *Stowarzyszenie Oławska Telewizja Kablowa*,
C-367/15, EU:C:2017:36, para 22.

States with regard to the means of enforcing intellectual property rights so as to ensure a high, equivalent, and homogeneous level of protection in the internal market (Recital 10).[18] It is in order to realize that objective, which may also be discerned in the wording of Recitals 17 and 26 in the preamble thereof,[19] that this piece of legislation concerns all the measures, procedures, and remedies necessary to ensure the enforcement of intellectual property rights.[20] The objective—to ensure a high level of protection of intellectual property—is in line with Article 17(2) of the EU Charter.[21]

2.2 Autonomous concepts of EU law

No reference to the laws of individual Member States—When a certain provision in an EU directive makes no reference to national legislation, then relevant concepts are not to be defined at the national level, but are rather to be intended as autonomous concepts of EU law. As such, they are to be given a uniform application throughout the EU. This is an expression of the principle of autonomy of EU law. As the Court clarified in *Ekro*, C-327/82:

The need for a uniform application of Community law and the principle of equality require that the terms of a provision of Community law which makes no express reference to the law of the Member States for the purpose of determining its meaning and scope must normally be given an independent and uniform interpretation throughout the Community; that interpretation must take into account the context of the provision and the purpose of the relevant regulations.[22]

Increased harmonization—The CJEU has often employed this standard in its copyright case law, with the practical effect of strengthening harmonization of copyright laws across the EU. In one of the first decisions concerning the 1992 Rental and Lending Rights Directive, *SENA*, C-245/00, the Court addressed the concept of 'equitable remuneration' in Article 8(2) thereof. It noted that, since that provision makes no reference to the laws of EU Member States, pursuant to the principle of the autonomy of EU law, equitable remuneration is 'a concept that must be interpreted uniformly in all Member States'.[23] However, lacking any EU criteria for determining what constitutes uniform equitable remuneration, it is for the Member States alone to identify, in their own territory, the most relevant criteria for ensuring, within the limits imposed by EU law and the 1992 Rental and Lending Rights Directive, adherence to that EU concept.[24] The same reasoning may be discerned in *VEWA*, C-271/10, with reference to the notion of 'remuneration' in Article 5(1) of the 1992 Rental and Lending Rights Directive.[25] Over time the Court has applied the principle of autonomous interpretation and uniform application in relation to different concepts.

Specific areas of application—In relation to its construction of economic rights, the CJEU referred to the need to consider the notion of 'public' within Article 3(1) of the InfoSoc Directive as an autonomous concept of EU law in its first decision on the right of communication to the public (*SGAE*, C-306/05[26]). It achieved a similar conclusion with regard to the notions of 'reproduction' (*Football Association Premier League and*

[18] *Diageo Brands*, C-681/13, EU:C:2015:471, para 71.
[19] *Liffers*, C-99/15, EU:C:2016:173, para 24.
[20] *Diageo Brands*, C-681/13, EU:C:2015:471, para 71.
[21] *United Video Properties*, C-57/15, EU:C:2016:611, para 27.
[22] *Ekro*, C-327/82, EU:C:1984:11, para 11.
[23] *SENA*, C-245/00, EU:C:2003:68, para 24.   [24] Ibid, para 34.
[25] *VEWA*, C-271/10, EU:C:2011:442, paras 25–26.
[26] *SGAE*, C-306/05, EU:C:2006:764, para 31.

Others, C-429/08[27]) and 'reproduction in part' (*Infopaq*, C-5/08[28]) within Article 2 of the InfoSoc Directive, and the notion of 'distribution' (*Donner*, C-5/11;[29] *Dimensione Direct Sales and Labianca*, C-516/13[30]) within Article 4 of the same directive. With reference to the right of distribution, in *UsedSoft*, C-128/11, the Court clarified that the notion of 'sale' within Article 4(2) of the Software Directive is to be regarded as an autonomous concept of EU law.[31] Similarly, in *ITV Broadcasting*, C-275/15, the CJEU found that the notion of 'access to cable of broadcasting services' within Article 9 of the InfoSoc Directive is an autonomous concept of EU law.[32] Recently, in his Opinion in *Levola Hengelo*, C-310/17 (in progress), AG Wathelet held that 'work' under the InfoSoc Directive is also an autonomous concept of EU law.[33]

A similar pattern may be discerned with reference to exceptions and limitations. The CJEU has referred to the following as autonomous concepts of EU law: 'fair compensation' for private copying within Article 5(2)(b) of the InfoSoc Directive (*Padawan*, C-467/08;[34] *Hewlett-Packard Belgium*, C-572/13;[35] *EGEDA and Others*, C-470/14[36]); 'by means of its own facilities' within Article 5(2)(d) of the InfoSoc Directive (*DR and TV2 Danmark*, C-510/10[37]); and 'parody' under Article 5(3)(k) of the InfoSoc Directive (*Deckmyn*, C-201/13[38]).

2.3 Effectiveness

Combination with other standards—The principle of effectiveness has often been employed together with other standards, including proportionality and fair balance and, to a lesser extent, interpretation of provisions in EU directives in a way that is compatible with fundamental rights as envisaged in the EU Charter. These correlations are not surprising when reference to effectiveness is found in cases concerning enforcement and remedies: it is Article 3 of the Enforcement Directive (read in light of Recitals 3 and 10 in the preamble thereof)[39] that imposes on EU Member States the duty to provide that measures, procedures, and remedies necessary to ensure the enforcement of the intellectual property rights are fair, equitable, not unnecessarily complicated or costly or such as to entail unreasonable time-limits or unwarranted delays, effective, proportionate, and dissuasive and applied in such a manner as to avoid the creation of barriers to legitimate trade and to provide for safeguards against their abuse.

---

[27] *Football Association Premier League and Others*, C-403/08 and C-429/08, EU:C:2011:631, para 154.
[28] *Infopaq International*, C-5/08, EU:C:2009:465, paras 27–29. For a critical appraisal of the use of this principle in this ruling, see S Vousden, '*Infopaq* and the Europeanisation of copyright law' (2010) 1(2) WIPOJ 197, 199.
[29] *Donner*, C-5/11, EU:C:2012:370, para 25.
[30] *Dimensione Direct Sales and Labianca*, C-516/13, EU:C:2015:315, para 22.
[31] *UsedSoft*, C-128/11, EU:C:2012:407, para 40.
[32] *ITV Broadcasting*, C-275/15, EU:C:2017:144, para 18.
[33] Opinion of Advocate General Melchior Wathelet in *Levola Hengelo*, C-310/17, EU:C:2018:618, paras 37–39.
[34] *Padawan*, C-467/08, EU:C:2010:620, para 37.
[35] *Hewlett-Packard Belgium*, C-572/13, EU:C:2015:750, para 35.
[36] *EGEDA and Others*, C-470/14, EU:C:2016:418, para 38.
[37] *DR and TV2 Danmark*, C-510/10, EU:C:2012:244, para 34.
[38] *Deckmyn and Vrijheidsfonds*, C-201/13, EU:C:2014:2132, para 15.
[39] *Stowarzyszenie Oławska Telewizja Kablowa*, C-367/15, EU:C:2017:36, paras 21–22. In relation to effectiveness of provisions of the Enforcement Directive, see *SNB-REACT*, C-521/17, EU:C:2018:639, para 32 (to be noted that this is a case whose background national proceedings related to trade mark, rather than copyright).

Promusicae—In *Promusicae*, C-275/06, the CJEU was asked whether EU law (more specifically, Articles 15(2) and 18 of the E-commerce Directive, Article 8(1) and (2) of the InfoSoc Directive, Article 8 of the Enforcement Directive, and Articles 17(2) and 47 of the EU Charter) allows Member States to limit to certain specific contexts (criminal investigations, public security, and national defence) the duty of operators of electronic communications networks and services, providers of access to telecommunications networks, and providers of data storage services to retain and make available connection and traffic data generated by the communications established during the supply of an information society service.

The CJEU acknowledged that the purpose of those directives is ensuring, especially in the information society, effective protection of industrial property, in particular copyright. However, the protection afforded under such legislation is without prejudice to other types of protection, including personal data.[40] As regards the EU Charter, while this recognizes both intellectual property as a fundamental right within the right to property and the right to effective judicial protection, it also mandates protection of personal data and private life. Effective protection of copyright should not be considered in isolation, but rather as part of a mechanism that requires the balancing of different rights and interests. This is so because EU law requires Member States, when transposing those EU directives, and national courts and authorities, when interpreting them, to strike a fair balance between the various fundamental rights protected by the EU legal order. This also requires that due consideration be paid to the general EU principle of proportionality.[41] Consequently, EU law does not impose such a duty of disclosure. Nonetheless it cannot be concluded that EU law forbids Member States from envisaging such a duty.[42]

Enforcement and its effectiveness—Interpretation of the Enforcement Directive has required consideration of the principle of effectiveness on a number of occasions. For instance, the right to information within Article 8(1) of the Enforcement Directive has been considered to be aimed at benefiting the copyright holder in the context of proceedings concerning an infringement of their right to property and, more generally, as an application and implementation of the fundamental right to an effective remedy as guaranteed in Article 47 of the EU Charter. Thus, its recognition ensures the effective exercise of the fundamental right to property, which includes intellectual property in Article 17(2) of the EU Charter.[43]

Other areas in which effectiveness has been considered—The context of enforcement is not the only one in which effectiveness has been considered. The Court has also referred to it in the broader context of interpretation of national law in light of EU law, with regard to economic rights and exceptions and limitations, and in the application of EU law to acts committed in third countries but targeting the EU. Examples of these instances are provided below.

Interpretation of national law—A general principle of EU law is that national law is to be interpreted in light of, and so to achieve, the objectives of the relevant piece of EU legislation (see further in Section 2.8). In *VG Wort*, C-457/11, one of the questions referred to the CJEU was whether in the period comprised between the date of entry into force of the InfoSoc Directive and the date on which the directive was transposed

---

[40] *Promusicae*, C-275/06, EU:C:2008:54, para 57.   [41] Ibid, para 70.
[42] *LSG-Gesellschaft zur Wahrnehmung von Leistungsschutzrechten*, C-557/07, EU:C:2009:107, para 41.
[43] *Coty Germany*, C-580/13, EU:C:2015:485, para 29. See also *NEW WAVE CZ*, C-427/15, EU:C:2017:18.

into national (German) law, the doing of acts falling in principle under the scope of that piece of EU legislation would be affected by it. The Court answered in the negative, noting that the directive has no retroactive effect and that the general obligation owed by national courts to interpret domestic law in conformity with a directive exists only once the period for its transposition has expired.[44] This obligation is inherent in the system of the TFEU, 'since it permits national courts, for the matters within their jurisdiction, to ensure the full effectiveness of European Union law when they determine the disputes before them'.[45]

Economic rights—In *Peek & Cloppenburg*, C-456/06, in constructing the right of distribution within Article 4 of the InfoSoc Directive, the CJEU noted that Recitals 9 and 11 state that copyright harmonization should achieve a high level of protection, that authors must receive an appropriate reward for the use of their work, and that the system for the protection of copyright must be rigorous and effective. Such goals may be only fulfilled within the framework put in place by the EU legislature. This means that the EU legislature would need to amend, if necessary, EU rules on protection of intellectual property if it considered that protection of authors is not assured to an adequate level by the legislation in force.[46] With regard to the right of distribution in the context of the Software Directive, the Court dismissed the idea that a contract denominated as a 'licence' could not be regarded as a 'sale' if the actual conditions are those of the latter rather than the former:

[I]f the term 'sale' within the meaning of Article 4(2) of the Software Directive were not given a broad interpretation as encompassing all forms of product marketing characterized by the grant of a right to use a copy of a computer program, for an unlimited period, in return for payment of a fee designed to enable the copyright holder to obtain a remuneration corresponding to the economic value of the copy of the work of which he is the proprietor, then the effectiveness of that provision would be undermined, since suppliers would merely have to call the contract a 'licence' rather than a 'sale' in order to circumvent the rule of exhaustion and divest it of all scope.[47]

Exceptions and limitations—The CJEU has also considered effectiveness in the context of exceptions and limitations. In *Football Association Premier League and Others*, C-403/08 and C-429/08, for instance, with regard to the temporary copies exemption within Article 5(1) of the InfoSoc Directive, the Court noted how the interpretation of relevant conditions therein 'must enable the effectiveness of the exception thereby established to be safeguarded and permit observance of the exception's purpose'.[48] An identical reasoning may be discerned in other cases, including: *Eugen Ulmer*, C-117/13, in relation to digitization of works in library collections and Article 5(3)(n) of the InfoSoc Directive;[49] *Deckmyn*, C-201/13, in relation to parody under Article 5(3)(k) of the InfoSoc Directive;[50] *Painer*, C-145/10, with regard to the quotation exception within Article 5(3)(d) of the InfoSoc Directive. In the latter, the Court held that:

[W]hile the conditions set out in Article 5(3)(d) of Directive 2001/29 must ... be interpreted strictly, since that provision is a derogation from the general rule established by that directive, the

[44] *VG Wort*, C-457/11, EU:C:2013:426, paras 26–27.   [45] Ibid, para 25.
[46] *Peek & Cloppenburg*, C-456/06, EU:C:2008:232, paras 37–39.
[47] *UsedSoft*, C-128/11, EU:C:2012:407, para 49.
[48] *Football Association Premier League and Others*, C-403/08 and C-429/08, EU:C:2011:631, para 163.
[49] *Eugen Ulmer*, C-117/13, EU:C:2014:2196, para 32.
[50] *Deckmyn and Vrijheidsfonds*, C-201/13, EU:C:2014:2132, para 23.

fact remains that the interpretation of those conditions must also enable the effectiveness of the exception thereby established to be safeguarded and its purpose to be observed.[51]

By contrast, in other cases effectiveness of the limitation or exception has taken a back seat to other goals. For example, in *Stichting de Thuiskopie*, C-462/09, the Court noted how Article 5(2)(b) (read in light of Recital 35 in the preamble) and 5(5) (in particular the three-step test requirement that the legitimate interests of a rightholder are not unduly prejudiced) of the InfoSoc Directive requires that effective recovery of the fair compensation must be guaranteed to compensate the authors harmed by the doing of unauthorized acts of reproduction pursuant to a private copying limitation.[52] The Court confirmed this approach in *Amazon.com International Sales and Others*, C-521/11;[53] *Austro-Mechana*, C-572/14;[54] and *Microsoft Mobile Sales International and Others*, C-110/15.[55]

Acts committed in third countries but targeting the EU—In *L'Oréal and Others*, C-324/09, the Court had to consider whether the proprietor of a trade mark registered in an EU Member State or at the EU level may be able to prevent, under relevant provisions of EU trade mark instruments, the offer for sale, on an online marketplace, of goods bearing that trade mark which have not been put on the market in the EEA (for national trade marks) or in the EU (for the EU trade mark), or whether it is sufficient if the offer for sale is targeted at consumers located in the territory covered by the trade mark. Answering the latter in the affirmative, the CJEU noted that, if it were otherwise, operators of online marketplaces targeting EU-based consumers but located in a third state would, so far as offers for sale of that type are concerned, have no obligation to comply with EU intellectual property rules. Such a situation would have an impact on the effectiveness (*effet utile*) of those rules.[56] The same reasoning may be discerned also in the copyright context. In *Football Dataco*, C-173/11, the Court reasoned in this sense in relation to holders of database rights with regard to unauthorized acts of reutilization of the content of a database performed in a third country, yet targeting the public in an EU Member State. If the Database Directive were inapplicable, this would have an impact on the effectiveness of the protection under the national law concerned conferred on the database by that piece of EU legislation.[57]

2.4 Proportionality

A general principle of EU law and a principle in EU copyright directives—The Court has referred to the principle of proportionality as both a general principle of EU law, whose protection is also mandated on a fundamental rights basis by Article 52 of the EU Charter,[58] and a principle enshrined in relevant EU copyright directives. The latter is for instance the case of Articles 3 and 14 of the Enforcement Directive, as well as of

---

[51] *Painer*, C-145/10, EU:C:2011:798, para 133.
[52] *Stichting de Thuiskopie*, C-462/09, EU:C:2011:397, paras 33–34.
[53] *Amazon.com International Sales and Others*, C-521/11, EU:C:2013:515, para 31.
[54] *Austro-Mechana*, C-572/14, EU:C:2016:286, para 20.
[55] *Microsoft Mobile Sales International and Others*, C-110/15, EU:C:2016:717, para 37.
[56] *L'Oréal and Others*, C-324/09, EU:C:2011:474, para 62.
[57] *Football Dataco and Others*, C-173/11, EU:C:2012:642, para 45.
[58] Proportionality is also relevant in the context of the European Convention for the Protection of Human Rights and Fundamental Freedoms: for a discussion, see J Christoffersen, 'Human rights and balancing: the principle of proportionality', in Geiger (ed), *Research Handbook on Human Rights and Intellectual Property* (Edward Elgar:2015), 19–51.

the InfoSoc Directive with regard to the legal protection of technological measures as per Recital 48 and Article 6 thereof.

Enforcement—Article 3 of the Enforcement Directive requires that measures referred to in that directive be fair and proportionate and not excessively costly. The Court has considered proportionality within the meaning of this provision to rule out that EU law would allow the enactment of national provisions requiring an intermediary provider to actively monitor all the data of each of its customers in order to prevent any future infringement of intellectual property rights (*Scarlet Extended*, C-70/10,[59] and *SABAM*, C-360/10[60]). Still in the context of injunctions, referring to *L'Oréal and Others*, C-324/09,[61] in *Tommy Hilfiger*, C-494/15 (this being another case whose background proceedings related to trade mark, rather than copyright law), the CJEU reiterated that the requirement of an injunction be proportionate requires that it does not create barriers to legitimate trade. While an intermediary may not be required to exercise general and permanent oversight over its customers, it may be forced to take measures, which contribute to avoiding new infringements of the same nature by the same market-trader from taking place.[62] The Court also referred to proportionality in Article 3 of the Enforcement Directive, though without particular elaboration, in relation to the issue of damages (*Stowarzyszenie Oławska Telewizja Kablowa*, C-367/15[63]).

With regard to Article 14 of the Enforcement Directive, this provision requires that legal costs that the unsuccessful party will have to bear must be 'proportionate'. In *United Video Properties*, C-57/15 (a case whose background national proceedings were in the patent field), the Court held that the question of whether those costs are proportionate cannot be assessed independently of the costs that the successful party actually incurred in respect of the assistance of a lawyer, provided they are reasonable. Furthermore:

If the requirement of proportionality does not imply that the unsuccessful party must necessarily reimburse the entirety of the costs incurred by the other party, it does however mean that the successful party should have the right to reimbursement of, at the very least, a significant and appropriate part of the reasonable costs actually incurred by that party.[64]

Proportionality as a general EU law principle—As mentioned, the Court has also referred to proportionality as a general principle of EU law, which also finds its application in the field of copyright and does so irrespective of positive references in relevant directives.[65] Proportionality is also referred to in the EU Charter. Article 52 thereof states that any limitation on the exercise of the rights and freedoms recognized by that instrument must be provided for by law and respect the essence of those rights and freedoms. Subject to the principle of proportionality, limitations may be made only if they are necessary and genuinely meet objectives of general interest recognized by the EU or the need to protect the rights and freedoms of others. In this sense,

---

[59] *Scarlet Extended*, C-70/10, EU:C:2011:771, para 36.
[60] *SABAM*, C-360/10, EU:C:2012:85, para 34.
[61] *L'Oréal and Others*, C-324/09, EU:C:2011:474, paras 138–141.
[62] *Hilfiger*, C-494/15, EU:C:2016:528, para 34.
[63] *Stowarzyszenie Oławska Telewizja Kablowa*, C-367/15, EU:C:2017:36, para 21.
[64] *United Video Properties*, C-57/15, EU:C:2016:611, para 29. On the issue of costs, see also *Diageo Brands*, C-681/13, EU:C:2015:471, paras 69–80.
[65] Cf O Fischman Afori, 'Proportionality: a new mega standard in European copyright law' (2014) 45(8) IIC 889, 890, suggesting instead that '[t]he proportionality test was introduced into copyright law through the framework of remedies'.

proportionality would serve to achieve a fair balance of contrasting rights and inter-ests[66] (see further Section 2.5).

The proportionality assessment has been identified as relevant, on the one hand, to the evaluation of the appropriateness of national transpositions of EU directives and, on the other hand, to the restriction to free movement principles resulting from copy-right protection. The examples below serve to illustrate applications of proportionality in this sense.

In *Laserdisken*, C-479/04, the Court addressed the compatibility of the rule of re-gional exhaustion within Article 4(2) of the InfoSoc Directive with the principle of proportionality. The CJEU observed that this is a general principle of EU law, which 'requires that measures implemented through Community provisions be appropriate for attaining the objective pursued and must not go beyond what is necessary to achieve it'.[67] Moving on from this, the Court explored the rationale of EU harmonization of national exhaustion rules, which is an internal market one (see also Chapter 4, Section 3.2, and Chapter 7, Section 2): 'differences in the national laws governing exhaustion of the right of distribution are likely to affect directly the smooth functioning of the internal market. Accordingly, the objective of harmonization in this area is that of removing impediments to free movement.'[68] The CJEU then noted the objectives un-derlying adoption of the InfoSoc Directive, which include: preserving and developing creativity in the interests of, inter alia, authors, performers, producers, and consumers (Recital 9); protecting intellectual property in order to guarantee an appropriate re-ward for the use of works and to provide the opportunity for satisfactory returns on investment (Recital 10); and providing a rigorous and effective system of protection to ensure that European cultural creativity and production receive the necessary resources and of safeguarding the independence and dignity of artistic creators and performers (Recital 11).[69] All these considerations led the Court to conclude that the provision in Article 4(2) of the InfoSoc Directive would not be contrary to the general EU principle of proportionality.[70]

In *Promusicae*, C-275/06, the CJEU suggested that national transpositions of EU directives must ensure that a fair balance be struck between different fundamental rights protected under EU law. This obligation also applies to national authorities and courts when interpreting and applying resulting provisions. It is indeed required that interpretation of Member States' legislation adopted to comply with EU law ob-ligations is compatible with fundamental rights as recognized by the EU legal order and general EU principles such as the principle of proportionality.[71] The reference to proportionality in this decision subsequently allowed the CJEU to conclude, in *LSG-Gesellschaft zur Wahrnehmung von Leistungsschutzrechten*, C-557/07, that it would not be contrary to Article 8(3) of the Enforcement Directive, read in conjunction with Article 15(1) of Directive 2002/58[72] (Directive on privacy and electronic communi-cations), to implement a national provision that imposes an obligation to disclose to private third parties personal data relating to internet traffic in order to enable them to

---

[66] In this sense, C Geiger, 'Intellectual "property" after the Treaty of Lisbon: towards a different approach in the new European legal order?' (2010) 32(6) EIPR 255, 257.

[67] *Laserdisken*, C-479/04, EU:C:2006:549, para 53.

[68] Ibid, para 56.   [69] Ibid, para 57.   [70] Ibid, para 58.

[71] *Promusicae*, C-275/06, EU:C:2008:54, para 70.

[72] Directive 2002/58/EC of the European Parliament and of the Council of 12 July 2002 con-cerning the processing of personal data and the protection of privacy in the electronic communica-tions sector, OJ L 201, 31 July 2002, 37–47.

bring civil proceedings for copyright infringements. However, such provision must be interpreted and applied by competent authorities and courts in a way compatible with fundamental rights and general EU law principles, including proportionality.[73]

Proportionality assessment—Similarly, in *Flos*, C-168/09, the CJEU was asked to clarify whether Article 17 of Directive 98/71[74] (Design Directive) precludes national legislation which—either for a substantial period or *tout court*—excluded from copyright protection designs that, although meeting all the requirements to be eligible for copyright protection, had entered the public domain before the date of entry into force of that legislation. Answering this question in the affirmative, the Court elaborated further on how proportionality is to be understood in a copyright context. According to the Court, the test of proportionality is a two-pronged one: it requires consideration of whether, on the one hand, the national provision at issue is appropriate for attaining the objective pursued by the national law and, on the other hand, whether it is also necessary for that purpose. In the case at issue, ie one concerning the lawfulness of a national transitional period, this translates into ensuring that:

a balance is struck between, on the one hand, the acquired rights and legitimate expectations of the third parties concerned and, on the other, the interests of the rightholders. Care must also be taken to make sure that the measure does not go beyond what is needed to ensure that that balance is struck.[75]

In *Painer*, C-145/10, the Court confirmed that this is the correct understanding of proportionality and that it represents one of the limits imposed by EU law on Member States' discretion when transposing Article 5(3)(e) of the InfoSoc Directive.[76]

In *Bonnier Audio and Others*, C-461/10, the CJEU considered proportionality in order to determine whether application of a certain national provision laying down an obligation to communicate personal data to private persons in civil proceedings would be compatible with EU law. It noted how the legislation at issue required, among other things, that for an order for disclosure of this kind there must be clear evidence of an infringement of an intellectual property right, that the information may be regarded as facilitating the investigation into an infringement, and that the reasons for the measure outweigh the nuisance or other harm which the measure may entail for the person affected by it or for some other conflicting interest. The Court concluded that such a system would allow national courts to weigh the conflicting interests and take into due account the requirements of the principle of proportionality.[77]

In *Donner*, C-5/11, the Court had the opportunity to assess the scope of the right of distribution in light of the general principle of proportionality. The EU internal market is governed by the principle of free movement of goods (Article 34 TFEU). However, application of this principle is not absolute and restrictions to the free movement of goods may be justified under Article 36 TFEU for reasons relating to the protection of industrial and commercial property. The Court had to consider criminal prosecution for the offence of aiding and abetting the unauthorized distribution of copies of copyright works, and whether Articles 34 and 36 TFEU would preclude it. The referral related to the situation in which copies of such works are distributed to the

---

[73] *LSG-Gesellschaft zur Wahrnehmung von Leistungsschutzrechten*, C-557/07, EU:C:2009:107, para 29.
[74] Directive 98/71/EC of the European Parliament and of the Council of 13 October 1998 on the legal protection of designs, OJ L 289, 28 October 1998, 28–35.
[75] *Flos*, C-168/09, EU:C:2011:29, para 57.
[76] *Painer*, C-145/10, EU:C:2011:798, paras 104–105.
[77] *Bonnier Audio and Others*, C-461/10, EU:C:2012:219, paras 58–59.

public on the territory of that Member State in the context of a sale aimed specifically at the public of that State, but concluded in another Member State where those works are not protected or the protection is not enforceable against third parties. The CJEU answered in the negative, holding that the application of provisions of this kind may be considered necessary to protect the specific subject matter of the copyright, which confers inter alia the exclusive right of exploitation. The restriction on the free movement of goods resulting therefrom is accordingly justified and proportionate to the objective pursued, in circumstances such as those of the main proceedings where the accused intentionally, or at the very least knowingly, engaged in operations giving rise to the distribution of protected works to the public on the territory of a Member State in which the copyright enjoyed full protection, thereby infringing on the exclusive right of the copyright proprietor.[78]

Proportionality and fundamental rights—In *UPC Telekabel*, C-314/12, the CJEU specifically conducted an assessment in light of fundamental rights and the principle of proportionality. In considering whether a particular type of intermediary injunction, ie blocking injunctions, would be compatible with EU law, the CJEU noted that the rights at issue in a context of this kind would be copyright protection (Article 17(2) of the EU Charter), freedom to conduct a business (Article 16 of the EU Charter), and freedom of expression and information (Article 11 of the EU Charter). When the addressee of an injunction chooses the measures to be adopted in order to comply with that injunction, they must ensure compliance with the fundamental right of internet users to freedom of information. This requires that the measures adopted be strictly targeted: they must serve to bring an end to a third party's infringement of copyright or of a related right but without thereby affecting internet users who are using the provider's services in order to access information lawfully. Failing that, the provider's interference in the freedom of information of those users would be unjustified in the light of the objective pursued, and it should be possible for a court to repress any abuses thereof.[79]

2.5 Fair balance of different rights and interests

The EU Charter and its status—Another principle that the CJEU has employed in its case law, often in combination with or as an expression of the principle of proportionality to reflect the constitutional dimension of fundamental rights after the Treaty of Lisbon, and even—according to some commentators—to lend rhetorical coherence to the Court's harmonizing 'agenda',[80] is that of striking a fair balance between different, conflicting rights.

SENA—The first reference in a CJEU judgment to the need to balance different and potentially conflicting rights and interests may be discerned in *SENA*, C-245/00. Noting that it is for the Member States—rather than the EU judicature—to

---

[78] *Donner*, C-5/11, EU:C:2012:370, para 36.
[79] *UPC Telekabel Wien*, C-314/12, EU:C:2014:192, paras 56–57.
[80] In this sense, J Griffiths, 'Constitutionalising or harmonising? The Court of Justice, the right to property and European copyright law' (2013) 38(1) EL Rev 65, 71. Also considering references to the EU Charter by the CJEU as not affecting substantially the interpretation and construction of relevant EU provisions, see T Mylly, 'The constitutionalization of the European legal order: Impact of human rights on intellectual property in the EU', in Geiger (ed), *Research Handbook* 123–6. For more generous considerations regarding the Court's engagement with the EU Charter, see D Voorhoof, 'Freedom of expression and the right to information: Implications for copyright', in Geiger (ed), *Research Handbook* 342–7.

determine what constitutes equitable remuneration under the 1992 Rental and Lending Rights Directive, the CJEU also recalled that Member States must exercise this discretion within the limits set by that directive. By requiring that such remuneration be equitable (meaning 'fair'[81]), EU law mandates Member States to lay down rules for equitable remuneration that enable a proper balance to be achieved between the interests of performers and producers in obtaining remuneration for the broadcast of a particular phonogram and the interests of third parties in being able to broadcast the phonogram on terms that are reasonable. This requires the remuneration for the use of a commercial phonogram to reflect the value of that use in trade.[82] For broadcasting purposes, this means taking into account the criteria set out in Recital 17 of the preamble to the Satellite and Cable Directive, including the actual audience, the potential audience, and the language version of the broadcast at issue.[83]

Fair balance in national transpositions and applications of EU legislation—It is therefore with regard to Member States' duties when *transposing* relevant EU legislation and national authorities and courts when *interpreting* resulting national provisions that a duty of balancing, fairly, different rights and interests arises. The CJEU made this particularly clear in *Promusicae*, C-275/06, and subsequent case law, including *LSG-Gesellschaft zur Wahrnehmung von Leistungsschutzrechten*, C-557/07,[84] *Bonnier Audio and Others*, C-461/10,[85] *Deckmyn and Vrijheidsfonds*, C-201/13,[86] *Coty Germany*, C-580/13,[87] and *Mc Fadden*, C-484/14.[88] In *Promusicae*, C-275/06, the Court moved from the peculiar nature of provisions in EU directives to set out obligations for EU Member States:

As to those directives, their provisions are relatively general, since they have to be applied to a large number of different situations which may arise in any of the Member States. They therefore logically include rules which leave the Member States with the necessary discretion to define transposition measures which may be adapted to the various situations possible ... That being so, the Member States must, when transposing the directives mentioned above, take care to rely on an interpretation of the directives which allows a fair balance to be struck between the various fundamental rights protected by the Community legal order. Further, when implementing the measures transposing those directives, the authorities and courts of the Member States must not only interpret their national law in a manner consistent with those directives but also make sure that they do not rely on an interpretation of them which would be in conflict with those fundamental rights or with the other general principles of Community law, such as the principle of proportionality.[89]

Fair balance as proportionality—At times the Court has conflated the fair balance and proportionality assessments. For instance, in *Flos*, C-168/09, fulfilment of the requirements proper to proportionality—these being necessity and appropriateness of

---

[81] *VEWA*, C-271/10, EU:C:2011:442, paras 29–30.
[82] *SENA*, C-245/00, EU:C:2003:68, paras 36–37. In the same sense, see *Lagardère Active Broadcast*, C-192/04, EU:C:2005:475, paras 49–50.
[83] *Lagardère Active Broadcast*, C-192/04, EU:C:2005:475, para 51.
[84] *LSG-Gesellschaft zur Wahrnehmung von Leistungsschutzrechten*, C-557/07, EU:C:2009:107, para 28.
[85] *Bonnier Audio and Others*, C-461/10, EU:C:2012:219, para 56.
[86] *Deckmyn and Vrijheidsfonds*, C-201/13, EU:C:2014:2132, paras 26–33.
[87] *Coty Germany*, C-580/13, EU:C:2015:485, para 34.
[88] *Mc Fadden*, C-484/14, EU:C:2016:689, C-484/14, para 83.
[89] *Promusicae*, C-275/06, EU:C:2008:54, paras 67–68.

the measure at issue—would lead to a finding that an appropriate balance has been struck:

[T]he legislative measure adopted by the Member State concerned must be appropriate for attaining the objective pursued by the national law and necessary for that purpose—namely ensuring that a balance is struck between, on the one hand, the acquired rights and legitimate expectations of the third parties concerned and, on the other, the interests of the rightholders. Care must also be taken to make sure that the measure does not go beyond what is needed to ensure that that balance is struck.[90]

Fair balance and exceptions and limitations—A 'fair balance' requirement is also present with regard to exceptions and limitations in the InfoSoc Directive. Recital 31 in the preamble thereof states that '[a] fair balance of rights and interests between the different categories of rightholders, as well as between the different categories of rightholders and users of protected subject matter must be safeguarded'. Reference to this principle has occurred on a number of occasions. At times the Court has highlighted how striking a fair balance is an expression of the more general principle of effectiveness. It did so in *Football Association Premier League and Others*, C-403/08 and C-429/08 (and reiterated it in *Public Relations Consultants Association*, C-360/13[91]), to stress that a copyright exception (in that particular case: the temporary copies exemption within Article 5(1) of the InfoSoc Directive) must allow and ensure the development and operation of new technologies and safeguard a fair balance between, on the one hand, the rights and interests of rightholders and, on the other hand, of users of protected works who wish to avail themselves of those new technologies.[92] In relation to private copying, the need to maintain a fair balance has been considered by the Court when determining who should be responsible for paying the fair compensation for private copying and how fair compensation mechanisms ought to work (*Padawan*, C-467/08;[93] *Stichting de Thuiskopie*, C-462/09;[94] *Amazon.com International Sales and Others*, C-521/11;[95] *ACI Adam and Others*, C-435/12;[96] *Copydan Båndkopi*, C-463/12;[97] *Hewlett-Packard Belgium*, C-572/13;[98] *Austro-Mechana*, C-572/14;[99] *EGEDA and Others*, C-470/14;[100] *Microsoft Mobile Sales International and Others*, C-110/15[101]).

Fair balance set by the EU legislature—On other occasions, the Court has referred to certain choices made by the EU legislature to conclude that the fair balance had been set at the legislative level. For instance, in *Painer*, C-145/10, the CJEU observed how quotation within Article 5(3)(d) of the InfoSoc Directive:

is intended to strike a fair balance between the right to freedom of expression of users of a work or other protected subject matter and the right of reproduction conferred on authors. That fair balance is struck, in this case, by favouring the exercise of the users' right to freedom of expression over the interest of the author in being able to prevent the reproduction of extracts from

---

[90] *Flos*, C-168/09, EU:C:2011:29, para 57.
[91] *Public Relations Consultants Association*, C-360/13, EU:C:2014:1195, para 24.
[92] *Football Association Premier League and Others*, C-403/08 and C-429/08, EU:C:2011:631, paras 163–164.
[93] *Padawan*, C-467/08, EU:C:2010:620, paras 43–50.
[94] *Stichting de Thuiskopie*, C-462/09, EU:C:2011:397, paras 25–29.
[95] *Amazon.com International Sales and Others*, C-521/11, EU:C:2013:515, paras 25–37.
[96] *ACI Adam and Others*, C-435/12, EU:C:2014:254, paras 52–53.
[97] *Copydan Båndkopi*, C-463/12, EU:C:2015:144, paras 53–54.
[98] *Hewlett-Packard Belgium*, C-572/13, EU:C:2015:750, paras 85–86.
[99] *Austro-Mechana*, C-572/14, EU:C:2016:286, para 22.
[100] *EGEDA and Others*, C-470/14, EU:C:2016:418, paras 35–36.
[101] *Microsoft Mobile Sales International and Others*, C-110/15, EU:C:2016:717, para 29.

his work which has already been lawfully made available to the public, whilst ensuring that the author has the right, in principle, to have his name indicated.[102]

A similar reasoning may be discerned in *Eugen Ulmer*, C-117/13, in relation to Article 5(3)(n) of the InfoSoc Directive,[103] and in *Ryanair*, C-30/14, with regard to the general scheme of the Database Directive ('that directive sets out to achieve a balance between the rights of the person who created a database and the rights of lawful users of such a database, that is third parties authorised by that person to use the database').[104]

Fundamental rights and the fair balance assessment—While reference to fundamental rights to ensure that a fair balance be struck has been made since *Promusicae*, C-275/06, it is in *Scarlet Extended*, C-70/10, that the Court has begun scrutinizing the interplay, in the copyright field, between different fundamental rights in a more material fashion (see further in Chapter 6, Section 1.1). This has been particularly true in relation to injunctions against intermediaries. In the seminal decision in *L'Oréal and Others*, C-324/09 (concerning injunctions under the third sentence of Article 11 of the Enforcement Directive), the CJEU stated that an injunction against an intermediary needs to ensure the protection of intellectual property without posing obstacles to legitimate trade.[105] In *Scarlet Extended*, C-70/10, the Court gave substance to the requirement of taking fundamental rights into account: moving from the need to balance copyright protection with other rights, it made it clear that, as regards the fundamental rights at stake in a case like the one at issue (filtering obligations of internet service providers, ISPs) a fair balance is to be struck not between fundamental rights in general but, specifically, 'between the protection of the intellectual property right enjoyed by copyright holders and that of the freedom to conduct a business enjoyed by operators such as ISPs pursuant to Article 16 of the EU Charter'.[106]

A similar approach has also been employed in *UPC Telekabel*, C-314/12, and *Mc Fadden*, C-484/14 (both cases concerning injunctions against intermediaries). There the Court observed how the rights at stake, and for which a fair balance would be needed, are copyright protection, freedom to conduct a business, and freedom of expression/information.[107]

Similarly, in *GS Media*, C-160/15, the CJEU highlighted the fundamental rights dimensions of the notion of 'fair balance', when it stated:

[I]t follows from recitals 3 and 31 of Directive 2001/29 that the harmonisation effected by it is to maintain, in particular in the electronic environment, a fair balance between, on one hand, the interests of copyright holders and related rights in protecting their intellectual property rights, safeguarded by Article 17(2) of the Charter of Fundamental Rights of the European Union ('the Charter') and, on the other, the protection of the interests and fundamental rights of users of protected objects, in particular their freedom of expression and of information, safeguarded by Article 11 of the Charter, and of the general interest.[108]

---

[102] *Painer*, C-145/10, EU:C:2011:798, paras 134–135.
[103] *Eugen Ulmer*, C-117/13, EU:C:2014:2196, para 31.
[104] *Ryanair*, C-30/14, EU:C:2015:10, para 40.
[105] *L'Oréal and Others*, C-324/09, EU:C:2011:474, paras 138–141. In the same sense, see also *Tommy Hilfiger*, C-494/15, EU:C:2016:528, para 34.
[106] *Scarlet Extended*, C-70/10, EU:C:2011:771, paras 44–45. In the same sense, see also *SABAM*, C-360/10, EU:C:2012:85, paras 43–44.
[107] *UPC Telekabel Wien*, C-314/12, EU:C:2014:192, paras 46–47; *Mc Fadden*, C-484/14, EU:C:2016:689, paras 88–89.
[108] *GS Media*, C-160/15, EU:C:2016:644, para 31.

A similar approach may be discerned in *Renckhoff*, C-161/17, although the Court relied on it to exclude that the unauthorized online re-posting of copyright works or protected subject matter already available, freely and with the permission of the rightholder on a third-party website, should be treated in the same way as linking to lawful and freely accessible content.[109]

2.6 Interpretation in light of international instruments

International instruments—The Court has often relied on international instruments (or even the WIPO Glossary![110]) to undertake the proper interpretation of EU law. This is not surprising, considering that legislation such as the InfoSoc Directive was adopted to implement the WIPO Internet Treaties (Recital 15). Article 1(2) of the WIPO Copyright Treaty requires compliance with Articles 1 to 21 of the Berne Convention, and the Court has indeed often referred to the provisions contained in the Convention. This has allowed the CJEU to achieve important, yet at times controversial, outcomes: in *Infopaq International*, C-5/08,[111] it helped the Court de facto to harmonize the standard of originality beyond the legislative harmonization which occurred for software, databases, and photographs in the Software Directive, Database Directive, and Term Directive (see further Chapter 4, Section 1.1). In *SGAE*, C-306/05,[112] the CJEU introduced the concept of a 'new public' in relation to the right of communication to the public (though, admittedly, by relying on a non-binding and allegedly incorrect former version of the WIPO Guide to the Berne Convention, rather than the Convention itself—see further Chapter 4, Section 2.2).

SENA—The first reference to international law may be discerned in *SENA*, C-245/00, a case concerning the 1992 Rental and Lending Rights Directive. In order to provide guidance on the correct interpretation of the concept of 'equitable remuneration', the Court found the source of inspiration for Article 8(2) of that directive in Article 12 of the 1961 Rome Convention for the Protection of Performers, Producers of Phonograms and Broadcasting Organisations. Article 12 provides that the payment of equitable remuneration and the conditions for sharing that remuneration are, absent an agreement between the various parties concerned, to be established by domestic law. As a result, the role of the Court may only be to call upon the Member States to ensure the greatest possible adherence to equitable remuneration.[113]

Functions performed by this principle—Overall, references to international law may be said to have performed three different tasks: first, they have helped the Court interpret relevant EU provisions; second, they have served to appreciate the freedom left to the EU legislature with regard to the regulation of certain issues; finally, they have helped define the freedom left to individual Member States in respect of areas harmonized at the EU level.

The first group of decisions is expression of the settled principle that EU legislation must, as far as possible, be interpreted in a manner that is consistent with international

---

[109] *Renckhoff*, C-161/17, EU:C:2018:634, para 41, also referring to the rights protected under the EU Charter.

[110] This was the case in *Phonographic Performance (Ireland)*, C-162/10, EU:C:2012:141, para 34, in relation to the concept of communication to the public.

[111] *Infopaq International*, C-5/08, EU:C:2009:465, paras 32–37.

[112] *SGAE*, C-306/05, EU:C:2006:764, paras 35 and 40–41.

[113] *SENA*, C-245/00, EU:C:2003:68, paras 35–36. Also in the field of related rights, see *SCF*, C-135/10, EU:C:2012:140, para 51.

law, in particular where its provisions are intended specifically to give effect to an international agreement. The Court has referred to this obligation in a number of decisions,
notably those on: the construction of the scope of copyright protection (recalling that
copyright protection extends to expressions and not to ideas, procedures, methods of
operation, or mathematical concepts as such in *SAS Institute*, C-406/10[114]); economic
rights, such as the rights of reproduction within Article 2 of the InfoSoc Directive
(*Infopaq International*, C-5/08[115]), communication to the public within Article 3(1)
of the InfoSoc Directive (*SGAE*, C-306/05;[116] *Football Association Premier League and
Others*, C-403/08 and C-429/08;[117] *SCF*, C-135/10[118]), and distribution within Article
4 of the InfoSoc Directive (*Peek & Cloppenburg*, C-456/06;[119] *Donner*, C-5/11;[120] *Art
& Allposters International*, C-419/13;[121] *Dimensione Direct Sales and Labianca*, C-516/
13[122]); exceptions and limitations within Article 5 of the InfoSoc Directive (*DR and
TV2 Danmark*, C-510/10[123]); and copyright protection in databases (*Football Dataco
and Others*, C-604/10[124]).

With regard to the second group, it may be recalled that in *Laserdisken*, C-479/
04, reference to the WIPO Internet Treaties led the Court to rule out the possibility that international law would pose any constraints on the choice of specific
rules of exhaustion for the right of distribution within Article 4(2) of the InfoSoc
Directive.[125]

An example of the third kind of situation is *Luksan*, C-277/10, in which the Court
was called to address whether an individual EU Member State could exclude the principal director from being recognized as the author of a cinematographic work. Article
14*bis* of the Berne Convention allows national legislation to deny the principal director certain rights to exploit a cinematographic work, such as the reproduction right
and the right of communication to the public. However, Article 2(1) of the Term
Directive sets out, under the heading 'Cinematographic or audiovisual works', the general rule that the principal director of a cinematographic work is to be considered its
author or one of its authors, Member States being free to designate other co-authors.
This led to the conclusion that:

[i]n providing that the principal director of a cinematographic work is to be considered its
author or one of its authors, the European Union legislature exercised the competence of the
European Union in the field of intellectual property. In those circumstances, the Member
States are no longer competent to adopt provisions compromising that European Union legis-
lation. Accordingly, they can no longer rely on the power granted by Article 14*bis* of the Berne
Convention.[126]

---

[114] *SAS Institute*, C-406/10, EU:C:2012:259, para 33.
[115] *Infopaq International*, C-5/08, EU:C:2009:465, para 32.
[116] *SGAE*, C-306/05, EU:C:2006:764, para 35.
[117] *Football Association Premier League and Others*, C-403/08 and C-429/08, EU:C:2011:631,
paras 189–190.
[118] *SCF*, C-135/10, EU:C:2012:140, para 51.
[119] *Peek & Cloppenburg*, C-456/06, EU:C:2008:232, para 30.
[120] *Donner*, C-5/11, EU:C:2012:370, para 23.
[121] *Art & Allposters International*, C-419/13, EU:C:2015:27, para 38.
[122] *Dimensione Direct Sales and Labianca*, C-516/13, EU:C:2015:315, para 23.
[123] *DR and TV2 Danmark*, C-510/10, EU:C:2012:244, para 29.
[124] *Football Dataco and Others*, C-604/10, EU:C:2012:115, para 31.
[125] *Laserdisken*, C-479/04, EU:C:2006:549, para 40.
[126] *Luksan*, C-277/10, EU:C:2012:65, para 64.

2.7 Interpretation in light of the wording and context of provisions

A basic interpretive principle—It is settled case law that, in interpreting a provision of EU law, it is necessary to consider not just its wording, but also the surrounding context and the objectives pursued by the rules of which it is part.[127] It is therefore not surprising that, in parallel with the requirement of a teleological interpretation of relevant EU provisions (see Section 2.8), the Court has referred to the need to interpret EU norms in light of their wording and context. This principle of legal interpretation is a basic one and in fact the Court has referred to it on several occasions.[128] At times, the CJEU has considered the context in which a certain provision appears.[129]

Corollaries—Corollaries enunciated by the Court, which are part of the standard discussed in this section are: first, that the same concepts found in different directives should have the same meaning, and, secondly, that different language versions of the same piece of EU legislation should be considered. Examples of the former include the decisions in *Luksan*, C-277/10 (presumption of transfer mechanisms[130]), *Football Association Premier League*, C-403/08 and C-429/08 (communication to the public[131]), *UsedSoft*, C-128/11 (exhaustion of the right of distribution[132]), and *Mc Fadden*, C-484/14 (information society service providers[133]). Examples of the latter are the judgments in *DR and TV2 Danmark*, C-510/10 (Recital 41 of the InfoSoc Directive[134]), *Eugen Ulmer*, C-117/13 (Article 5(3)(n) of the InfoSoc Directive[135]), and *Christie's France*, C-41/14 (Article 1(4) of the Resale Right Directive[136]). The Court has clarified that where there is divergence between two language versions of an EU legal text, the provision in question

---

[127] *SGAE*, C-306/05, EU:C:2006:764, para 34; *Infopaq International*, C-5/08, EU:C:2009:465, para 32; *Fundación Gala-Salvador Dalí and VEGAP*, C-518/08, EU:C:2010:191, para 25; *Bezpečnostní softwarová asociace*, C-393/09, EU:C:2010:816, para 30; *Circul Globus Bucureşti*, C-283/10, EU:C:2011:772, para 32; *Ryanair*, C-30/14, EU:C:2015:10, para 31; *Liffers*, C-99/15, EU:C:2016:173, para 14; *GS Media*, C-160/15, EU:C:2016:644, para 29; *NEW WAVE CZ*, C-427/15, EU:C:2017:18, para 19; *ITV Broadcasting*, C-275/15, EU:C:2017:144, para 18; *Stichting Brein*, C-527/15, EU:C:2017:300, para 26.

[128] *Laserdisken*, C-479/04, EU:C:2006:549, para 24; *SGAE*, C-306/05, EU:C:2006:764, para 34; *Peek & Cloppenburg*, C-456/06, EU:C:2008:232, para 34; *Directmedia Publishing*, C-304/07, EU:C:2008:552, para 35; *Sony Music Entertainment*, C-240/07, EU:C:2009:19, para 22; *Fundación Gala-Salvador Dalí and VEGAP*, C-518/08, EU:C:2010:191, para 26; *Padawan*, C-467/08, EU:C:2010:620, para 57; *Infopaq International*, C-5/08, EU:C:2009:465, paras 28 and 32; *Phonographic Performance (Ireland)*, C-162/10, EU:C:2012:141, para 61; *Football Association Premier League and Others*, C-403/08 and C-429/08, EU:C:2011:631, para 64; *Ryanair*, C-30/14, EU:C:2015:10, para 33; *ITV Broadcasting*, C-275/15, EU:C:2017:144, para 19; *SNB-REACT*, C-521/17, EU:C:2018:639, paras 30 and 41.

[129] *SGAE*, C-306/05, EU:C:2006:764, para 34; *Directmedia Publishing*, C-304/07, EU:C:2008:552, para 28; *Apis-Hristovich*, C-545/07, EU:C:2009:132, para 39; *Padawan*, C-467/08, EU:C:2010:620, para 32; *Football Association Premier League and Others*, C-403/08 and C-429/08, EU:C:2011:631, para 185; *Football Dataco and Others*, C-173/11, EU:C:2012:642, para 20.

[130] *Luksan*, C-277/10, EU:C:2012:65, para 85.

[131] *Football Association Premier League and Others*, C-403/08 and C-429/08, EU:C:2011:631, paras 187–188.

[132] *UsedSoft*, C-128/11, EU:C:2012:407, para 60.

[133] *Mc Fadden*, C-484/14, EU:C:2016:689, para 36.

[134] *DR and TV2 Danmark*, C-510/10, EU:C:2012:244, paras 38–45.

[135] *Eugen Ulmer*, C-117/13, EU:C:2014:2196, para 16.

[136] *Christie's France*, C-41/14, EU:C:2015:119, paras 25–26.

must be interpreted by reference to the purpose and general scheme of the rules of which it forms part.[137]

2.8 Interpretation in light of the objectives pursued by the piece of legislation at issue

Elements considered—Teleological interpretation of legal provisions is another basic legal interpretation method. The CJEU has employed it in close connection with the need to interpret norms in light of their wording and context. At times, in order to discern the objectives pursued by a certain piece of EU legislation, the Court has not only considered the relevant text at issue (notably the recitals in the preamble to a certain directive), but also the *travaux préparatoires*, in particular the original EU Commission's proposal (and its Explanatory Memorandum) for a certain piece of legislation that was eventually adopted.[138]

Overall the Court has often referred to the need to ensure that interpretation of relevant provisions complies with the objectives of the piece of legislation at issue. The first reference may be found in *Metro Metromusik*, C-200/96, with regard to the 1992 Rental and Lending Rights Directive.[139] With reference to the InfoSoc Directive, as will be discussed further in Chapter 4, consideration of the objectives pursued by that piece of legislation (guarantee of a high level of protection) has allowed the Court to interpret economic rights broadly.

The need for 'dynamism'—An aspect that has emerged, particularly in more recent cases, is consideration of the need, in order to comply with the objectives of a certain piece of legislation, for relevant provisions to be subjected to an evolutionary or 'dynamic' interpretation. This principle has been employed especially by AG Maciej Szpunar. In his Opinions in both *Vereniging Openbare Bibliotheken*, C-174/15, and *Verwertungsgesellschaft Rundfunk*, C-641/15, the AG expressed the view that 'it is imperative to give legal acts an interpretation which takes into account developments in technology, markets and behaviour and not to fix such acts in the past by adopting too rigid an interpretation':[140] a dynamic interpretation of the provisions of law, which is capable of adapting the wording thereof to the changing conditions, allows in fact the objective sought by the provisions at issue to be attained.[141]

2.9 Interpretation in light of fundamental rights as granted by the EU Charter

Status of the EU Charter and ECHR—The Court has also increasingly referred to the need to interpret relevant provisions in EU directives in light of fundamental rights

---

[137] *DR and TV2 Danmark*, C-510/10, EU:C:2012:244, para 45; *Christie's France*, C-41/14, EU:C:2015:119, para 26.

[138] See eg *Butterfly Music*, C-60/98, EU:C:1999:333, paras 19–20; *Fixtures Marketing*, C-444/02, EU:C:2004:697, para 22; *Lagardère Active Broadcast*, C-192/04, EU:C:2005:475, para 29; *SAS Institute*, C-406/10, EU:C:2012:259, para 41; *C More Entertainment*, C-279/13, EU:C:2015:199, para 26; *Vereniging Openbare Bibliotheken*, C-174/15, EU:C:2016:856, para 41.

[139] *Metronome Musik*, C-200/96, EU:C:1998:172, paras 22–23.

[140] Opinion of Advocate General Maciej Szpunar in *Vereniging Openbare Bibliotheken*, C-174/15, EU:C:2016:459, para 27.

[141] Opinion of Advocate General Maciej Szpunar in *Verwertungsgesellschaft Rundfunk*, C-641/15, EU:C:2016:795, para 35.

as protected in the EU Charter. At times, this has also been instrumental in achieving the fair balance between copyright protection and third-party interests and rights, as discussed in Section 2.5.

Since the 2007 Treaty of Lisbon the EU Charter has had the status of a primary EU law source, on the same footing as the Treaties. Article 6(1) TEU states in fact that '[t]he Union recognises the rights, freedoms and principles set out in the Charter of Fundamental Rights of the European Union ... which shall have the same legal value as the Treaties'. Article 6(3) also clarifies that fundamental rights, as guaranteed by the European Convention for the Protection of Human Rights and Fundamental Freedoms (ECHR)—to which the EU has expressly acceded (Article 6(2) TEU)—and as they result from the constitutional traditions common to the EU Member States, constitute general principles of EU law.

The result has been a process of constitutionalization carried out by the CJEU also in the field of copyright, although some critics have considered this process to be merely cosmetic and underlying a de facto harmonizing agenda on the side of the Court instead.[142] The EU Charter rights that have been considered more often are copyright protection within the right to property (Article 17(2)); freedom of expression/information (Article 11); freedom to conduct a business (Article 16); and protection of personal data (Article 8). It would be however parochial to think of these fundamental rights and freedoms as inherently at odds with each other, also because any balancing exercise is not only carried out externally: balancing mechanisms are also present internally. So, within copyright itself there are safeguards in the interest of third parties, including—to name only a few—the idea/expression dichotomy, originality (which should not be intended as a mundane requirement[143]), limited term of protection, standard of infringement, and exceptions and limitations.

Laserdisken—The first reference to a fundamental rights-oriented interpretation of EU copyright norms may be found, although the Court did not really elaborate upon it, in *Laserdisken*, C-479/04. There, the CJEU held that a restriction on the freedom to receive information pursuant to Article 10 ECHR (the decision does not contain any reference to the EU Charter, despite the fact that this was adopted in 2000) is justified in light of the need to protect intellectual property rights, including copyright, because these form part of the right to property.[144]

Promusicae—A more meaningful consideration of fundamental rights, also in light of the questions referred by the national court and with specific reference to the EU Charter, was undertaken in *Promusicae*, C-275/06. There the CJEU had to consider the interplay between copyright protection in Article 17(2) of the EU Charter and the right to an effective remedy within Article 47 of the EU Charter (copyright and the right to an effective remedy being considered general principles of EU law[145]), and the

---

[142] In this sense, see J Griffiths, 'Constitutionalising or harmonising?' 77. Also critically, see C Sganga and S Scalzini, 'From abuse of right to European copyright misuse: a new doctrine for EU copyright law' (2017) 48(4) IIC 405, 413. Advocating a constitutionalization of intellectual property through reliance on fundamental rights, see C Geiger, ' "Constitutionalising" intellectual property law? The influence of fundamental rights on intellectual property in the European Union' (2006) 37(4) IIC 371, 385–9.

[143] I also recently made this point in E Rosati, 'Why originality in copyright is not and should not be a meaningless requirement' (2018) 13(8) JIPLP 597. On copyright's internal safeguards, especially from a UK perspective, see further CJ Angelopoulos, 'Freedom of expression and copyright: the double balancing act' (2008) 2008/3 IPQ 328, 333–6.

[144] *Laserdisken*, C-479/04, EU:C:2006:549, para 65.

[145] *Promusicae*, C-275/06, EU:C:2008:54, para 62.

rights to private life within Article 7 of the EU Charter and protection of personal data within Article 8 of the EU Charter. The Court considered that balancing mechanisms are already envisaged in the directives subject to the reference for a preliminary ruling. However, EU Member States, when transposing relevant EU legislation into their own national laws, and national authorities and courts when interpreting resulting provisions, are under an obligation to rely on an interpretation of the directives which allows a fair balance to be struck between the various fundamental rights protected by the EU legal order, as well as general principles of EU law, including proportionality[146] and the respect of legitimate expectations and acquired rights.[147]

Intermediary injunctions—A concrete application of the balancing of different fundamental rights, prompted by the questions referred by national courts, may be discerned in cases like *Scarlet Extended*, C-70/10, and *SABAM*, C-360/10.[148] There, the Court applied the principles expressed in *Promusicae*, C-275/06, to the scenarios at issue (filtering injunctions), holding that it is indeed for national courts, when considering adoption of the measures requested by rightholders, to strike a fair balance between the protection of the intellectual property right enjoyed by these, freedom to conduct a business enjoyed by operators such as ISPs pursuant to Article 16 of the Charter, and also, freedom of expression/information and personal data enjoyed by customers of the ISPs under, respectively, Articles 11 and 8 of the EU Charter.[149]

UPC Telekabel Wien—The need for a similar balancing exercise has been reiterated and further elaborated in *UPC Telekabel Wien*, C-314/12, a case in which the CJEU considered the compatibility with the EU legal order of an injunction that would require an ISP to block access to an infringing website. The Court noted that establishing whether a blocking injunction, taken on the basis of Article 8(3) of the InfoSoc Directive, is consistent with EU law does indeed require consideration of the requirements that stem from the protection of the applicable fundamental rights, also including Article 51 of the EU Charter.[150] While an injunction of this kind would restrict an ISP's freedom to conduct its business, it would not infringe the very substance of such freedom,[151] in that it would allow it to determine the specific measures to be taken in order to achieve the result sought;[152] proving that the ISP has taken all reasonable measures would exonerate it from liability.[153] In any case, the ISP must also respect its customers' freedom of expression and information. This requires that the measures adopted be strictly targeted: they must serve to bring an end to a third party's infringement without affecting use of the service to access lawful information.[154] Even if the EU Charter does not mandate that copyright protection be absolute, the measures which are taken by an ISP in the context of implementing an injunction must be sufficiently effective to ensure its genuine protection, and must have the effect of preventing unauthorized access to the protected subject matter or, at least, of making it difficult to achieve, as well as seriously discouraging the ISPs' customers from accessing the subject matter made available to them in breach of that fundamental right.[155]

---

[146] Ibid, para 68. In the same sense, see also *LSG-Gesellschaft zur Wahrnehmung von Leistungsschutzrechten*, C-557/07, EU:C:2009:107, para 28; *Bonnier Audio and Others*, C-461/10, EU:C:2012:219, para 56.

[147] *Flos*, C-168/09, EU:C:2011:29, para 50.

[148] BJ Jütte, 'The beginning of a (happy?) relationship: copyright and freedom of expression in Europe' (2016) 38(1) EIPR 11, 16, sees these cases as the first ones with the potential to initiate a discussion on the relation between copyright and freedom of expression.

[149] *Scarlet Extended*, C-70/10, EU:C:2011:771, paras 46–50; *SABAM*, C-360/10, EU:C:2012:85, C-360/10, paras 43–50.

[150] *UPC Telekabel Wien*, C-314/12, EU:C:2014:192, para 45.   [151] Ibid, paras 50–51.

[152] Ibid, para 52.   [153] Ibid, para 53.   [154] Ibid, para 56.   [155] Ibid, para 62.

the decision in *UPC Telekabel Wien*, C-314/12, remains that in which the Court has undertaken the most sophisticated and meaningful consideration of different fundamental rights. In other decisions, the CJEU has referred to fundamental rights without particular elaboration. This has been, for instance, the case of: freedom of the press (Article 10 ECHR and Article 11 of the EU Charter) in relation to public security in *Painer*, C-145/10;[156] lack of recognition of the director of a cinematographic work as an author as deprivation of intellectual property protection in relation to Article 17(2) in *Luksan*, C-277/10;[157] parody as part of freedom of expression within Article 11 of the Charter and the principle of non-discrimination within Article 21(1) of the EU Charter in *Deckmyn and Vrijheidsfonds*, C-201/13.[158]

Private copying—In relation to the fair compensation requirement for private copying and the right to equal treatment under Article 20 of the EU Charter, the CJEU dealt with it briefly in *VG Wort*, C-457/11,[159] but engaged with it more substantially in *Copydan Båndkopi*, C-463/12. The Court noted that this right, which is also a general principle of EU law, requires that comparable situations must not be treated differently and that different situations must not be treated in the same way unless such treatment is objectively justified.[160] In relation to the fair compensation requirement, this means that Member States cannot lay down detailed fair compensation rules which would discriminate, without any justification, between the different categories of economic operators marketing comparable goods covered by the private copying exception or between the different categories of users of protected subject matter.[161]

2.10 Preventive nature of economic rights

An increasingly relevant standard—This is a standard that has not appeared too frequently, though the frequency with which the Court has referred to it has increased recently. The first reference is found in *SCF*, C-135/10. In that case, the Court contrasted the nature of the rights harmonized by the InfoSoc Directive (right of communication to the public) with those harmonized by the 1992 Rental and Lending Rights Directive (notably broadcasters' rights). While the right under Article 8(2) of the 1992 Rental and Lending Rights Directive is compensatory in nature and may not be exercised before a phonogram is published for commercial purposes, or before a reproduction of such a phonogram has been used for communication to the public by a user, the right of communication to the public under Article 3(1) of the InfoSoc Directive is preventive in nature and allows authors to intervene between possible users of their work and the communication to the public which such users might contemplate performing, in order to prohibit such use.[162] The preventive nature of the right of communication to the public has also been reiterated in more recent case law, including *Reha Training*, C-117/15;[163]

---

[156] *Painer*, C-145/10, EU:C:2011:798, paras 114–115.
[157] *Luksan*, C-277/10, EU:C:2012:65, para 68.
[158] *Deckmyn and Vrijheidsfonds*, C-201/13, EU:C:2014:2132, C-201/13, paras 25 and 30.
[159] *VG Wort*, C-457/11, EU:C:2013:426, para 73.
[160] *Copydan Båndkopi*, C-463/12, EU:C:2015:144, para 32.
[161] Ibid, para 33. In the same sense, see also *Microsoft Mobile Sales International and Others*, C-110/15, EU:C:2016:717, paras 44–46.
[162] *SCF*, C-135/10, EU:C:2012:140, para 75. In the same sense, see also *Vereniging Openbare Bibliotheken*, C-174/15, EU:C:2016:856, para 59.
[163] *Reha Training*, C-117/15, EU:C:2016:379, para 30.

GS Media, C-160/15;[164] *Stichting Brein*, C-527/15;[165] *Stichting Brein*, C-610/15;[166] and *Renckhoff*, C-161/17.[167]

Over time, however, the CJEU has refined this principle further, and used it to define the nature of the rights harmonized under the InfoSoc Directive and the nature of consent that authors are to grant for the use of their works or subject matter. Consideration of economic rights as preventive in nature has allowed the Court to clarify that any reproduction or communication to the public of a work by a third party requires the prior consent of its author.[168] The preventive nature of economic rights means that authors have a right that allows them to consent to or prevent the doing of restricted acts. Consent, however, does not necessarily need to be explicit all the time.[169]

2.11 Strict interpretation of exceptions and limitations

Derogations from general rules—It is settled CJEU case law that the provisions of a directive which derogate from a general principle established by EU legislation must be interpreted strictly.[170] In the field of copyright, the Court has given effect to this principle in relation to both the special rule of jurisdiction in Article 7(2) of the Brussels I Regulation recast (previously, Article 5(3) of the Brussels I Regulation)[171]— contrasted to the general rule applicable to all causes of action encompassed in the regulation—and exceptions and limitations. The principle according to which exceptions and limitations are to receive strict interpretation is linked to consideration of them as derogation from the general rule that authors' original creations are deserving of protection. In the context of the InfoSoc Directive, this is also linked to the objective of that directive, ie granting a high level of protection.

Infopaq International—A significant engagement with the principle of strict interpretation of exceptions and limitations may be found in *Infopaq International*, C-5/08, in relation to the temporary copies exception in Article 5(1) of the InfoSoc Directive. The Court noted that such provision must be interpreted strictly in that it derogates from the general principle established by that directive, namely that authorization from the rightholder is required for any reproduction of a protected work.[172] In addition, the three-step test in Article 5(5) of the InfoSoc Directive mandates that exceptions and limitations be applied only in certain special cases, which do not conflict with a normal

---

[164] *GS Media*, C-160/15, EU:C:2016:644, para 28.

[165] *Stichting Brein*, C-527/15, EU:C:2017:300, para 25.

[166] *Stichting Brein*, C-610/15, EU:C:2017:456, para 20.

[167] *Renckhoff*, C-161/17, EU:C:2018:634, para 29.

[168] *Infopaq International*, C-5/08, EU:C:2009:465, paras 57 and 74; *Football Association Premier League and Others*, C-403/08 and C-429/08, EU:C:2011:631, para 162; *SCF*, C-135/10, EU:C:2012:140, para 75; *Svensson and Others*, C-466/12, EU:C:2014:76, para 15; *Soulier and Doke*, C-301/15, EU:C:2016:878, para 33; *Renckhoff*, C-161/17, EU:C:2018:634, paras 30–31.

[169] *Soulier and Doke*, C-301/15, EU:C:2016:878, para 35.

[170] *Kapper*, C-476/01, EU:C:2004:261, para 72, and *Commission v Spain*, C-36/05, EU:C:2006:672, para 31.

[171] *Pinckney*, C-170/12, EU:C:2013:635, para 25; *Hi Hotel HCF*, C-387/12, EU:C:2014:215, para 26; *Hejduk*, C-441/13, EU:C:2015:28, para 16.

[172] *Infopaq International*, C-5/08, EU:C:2009:465, para 57. In the same sense, see also *Football Association Premier League and Others*, C-403/08 and C-429/08, EU:C:2011:631, para 162; *Infopaq International*, C-302/10, EU:C:2012:16, para 27; *ACI Adam and Others*, C-435/12, EU:C:2014:254, para 22; *Public Relations Consultants Association*, C-360/13, EU:C:2014:1195, para 23; *Deckmyn and Vrijheidsfonds*, C-201/13, EU:C:2014:2132, para 22; *Ranks and Vasiļevičs*, C-166/15, EU:C:2016:762, para 42; *AKM*, C-138/16, EU:C:2017:218, para 37; *VCAST*, C-265/16, EU:C:2017:913, para 32.

exploitation of the work or other subject matter and do not unreasonably prejudice the legitimate interests of the rightholder.[173]

In any case, the Court has also clarified that, with particular regard to the exemption for temporary copies, that provision must allow and ensure the development and operation of new technologies, and safeguard a fair balance between the rights and interests of rightholders and users of protected works who wish to avail themselves of those technologies.[174] More generally, exceptions and limitations must be interpreted in such a way that their effectiveness is safeguarded and its purpose may be observed.[175] These final considerations support the proposition, advanced by some commentators, that the three-step test in Article 5(5) of the InfoSoc Directive (see further Chapter 5, Section 4) should not be intended as solely aimed at requiring a narrow interpretation of Article 5 exceptions and limitations, but rather as also having an 'enabling' function.[176]

3. Data-Based Case Law (DBCL)—with Carlo Maria Rosati, MD

A statistical search for relations between standards—The analysis earlier in this chapter has focused on the meaning and content of the standards that the CJEU has most significantly employed in its copyright case law, selected as detailed in Chapter 1, Section 4. As mentioned, several of them have been referred to and applied in combination with other standards. But, if we were to perform a statistical analysis of such principles, what would be the meaning of relations between them? In particular: are there pairs of standards which are likely to be used together/in combination or, on the contrary, pairs of standards that are unlikely to be used together in the same decision by the CJEU?

Together with Carlo Maria Rosati, MD[*] we performed the following analysis. We found that the following eleven policies and principles were employed (or not employed) by the CJEU in taking its decisions:

1. High level of protection (G);
2. Autonomous concepts of EU law (G);
3. Effectiveness (G);
4. Proportionality (G);
5. Fair balance of different rights and interests (G);
6. Interpretation in light of international instruments (G);
7. Interpretation in light of wording and context of provisions (G);
8. Interpretation in light of objectives pursued by legislation at issue (G);

---

[173] *ACI Adam and Others*, C-435/12, EU:C:2014:254, para 24.

[174] *Football Association Premier League and Others*, C-403/08 and C-429/08, para 164; *Public Relations Consultants Association*, C-360/13, EU:C:2014:1195, para 24.

[175] *Football Association Premier League and Others*, C-403/08 and C-429/08, paras 162–163; *Painer*, C-145/10, EU:C:2011:798, para 133; *Vereniging Openbare Bibliotheken*, C-174/15, EU:C:2016:856, para 50. For a discussion of the Court's approach to exceptions and limitations, see also JP Quintais, *Copyright in the Age of Online Access—Alternative Compensation Systems in EU Law* (Wolters Kluwer:2017), 199–205.

[176] With regard to the international three-step test, see further and *ex multis*: WF Patry, *Patry on Fair Use* (Thomson Reuters:2018), 2018 edn, §8.2, and the literature cited therein; C Geiger, RM Hilty, J Griffiths, and U Suthersanen, 'Declaration on a balanced interpretation of the "three-step test" in copyright law' (2010) 1(2) JIPITEC 119; C Geiger, DJ Gervais, and M Senftleben, 'Understanding the "three-step test"', in DJ Gervais (ed), *International Intellectual Property – A Handbook of Contemporary Research* (Edward Elgar:2015), 183–8, also providing examples from national legislation and case law. See further in Chapter 5, Section 5.

[*] University of Michigan, Ann Arbor (MI, USA). Email: carlo.m.rosati@gmail.com.

9. Interpretation in light of fundamental rights as granted by the EU Charter of Fundamental Rights (G);
10. Preventive nature of economic rights (S);
11. Strict interpretation of exceptions and limitations (S).

Such standards are either general (G) or specific (S), as detailed above.

When looking at a possible positive vs negative association between standards (where positive association = more likely to be used together than would be expected by pure chance, and negative association = less likely to be used together than would be expected by pure chance, respectively), we performed a pairwise analysis among all the possible non-ordered couples of standards (eleven standards, so giving fifty-five non-ordered pairs of standard).

For each pair of standards (eg Standard A and Standard B), we examined the related 2x2 contingency table:

		Did the Court employ Standard B?	
		Yes	No
Did the Court employ Standard A?	Yes	a	b
	No	c	d

where:

- a is the number of decisions where the CJEU employed both Standard A and Standard B;
- b is the number of decisions where the CJEU employed Standard A, but not Standard B;
- c is the number of decisions where the CJEU employed Standard B, but not Standard A;
- d is the number of decisions where the CJEU employed neither Standard A nor Standard B.

We analyzed each 2x2 contingency table with Fisher exact test.

For each pair of standards, we defined:

- No association: p value of Fisher exact test of the related 2x2 contingency table $\geq$ 0.05 (ie the two standards are used independently of each other);
- Weak association: p value of Fisher exact test of the related 2x2 contingency table < 0.05 but ≥ 0.01;
- Strong association: p value of Fisher exact test of the related 2x2 contingency table < 0.01.

Any weak or strong association between two standards was then classified as positive (vs negative) if those two standards were more (vs less, respectively) likely to be used together than would be expected by pure chance.

All analysis was performed using the open source software for statistical computing and graphics R (<https://www.r-project.org/>).

Findings—Our findings were that:

- A strong positive association exists between:
  - A high level of protection and interpretation in light of the objectives pursued by legislation at issue;
  - Effectiveness and proportionality;

- Effectiveness and fair balance of different rights and interests;
- Effectiveness and interpretation in light of fundamental rights as granted by the EU Charter;
- Proportionality and interpretation in light of fundamental rights as granted by the EU Charter;
- Interpretation in light of wording and context of provisions and interpretation in light of the objectives pursued by legislation at issue;
- Fair balance of different rights and interests and interpretation in light of fundamental rights as granted by the EU Charter.
- A weak positive association exists between:
  - A high level of protection and interpretation in light of wording and context of provisions;
  - A high level of protection and preventive nature of economic rights;
  - Autonomous concepts of EU law and interpretation in light of international instruments;
  - Proportionality and fair balance of different rights and interests.
- No weak negative association was found.
- A strong negative association exists between:
  - Fair balance of different rights and interests and interpretation in light of international instruments.

Although at this stage we cannot validate our model, we anticipate that the associations detailed above may be expected to occur also in future case law of the Court. This may serve parties to proceedings in which a CJEU referral is being considered or has been made, as well as interested stakeholders, to anticipate—at least to some extent—the outcome of referrals.

We represented our findings (strong/weak positive/negative associations within pairs of standards) in Figure 2.2.[177]

We also considered three distinct areas of copyright decisions: economic rights, exceptions and limitations, and enforcement. With the same method explained above, we investigated whether there are certain principles that are more likely to be employed by the CJEU when deciding cases in these three areas. We concluded in the affirmative. As detailed above, our findings below may help enhance the predictability of the outcome of CJEU referrals.

Standards in case law on economic rights—With regard to decisions in the area of economic rights, the standards that have been employed most frequently are interpretation in light of the objectives pursued by the piece of legislation at issue and the need to guarantee a high level of protection. The results are shown in Figure 2.3.[178]

Standards in case law on exceptions and limitations—With regard to decisions in the area of exceptions and limitations, the standards that have been employed most frequently are the need to guarantee a fair balance of different interests and rights and to interpret relevant provisions in light of the objectives pursued by the relevant piece of legislation. The results are shown in Figure 2.4.[179]

Standards in case law on enforcement—Finally, in the area of enforcement, the standards that have been employed most frequently are proportionality, effectiveness, and the need to provide a fair balance of different rights and interests. The results are shown in Figure 2.5.[180]

---

[177] Up-to-date as of August 2018. Pending cases were excluded from the analysis.
[178] Ibid.   [179] Ibid.   [180] Ibid.

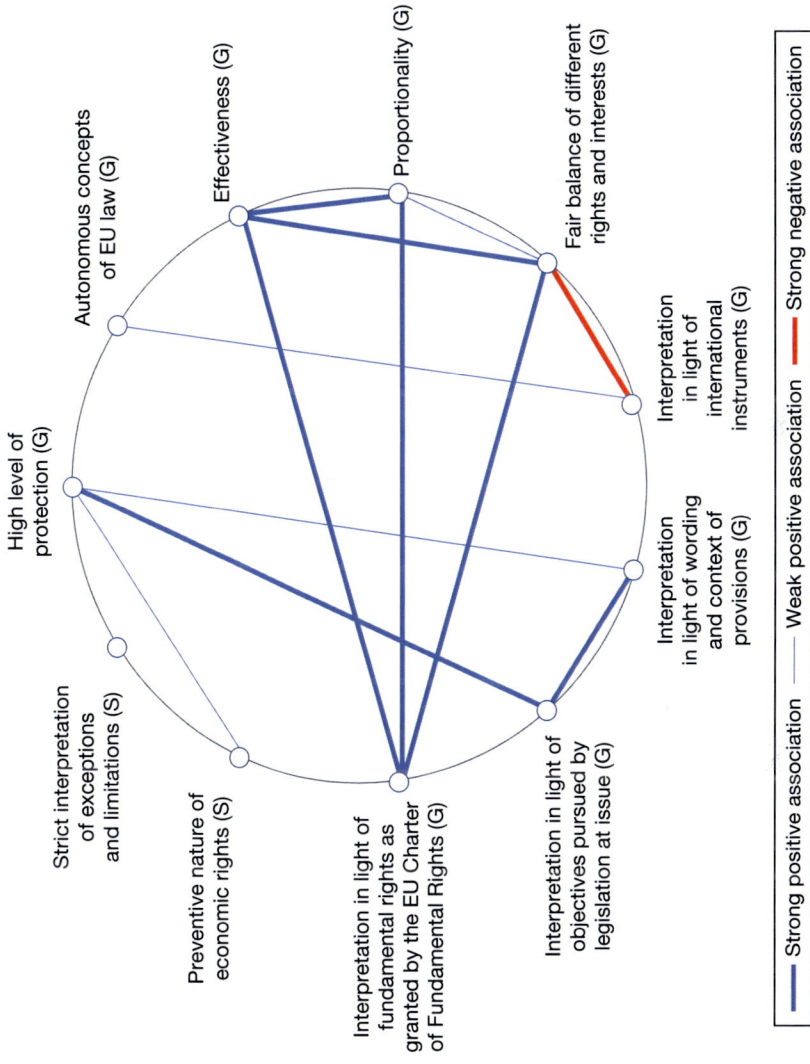

Figure 2.2 Rosati & Rosati EU copyright DBCL (2018)

Autonomous concepts of EU law (G)

Effectiveness (G)

Proportionality (G)

Fair balance of different rights and interests (G)

Interpretation in light of international instruments (G)

High level of protection (G)

Interpretation in light of wording and context of provisions (G)

Strict interpretation of exceptions and limitations (S)

Preventive nature of economic rights (S)

Interpretation in light of fundamental rights as granted by the EU Charter of Fundamental Rights (G)

Interpretation in light of objectives pursued by legislation at issue (G)

—— Strong positive association —— Weak positive association —— Strong negative association

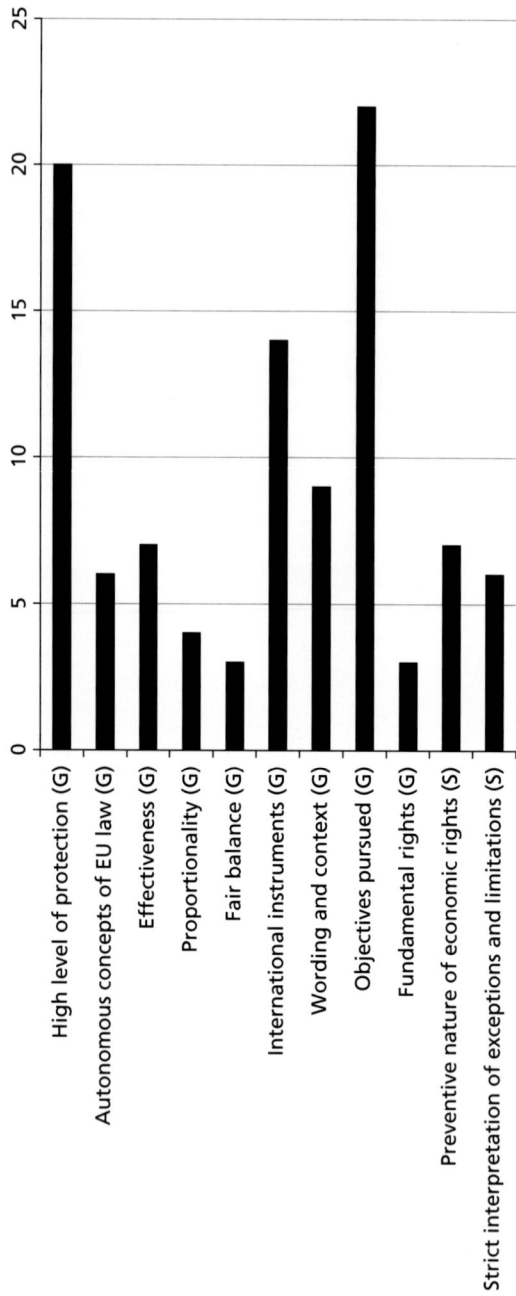

Figure 2.3 Standards employed in preliminary rulings concerning economic rights (1998–2018)

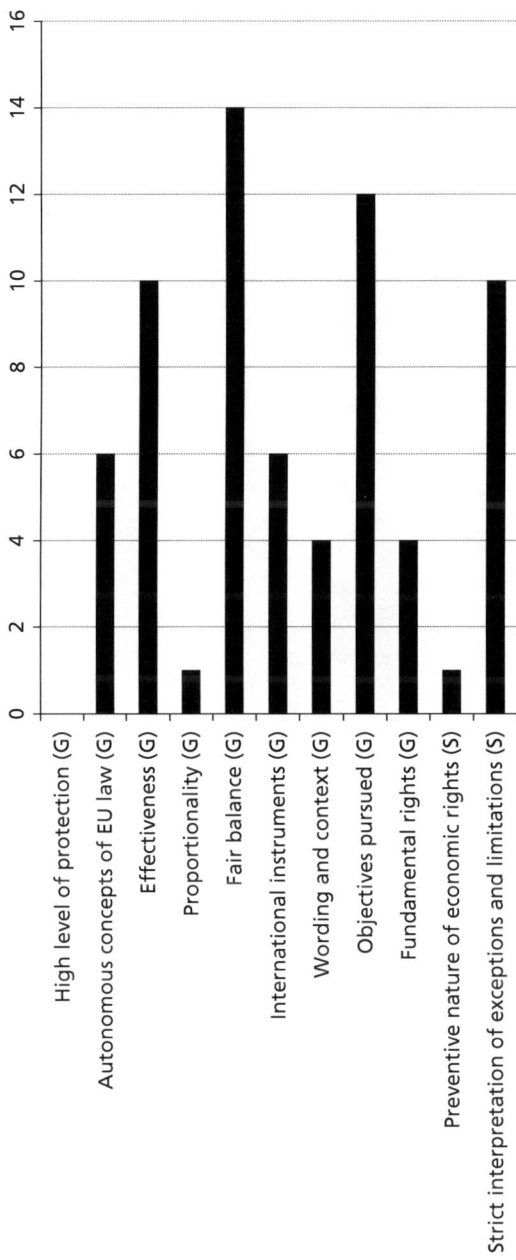

Figure 2.4 Standards employed in preliminary rulings concerning exceptions and limitations (1998–2018)

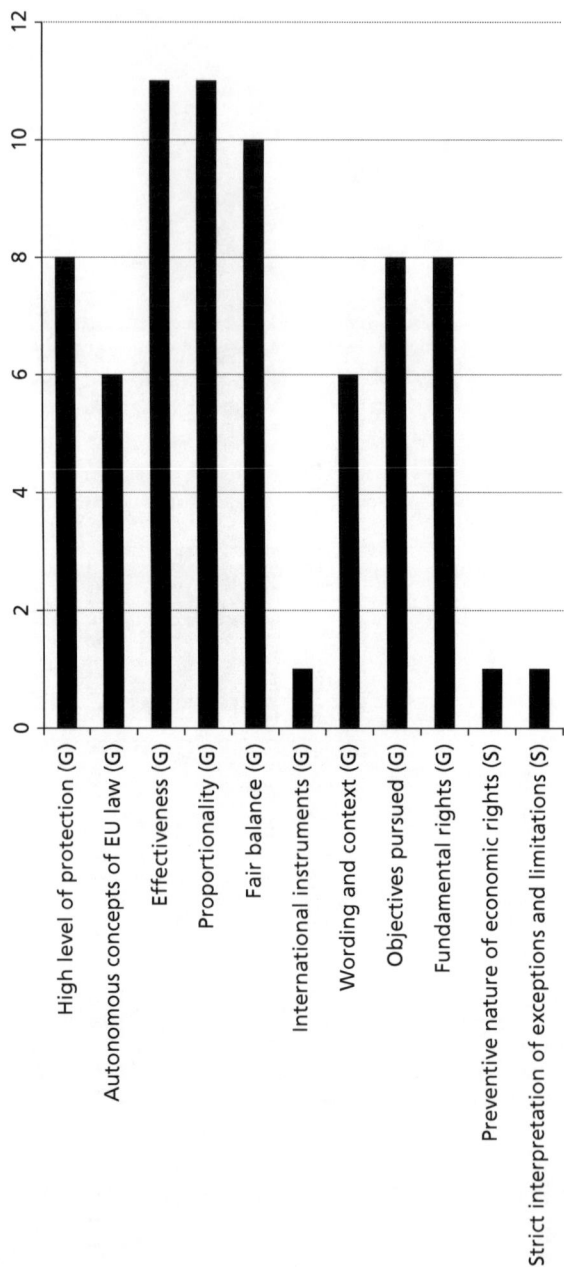

Figure 2.5 Standards employed in preliminary rulings concerning enforcement (1998–2018)

Conclusion

In developing its approach to the interpretation of copyright provisions in relevant EU directives, the CJEU has relied on a number of key standards. This chapter has mapped them and discussed their meaning and content. It has also provided a statistical analysis of relevant decisions (data-based copyright case law—DBCL), aimed at showing relevant relations between different standards. This work will be useful to appreciate the impact of CJEU activity in the area of copyright, and understand the implications thereof. The next part will focus on the analysis of relevant decisions in a number of distinct areas: as will be shown, developments occurring at different levels are not surprising if one considers the underlying standards that have helped the Court to achieve certain outcomes.

PART II

BEYOND THE LAW?
A CJEU-MADE
COPYRIGHT SYSTEM

Over time, reliance on the standards discussed in the previous chapter has paved the way for two trends. On the one hand, the CJEU has been displaying an increasing reluctance towards tolerating diverging national approaches in areas harmonized by relevant EU directives. On the other hand, the Court has been pushing the boundaries of harmonization beyond the literal wording of EU copyright provisions. These aspects are interconnected and closely dependent on each other: the de facto harmonization of copyright law is possible *because* less flexibility is granted to Member States, and vice versa. The twofold phenomenon of decreased flexibility and greater harmonization may be appreciated in different areas of EU copyright, and raises the more fundamental question whether, in acting as material EU copyright legislator, the Court has been exceeding its competence as interpreter of EU law.[1]

Following a description of the emerging doctrine of EU preemption, the next chapter will discuss how AGs and the CJEU have relied upon this concept to hold that national approaches departing from the text of copyright directives would be incompatible with EU law. This has occurred in respect of economic rights and exceptions and limitations (notably private copying), as well as national legislative initiatives, for example in the area of out-of-commerce works. The second part of Chapter 3 will consider a number of issues within the areas of economic rights and exceptions and limitations to show how the Court has followed similar approaches and, in doing so, achieved greater harmonization than would appear from a literal reading of the provisions in relevant directives. In conclusion, if not an express 'agenda', there seem to be at least common patterns that the CJEU has been relying upon to construe its own copyright system, informed by a logic of high protection, more homogeneous approaches across the EU, and an overarching internal market-building goal.

Chapters 4, 5, and 6 will analyze CJEU activity in three distinct areas: economic rights (Chapter 4); exceptions and limitations (Chapter 5); and enforcement

---

[1] Also discussing this, see A Ramalho, *The Competence of the European Union in Copyright Lawmaking—A normative perspective of EU powers for copyright harmonization* (Springer:2016), 59–60.

(Chapter 6). The objective of these chapters is to present the reader with an understanding of both the current state of the law and the mechanisms and rationales that have guided the evolution which has taken place in the areas of economic rights, exceptions and limitations, and enforcement, respectively. In this sense, the role of some of the principles discussed in Chapter 2 may be regarded as pivotal to such a process.

3

Towards Less Flexibility

EU Preemption

Introduction

Supremacy and preemption of EU law—Supremacy of EU law over EU Member States' laws is one of the cornerstones of the overall EU integration process and denotes the superiority of the EU legal order over national legal orders.[1] The doctrine of EU preemption is closely associated with EU supremacy, yet remains distinct from it:

Supremacy denotes the superior hierarchical status of the Union legal *order* over the national legal orders and thus gives European law the *capacity* to preempt national law. The doctrine of preemption, on the other hand, denotes the *actual degree* to which national law will be set aside by European law.[2]

According to some commentators,[3] preemption has received an embryonic codification in Article 2(1)–(2) TFEU:

1. When the Treaties confer on the Union exclusive competence in a specific area, only the Union may legislate and adopt legally binding acts, the Member States being able to do so themselves only if so empowered by the Union or for the implementation of Union acts.
2. When the Treaties confer on the Union a competence shared with the Member States in a specific area, the Union and the Member States may legislate and adopt legally binding acts in that area. The Member States shall exercise their competence to the extent that the Union has not exercised its competence. The Member States shall again exercise their competence to the extent that the Union has decided to cease exercising its competence.

There are three main types of preemption: 'field preemption' (EU law is considered to have a monopoly, and national laws—irrespective of whether they conflict with EU measures—can only be enacted with the authorization of EU law); 'rule preemption' (national measures can be adopted but will be set aside if they conflict with an EU law provision); and 'obstacle preemption' (EU Member States can adopt measures but these cannot obstruct the effectiveness of EU policies).[4] EU Member States remain free to adopt policies and legislate in areas for which no EU competence has been delegated, within the framework of international obligations (if any).

Preemption in copyright—Intellectual property, including copyright, is an area of shared competence between the EU and its Member States. This means that, once the EU has exercised its competence in a certain field and adopted rules on a particular matter, EU Member States may no longer legislate. This should not be intended as an overall ban to legislate in relation to a certain area as a whole, but only as preemption

---

[1] See the critical analysis in C Barnard and S Peers (eds), *European Union Law* (OUP:2018), 2nd edn 72–6.

[2] R Schütze, *European Constitutional Law* (CUP:2012), 364 (emphasis in the original).

[3] D Chalmers, G Davies, and G Monti, *European Union Law* (CUP:2014), 3rd edn, 210.

[4] R Schütze, 'Supremacy without preemption? The very slowly emergent doctrine of preemption' (2006) 43 CML Rev 1023, 1038, also referred to in Chalmers et al, *European Union Law* 209 and 211.

from legislating in relation to the elements of the EU action in question.[5] Although discussion on preemption in other areas of EU law appears to be reasonably well established,[6] the same has been hardly the case of intellectual property and copyright. On the one hand, scholarship has not really engaged with questions of preemption; rather, it has advanced the idea that EU copyright law—in particular the InfoSoc Directive with regard to available exceptions and limitations under Article 5 therein—allows a substantial degree of flexibility.[7] On the other hand, Member States' transpositions of relevant directives have often occurred through the adoption, by individual legislatures, of language departing from that of the corresponding EU provisions or envisaging a different scope altogether of resulting national provisions.

Choice(s) left to EU Member States—Whilst it is true that Article 288(3) TFEU allows national authorities to determine the form and methods to achieve the result mandated by a certain EU directive, the choice between different approaches to national transpositions is not always something left to the complete discretion of EU Member States. There are provisions of EU law that actually provide a choice between copying and elaboration (minimalistic and non-minimalistic methods of transposition), but this is not always the case.[8] For instance, in the field of exceptions and limitations under Article 5 of the InfoSoc Directive, while all exceptions and limitations (with the exclusion of Article 5(1)) are optional for Member States to transpose, the individual language requires different approaches to national transpositions. Overall, it would appear that, except where expressly so provided (eg Article 5(2)(c) which refers to 'specific acts of reproduction' to be defined at the national level), the InfoSoc Directive does not allow Member States to alter the scope of the exceptions and limitations that they have decided to import into national copyright regimes. This means that exceptions and limitations like those provided in Articles 5(2)(a), (b), (d), and (e), and Articles 5(3)(b), (d), (f), (h), (k) (after the decision in *Deckmyn*, C-201/13), (i), and (m) require EU Member States that have decided to import them into their national laws to reproduce the very language of the directive. Even in those cases (Articles 5(3)(f), (h), (i), and (m)) where the conjunction 'or' is employed, this should be interpreted as exemplifying the possible uses of a work or other protected subject matter, rather than setting distinct options.[9] This, however, is not what has occurred at the level of individual Member States, the result being an unsatisfactory attempt to establish an internal market for permitted uses of protected works and subject matter.[10]

---

[5] TEU, Protocol No 25 on the exercise of shared competences, OJ 115, 9 May 2008, 307. See further Barnard and Peers (eds), *European Union Law* 109.

[6] Chalmers et al, *European Union Law* 210–15.

[7] See eg B Hugenholtz and MRF Sentleben, *Fair Use in Europe. In Search of Flexibilities* (2012), Amsterdam Law School Research Paper No 2012-39; Institute for Information Law Research Paper No 2012-33, available at <https://papers.ssrn.com/sol3/papers.cfm?abstract_id=2013239> (last accessed 15 August 2018).

[8] See the interesting discussion in R Král, 'On the choice of methods of transposition of EU Directives' (2016) 41(2) EL Rev 220.

[9] See further E Rosati, 'Copyright in the EU: in search of (in)flexibilities' (2014) 9(7) JIPLP 585, 592–3. See also MRF Senftleben, *Copyright limitations, and the Three-Step Test: An analysis of the three-step test and EC copyright law* (Kluwer Law International:2004), 281, holding the view that the framework set out in Article 5 should be copied as precisely as possible: 'By doing so, a further fragmentation of copyright law in the EU can be prevented. If all member states would literally reproduce the cases they wish to include in national law and subject these cases to the three-step test, a uniform framework would indeed be established.'

[10] See also the helpful analysis of national implementations of Article 5 exceptions and limitations in M Favale, 'Fine-tuning European copyright law to strike a balance between the rights of owners and users' (2008) 33(5) EL Rev 687, 697–705.

Recent CJEU approach—Especially in more recent cases, the CJEU appears to have dispelled what could indeed be considered a 'myth' of EU copyright law—that of its inherent and substantial flexibility. Although neither the Court nor the AGs have systematically developed a system of EU preemption in EU copyright, the application of preemption has been material, prompted by the objective of achieving certain, internal market-rooted, outcomes for questions referred by national courts. The practical, result-oriented use of EU preemption may be seen in the area of economic rights with regard to the scope of national implementations of, for example, the InfoSoc Directive; exceptions and limitations (notably national private copying provisions); and independent national legislative initiatives, such as the one at issue in *Soulier and Doke*, C-301/15, concerning the 2012 French law on the exploitation of out-of-commerce works.[11] As of today, this case admittedly represents the most sophisticated and explicit use of EU preemption by the Court and—in even more express terms—by AG Wathelet in his Opinion.[12] A recent demonstration that EU copyright directives preempt Member States from altering the scope of matters harmonized at the EU level may be clearly discerned also in the Opinion of AG Wathelet in *Levola Hengelo*, C-310/17 (at the time of writing the case is still pending before the CJEU). The analysis will therefore begin with the AG Opinion in this case, before turning to *Soulier and Doke*, C-301/15.

1. The Opinion of Advocate General Wathelet in *Levola Hengelo*

Issues—This referral from the Netherlands asked the CJEU to clarify whether EU law precludes the taste of a food product (the taste of a spreadable cheese in the background national proceedings)—as its author's own intellectual creation—being granted copyright protection. The referring court is seeking clarification on a number of core copyright issues that, so far, have not really been addressed by the CJEU. In particular, the Dutch court asked the CJEU to weigh in on what qualifies as a protectable work under Article 2(1) of the Berne Convention, including whether the notion of work is affected by the (possible) instability of a food product and/or the subjective nature of the taste experience.

The AG Opinion—In his Opinion in this case, AG Wathelet advised the CJEU to rule that the taste of a cheese is not eligible for copyright protection as a 'work' under the InfoSoc Directive. To reach this conclusion, the Opinion tackles what is meant by 'work' under that piece of EU legislation. Although the InfoSoc Directive does not contain a definition of 'work', this should be regarded as an autonomous concept of EU law that mandates uniform application throughout the EU. According to the AG, Member States may not grant protection to objects as 'works' under the InfoSoc Directive beyond what the directive itself envisages.[13] This is a clear, albeit implicit, application of preemption. Consideration of a certain concept as autonomous means that diverging national approaches are not allowed: the only permissible approach is the one mandated at the EU level.

---

[11] Loi n° 2012-287 du 1er mars 2012 relative à l'exploitation numérique des livres indisponibles du XXe siècle, JORF No 0053 of 2 March 2012, 3986.

[12] Opinion of Advocate General Melchior Wathelet in *Soulier and Doke*, C-301/15, EU:C:2016:536.

[13] Opinion of Advocate General Melchior Wathelet in *Levola Hengelo*, C-310/17, EU:C:2018:618, para 40.

Should the CJEU decide to follow the Opinion of its AG, this would mean that an approach like the one adopted by the Dutch Supreme Court in *Kecofa v Lancôme*,[14] in which copyright was found to subsist in the smell of a perfume, would no longer be possible or tolerated. Already at the time when the Dutch judgment was issued (2006) some commentators noted that disparities in the protection *tout court* of certain subject matter across the EU would raise free movement issues[15] (see further Chapter 4, Section 1.1).

2. *Soulier and Doke*: Preemption as an Integral Part of the EU Copyright System

The case—This reference for a preliminary ruling was made by the French Council of State and concerned the compatibility with the InfoSoc Directive of a law (Loi No 2012-287) enacted in France in 2012 to allow and regulate the digital exploitation of out-of-print twentieth-century books.[16] The French legislature introduced into the Code de la propriété intellectuelle (CPI) a new chapter—Chapter IV (Articles L 134-1–L 134-9, subsequently amended)—to Title III of Book I.[17] The CPI provisions envisage a system of non-voluntary collective licensing[18] and vest approved collecting societies with the right to authorize the reproduction and representation in digital form of out-of-print books (these being published in France before 1 January 2001, no longer commercially distributed by a publisher, and not published in print or digital format), while allowing the authors of those books, or their successors in title (including publishers), to oppose or put an end to that practice, subject to certain conditions.[19] Pursuant to the relevant implementing decree, the right to authorize the reproduction or performance of those books in digital format would be exercised, six months after their registration in a publicly accessible database for which the National Library of France would be responsible, by collecting societies approved by the French Ministry of Culture.[20] Overall, this initiative should be seen in parallel to—yet not as a direct consequence of—EU-promoted stakeholder dialogue around digitization issues under the umbrella of the Digital Agenda for Europe. This resulted in the conclusion, in 2011, of a Memorandum of Understanding on the digitization of out-of-commerce works and mass digitization projects.[21] The underlying objective would be to serve

---

[14] Hoge Raad, *Kecofa BV v Lancôme Parfums et Beauté et Cie SNC*, C04/327HR, NL:HR:2006:AU8940. The French Court of Cassation rejected instead the idea that copyright could vest in a perfume: Cour de Cassation, *Bsiri-Barbir v Haarmann & Reimer*, 13 June 2006, [2006] 28 ECDR 380.

[15] C Seville, 'Copyright in perfumes: smelling a rat' (2007) 66(1) CLJ 49, 51.

[16] Loi n° 2012-287 du 1er mars 2012 relative à l'exploitation numérique des livres indisponibles du XXe siècle, JORF No 0053 of 2 March 2012, 3986.

[17] Code de la propriété intellectuelle, consolidated text as of 1 August 2018.

[18] As explained by O Bulayenko, 'Permissibility of non-voluntary collective management of copyright under EU law—The case of the French law on out-of-commerce books' (2016) 7(1) JIPITEC 51, 61, the mechanism at issue should not be equated to mandatory collective management.

[19] S Nérisson, 'Collective management and exclusive rights: friends or foes?', in P Torremans (ed), *Research Handbook on Copyright Law* (Edward Elgar:2017), 2nd edn, 440–1, submits that the opting-out mechanism envisaged by the French scheme may be contrary to Article 5(2) of the Berne Convention, in that it could be considered as akin to a forbidden formality.

[20] For criticisms of the French initiative, see C Sganga, 'The eloquent silence of *Soulier and Doke*' (2017) 12(4) JIPLP 321, 324–5.

[21] Memorandum of Understanding Key Principles on the Digitisation and Making Available of Out-of-Commerce Works (2011), available at <http://ec.europa.eu/internal_market/copyright/docs/copyright-infso/20110920-mou_en.pdf> (last accessed 15 August 2018).

as a blueprint for collective licensing agreements negotiated amongst rightholders, libraries, and collecting societies.[22]

Further to the enactment of the *Loi*, two authors lodged an application with the Council of State, seeking the annulment for misuse of powers of Law No 2012-287 implementing decree, on grounds that such a piece of legislation would not be compatible with the limitations and exceptions to exclusive rights as exhaustively set out in the InfoSoc Directive. Among other things, Articles 2(a) and 3(1) of the InfoSoc Directive provide that *authors*—not collecting societies—have the right to authorize the reproduction and communication to the public of their works. The Council of State asked the CJEU whether Articles 2 and 5 of the InfoSoc Directive preclude legislation, such as that established in Articles L 134-1–L 134-9 CPI.

The decision—Having clarified that the provisions in Article 5 would not be relevant to the case at issue, the CJEU noted that the French legislation would require consideration of the rights of reproduction and communication to the public. The actual question referred by the French court should therefore be read as asking whether Article 2(a) and Article 3(1) of the InfoSoc Directive preclude national legislation that gives an approved collecting society the right to authorize the reproduction and communication to the public, in digital form, of out-of-print books, while allowing the authors of those books or their successors in title to oppose or put an end to that practice on the conditions that that legislation lays down.

Implied and express consent—The Court noted that, in line with the provisions in the Berne Convention, the protection conferred by Articles 2(a) and 3(1) of the InfoSoc Directive must be given a broad interpretation. Such protection includes the enjoyment of rights, but also their *exercise*. InfoSoc economic rights are preventive in nature, in the sense that any reproduction or communication to the public of a work by a third party requires the prior consent of its author. Neither Article 2(a) nor Article 3(1) specify the way in which the prior consent of the author must be expressed. Those provisions do not require that such consent necessarily be expressed. Hence, those provisions also allow that consent be implied.

However, from the objective of increased protection of authors within Recital 9 in the preamble to the InfoSoc Directive it follows that the circumstances in which implicit consent can be admitted must be strictly defined. This is required in order not to deprive of effect the very principle of the author's prior consent. All this implies that authors must be individually informed of the future third-party use of their works and the means available to prohibit it if so they wish. In the absence of any actual prior information relating to that future use, authors are not in a position to prohibit such use, so that the very existence of implicit consent appears purely hypothetical in that regard. Thus, without guarantees that authors are actually informed as to the envisaged use of their works and the means at their disposal to prohibit it, it is virtually impossible for them to adopt any position whatsoever as to such use.[23]

Information mechanisms—The Court considered that the national legislation at issue would not offer a mechanism ensuring that authors are actually and individually informed. Therefore, it is not inconceivable that some of the authors concerned would not, in reality, even be aware of the envisaged use of their works and that, therefore, they would not be able to adopt a position, one way or the other, thereon. In those circumstances, a mere lack of opposition on their part cannot be regarded as the expression of their implicit consent to that use.

---

[22] Sganga, 'The eloquent silence' 322–3.
[23] *Soulier and Doke*, C-301/15, EU:C:2016:878, paras 31–40.

In all this, however, the Court did not place an absolute ban on future national legislative interventions on out-of-commerce works based on the InfoSoc Directive.[24] The Court added in fact that the InfoSoc Directive does not prohibit Member States from granting certain rights or certain benefits to third parties, such as publishers, as long as those rights and benefits do not harm the rights which that directive gives exclusively to authors. When the author of a work decides to put an end to the future exploitation of that work in a digital format, that right must be capable of being exercised without having to depend, in certain cases, on the concurrent will of persons other than those to whom that author had given prior authorization to proceed with such a digital exploitation and, thus, on the agreement of the publisher holding only the rights of exploitation of that work in a printed format and without being subject to any particular formality.[25]

The function of the author principle—In *Soulier and Doke*, C-301/15, the CJEU relied on standards employed in several other decisions, these being that economic rights must be interpreted broadly and considered preventive in nature (see Chapter 2, Sections 2.1 and 2.10). However, reliance on the so-called author principle—which the CJEU had already employed in *Hewlett-Packard Belgium*, C-572/13 (on which see further Chapter 5, Section 3.2.4) and implicitly relied upon in *Renckhoff*, C-161/17— served the Court to push the boundaries of EU harmonization further and, in doing so, restrict Member States' legislative freedom. It should be noted, however, that in the aftermath of *Soulier and Doke*, C-301/15, the relevant CPI provisions have remained in place although the Council of State declared the decree implementing the provisions in Articles 134-1–134-9 CPI, which was subject to the action before this court, invalid due to misuse of powers (*excès de pouvoir*).[26]

Implied application of EU preemption—Although it did not refer explicitly to the notion of EU preemption, the CJEU embraced it. In this sense, there is no contradiction between the CJEU judgment and the Opinion of AG Wathelet, which rejects the view that the national legislation at issue would not affect the protection of copyright because it simply constitutes an arrangement for managing certain rights that the InfoSoc Directive does not preclude. In possibly more explicit terms than those used by the Court, AG Wathelet dismissed the argument that the legislation at issue would not leave the protection of copyright untouched. According to the AG, this interpretation would be contrary to Articles (2)(a) and Article 3(1) of the InfoSoc Directive. In providing for the authors' exclusive right to authorize or prohibit the reproduction and communication to the public of their works, those provisions also concern the way in which those rights are exercised by the author.

Noting that the InfoSoc Directive neither harmonizes nor prejudices the *arrangements* concerning the management of copyright which exist in Member States, the AG also found that the EU legislature, in providing that authors enjoy, in principle, exclusive rights to authorize or prohibit the reproduction of their work and its

---

[24] Ibid, para 45.   [25] Ibid, paras 49–50.

[26] Conseil d'État, 10ème–9ème chambres réunies, 7 June 2017, 368208, FR:CECHR:2017: 368208.20170607. On whether the invalidity has effects *ex tunc* or *ex nunc*, see further E Rosati, 'French Conseil d'État invalidates decrees implementing law on out-of-commerce works' (8 June 2017), The IPKat, available at <http://ipkitten.blogspot.com/2017/06/french-counseil-detat-invalidates.html> (last accessed 15 August 2018), and FM Pirou, 'The ruling of the Court of Justice in *Soulier* revisited' (2 October 2017) Kluwer Copyright Blog, available at <http://copyrightblog. kluweriplaw.com/2017/10/02/ruling-court-justice-soulier-revisited/#_ftnref1> (last accessed 15 August 2018).

communication to the public, exercised its competence in the field of intellectual property.[27] This means that:

[i]n those circumstances, the Member States can no longer adopt management arrangements which compromise EU legislation, even if this is done with the intention of furthering a public interest objective. Before management of the rights of reproduction and communication to the public can be taken into consideration, the holder of those exclusive rights must have authorised a management organisation to manage his rights.[28]

Both the AG in his Opinion and the Court in its judgment considered it key whether authors have and have had the possibility to express their individual consent. In this sense, the analysis of the 2012 French law may be replicated in other instances of national legislation that do not foresee a consent mechanism of this kind, eg non-voluntary collective licensing schemes in general.[29]

3. The Scope of Economic Rights: The Case of Communication and Making Available to the Public

The InfoSoc Directive—A similar limitation to Member States' freedom may be found in relation to the scope of the exclusive rights harmonized at the EU level, notably the rights of communication and making available to the public pursuant to Article 3(1)–(2) of the InfoSoc Directive:

1. Member States shall provide authors with the exclusive right to authorise or prohibit any communication to the public of their works, by wire or wireless means, including the making available to the public of their works in such a way that members of the public may access them from a place and at a time individually chosen by them.
2. Member States shall provide for the exclusive right to authorise or prohibit the making available to the public, by wire or wireless means, in such a way that members of the public may access them from a place and at a time individually chosen by them:
   (a) for performers, of fixations of their performances;
   (b) for phonogram producers, of their phonograms;
   (c) for the producers of the first fixations of films, of the original and copies of their films;
   (d) for broadcasting organisations, of fixations of their broadcasts, whether these broadcasts are transmitted by wire or over the air, including by cable or satellite.

Broader scope of national rights?—In both *Svensson and Others*, C-466/12, and *C More Entertainment*, C-279/13, one of the questions referred by the national courts—the Svea hovrätt and the Högsta domstolen (both Sweden), respectively—was whether it is possible for a Member State to give broader protection to authors' rights by

---

[27] Opinion of Advocate General Wathelet in *Soulier and Doke*, C-301/15, EU:C:2016:536, paras 55–56.
[28] Ibid, para 57.
[29] A potential example might be, still in France and as discussed at more length in E Rosati, 'The CJEU decision in *Soulier*: what does it mean for laws other than the French one on out-of-print books?' (17 November 2016), The IPKat, available at <http://ipkitten.blogspot.com/2016/11/the-cjeu-decision-in-soulier-what-does.html> (last accessed 15 August 2018), Loi n° 2016-925 du 7 juillet 2016 relative à la liberté de la création, à l'architecture et au patrimoine, JORF No 0158 of 8 July 2016. With regard to non-voluntary collective licensing schemes, see AP Ringelhann and M Mimler, 'Digital exploitation of out-of-print books and copyright law: French licensing mechanism for out-of-print books under CJEU scrutiny' (2017) 39(3) EIPR 190, 192–3 and M Gera, 'A tectonic shift in the European system of collective management of copyright? Possible effects of the *Soulier & Doke* decision' (2017) 39(5) EIPR 261, 263–4.

enabling communication/making available to the public to cover a greater range of acts than provided for in Article 3 of the InfoSoc Directive. In both instances the CJEU answered in the negative, although in different terms.

Svensson and Others—In *Svensson and Others*, C-466/12, the Court justified its response by reference to the goals of harmonization (Recitals 1, 6, and 7 in the preamble to the InfoSoc Directive), notably remedying the legislative differences and legal uncertainty that existed among Member States in relation to copyright protection prior to the adoption of the InfoSoc Directive. According to the Court, acceptance of the proposition that a Member State may grant broader protection to copyright holders by laying down that the concept of communication/making available to the public also includes activities other than those referred to in Article 3 of the InfoSoc Directive would have the effect of creating legislative differences and thus, for third parties, legal uncertainty. As a result, the goal pursued by EU legislature when adopting the InfoSoc Directive would inevitably be undermined if the concept of communication/making available to the public were to be construed in different EU Member States as including a wider range of activities than those referred to in Article 3(1) of that directive.[30]

C More Entertainment—The Court also acknowledged that the InfoSoc Directive is not a complete harmonization instrument: Recital 7 in the preamble thereof indicates in fact that the directive does not have the objective of removing or preventing differences that do not adversely affect the functioning of the internal market. In *C More Entertainment*, C-279/13, the meaning of this recital became clearer. The Court interpreted it as somewhat limiting EU law's influence in the area of the making available right. In particular with regard to broadcasters' rights over fixations of their broadcasts, the CJEU concluded that neither Article 3(2) of the InfoSoc Directive nor any other provision in that directive prevents or removes differences between Member States' laws as regards the extent of the protection which they may grant broadcasters with regard to certain acts, such as internet live streaming, which are not expressly referred to in that provision.[31]

The Court's conclusion in this case is not in contradiction with the one in *Svensson and Others*, C-466/12; rather, it shapes further the substantial scope of EU preemption in the area of economic rights, by clarifying that Member States' freedom is limited only where and insofar as harmonization has occurred at the EU level. If the relevant EU provisions only achieve a limited harmonization and build upon existing legislation, then national freedom remains available, although influenced by EU law.

In the case of the making available right, it is Recital 20 in the preamble to the InfoSoc Directive that explicitly states that such directive is based on principles and rules already laid down in earlier directives, including the Rental and Lending Rights Directive.[32] Recital 16 in the preamble to that directive leaves Member States precisely such freedom in the area of broadcasting rights:

---

[30] *Svensson and Others*, C-466/12, EU:C:2014:76, paras 34–35. See F Brison and S Depreeuw, 'The right of "communication to the public" in the European Union', in Torremans (ed), *Research Handbook* 101, speaking of 'maximal' harmonization undertaken by the InfoSoc Directive in respect of the right of communication to the public.

[31] *C More Entertainment*, C-279/13, EU:C:2015:199, paras 29–31.

[32] Ibid, para 32, referring to *Football Association Premier League and Others*, C-403/08 and C-429/08, EU:C:2011:631, para 187. See also *C More Entertainment*, C-279/13, EU:C:2015:199, para 35.

Member States should be able to provide for more far-reaching protection for owners of rights related to copyright than that required by the provisions laid down in this Directive in respect of broadcasting and communication to the public.

The implication of this approach is that, on the one hand, EU preemption operates where the EU legislature has exercised its competence and, on the other hand, in areas touched upon by EU law Member States' freedom continues to exist only where and insofar as EU law allows it.

4. The Scope of Exceptions and Limitations: The Case of Private Copying

Diverging and incompatible national approaches—A limitation of EU Member States' initiatives may also be discerned in the area of exceptions and limitations. In particular, and among other things, the several preliminary rulings on private copying under Article 5(2)(b) of the InfoSoc Directive[33] have given the CJEU the opportunity to ponder different national systems of private copying and setting guidelines which have led to a finding of de facto incompatibility between certain national approaches and the InfoSoc Directive (see also Chapter 5, Section 3.2). This has been, for instance, the case of Dutch, Belgian, and Italian legislation on private copying.

ACI Adam—In *ACI Adam*, C-435/12, the CJEU ruled that a private copying exception—like the one envisaged under Dutch law at the time when the referral was made—that would encompass reproductions from both lawful and unlawful sources would be contrary to Article 5(2)(b) of the InfoSoc Directive, read in combination with the three-step test in Article 5(5) therein. Among other things, the Court highlighted how, on the one hand, Member States have the option of introducing the different exceptions provided for in Article 5 of the InfoSoc Directive in accordance with their legal traditions and, on the other hand, once they have made the choice of introducing a certain exception, this must be applied coherently, so that they cannot undermine the objectives which that directive pursues with the aim of ensuring the proper functioning of the internal market.[34]

Accordingly, divergences in Member States' implementations of Article 5 exceptions and limitations would 'clearly be detrimental to the proper functioning of the internal market'.[35] The CJEU appeared to suggest that in the area of exceptions and limitations Member States' freedom (where it exists) would be *just* in the sense of limiting the scope of the resulting national exceptions or limitations, not also in the sense of extending it beyond the scope of what is provided in the relevant Article 5 exception or limitation. Such a conclusion would follow from Recital 32 in the preamble to the InfoSoc Directive, which states that, in providing an exhaustive enumeration of exceptions and limitations to the reproduction right and the right of communication to the public which takes due account of the different legal traditions in Member States,

---

[33] They are (in reverse chronological order): *VCAST*, C-265/16, EU:C:2017:913; *Microsoft Mobile Sales International and Others*, C-110/15, EU:C:2016:717; *EGEDA and Others*, C-470/14, EU:C:2016:418; *Austro-Mechana*, C-572/14, EU:C:2016:286; *Hewlett-Packard Belgium*, C-572/13, EU:C:2015:750; *Copydan Båndkopi*, C-463/12, EU:C:2015:144; *Eugen Ulmer*, C-117/13, EU:C:2014:2196; *ACI Adam and Others*, C-435/12, EU:C:2014:254; *Amazon.com International Sales and Others*, C-521/11, EU:C:2013:515; *VG Wort*, C-457/11, EU:C:2013:426; *Luksan*, C-277/10, EU:C:2012:65; *Stichting de Thuiskopie*, C-462/09, EU:C:2011:397; and *Padawan*, C-467/08, EU:C:2010:620.
[34] *ACI Adam and Others*, C-435/12, EU:C:2014:254, para 34.   [35] Ibid, para 35.

while, at the same time, aiming to ensure a functioning internal market, 'Member States should arrive at a coherent application of these exceptions and limitations'.[36]

Inconsistent scope—Although the Court did not make an express reference to it, the conclusion reached in *ACI Adam*, C-435/12, is in line with earlier case law, notably the decision in *Padawan*, C-467/08. There the CJEU had suggested that, unless the InfoSoc Directive leaves it to Member States to fine-tune the breadth of resulting exceptions and limitations, it is not possible for them to alter the scope of the exceptions and limitations that they have decided to transpose into their national regimes. More specifically, an interpretation according to which EU Member States that have introduced into their national law an exception pursuant to the list under Article 5 of the InfoSoc Directive, 'are free to determine the limits in an inconsistent and unharmonised manner which may vary from one Member State to another, would be incompatible with the objective of that directive, as set out in the preceding paragraph'.[37]

Hewlett-Packard Belgium—A similar approach to the one adopted in *ACI Adam*, C-435/12, with regard to Member States' freedom may be also discerned in *Hewlett-Packard Belgium*, C-572/13. This reference for a preliminary ruling originated in the context of litigation between Hewlett-Packard (HP) and collective management rights organization Reprobel over the level of fair compensation for reprography and private copying pursuant to the Belgian implementations of, respectively, Article 5(2)(a) and (b) of the InfoSoc Directive. Both copyright exceptions are subject to the requirement that rightholders receive fair compensation. As explained by Recital 35 in the preamble to the InfoSoc Directive, fair compensation is intended to compensate rightholders adequately for the use made of their protected works. Although Member States retain a certain freedom in determining the level and modalities of fair compensation, account should be taken of the particular circumstances of each case. Recital 35 mandates that '[w]hen evaluating these circumstances, a valuable criterion would be the possible *harm* to the rightholders resulting from the act in question' (emphasis added).

Among the questions referred by the Brussels Court of Appeal was whether EU Member States—as was the case of Belgium at the time of the referral—may allocate half of the fair compensation due to rightholders to the publishers of works created by authors, the publishers being under no obligation whatsoever to ensure that the authors benefit, even indirectly, from some of the compensation of which they have been deprived. The Court answered in the negative, noting at the outset that compensation for reprography and private copying should normally be payable to reproduction rightholders.[38] The InfoSoc Directive does not recognize publishers as reproduction rightholders. In addition, as the rationale of the fair compensation requirement is to compensate rightholders for the harm caused by unauthorized acts of reproduction, publishers cannot be directly entitled to any fair compensation: not being among reproduction rightholders, they do not suffer any harm (see further Chapter 5, Section 3.2.4).[39]

Limited national freedom—The national systems of fair compensation have come under the scrutiny of the CJEU on several other occasions. The string of CJEU decisions highlights how this is an area in which Member States enjoy significant discretion and yet are subject to a number of principles, including ultimately that the level

[36] Ibid, para 27.
[37] *Padawan*, C-467/08, EU:C:2010:620, para 36. In the same sense, see also *DR and TV2 Danmark*, C-510/10, EU:C:2012:244, para 36.
[38] *Hewlett-Packard Belgium*, C-572/13, EU:C:2015:750, para 45.
[39] Ibid, paras 47–48.

of compensation must be linked to the harm caused to rightholders by the making of private copies,[40] and that it is the natural person doing the unauthorized acts of reproduction who is ultimately responsible for the payment of the fair compensation.[41] Only if certain conditions are satisfied is it possible to apply a levy on blanket media.[42] The CJEU has employed these two key principles to issue a number of judgments that have resulted in the incompatibility of certain national systems of private copying and private copying levies with the only seemingly loose language of Article 5(2)(b).

5. Consequences of Incorrect Transpositions of EU Directives

As mentioned earlier, there are provisions in EU directives that are drafted in such a way that EU Member States enjoy limited freedom when transposing them into national legal systems. The question that arises is therefore whether provisions of this kind may be directly relied upon before the courts of a Member State that has failed to implement them correctly. The CJEU has clarified that this might be the case when, in the context of an action against any entity or body subject to the control or authority of the Member State at issue, a provision in an EU directive imposes on EU Member States, in unequivocal terms, well-defined obligations as to the result to be achieved that is not coupled with any condition regarding application of the rule laid down therein (direct vertical effect).[43]

OSA—The issue of direct effect of EU directives has been tackled in a copyright context in *OSA*, C-351/12. That reference for a preliminary ruling from the Czech Republic asked the CJEU, among other things, whether Article 3(1) of the InfoSoc Directive is unconditional enough and sufficiently precise for a certain individual or organization (a copyright collecting society in that case) to rely on in a dispute between individuals before a national court in case of incorrect transposition of that directive by a certain EU Member State. The CJEU answered in the negative. It is settled case law that even a clear, precise, and unconditional provision of a directive seeking to confer rights or impose obligations on individuals cannot of itself apply in proceedings exclusively between private parties (lack of direct horizontal effect).[44] It is true that a national court, when hearing a case between individuals, is required, when applying the provisions of domestic law, to consider the whole body of rules of national law and to interpret them, so far as possible, in the light of the wording and purpose of the directive in order to achieve an outcome consistent with the objective pursued by the directive. However, this cannot serve as the basis for an interpretation of national law *contra legem*.[45] Also in the different context relating to the interpretation of EU law provisions that are relevant to the topic of compensation for injuries suffered as

---

[40] *Padawan*, C-467/08, EU:C:2010:620, paras 40 and 42; *Copydan Båndkopi*, C-463/12, EU:C:2015:144, para 21; *Microsoft Mobile Sales International and Others*, C-110/15, EU:C:2016:717, para 28.

[41] *Padawan*, C-467/08, EU:C:2010:620, para 45; *Stichting de Thuiskopie*, C-462/09, EU:C:2011:397, para 26; *Amazon.com International Sales and Others*, C-521/11, EU:C:2013:515, para 23; *Microsoft Mobile Sales International and Others*, C-110/15, EU:C:2016:717, para 30.

[42] *Padawan*, C-467/08, EU:C:2010:620, paras 46 and 52; *Stichting de Thuiskopie*, C-462/09, EU:C:2011:397, paras 27–28; *Amazon.com International Sales and Others*, C-521/11, EU:C:2013:515, paras 24–25, 28, 31, and 34; *Copydan Båndkopi*, C-463/12, EU:C:2015:144, paras 25, 44–47, and 52; *Microsoft Mobile Sales International and Others*, C-110/15, EU:C:2016:717, paras 31–37.

[43] See eg *Dominguez*, C-282/10, EU:C:2012:33, para 34.

[44] *Association de médiation sociale*, C-176-12, EU:C:2014:2, para 36.

[45] *OSA*, C-351/12, EU:C:2014:110, paras 42–48.

a result of a road traffic accident, the CJEU has recently confirmed the lack of direct horizontal effect of EU directives that have not been correctly transposed by a certain EU Member State:

EU law, in particular Article 288 TFEU, must be interpreted as meaning that a national court, hearing a dispute between private persons, which finds that it is unable to interpret the provisions of its national law that are contrary to a provision of a directive that satisfies all the conditions required for it to produce direct effect in a manner that is compatible with that provision, is not obliged, solely on the basis of EU law, to disapply those provisions of national law and a clause to be found, as a consequence of those provisions of national law, in an insurance contract.[46]

In that case, the Court also stressed how a party adversely affected by the incompatibility of national law with EU law or a person subrogated to the rights of that party could however rely on *Francovich and Others*, C-6/90 and C-9/90,[47] in order to obtain from the relevant Member State, if justified, compensation for any loss sustained.[48]

The contrary view of AG Sharpston—The conclusion of the CJEU in *OSA*, C-351/12, differs from the view that AG Sharpston had taken in her Opinion in the same case. The AG observed that, first, when national courts apply domestic law, they are bound to interpret it, so far as possible, in the light of the wording and purpose of any relevant directive, in order to achieve the result sought by the directive (*Marleasing* principle[49]). That obligation is inherent in the Treaty system and enables national courts to ensure the full effectiveness of EU law when they determine disputes within their jurisdiction. Only if such an approach is not possible, for example because it would lead to an interpretation *contra legem*, is it necessary to consider whether a relevant provision of a directive has direct effect and, if so, whether that direct effect may be relied on against a party to the national dispute. The AG also stressed that it is for national courts to do whatever lies within their jurisdiction, for example taking the whole body of domestic law into consideration and applying the interpretative methods recognized by it, to ensure that the InfoSoc Directive is fully effective, and thus achieve outcomes consistent with the objectives pursued by it. She concluded that an interpretation of national law that would be inconsistent with the directive is not permissible.[50] The AG did not state expressly what the legal consequences of incorrect implementations of the InfoSoc Directive would be. However, she appeared to agree with OSA's suggestion that this would be disapplication of incorrect national provisions.[51]

Conclusion

The discussion undertaken in this chapter has focused on some of the effects of CJEU activity in the area of copyright, specifically those relating to EU Member States' freedom in areas harmonized by relevant directives. It has done so by discussing selected examples relating to national legislative initiatives, the scope of economic rights,

---

[46] *Smith*, C-122/17, EU:C:2018:631, para 57.
[47] *Francovich and Others*, C-6/90 and C-9/90, EU:C:1991:428.
[48] *Smith*, C-122/17, EU:C:2018:631, para 56.
[49] *Marleasing*, C-106/89, EU:C:1990:395, para 7.
[50] Opinion of Advocate General Eleanor Sharpston in *OSA*, C-351/12, EU:C:2013:749, paras 44–47.
[51] Ibid, paras 38 and 43.

and the construction of exceptions and limitations. Of course, the impact of CJEU case law is broader than this. It essentially consists of an activity that has extended the boundaries of harmonization further than relevant legislation alone has done and, in doing so, resulted in the substantial construction of areas for which the legislative framework may be regarded as fairly thin. The following chapters will explore the work of the Court in the areas of: economic rights, exceptions and limitations, and enforcement, respectively.

4

The Construction of Economic Rights in the InfoSoc Directive

Introduction

The activity of the Court has not just resulted in a limitation of Member States' freedom to adopt certain initiatives or shape the scope of economic rights and related exceptions and limitations but also, and possibly more evidently, in an interpretative work that has led both to the further harmonization of areas formally touched upon by legislation and the employment of concepts that are either undefined or not even present in relevant legislation. In this sense, CJEU case law has resulted in an evolution of the copyright system. Overall, this has been possible through the Court's reliance on the standards discussed in Chapter 2, as well as overriding internal market concerns. Although the EU legislature has undertaken the harmonization of exclusive rights in relation to specific subject matter, this chapter only focuses on the horizontal harmonization of economic rights in the InfoSoc Directive, ie the rights of reproduction, communication to the public, and distribution.

1. The Right of Reproduction and the De Facto Harmonization of the Originality Standard

Origin and content of the provision—Article 2 of the InfoSoc Directive has brought about a horizontal harmonization of the right of reproduction, which goes beyond the wording of Article 9(1) of the Berne Convention.[1] While the latter provides that authors of literary and artistic works shall have the exclusive right of authorizing the reproduction of these works, in any manner or form, Article 2 of the InfoSoc Directive provides a broad description—not a definition[2]—of reproduction as the right:

to authorise or prohibit direct or indirect, temporary or permanent reproduction by any means and in any form, in whole or in part:

(a) for authors, of their works;
(b) for performers, of fixations of their performances;
(c) for phonogram producers, of their phonograms;
(d) for the producers of the first fixations of films, in respect of the original and copies of their films;
(e) for broadcasting organisations, of fixations of their broadcasts, whether those broadcasts are transmitted by wire or over the air, including by cable or satellite.

Reproduction 'in part' in *Infopaq International*—The notion of reproduction 'in part' has been at the centre of the reference in *Infopaq International*, C-5/08, by which the

---

[1] M Lehmann, 'The EC Directive on the harmonisation of certain aspects of copyright and related rights in the information society—a short comment' (2003) 34(5) IIC 521, 523.
[2] *Infopaq International*, C-5/08, EU:C:2009:465, para 31.

CJEU also carried out the de facto harmonization of the originality requirement for works falling under the scope of the InfoSoc Directive. The Højesteret (Denmark) had asked the Court to clarify what is intended by reproduction 'in part', so as to be able to rule in the proceedings that a professional association of Danish daily newspaper publishers had brought against a media monitoring and analysis business that provided its customers with unauthorized reproductions of extracts of eleven words from selected Danish newspapers. Could the reproduction of such short extracts qualify as reproduction 'in part' within the meaning of the provisions by which Denmark had transposed Article 2 of the InfoSoc Directive into its own national law?

The Court noted at the outset that the notion of reproduction 'in part' should be given an autonomous and uniform interpretation throughout the EU, in that the directive does define neither 'reproduction' nor reproduction 'in part' (in its subsequent ruling in *Football Association Premier League and Others*, C-403/08 and C-429/08, the Court held that also 'reproduction' must be given an autonomous and uniform interpretation throughout the EU[3]). The meaning must be one that has regard to the wording and context of Article 2, as well as the overall objectives of the InfoSoc Directive and international law.[4]

The right of reproduction is intended to cover a 'work'.[5] This is a concept derived from the Berne Convention, which implies (the Convention does not provide a specific definition) that subject matter is protected if it is sufficiently original in the sense that it is an intellectual creation. The Court then observed that the EU legislature provided a limited harmonization of the standard of originality in respect of software (Article 1(3) of the 1991 Software Directive, now Article 1(3) of the Software Directive), photographs (Article 6 of Council Directive 93/98, now Article 6 of the Term Directive), and databases (Article 3(1) of the Database Directive), and defined it as the 'author's own intellectual creation'.[6] The InfoSoc Directive is based on the same principles as those directives (according to the Court this would be evidenced by Recitals 4, 9 to 11, and 20 in the preamble to the directive).[7] Hence a work is protected under the InfoSoc Directive if it is original in the sense that it is its author's own intellectual creation.[8]

Originality—The discussion of originality served the Court in tackling the question referred by the Danish court, ie when there is reproduction 'in part' of a work. The CJEU explained in fact that the InfoSoc Directive does not differentiate between the taking of a work as a whole or in part for the sake of applying Article 2. Thus, the concept of reproduction 'in part' should not be intended in a quantitative sense.[9] There is reproduction—whether as a whole or 'in part'—when what is being reproduced is sufficiently original in the sense that it is its author's own intellectual creation.[10] Such

---

[3] *Football Association Premier League and Others*, C-403/08 and C-429/08, EU:C:2011:631, para 154.

[4] *Infopaq International*, C-5/08, EU:C:2009:465, para 32.   [5] Ibid, para 33.

[6] Before *Infopaq International*, C-5/08 and its progeny, M van Eechoud, PB Hugenholtz, S van Gompel, L Guibault, and N Helberger, *Harmonizing European Copyright Law—The Challenges of Better Lawmaking* (Wolters Kluwer:2009), 41, wondered whether the meaning of the phrase 'author's own intellectual creation' in those directives should be the same or whether, instead, the standard for photographs should be higher, given the reference in Article 6 of the Term Directive to the requirement that the author's own intellectual creation reflect their personality.

[7] For a criticism of the succinct reasoning in this part, see S Vousden, '*Infopaq* and the Europeanisation of copyright law' (2010) 1(2) WIPOJ 197, 200.

[8] *Infopaq International*, C-5/08, EU:C:2009:465, paras 34–37.

[9] S Depreeuw, *The Variable Scope of the Exclusive Economic Rights in Copyright* (Wolters Kluwer:2014), 203.

[10] *Infopaq International*, C-5/08, EU:C:2009:465, paras 38–39 and 48.

a broad definition of reproduction 'in part'—which may well extend to the copying of short extracts of a work,[11] as long as the choice, sequence, and combination of words is sufficiently original[12]—is, according to the CJEU, in line with the objective of the InfoSoc Directive to introduce a high level of protection of authors.[13]

1.1 'Originality' of a work

Lower threshold to infringement?—The outcome in *Infopaq International*, C-5/08, has given rise to an intense discussion as regards the role of the CJEU, including what has been labelled by some as 'harmonization by stealth'.[14] In addition, the broad scope of reproduction and reproduction 'in part' might have meant an extension of copyright protection, up to the point that copyright owners can license or prohibit third-party reproductions of very small excerpts of the works to which they own the rights. While this fear might have been justified in the immediate aftermath of the decision in *Infopaq International*, C-5/08, subsequent CJEU case law suggests that this concern is exaggerated. In particular, the way in which the Court has further defined 'author's own intellectual creation' is such that the bar to protection has been raised at the EU level. The result is not just that satisfying this requirement may not be a given, but also that Member States which traditionally have had a looser understanding of originality have been required to move away from a definition of originality as 'sufficient skill, labour or effort' (see further Chapter 7, Section 4.1).[15]

Admissibility of different originality standards—In addition, the ruling in *Infopaq International*, C-5/08, has seemingly removed the possibility of envisaging different standards of protection for different subject matter.[16] In *Flos*, C-168/09, the CJEU held that, while unregistered designs in the public domain are outside the scope of Article 17 of the Design Directive, they might nonetheless qualify for copyright protection under the InfoSoc Directive 'if the conditions for that directive's application are met',[17] ie if they are their author's own intellectual creation.[18] Article 17 of the Design Directive in principle leaves EU Member States free to determine in what conditions copyright protection would arise in respect of designs protected by design rights:

---

[11] Ibid, paras 47 and 49–50.   [12] Ibid, para 45.

[13] Ibid, paras 40–43. See also *Nintendo and Others*, C-355/12, EU:C:2014:25, paras 21–22.

[14] L Bently, *Harmonization by Stealth: Copyright and the ECJ*, Fordham IP Conference 2010, available at <http://fordhamipconference.com/wp-content/uploads/2010/08/Bently_Harmonization.pdf> (last accessed 15 August 2018). Also discussing *Infopaq International*, C-5/08, from the perspective of CJEU activism, see J Griffiths, 'The role of the Court of Justice in the development of European Union copyright law', in I Stamatoudi and P Torremans (eds), *EU Copyright Law—A Commentary* (Edward Elgar:2014), §§20.06–20.16.

[15] See further E Rosati, *Originality in EU Copyright—Full Harmonization through Case Law* (Edward Elgar:2013), 108–11; E Derclaye, '*Infopaq International A/S v Danske Dagblades Forening* (C-5/08): wonderful or worrisome? The impact of the ECJ ruling in Infopaq on UK copyright law' (2010) 32(5) EIPR 247, 248–50; C Handig, 'The "sweat of the brow" is not enough!—more than a blueprint of the European copyright term "work"' (2013) 35(6) EIPR 334, 336–7; and D Liu, 'Of originality: originality in English copyright law: past and present' (2014) 36(6) EIPR 376, 385–8. Cf, discussing critically whether that would actually be the case, A Rahmatian, 'Originality in UK copyright law: the old "skill and labour" doctrine under pressure' (2013) 44(1) IIC 4, 15–16.

[16] See also the discussion in TE Synodinou, 'The foundations of the concept of work in European copyright law', in TE Synodinou (ed), *Codification of European Copyright Law—Challenges and Perspectives* (Wolters Kluwer:2012), 98–9.

[17] *Flos*, C-168/09, EU:C:2011:29, para 34.

[18] On the particular outcome of *Flos*, C-168/09, see, critically, L Bently, 'The return of industrial copyright?' (2012) 34(10) EIPR 654, 660–1.

A design protected by a design right registered in or in respect of a Member State in accordance with this Directive shall also be eligible for protection under the law of copyright of that State as from the date on which the design was created or fixed in any form. The extent to which, and the conditions under which, such a protection is conferred, including the level of originality required, shall be determined by each Member State.

However, in *Flos*, C-168/09, the CJEU seemed to take a different approach. This was a reference from Italy asking about the compatibility with EU law of certain Italian provisions that the Court of First Instance of Milan had deemed potentially incompatible with the principle of cumulation envisaged under EU law. The Italian approach to copyright protection of designs has been traditionally rooted within the principle of *scindibilità* (separability). The CJEU held that EU law prohibits Member States from denying copyright protection to designs that meet the requirements for copyright protection—including designs other than registered ones (subject to Article 17)—and suggested (albeit rather ambiguously) that Member States cannot set any particular requirements as to how protection is to be secured. The implication of all this may be that, if a design is eligible for protection under the InfoSoc Directive and is, as such, original in the sense clarified by the CJEU, Member States cannot deny such protection. Such a reading of the *Flos* case is the one that AG Jääskinen proposed in *Donner*, C-5/11:

[T]he judgment in *Flos* indicates that the items here in issue, although unprotected under Italian copyright law during the relevant period, were entitled to protection under EU copyright law.[19]

By 'EU copyright law' what is meant is the InfoSoc Directive. In *Flos*, C-168/09, the CJEU stated:

[I]t is conceivable that copyright protection for works which may be unregistered designs could arise under other directives concerning copyright, in particular Directive 2001/29, if the conditions for that directive's application are met, a matter which falls to be determined by the national court.[20]

The *Flos* decision has given rise to contrasting interpretations, and prompted the Portuguese Supreme Court to make a reference to the CJEU, *Cofemel*, C-683/17 (in progress), which seeks guidance regarding the conditions for copyright protection in works of applied art and industrial models and designs.[21]

Higher threshold to protection—In the first decision after *Infopaq International*, C-5/08, *Bezpečnostní softwarová asociace*, C-393/09, the CJEU elaborated further on the notion of 'author's own intellectual creation' by discussing copyright protection of graphic user interfaces. It clarified that 'creation' is to be intended as requiring 'creativity': the standard of originality mandates in fact that the author has expressed 'his creativity in an original manner'.[22] Such an understanding of originality has been confirmed in *Football Association Premier League and Others*, C-403/08 and C-429/08: originality as 'author's own intellectual creation' requires exerting 'creative freedom', this being something that football matches—being subject to the rules of the game—do

---

[19] Opinion of Advocate General Niilo Jääskinen in *Donner*, C-5/11, EU:C:2012:195, para 31.

[20] *Flos*, C-168/09, EU:C:2011:29, para 34.

[21] See further E Rosati, 'When does copyright protection arise in works of applied art and industrial models and designs? A new CJEU reference' (25 January 2018), The IPKat, available at <http://ipkitten.blogspot.com/2018/01/when-does-copyright-protection-arise-in.html> (last accessed 15 August 2018), and T Rendas, 'Copyright protection of designs in the EU: how many originality standards is too many?' (2018) 13(6) JIPLP 439.

[22] *Bezpečnostní softwarová asociace*, C-393/09, EU:C:2010:816, para 50.

not possess.[23] The CJEU refined further its construction of the standard of protection in its subsequent decision in *Painer*, C-145/10. In relation to the originality requirement for photographs, in particular portrait photographs, what is required is for the author 'to express his creative abilities in the production of the work by making free and creative choices, so that he 'can stamp the work created with his "personal touch"'.[24] It is therefore apparent that the EU standard of originality, as also acknowledged by AG Mengozzi in his Opinion in *Football Dataco and Others*, C-604/10, entails a ' "creative" aspect, and it is not sufficient that the creation of [the work] required labour and skill'.[25]

More than just 'skill, labour or effort'—Despite some reluctance on the part of courts in Member States like the UK, there is little doubt that originality as 'author's own intellectual creation' mandates a certain degree of creativity and the display of the author's personality.[26] Unlike other EU Member States following the *droit d'auteur* approach to copyright protection, in the UK traditionally the understanding of the originality requirement has been a loose one (see further Chapter 7, Section 4.1). In 2010, the High Court of England and Wales stated that originality involves the application of skill or labour in the creation of a work. The skill or labour need not be directed to the creation of particular modes of expression, in that it can be deployed in the selection or choice of what should be included in the work.[27] In this sense, that court did not consider the CJEU decision in *Infopaq International*, C-5/08, as having prompted a change in the approach to originality, although it conceded that the full implications of that decision had yet to be worked out.[28] However, more recent decisions suggest a different approach. For instance, in a 2017 judgment concerning availability of copyright protection for TV formats, the High Court of England and Wales stated that the requirement of originality under the Copyright, Designs and Patents Act 1988 (CDPA) 'is that the work must be an expression of the author's own intellectual creation ... This does not, however, mean that every constituent aspect of a work must be original. The work must be taken as a whole, and can include parts that are neither novel nor ingenious.'[29]

Floodgates to open?—Overall, through its case law the CJEU has, on the one hand, adopted a broad understanding of the concept of reproduction and, on the other hand, by elaborating on the concept of 'author's own intellectual creation', carried out a de

---

[23] *Football Association Premier League and Others*, C-403/08 and C-429/08, EU:C:2011:631, para 98.

[24] *Painer*, C-145/10, EU:C:2011:798, paras 89 and 92.

[25] Opinion of Advocate General Paolo Mengozzi in *Football Dataco Ltd and Others*, C-604/10, EU:C:2011:848, para 35. But see A Rahmatian, 'Originality in UK copyright law', suggesting a different reading of the string of CJEU originality cases with regard to Member States that have traditionally intended originality as just requiring sufficient skill, labour, or effort.

[26] This might have implications for the protection of works created by Artificial Intelligence: see further the discussion in A Guadamuz, 'Do androids dream of electric copyright? Comparative analysis of originality in artificial intelligence generated works' (2017) 2017/2 IPQ 169, 178–80; E Rosati, 'The *Monkey Selfie* case and the concept of authorship: an EU perspective' (2017) 12(12) JIPLP 973, 976.

[27] *Newspaper Licensing Agency Ltd and Others v Meltwater Holding BV and Others* [2010] EWHC 3099 (Ch) (26 November 2010), para 30, referring to: *Interlego AG v Tyco Industries* [1989] 1 AC 217, paras 259–263; *Walter v Lane* [1900] AC 539; *Express Newspapers Plc v News (UK) Limited* [1990] 1 WLR 1320.

[28] Ibid, para 81.

[29] *Banner Universal Motion Pictures Ltd v Endemol Shine Group Ltd and Another* [2017] EWHC 2600 (Ch) (19 October 2017), para 26, referring to *SAS Institute Inc v World Programming Ltd* [2013] EWCA Civ 1482 (21 November 2013), paras 29–37.

facto harmonization of the originality requirement for works falling under the scope of the InfoSoc Directive, by setting a relatively high threshold to protection. In this way, the Court constrained the potentially expansive stance of the scope of copyright protection as descending from *Infopaq International*, C-5/08. In doing so, however, the CJEU pushed harmonization of copyright laws further than the EU legislature had done.

1.2 Notion of 'work' under EU law

Ambiguities in existing case law—The judgments in *Infopaq International*, C-5/08; *Bezpečnostní softwarová asociace*, C-393/09; and *Football Association Premier League and Others*, C-403/08 and C-429/08, employ a rather problematic language, in the sense that they suggest—rather tautologically—that copyright protection would arise in relation to any subject matter that is sufficiently original. In *Infopaq International*, C-5/08, in fact, the Court held that 'copyright ... is liable to apply only in relation to a subject matter which is original in the sense that it is its author's own intellectual creation',[30] and in *Bezpečnostní softwarová asociace*, C-393/09, it found that a graphic user interface 'can, as a work, be protected by copyright if it is its author's own intellectual creation'.[31] In even more ambiguous terms, in *Football Association Premier League and Others*, C-403/08 and C-429/08, the CJEU stated that sporting events 'cannot be classified as works. To be so classified, the subject matter concerned would have to be original in the sense that it is its author's own intellectual creation'.[32]

All this might suggest that, in the Court's view, the primary—and even possibly the only—assessment to conduct is whether the subject matter in question is sufficiently original.[33] However, this would not be correct, as the subject matter at issue must be first considered a 'work'. This is a notion that, albeit referred to in the InfoSoc Directive, is not defined therein and on which the CJEU has not yet provided express guidance.[34]

The WIPO Guide to Berne—According to the WIPO Guide to the Berne Convention, although the general tone of the Convention suggests that 'it is not possible to speak about a complete definition' (BC-2.2.), 'the context in which the words "work" and "author" are used in the Convention—closely related to each other— indicates that only those productions qualify as works which are intellectual creations (and, consequently, only those persons qualify as authors whose intellectual creative activity brings such works into existence)'.[35] In general terms, it may be said that '[t]he term "production" ... only indicates that the protected object must have emerged from

---

[30] *Infopaq International*, C-5/08, EU:C:2009:465, para 37.
[31] *Bezpečnostní softwarová asociace*, C-393/09, EU:C:2010:816, para 46.
[32] *Football Association Premier League and Others*, C-403/08 and C-429/08, EU:C:2011:631, paras 96–97.
[33] See M van Eechoud, 'Along the road to uniformity—Diverse readings of the Court of Justice judgments on copyright work' (2012) 3(1) JIPITEC 60, 70 and literature cited therein.
[34] In the same sense, European Copyright Society, *Opinion on the pending reference before the CJEU in Case 310/17 (copyright protection of tastes)* (19 February 2018), available at <https://europeancopyrightsocietydotorg.files.wordpress.com/2018/03/ecs-opinion-on-protection-for-tastes-final1.pdf> (last accessed 15 August 2018), 2.
[35] World Intellectual Property Organization, *Guide to copyright and related rights treaties administered by WIPO and glossary of copyright and related rights terms* (2003), BC-2.2 and BC-2.3.

the mind of a person, left the sphere of the mind and become realized. This coincides with the term "expression" also contained in the definition'.[36]

'Work' as an autonomous concept of EU law—In his Opinion in *Levola Hengelo*, C-310/17 (at the time of writing, the case is still pending before the CJEU; for a background to the case, see Chapter 3, Section 1), AG Wathelet held that 'work' is to be intended as an autonomous concept of EU law that requires uniform application throughout the EU, and is to be defined in accordance with Article 2(1) of the Berne Convention. By harmonizing the conditions for protection of works, ie the originality standard, the CJEU has already ruled out that Member States could have different understandings of what qualifies as an original work.

Recalling in particular the decisions in *Infopaq International*, C-5/08; *Painer*, C-145/10; and *Football Dataco*, C-640/10, the AG in *Levola Hengelo*, C-310/17, noted that an 'object' is protectable if it is sufficiently original, in that sense that it is 'its author's own intellectual creation' which results from the marking of 'free and creative choices' so that the resulting 'object' displays the 'personal touch' of the author. Originality alone is not sufficient: it is also required that the 'object' in question is a 'work' within Article 2(1) of the Berne Convention. That provision includes a non-exhaustive list of protectable subject matter. Although it does not expressly exclude taste, smells, or perfumes, according to the AG the only types of works included therein are those that can be perceived through sight or hearing.[37] Hence, the taste of a food product—this being the subject matter at issue in the national background proceedings—would not be a work within the Berne Convention. In addition, an original expression would only be protectable by copyright if it is identifiable with sufficient precision and objectivity,[38] in a way similar to what the CJEU required in relation to the graphic representation requirement in trade mark law in its decision in *Sieckmann*, C-273/00.[39]

This last point raises a number of perplexities. In particular, even if the Opinion excludes that the InfoSoc Directive envisages a fixation requirement,[40] reference to the need for precision and objectivity of the subject matter implies that such a requirement be fulfilled instead. Would it be in fact possible to have subject matter that is precise and identifiable without it being also fixed in some material form? This may be problematic in that, first, the requirements for trade mark registration are—formally—different from those for copyright protection and, secondly, because in principle the Berne Convention (Article 2(2)) leaves it to individual signatories to determine whether to introduce a fixation requirement into their own copyright laws.[41]

Exhaustive and non-exhaustive lists of protectable works—In any case, should the CJEU state—as appears correct—that also the notion of 'work' is defined at the

---

[36] S von Lewinski, *International Copyright Law and Policy* (OUP:2008), §5.66. See also S Ricketson and JC Ginsburg, *International Copyright and Neighbouring Rights—The Berne Convention and Beyond* (OUP:2006), 2nd edn, Vol I, §§8.01–8.03.

[37] Arguing in the same sense, European Copyright Society, *Opinion on the pending reference before the CJEU in Case 310/17 (copyright protection of tastes)* (19 February 2018), available at <https://europeancopyrightsocietydotorg.files.wordpress.com/2018/03/ecs-opinion-on-protection-for-tastes-final1.pdf> (last accessed 15 August 2018), 6.

[38] Opinion of Advocate General Melchior Wathelet in *Levola Hengelo*, C-310/17, EU:C:2018:618, para 56.

[39] *Sieckmann*, C-273/00, EU:C:2002:748, para 55.

[40] Opinion of Advocate General Melchior Wathelet in *Levola Hengelo*, C-310/17, EU:C:2018:618, para 59.

[41] See further E Rosati, 'The AG Opinion in *Levola Hengelo*: more questions than answers?' (25 July 2018), The IPKat, available at <http://ipkitten.blogspot.com/2018/07/the-ag-opinion-in-levola-hengelo-more.html> (last accessed 15 August 2018).

EU level, then this would mean that the same type of subject matter is to be protected across the EU. On the one hand, this would prevent protection by means of copyright of subject matter that does not fall within the EU notion of 'work' and, on the other hand, it would prevent Member States from excluding protection for works that, instead, fall within the EU notion. In this sense, closed national systems of protectable works would be incompatible with EU law.[42] This conclusion is *also* prompted by the following consideration: if, on the one hand, we accept that solutions like that of the Dutch Supreme Court in *Kecofa v Lancôme*,[43] ie that copyright could vest in a perfume, may not be tolerated then, on the other hand, protection could not be denied in a certain work just because it does not belong to one of the categories envisaged by a certain Member State's list of protectable works (with regard to the UK, see further Chapter 7, Section 4.2). At the time when the Dutch judgment was issued (2006) some commentators noted that disparities in the protection *tout court* of certain subject matter across the EU would raise, inter alia, free movement issues:

> Dutch law is now out of step with that of all other EU member states. *Parfumeurs* welcomed the Dutch ruling, believing their work to be indubitably artistic. Such thinking sits comfortably with the Romantic vision of the author as uniquely entitled to proprietorship of created works, but this paradigm has been seriously challenged in post-modern times. It also draws on an aesthetic discourse of originality which cries loudly for protection but has a tendency to forget its own debts. TRÉSOR itself owes much to two earlier perfumes: Calvin Klein's ETERNITY and Sophia Grosjman's EXCLAMATION. In addition to the philosophical difficulties, there are practical problems. It will require considerable creativity to apply certain acts of copyright infringement (*e.g.* distribution, making available to the public) to fragrance, whose fundamental purpose is that it will be perceived not only by the wearer, but also by those in the vicinity. Furthermore, the ruling creates an unacceptable impediment to the free movement of goods within the EU. Harmonisation will be essential if the Dutch approach is maintained.[44]

The same would be true for works, possibly of a less conventional type, that are regarded as protectable in certain EU jurisdictions but not others. As a result, protection across the EU should be based on the same requirements and be subject to the same limitations.

1.3 The lawfulness of sampling: how far does the notion of 'reproduction in part' go?

Pelham and Others (the *Metall auf Metall* case)—A case currently pending before the CJEU (*Pelham and Others*, C-476/17) will serve to gauge the impact of *Infopaq International*, C-5/08, and its progeny in relation to the right of reproduction as applied to sampling musical content, ie taking part of a sound recording for re-use in a different song or piece.

The referral arose out of the longstanding and complex litigation in Germany concerning the unauthorized sampling by music producer Moses Pelham of a 2-second rhythmic sequence from Kraftwerk's 1977 song *Metall auf Metall* for use in his own 1997 *Nur Mir*. The sample featured in the latter's song (performed by Sabrina Setlur) is a continuous background loop. Following a number of lower courts' decisions and

---

[42] I argued this in E Rosati, 'Closed subject matter systems are no longer compatible with EU copyright' (2014) 12 GRUR Int 1112, 1112–18.

[43] Hoge Raad, *Kecofa BV v Lancôme Parfums et Beauté et Cie SNC*, C04/327HR, NL:HR:2006:AU8940.

[44] C Seville, 'Copyright in perfumes: smelling a rat' (2007) 66(1) CLJ 49, 51.

an instalment before the German Constitutional Court,[45] the case is now pending before Germany's Federal Court of Justice for the third time. This court decided to stay the proceedings and seek guidance from the CJEU on the correct interpretation of EU law with regard to the notion of 'reproduction in part' for phonograms under Article 2(c) of the InfoSoc Directive in order to determine whether a 2-second sample may fall within the scope of the right of reproduction. The question is whether a phonogram sampling an earlier phonogram is a copy of it within the meaning of Article 9(1)(b) of the Rental and Lending Rights Directive. Should the answer be in the affirmative, then the referring court asks whether the German 'free use' exception within §24(1) of the German Copyright Act (Urheberrechtsgesetz—UrhG) ('An independent work, created in the free use of the work of another person, may be published and exploited without the consent of the author of the work used.') is compatible with EU law; should the defendants be unable to rely on the 'free use' exception, whether the quotation exception within Article 5(3)(d) of the InfoSoc Directive might nonetheless shield them from liability on grounds that quotation would be a 'right', rather than just an exception; what role the rights granted by the EU Charter play, with particular regard to the interplay between Article 17(2) (copyright protection) and Article 13 (freedom of the arts) therein.[46]

It is expected that the outcome of this referral will serve to qualify further what is meant by 'reproduction in part' under Article 2 of the InfoSoc Directive, as well as understanding better the interplay between economic rights and exceptions and limitations, from a fundamental rights perspective.[47] This will be particularly important in a number of creative fields, especially music, where the lawfulness of practices like unlicensed sampling and remixing remains controversial.[48]

2. The Right of Communication to the Public

Overview of the right—The right of communication to the public within Article 3(1) of the InfoSoc Directive has been subject to a significant number of referrals since the first ruling in 2006 in *SGAE*, C-306/05.[49] By relying on international sources and a

---

[45] Bundesverfassungsgericht (*Metall auf Metall*) (1 BvR 1585/13), 31 May 2016.

[46] On the background national litigation, see further BJ Jütte and H Maier, 'A human right to sample—will the CJEU dance to the BGH-beat?' (2017) 12(9) JIPLP 784, in particular 789–96, and E Adeney, 'How much is too much? The gradual coalescence of the law on sampling' (2018) 2018/ 2 IPQ 91, 96–7 (also offering a comparative overview of the legal treatment of sampling of sound recordings).

[47] European Copyright Society, *Opinion of the European Copyright Society in relation to the pending reference before the CJEU in Case C-476/17*, Hutter v Pelham (2018), available at <https:// europeancopyrightsocietydotorg.files.wordpress.com/2018/03/opinion-metall-auf-metall-fin4.pdf> (last accessed 15 August 2018), §3.9, holding: 'Sampling ought to encroach upon the exclusive rights of a phonogram producer only if it significantly prejudices the economic interests of the right holder, i.e. if it prejudices the prospect of recouping a substantial investment in the production of the phonogram, through substitution of the original.'

[48] See also LT McDonagh, 'Is the creative use of musical works without a licence acceptable under copyright law?' (2012) 43(4) IIC 401, 418–19.

[49] They are (in chronological order): *SGAE*, C-306/05, EU:C:2006:764; *Organismos Sillogikis Diacheirisis Dimiourgon Theatrikon kai Optikoakoustikon Ergon*, C-136/09, EU:C:2010:151; *Circul Globus București*, C-283/10, EU:C:2011:772; *Football Association Premier League and Others*, C-403/08 and C-429/08, EU:C:2011:631; *Airfield and Canal Digitaal*, C-431/09, EU:C:2011:648; *SCF*, C-135/10, EU:C:2012:140; *Phonographic Performance (Ireland)*, C-162/10, EU:C:2012:141; *ITV Broadcasting*, C-607/11, EU:C:2013:147; *Svensson and Others*, C-466/12, EU:C:2014:76; *OSA*, C-351/12, EU:C:2014:110; *BestWater*, C-348/13, EU:C:2014:2315; *C More Entertainment*, C-279/13, EU:C:2015:199; *Sociedade Portuguesa de Autores CRL*, C-151/15, EU:C:2015:468; *SBS*

purpose-driven interpretation of the InfoSoc Directive, the CJEU has construed this exclusive right broadly and in such a way as to encompass, in certain conditions, different types of acts, including the making available of TV sets in certain contexts, linking to protected content, the provision of certain types of set-up boxes, indexing activities by a platform, and cloud-based recording services.[50]

Origin—At the international level the right of communication to the public received its first formulation in Article 11*bis* of the Berne Convention, as adopted in 1928 and later revised by the Brussels Act 1948.[51] The WIPO Copyright Treaty supplemented the Berne Convention[52] and introduced the concept of 'making available to the public'.[53]

Article 3(1) of the InfoSoc Directive—The wording of Article 3(1) of the InfoSoc Directive is derived from Article 8 of the WIPO Copyright Treaty.[54] However, Article 3(1) of the InfoSoc Directive does not define the concept of 'communication to the public'. This provision, in fact, only states that EU

Member States shall provide authors with the exclusive right to authorise or prohibit any communication to the public of their works, by wire or wireless means, including the making available to the public of their works in such a way that members of the public may access them from a place and at a time individually chosen by them.

Lacking a definition of the notion of 'communication to the public', the CJEU has sought to determine the meaning and scope of this concept in light of the objectives pursued by the InfoSoc Directive, notably ensuring a high level of protection of intellectual property (Recital 24) and for authors (see Chapter 2, Section 2.1).

In its rich body of case law on Article 3(1) of the InfoSoc Directive, the CJEU has consistently stated that the essential requirements of Article 3(1) are an 'act of communication', directed to a 'public'. In addition, the CJEU has also highlighted the importance of considering additional criteria, which are not autonomous and are interdependent, and may—in different situations—be present to widely varying

---

Belgium, C-325/14, EU:C:2015:764; *Reha Training*, C-117/15, EU:C:2016:379; *GS Media*, C-160/15, EU:C:2016:644; *Stichting Brein*, C-527/15, EU:C:2017:300; *AKM*, C-138/16, EU:C:2017:218; *Stichting Brein*, C-610/15, EU:C:2017:456; *VCAST*, C-265/16, EU:C:2017:913; and *Renckhoff*, C-161/17, EU:C:2018:634.

[50] According to some commentators, rather than a unified concept of communication to the public, in its case law the CJEU has created specific *sui generis* groups of communication to the public cases: see B Clark and S Tozzi, '"Communication to the public" under EU copyright law: an increasingly Delphic concept or intentional fragmentation?' (2016) 38(12) EIPR 715, 717.

[51] See World Intellectual Property Organization, *Guide to copyright and related rights treaties* BC-11*bis*.1.

[52] Article 1(4) of the WIPO Copyright Treaty mandates compliance with Articles 1 to 21 of and the Appendix to the Berne Convention.

[53] On the concept of making available within Article 8 of the WIPO Copyright Treaty, see MM Walter, 'Article 3 Right of communication to the public of works and right of making available to the public of other subject matter', in MM Walter and S von Lewinski, *European Copyright Law—A commentary* (2010:OUP), 975–80.

[54] It may be interesting to contrast EU law-making (and subsequent expansive interpretations of the CJEU) with the United States, which took the position that the existing rights of distribution and public performance under the US Act were sufficient to comply with the WIPO Copyright Treaty's making available right and no changes to the statute were needed in light of its new international obligations: see United States Copyright Office, *The Making Available Right in the United States—A Report of the Register of Copyrights* (February 2016), available at <https://www.copyright.gov/docs/making_available/making-available-right.pdf> (last accessed 15 August 2018), 15–18.

degrees. Such criteria must be applied both individually and in their interaction with one another.[55]

2.1 Requirements and criteria under Article 3(1) of the InfoSoc Directive

'Public' and 'new public'[56]—Starting from 'public', this is a concept that has not been straightforward to comprehend, also because the relevant understanding may change depending on the context.[57] In general terms, the notion of 'public' is that of an indeterminate and fairly large (above *de minimis*) number of people.[58] In the case of a communication concerning the same works as those covered by the initial communication and made with the same technical means (eg internet), the communication must be directed to a 'new' public. Derived from the interpretation given by the 1978 WIPO Guide to the Berne Convention of Article 11*bis*(1)(iii) of the Berne Convention as first employed by AG La Pergola in his Opinion in *EGEDA*, C-293/98,[59] the 'new public' that is relevant to the establishment of Article 3(1) applicability is the public which was not taken into account by the relevant rightholder when it authorized the initial communication to the public.[60]

Act of communication—With regard to the notion of 'act of communication', case law is now solidly oriented in the sense of requiring the mere making available of a copyright work—not also its actual transmission[61]—in such a way that the persons

---

[55] *SCF*, C-135/10, EU:C:2012:140, para 79; *Phonographic Performance (Ireland)*, C-162/10, EU:C:2012:141, para 30; *Reha Training*, C-117/15, EU:C:2016:379, para 35; *GS Media*, C-160/15, EU:C:2016:644, para 34; *Stichting Brein*, C-527/15, EU:C:2017:300, para 30; and *Stichting Brein*, C-610/15, EU:C:2017:456, para 25.

[56] Section 2.1 builds upon E Rosati, '*GS Media* and its implications for the construction of the right of communication to the public within EU copyright architecture' (2017) 54(4) CML Rev 1221, 1233–8 and E Rosati, 'The CJEU *Pirate Bay* judgment and its impact on the liability of online platforms' (2017) 39(12) EIPR 737.

[57] S Karapapa, 'The requirement for a "new public" in EU copyright law' (2017) 42(1) EL Rev 63, 66.

[58] *SGAE*, C-306/05, EU:C:2006:764, para 38; *SCF*, C-135/10, EU:C:2012:140, para 84; *Phonographic Performance (Ireland)*, C-162/10, EU:C:2012:141, para 33; *ITV Broadcasting*, C-607/11, EU:C:2013:147, para 32; *Svensson and Others*, C-466/12, EU:C:2014:76, para 21; *OSA*, C-351/12, EU:C:2014:110, para 27; *Sociedade Portuguesa de Autores CRL*, C-151/15, EU:C:2015:468, para 19; *SBS Belgium*, C-325/14, EU:C:2015:764, para 21; *GS Media*, C-160/15, EU:C:2016:644, para 36; *Stichting Brein*, C-527/15, EU:C:2017:300, para 45; *AKM*, C-138/16, EU:C:2017:218, para 24; and *Stichting Brein*, C-610/15, EU:C:2017:456, paras 27 and 42.

[59] Opinion of Advocate General Antonio Mario La Pergola in *EGEDA*, C-293/98, EU:C:1999:403, para 20. See further PB Hugenholtz and SC Van Velze, 'Communication to a new public? Three reasons why EU copyright law can do without a "new public"' (2016) 47(7) IIC 797, 802–3.

[60] *SGAE*, C-306/05, EU:C:2006:764, paras 40 and 42; *Organismos Sillogikis Diacheirisis Dimiourgon Theatrikon kai Optikoakoustikon Ergon*, C-136/09, EU:C:2010:151, para 39; *Football Association Premier League and Others*, C-403/08 and C-429/08, EU:C:2011:631, para 197, *Airfield and Canal Digitaal*, C-431/09, EU:C:2011:648, para 72; *Svensson and Others*, C-466/12, EU:C:2014:76, para 24; *OSA*, C-351/12, EU:C:2014:110, para 31; *Reha Training*, C-117/15, EU:C:2016:379, para 45; *GS Media*, C-160/15, EU:C:2016:644, para 37; *Stichting Brein*, C-527/15, EU:C:2017:300, para 47; *Stichting Brein*, C-610/15, EU:C:2017:456, para 28; and *Renckhoff*, C-161/17, EU:C:2018:634, para 24. But cf *AKM*, C-138/16, EU:C:2017:218, paras 26–27, suggesting that consideration of whether the communication at hand is addressed to a 'new public' is required *also* when the specific technical means used is different. On whether terms and conditions of use of a certain website might be relevant to determine whether the public targeted by the defendant's link is 'new', see (arguing in the negative) P McBride, 'The "new public" criterion after *Svensson*: the (ir)relevance of website terms and conditions' (2017) 2017/3 IPQ 262, 275–7.

[61] This was the case in *Circul Globus Bucureşti*, C-283/10, EU:C:2011:772, para 40; *Football Association Premier League and Others*, C-403/08 and C-429/08, EU:C:2011:631, paras 190,

forming the public may access it, irrespective of whether they avail themselves of such opportunity.[62]

Essential/indispensable (*incontournable*) intervention—In cases where the CJEU has held the making available of a work sufficient, the Court has also indicated the need to consider whether there is a necessary and deliberate intervention on the side of the user/defendant, without which third parties could not access the work at issue. More specifically, the user makes an act of communication when it intervenes—in full knowledge of the consequences of its action—to give access to a protected work to its customers, and does so, in particular, where, in the absence of that intervention, their customers would not, in principle, be able to enjoy the work.[63] In this sense, the intervention of the user/defendant must result from a role that is *incontournable*, ie an essential/indispensable role.[64]

With particular regard to the notion of essentiality/indispensability of one's own intervention, the Court has recently clarified that an intervention which *facilitates* access to unlicensed content that would otherwise be more difficult to locate qualifies as an essential/indispensable intervention. Over time the CJEU has dismissed attempts to interpret this criterion narrowly. A clear example is *GS Media*, C-160/15. In his Opinion in that case, AG Wathelet had excluded *tout court* that the unauthorized provision of a link to a copyright work—whether published with the consent of the rightholder or not—could be classified as an act of communication to the public. This would be so on consideration that, to establish an act of communication, the intervention of the 'hyperlinker' must be vital or indispensable in order to benefit from or enjoy the relevant copyright work. Hyperlinks posted on a website that direct to copyright works freely accessible on another website cannot be classified as an 'act of communication': the intervention of the operator of the website that posts the hyperlinks is not indispensable to the making available of the works in question to users.[65]

Provision of physical facilities—Another criterion considered by the CJEU is whether the user/defendant merely provides physical facilities or not. While the mere provision of physical facilities does not amount to an act of communication to the

---

193, and 207; *OSA*, C-351/12, EU:C:2014:110, para 25; *SBS Belgium*, C-325/14, EU:C:2015:764, para 16; and *Reha Training*, C-117/15, EU:C:2016:379, para 38.

[62] *SGAE*, C-306/05, EU:C:2006:764, para 43; *Svensson and Others*, C-466/12, EU:C:2014:76, para 19; *GS Media*, C-160/15, EU:C:2016:644, para 27; *Stichting Brein*, C-527/15, EU:C:2017:300, para 36; *AKM*, C-138/16, EU:C:2017:218, para 20; *Stichting Brein*, C-610/15, EU:C:2017:456, para 19; and *Renckhoff*, C-161/17, EU:C:2018:634, para 20. On the accessibility criterion, see, critically, J Koo, 'Away we Ziggo: the latest chapter in the EU communication to the public story' (2018) 13(7) JIPLP 542, 545–6.

[63] *SGAE*, C-306/05, EU:C:2006:764, para 42; *Football Association Premier League and Others*, C-403/08 and C-429/08, EU:C:2011:631, paras 194 and 195; *Airfield and Canal Digitaal*, C-431/09, EU:C:2011:648, para 79; *SCF*, C-135/10, EU:C:2012:140, para 82; *Phonographic Performance (Ireland)*, C-162/10, EU:C:2012:141, para 31; *Reha Training*, C-117/15, EU:C:2016:379, para 46; *GS Media*, C-160/15, EU:C:2016:644, para 35; *Stichting Brein*, C-527/15, EU:C:2017:300, para 31; and *Stichting Brein*, C-610/15, EU:C:2017:456, para 26.

[64] While in the original language version (French) of relevant judgments use of the adjective 'incontournable' is consistent, in the English versions that is not always the case: eg, in *Reha Training*, C-117/15, EU:C:2016:379, para 46, and *GS Media*, C-160/15, EU:C:2016:644, para 35, the adjective 'indispensable' is used, while in *Stichting Brein*, C-527/15, EU:C:2017:300, para 31, and *Stichting Brein*, C-610/15, EU:C:2017:456, para 26 the adjective 'essential' is employed. See, however, GF Frosio, 'To filter or not to filter? That is the question in EU copyright reform' (2018) 36(2) AELJ 101, 114, suggesting that there would be a difference between the standards of 'indispensability' and 'essentiality' of one's own role.

[65] Opinion of Advocate General Melchior Wathelet in *GS Media*, C-160/15, EU:C:2016:221, paras 57–60.

public (Recital 27), the installation of such facilities may make the public access to copyright works technically possible, and thus fall within the scope of Article 3(1) of the InfoSoc Directive.[66]

Profit-making intention and presumption of knowledge—In addition to the requirements of an act of communication directed to a public, the Court has also considered—from time to time—other non-autonomous and interdependent criteria (having no clear textual basis), necessary to undertake an individual assessment of the case at issue. Such criteria may, in different situations, be present to widely varying degrees. They must be applied both individually and in their interaction with one another.[67]

In *GS Media*, C-160/15 (see further Section 2.2), the Court, among other things, relied in particular on the 'profit-making' character of the communication at issue to determine potential liability of the 'hyperlinker' for the posting of links to unlicensed content. Prior to *GS Media*, C-160/15, the profit-making character of the communication at issue had not been given the centrality that it did instead acquire in that case: in *Reha Training*, C-117/15, for instance, the Grand Chamber of the CJEU considered that this criterion, while not irrelevant, would not be however decisive.[68] In *GS Media*, C-160/15, instead, the Court adopted a rebuttable presumption that

when the posting of hyperlinks is carried out for profit, it can be expected that the person who posted such a link carries out the necessary checks to ensure that the work concerned is not illegally published on the website to which those hyperlinks lead, so that it must be presumed that that posting has occurred with the full knowledge of the protected nature of that work and the possible lack of consent to publication on the internet by the copyright holder.[69]

Overall, in the context of communication to the public by linking, the Court deemed it necessary to move towards an assessment in which the subjective element is decisive to determine prima facie liability.[70]

Profit-making intention with regard to the act of communication or its context?—The operation of this presumption was confirmed in the subsequent ruling in *Stichting Brein*, C-527/15.[71] As discussed at greater length elsewhere, it might not be self-evident whether the presence of a profit-making intention should be assessed in relation to the specific act of communication at hand, or the broader context in which such an act is performed (see also Section 2.4.1). Although both alternatives are plausible, consideration of the context in which the relevant link is provided is more in line with existing CJEU case law, both preceding and following *GS Media*, C-160/15.[72] In *SGAE*, C-306/

---

[66] *SGAE*, C-306/05, EU:C:2006:764, paras 45–47.

[67] *GS Media*, C-160/15, EU:C:2016:644, para 34, referring to *SCF*, C-135/10, EU:C:2012:140, para 79; *Phonographic Performance (Ireland)*, C-162/10, EU:C:2012:141, para 30; and *Reha Training*, C-117/15, EU:C:2016:379, para 35.

[68] *Reha Training*, C-117/15, EU:C:2016:379, para 49, referring to *ITV Broadcasting and Others*, C-607/11, EU:C:2013:147, para 43, and *Football Association Premier League and Others*, C-403/08 and C-429/08, EU:C:2011:631, para 204. Commenting favourably on the consideration of the profit-making character of the communication at issue, see P Mysoor, 'Unpacking the right of communication to the public: a closer look at international and EU copyright law' (2013) 2013/2 IPQ 166, 182.

[69] *GS Media*, C-160/15, EU:C:2016:644, para 51.

[70] On this, see, critically, TE Synodinou, 'Decoding the Kodi box: to link or not to link?' (2017) 39(12) EIPR 733, 735.

[71] *Stichting Brein*, C-527/15, EU:C:2017:300, paras 49 and 51.

[72] Rosati, '*GS Media* and its implications' 1237–8. In a similar sense, see also B Clark and J Dickinson, 'Theseus and the labyrinth? An overview of "communication to the public" under EU copyright law: after *Reha Training* and *GS Media* where are we now and where do we go from here?' (2017) 39(5) EIPR 265, 269–70. Submitting instead that the profit-making intention of the 'hyperlinker' is to be appreciated with regard to the particular act of hyperlinking, see T Rendas, 'How Playboy photos compromised EU copyright law: the *GS Media* judgment' (2017) J Internet L 11, 14.

05; *Football Association Premier League and Others*, C-403/08; and C-429/08, and *Reha Training*, C-117/15, in fact, the Court considered that the profit-making nature of the communication would be apparent from the fact that the defendants transmitted the relevant works in their own establishment (hotels, a public house, and a rehabilitation centre, respectively) in order to benefit therefrom and attract customers to whom the works transmitted are of interest.[73] In *Stichting Brein*, C-527/15, the CJEU identified the profit-making intention of the defendant where the relevant multimedia player 'is supplied with a view to making a profit, the price for the multimedia player being paid in particular to obtain direct access to protected works available on streaming websites without the consent of the copyright holders'.[74]

Communication to the public in a map—Figure 4.1 provides an illustration of the construction and scope of the right of communication to the public under Article 3(1) of the InfoSoc Directive in CJEU case law, and potential liability for the doing of unauthorized acts of communication to the public:[75]

2.2 Communication to the public and linking

Svensson and Others—In its 2014 decision in *Svensson and Others*, C-466/12, the CJEU ruled that, at certain conditions, the provision of a hyperlink to a work hosted on a third-party website falls within the scope of copyright protection.[76] More specifically, linking to protected content may be regarded as an act of communication to the public within Article 3(1) of the InfoSoc Directive. Qualification of linking as an act of communication to the public means that, when the link in question is provided without permission from the relevant rightholder, this activity could amount, prima facie, to copyright infringement. Whether the act in question is an actual infringement depends on additional considerations, including whether the work at hand is protected by copyright in the first place, and whether the defendant may successfully invoke one or more copyright defences available under the applicable national copyright regime.

The main question of the referring court, the Svea Court of Appeal (Sweden), in *Svensson and Others*, C-466/12, was whether the provision of a hyperlink to a work *lawfully* made available on a certain website where it is *freely* accessible is to be regarded as an act of communication to the public within Article 3(1) of the InfoSoc Directive.[77]

---

[73] *SGAE*, C-306/05, EU:C:2006:764, para 44; *Football Association Premier League and Others*, C-403/08 and C-429/08, EU:C:2011:631, paras 205–206; *Reha Training*, C-117/15, EU:C:2016:379, paras 63–64.

[74] *Stichting Brein*, C-527/15, EU:C:2017:300, para 51.

[75] The diagram was first published in E Rosati, 'The right of communication to the public … in a chart' (24 July 2017), The IPKat, available at <http://ipkitten.blogspot.com/2017/07/the-right-of-communication-to-public-in.html> (last accessed 15 August 2018). For other visual representations of the right of communication to the public under EU copyright law, see O Butriy, 'Letters on copyright law: Hyperlinking and content embedding as 'communication to the public' in the digital space' (28 January 2017), available at <https://www.linkedin.com/pulse/letters-copyright-law-hyperlinking-content-embedding-public-butriy/?trk=hp-feed-article-title-publish> (last accessed 15 August 2018), and JP Quintais, *Untangling the hyperlinking Web: In search of the online right of communication to the public* (2018) Amsterdam Law School Research Paper No. 2018-16, available at <https://papers.ssrn.com/sol3/papers.cfm?abstract_id=3199733> (last accessed 15 August 2018), 15.

[76] Prior to this landmark CJEU decision, commentators (and case law) considered acts of linking within the framework of the right of reproduction or within the scope of accessory liability: see A Strowel, 'Secondary liability for copyright infringement with regard to hyperlinks', in A Strowel (ed), *Peer-to-Peer File Sharing and Secondary Liability in Copyright Law* (Edward Elgar:2009), 76–88.

[77] Already answering potentially in the affirmative prior to the *Svensson* decision, see MM Walter, 'Article 3 Right of communication', in Walter and Lewinski, *European Copyright Law* 985.

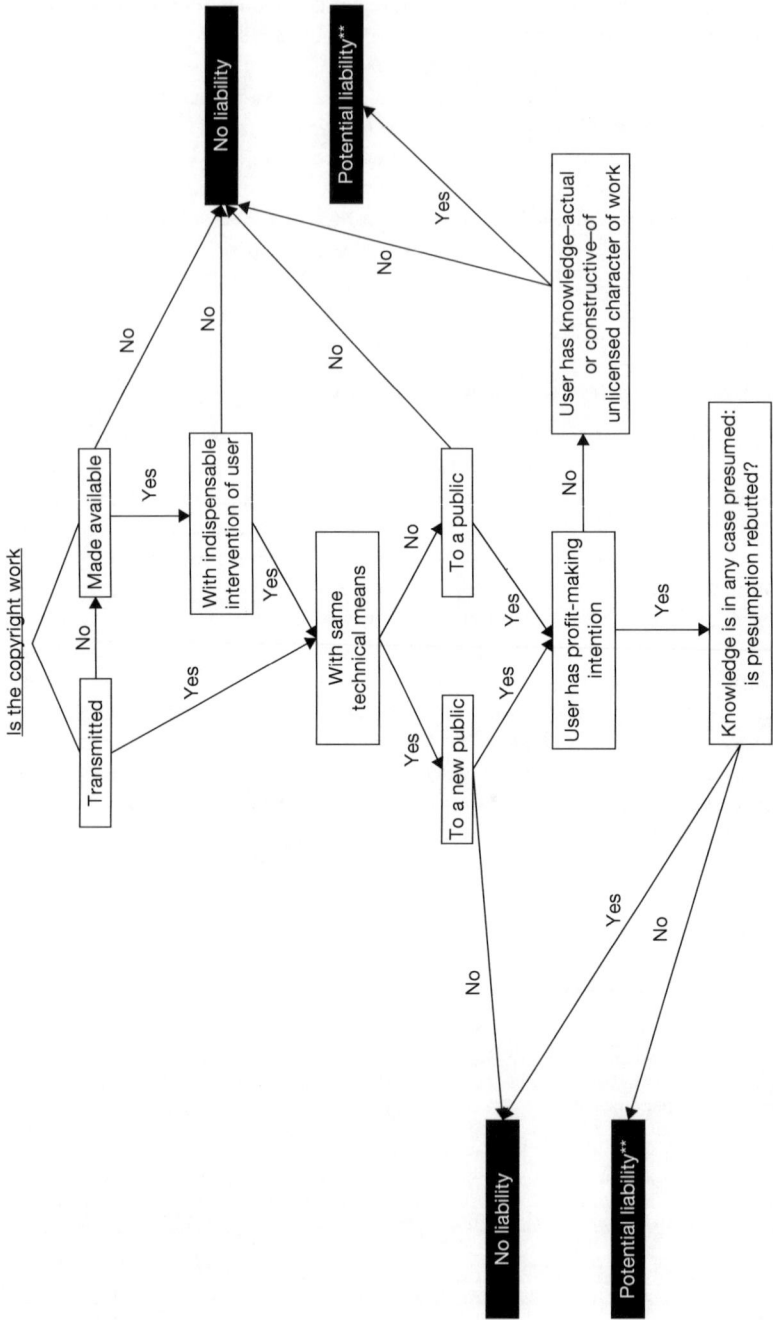

Figure 4.1 Right of communication to the public—Potential liability under Article 3(1) InfoSoc Directive

* Note that the mere provision of physical facilities falls outside Article 3(1).
** Whether user/defendant is actually liable depends on further considerations, including whether any exceptions apply.

This reference for a preliminary ruling had been made in the context of proceedings between a number of journalists and media monitoring provider Retriever, and concerned their request for compensation for the alleged harm suffered as a result of the inclusion, on the latter's website, of hyperlinks redirecting users to press articles (in which the applicants held the copyright) freely accessible on the *Göteborgs-Posten* website.

Act of communication—In its decision the CJEU noted that the concept of communication to the public within Article 3(1) of the InfoSoc Directive includes two cumulative criteria: an 'act of communication' of a work, directed to a 'public'.[78] As regards the first condition, the Court paid lip-service to the requirement that this concept be construed broadly in order to ensure, in accordance with—inter alia—Recitals 4, 9, and 23 in the preamble to the InfoSoc Directive, a high level of protection for rightholders. The provision, on a website, of hyperlinks to protected works published without any access restrictions on another site affords users of the first site direct access to those works, and therefore amounts to an 'act of communication'.[79]

Need for a 'new public'—Turning to the second condition, ie that the communication is directed to a 'public', the CJEU recalled that the term 'public' refers to an indeterminate number of potential recipients and implies a fairly large number of persons.[80] However, an act of communication within Article 3(1) of the InfoSoc Directive requires that a communication concerning the same works as those covered by the initial communication and made by the same technical means (ie internet), must also be directed to a 'new' public. This is a public that was not taken into account by the relevant rightholder when they authorized the initial communication to the public.[81]

The 'new public' requirement as an implied licence—The CJEU concluded that the provision of a hyperlink to a work *lawfully* and *freely* accessible on a third-party website does not fall within the scope of Article 3(1) of the InfoSoc Directive. This is because the public targeted by the initial communication consists of all potential visitors to the site concerned. As such, the hyperlink would not communicate the work to a public not taken into account by the relevant rightholder at the time of authorizing the initial communication.[82] Lacking a 'new' public, no infringing act is deemed to occur. In this sense, the requirement that the public targeted by the act of linking be new means overcoming something that, on the side of the relevant rightholder, may be regarded as an implied licence. Of course, this argument holds true if the content made available

---

[78] *Svensson and Others*, C-466/12, EU:C:2014:76, para 16, referring to *ITV Broadcasting*, C-607/11, EU:C:2013:147, paras 21 and 31.

[79] In its opinion prior to the CJEU judgment, the European Copyright Society had held the view that linking could not qualify as an act of communication to the public, also on consideration that a transmission of a work—as opposed to its mere accessibility—would be required under Article 3(1) of the InfoSoc Directive: see European Copyright Society, *Opinion on the Reference to the CJEU in Case C466/12 Svensson* (15 February 2013), available at <https://europeancopyrightsocietydotorg.files.wordpress.com/2015/12/european-copyright-society-opinion-on-svensson-first-signatoriespaginatedv31.pdf> (last accessed 15 August 2018), 2–4. See, *contra*, Association Littéraire et Artistique Internationale, *Report and Opinion on the making available and communication to the public in the internet environment—focus on linking techniques on the Internet* (16 September 2013), available at <http://www.alai.org/en/assets/files/resolutions/making-available-right-report-opinion.pdf> (last accessed 15 August 2018).

[80] *Svensson and Others*, C-466/12, EU:C:2014:76, para 21, referring to *SGAE*, C-306/05, EU:C:2006:479, paras 37–38, and *ITV Broadcasting*, C-607/11, EU:C:2013:147, para 32.

[81] *Svensson and Others*, C-466/12, EU:C:2014:76, para 24, recalling (by analogy) *SGAE*, C-306/05, EU:C:2006:479, paras 40 and 42; *Organismos Sillogikis Diacheirisis Dimiourgon Theatrikon kai Optikoakoustikon Ergon* C-136/09, EU:C:2010:151, para 38; and *ITV Broadcasting*, C-607/11, EU:C:2013:147, para 39.

[82] *Svensson and Others*, C-466/12, EU:C:2014:76, paras 25–28.

online and linked to has been published with the consent of the relevant rightholder.[83] The CJEU itself framed the 'new public' requirement within a licensing perspective. In *Soulier and Doke*, C-301/15, in referring to its earlier decision in *Svensson and Others*, C-466/12, it held in fact that,

in a situation in which an author had given prior, explicit and unreserved authorisation to the pub-lication of his articles on the website of a newspaper publisher, without making use of technological measures restricting access to those works from other websites, that author could be regarded, in essence, as having authorised the communication of those works to the general internet public.[84]

According to some commentators, employment of the 'new public' requirement would be based on an incorrect interpretation of international law (see further Section 2.1), and would result in an undue (cf Article 3(3) of the InfoSoc Directive) exhaustion of the right of communication to the public.[85]

BestWater—The Court confirmed the approach taken in *Svensson and Others*, C-466/12, in the subsequent 2014 order in *BestWater*, C-348/13, in which it indicated that the provision of a link to content that is freely accessible on a third-party website does not fall within the scope of Article 3(1) of the InfoSoc Directive. In that case the Court failed to address the fact that the content linked to and embedded on the defendant's page had been uploaded on YouTube without the authorization of the rele-vant copyright holder.[86] Hence, even after *BestWater*, C-348/13, it remained unclear what the treatment of linking to protected content available on a third-party website and first communicated without the consent of the relevant rightholder, ie unlicensed content, would be.[87] Logically, if one followed the reasoning of the CJEU in *Svensson* alone and fully, then linking of this kind would *always* be regarded as an act falling within the scope of Article 3(1) of the InfoSoc Directive and, for linking that in-volves embedding/framing, also issues of reproduction—which the CJEU has not yet addressed—would come into consideration.[88] The relevant rightholder, in fact, would

---

[83] Among the first commentators to frame the 'new public' requirement within an implied li-cence perspective are: JC Ginsburg, 'Hyperlinking and infringement: The CJEU decides (sort of)' (17 March 2014), available at <https://www.mediainstitute.org/2014/03/17/hyperlinking-and-infringement-the-cjeu-decides-sort-of/> (last accessed 15 August 2018), and E Arezzo, 'Hyperlinks and making available right in the European Union—what future for the Internet after *Svensson*?' (2014) 45(5) IIC 524, 543.

[84] *Soulier and Doke*, C-301/15, EU:C:2016:878, para 36.

[85] Association Littéraire et Artistique Internationale, *Opinion proposed to the Executive Committee and adopted at its meeting, 17 September 2014 on the criterion 'New Public', developed by the Court of Justice of the European Union (CJEU), put in the context of making available and communication to the public* (17 September 2014), available at <http://www.alai.org/en/assets/files/resolutions/2014-opinion-new-public.pdf> (last accessed 15 August 2018), 2. See also J Rosén, 'How much communi-cation to the public is "communication to the public"?', in IA Stamatoudi (ed), *New Developments in EU and International Copyright Law* (Wolters Kluwer:2016), 341–7, holding that the CJEU approach in *Svensson and Others*, C-466/12, would be incompatible with international law and EU directives.

[86] Also noting the ambiguity of the decision and the 'rivers of ink' wasted in vain commenting this ruling, see A Bellan, *Linking e comunicazione al pubblico nel sistema della Corte di Giustizia dell'Unione Europea* (2016), Tesi di dottorato—Scuola di Dottorato in Scienze Giuridiche, Dipartimento di Diritto Privato e Storia del Diritto (Università degli Studi di Milano—Facoltà di Giurisprudenza), Curriculum di Diritto Industriale: Ciclo XXVIII, 88–9.

[87] Also outlining the interpretative doubts left by the decisions in *Svensson and Others*, C-466/12, and *BestWater*, C-348/13, see M Leistner, 'Copyright at the interface between EU law and national law: definition of "work" and "right of communication to the public" (2015) 10(8) JIPLP 626, 636.

[88] For a discussion of linking and the right of reproduction, see T Pihlajarinne, 'Should we bury the con-cept of reproduction—towards principle-based assessment in copyright law?' (2017) 48(8) IIC 953, 961–5. As early as 1996 JH Spoor, 'The copyright approach to copying on the internet: (over)stretching the repro-duction right?' in PB Hugenholtz (ed), *The Future of Copyright in a Digital Environment* (Kluwer:1996), 78–9, warned against the risks of an overly broad scope of the right of reproduction online.

have had no public in mind, since they never authorized the making available of their work in the first place. Accordingly, linking to content of this kind should always be regarded as an act of communication to a 'new public'. Yet, when the opportunity arose to address this particular scenario (in *GS Media*, C-160/15), AG Wathelet first and, then, the CJEU took a different direction.[89]

GS Media—This case originated as a reference for a preliminary ruling from the Dutch Supreme Court, which made it in the context of proceedings between the publisher of *Playboy* magazine and GS Media. The case related to the publication by the defendant GS Media on a website that it operated (GeenStijl) of hyperlinks to other websites hosting unpublished photographs of Dutch TV personality Britt Dekker, that had been taken for a forthcoming issue of *Playboy*. In 2011 (prior to the publication of the *Playboy* issue in question) GS Media published a report containing a hyperlink to an Australian data-storage website, where the photographs were freely accessible and available for download.[90] As explained by AG Wathelet, the report carried the title '[obscenity] leaked! Nude photos … Dekker'. The report, which also included part of one of the photographs in the top left-hand corner, ended with the following words: 'And now the link with the pics you've been waiting for. Whoever [obscenity] first, [obscenity] first. HERE …'. By clicking on a hyperlink, indicated by 'HERE', readers would be directed to an Australian data-storage website called Filefactory.com. By clicking on the following hyperlink, they could open a new window that contained the button 'DOWNLOAD NOW'. As shown in Figure 4.2, by clicking on the button, the readers opened a file in zip format containing eleven files in PDF format, each of which contained one of the photographs.[91]

Despite Sanoma's demands, GS Media refused to remove the hyperlink in question. Although the photographs were eventually deleted on the filefactory.com website, they were subsequently made available at another online location. GS Media published two further reports with new hyperlinks to Dekker's photographs.

Sanoma succeeded in its actions before the Amsterdam District Court and the Amsterdam Court of Appeal, although these courts considered different aspects. The former held that, by posting those hyperlinks, GS Media's conduct had been unlawful because it encouraged visitors to GeenStijl to view the photographs unlawfully posted elsewhere and which, without those hyperlinks, would have not been easy to find. In contrast, the appellate court held that, on the one hand, GS Media had infringed copyright by posting a cut-out of one of the photographs on its own website but, on the other hand, had not made the photographs available to the public by posting the hyperlinks on its website.[92]

The decision of the Court of Appeal was appealed before the Supreme Court, which decided to stay the proceedings and refer the case to the CJEU for a preliminary ruling asking whether: the provision on a website of a hyperlink to another website operated by a third party, which is accessible to the general internet public and on which works protected by copyright are made available to the public, without the authorization of the copyright holder constitutes an act of communication to the public; the fact that the person who posts the hyperlink to a website is or ought to be aware of the lack of

---

[89] In their interesting analysis JC Ginsburg and LA Budiardjo, 'Liability for providing hyperlinks to copyright-infringing content: international and comparative law perspectives' (2018) 41 Colum JL & Arts 153, 169–70, submit that post-*Svensson* case law might have reduced the centrality of the 'new public' criterion.

[90] AG Wathelet noted that whether this was the case was not entirely clear: Opinion of Advocate General Melchior Wathelet in *GS Media*, C-160/15, EU:C:2016:221, para 71.

[91] Ibid, para 10.   [92] *GS Media*, C-160/15, EU:C:2016:644, paras 17–18.

77 files · 61 km   206536 leden / 5332 stijllozen   Social:

Fucking uitgelekt! Naaktfotoos Britt Dekker

Ach nee. Hoe KAN dat nou goedverdoemme telkens weer? Het is toch niet te gleuven? Na Amanda Krabbé zijn de kroonjuwelen van het blootblad wederom op straat komen te liggen. Het is één grote lektober daar bij de Playboy. Ook de blootplaatjes van Britt Dekker zijn nu uitgelekt. Amper drie weken na de naaqtshoot op een appeltjesbruin Canarisch Eiland (deze) liggen de fapfotoos van het Pareltje van Purmereutel open en bloot op straat. Je zou toch denken dat ze daar bij de Sanoma enige maatregelen getroffen hebben na het vorige lek. Personeel op straat flikkeren, toegangspasjes doormidden knippen, logins voor het CMS onklaar maken, het fotomateriaal 24/7 laten bewaken door een homofiele Men's Health-lezer (is dat dubbelop? - ff uitzoeken). Maar nee. Niets van dat alles. Het lijkt wel of ze het erom doen? Mensen. Dit is toch geen toeval meer? Ennieweetjes. Vanavond een totaal ontredderde en hoofdschuddende PB-hoofdredacteur Jan Heemskerk - die er ook niks van snapt - in RTL Boulevard en Shownieuws. En dan nu het linkje met pics waar u op zat te wachten. Wie het eerst fapt, die het eerst komt. HIERRR. De bloeddoddige mevrouw Dekker complimenteren met het keurig aangeharkte voortuintje kan daar. Pritt ♥ Britt.
Update. Vooruit dan.

Pritt Stift | 27-10-11 | 07:59 | Link | 156 reacties |

HEADLINES

29-11

Opstelten praat aantoonbaar poep

NOS vervangt wereldberoemd sportmeisje

Figure 4.2 Screenshot of the GeenStijl website linking to leaked images of Britt Dekker for *Playboy* magazine

(source: http://www.ie-forum.nl/artikelen/hyperlinken-naaktfoto-039-s-playboy-onder-omstandigheden-niet-toegestaan-1)

consent by the copyright holder for the initial communication of the works on that website is important for the purpose of Article 3(1) of InfoSoc Directive; the fact that a hyperlink has facilitated access to the works in question is relevant in accordance with Article 3(1).

Criteria to consider to determine liability for linking to unlicensed content—The CJEU held that the provision of a hyperlink (but it would appear that the same reasoning applies to other types of links[93]) to a copyright work that is freely accessible and was initially published without the rightholder's consent on another website does not constitute a communication to the public, as long as the person who posts that link does not seek financial gain and acts without knowledge that such work has been published without a licence from the relevant rightholder.

The CJEU began its analysis with a general discussion of the preventative nature of the right of communication to the public.[94] It mentioned the lack of a definition in the body of the InfoSoc Directive and, hence, the need to refer to the objectives pursued by this piece of EU legislation: high level of protection of authors, but also a fair balance of contrasting rights and interests, as also protected by the EU Charter. Having recalled the requirement under Article 3(1) of the InfoSoc Directive,[95] it noted

[93] According to M Leistner, 'Copyright law on the internet in need of reform: hyperlinks, online platforms and aggregators' (2017) 12(2) JIPLP 136, 138–9, not all links should be treated the same, and the provider of a framed link should be under more than a merely minimal duty to check the lawfulness of the posted material. See also the discussion in J Axhamn, 'Internet linking and the notion of 'new public' (2014) 2014/2 NIR 110, 126–8.

[94] *GS Media*, C-160/15, EU:C:2016:644, para 28.

[95] Ibid, paras 30–32, referring to *Svensson and Others*, C-466/12, EU:C:2014:76, para 16; *SBS Belgium*, C-325/14, EU:C:2015:764, para 15; and *Reha Training)*, C-117/15, EU:C:2016:379, para 37.

how an individual assessment is to be undertaken in specific instances by considering several complementary criteria. These are not autonomous and are interdependent, and may, in different situations, be present to widely varying degrees. They must be applied both individually and in their interaction with one another. One such criterion is the indispensable role played by the user and the deliberate nature of its intervention: the user makes an act of communication when it intervenes, in full knowledge of the consequences of its action, to give access to a protected work to its customers, and does so, in particular, where, in the absence of that intervention, its customers would not, in principle, be able to enjoy the work.[96] Other criteria include: a communication using specific technical means;[97] different from those previously used or, failing that, to a 'new public'; and the profit-making nature of the communication. According to the court it is in the light, in particular, of these criteria that a situation like the one at issue in the background proceedings should be assessed.[98] Reviewing earlier case law, the CJEU noted how from this it could not be inferred that, lacking the relevant rightholder's consent, a link would invariably amount to an unauthorized act of communication to the public.[99]

Importance of the internet—In light of this conclusion, the court made two observations. First, the internet is of particular importance to freedom of expression and of information, and hyperlinks contribute to its sound operation as well as to the exchange of opinions and information in a network characterized by the very availability of immense amounts of information. Second, it may be difficult, in particular for individuals who wish to post such links, to ascertain whether the website to which those links are expected to lead provides access to works which are protected and, if necessary, whether the copyright holders of those works have consented to their posting on the internet. Checking is all the more difficult where those rights have been subject to sub-licences. Moreover, the content of a website to which a hyperlink enables access may be changed after the creation of that link, including the protected works, without the person who created that link necessarily being aware of it.

Intervention in full knowledge of the consequences—Thus, in order to determine whether the provision of a hyperlink to unlicensed content amounts to an act of communication to the public, the CJEU considered the complementary criteria mentioned earlier in the chapter, notably the profit-making intention and the subjective state of mind of the 'hyperlinker'. According to the court, when the provision of a hyperlink to a work freely available on another website is carried out by a person who, in so doing, does not pursue a profit, it is necessary to consider that such person is unaware that the work had been published on the internet without the consent of the relevant rightholder. In other words, in such circumstances, the link provider does not intervene in full knowledge of the consequences of their conduct.

Conversely, the provision of a hyperlink to protected content would amount to an act of communication to the public in the following situations. First, when the 'hyperlinker' knows or ought to have known that the hyperlink posted would provide access to a work unlawfully placed on the internet, for example owing to the fact that they were notified to this effect by the relevant rightholder. Second, when the

---

[96] *GS Media*, paras 33–35, also referring (para 34) to *SCF*, C-135/10, EU:C:2012:140, para 79; *Phonographic Performance (Ireland)*, C-162/10, EU:C:2012:141, para 30; and *Reha Training*, C-117/15, EU:C:2016:379, para 35.

[97] As noted by Leistner, 'Copyright at the interface between EU law and national law' 634, the definition of the same technical means has been rather generous in CJEU case law: for instance, on the internet all potential and different forms of communication constitute the same technical means.

[98] *GS Media*, C-160/15, EU:C:2016:644, paras 36–39.   [99] Ibid, para 43.

hyperlink at issue allows users of the website on which they are posted to circumvent the restrictions taken by the site where the protected work is posted in order to restrict the public's access to their own subscribers.[100] While the latter scenario also leads to a finding of copyright infringement, the same might not be true in relation to the former. In fact, as the CJEU explained at paragraph 53, liability of the 'hyperlinker' would follow not only from knowledge that the content linked to is unlicensed, but also from the impossibility of successfully invoking a defence allowed by Article 5(3) of the InfoSoc Directive and available under the applicable national copyright regime.[101]

Rebuttable presumption of knowledge for for-profit link providers—The Court also added a *presumptio iuris tantum* (ie rebuttable):

when the posting of hyperlinks is carried out for profit, it can be expected that the person who posted such a link carries out the necessary checks to ensure that the work concerned is not illegally published on the website to which those hyperlinks lead, so that it must be presumed that that posting has occurred with the full knowledge of the protected nature of that work and the possible lack of consent to publication on the internet by the copyright holder.[102]

In the case at hand, the defendant provided the hyperlinks for profit, yet knowing that the photos had been published without the copyright holders' permission. The Court found that a situation of this kind would clearly be one of prima facie copyright infringement,[103] although it failed to clarify whether the profit-making intention should relate to the provision of the link per se or, rather, the overall context in which the link is provided. Should one consider whether the relevant link is provided with the intention to make a profit? Or should one rather consider the surrounding environment to the relevant link, for example, whether it is provided on a website that is operated for profit? Although both alternatives are plausible, consideration of the context in which the relevant link is provided is more in line with earlier CJEU case law.

In both *SGAE*, C-306/05, and *Football Association Premier League and Others*, C-403/08 and C-429/08, the CJEU considered that the profit-making nature of the communication was apparent from the fact that the defendants transmitted the relevant works in their own establishment (hotels and a public house, respectively) in order to benefit therefrom and to attract customers to whom the works transmitted are of interest.[104] Yet, the fact that the link at issue appears on a commercial website might result in the profit-making intention being present in the majority of cases and, with it, the presumption of knowledge (see further Section 2.4.1).

Linking in a table—Following the CJEU decision in *GS Media*, C-160/15, the legal treatment of linking under Article 3(1) of the InfoSoc Directive is summarized in Table 4.1.[105]

2.3 Communication to the public and platform liability

Liability of platform operators—In its 2017 judgment in *Stichting Brein*, C-610/15, the CJEU further developed its construction of the right of communication to the

---

[100] Ibid, paras 46–50.   [101] Ibid, para 53.   [102] Ibid, para 51.
[103] Ibid, para 54.
[104] See *SGAE*, C-306/05, EU:C:2006:764, para 44, and *Football Association Premier League and Others*, C-403/08 and C-429/08, EU:C:2011:631, paras 205–206.
[105] This table was first published in E Rosati, 'Linking after *GS Media* ... in a table' (10 September 2016), The IPKat, available at <http://ipkitten.blogspot.com/2016/09/linking-after-gs-media-in-table.html> (last accessed 15 August 2018).

Table 4.1 Linking after *GS Media*

Accessibility of content	Content published with rightholder's consent	Profit-making intention	Knowledge that content linked to is unlawful	Act of communication to the public	Potential infringement
Freely accessible	Yes	n/a	n/a	No (*Svensson*, *GS Media*)	No
Not freely accessible	Yes	n/a	n/a	Yes (*BestWater*, *GS Media*)	Yes
Freely accessible	No	No	No	No (*GS Media*)	No
Freely accessible	No	No	Yes (eg because notified)	Yes (*GS Media*)	Yes*
Freely accessible	No	Yes	Presumed (rebuttable presumption)	Yes (*GS Media*)	Yes*
Not freely accessible	No	n/a	n/a	Yes	Yes

*If rightholder notifies link provider (without prior knowledge of unlawfulness) that content linked to is unlawful and he refuses to remove the link, and exceptions and limitations in Article 5(3) of the InfoSoc Directive are inapplicable.

public within Article 3(1) of the InfoSoc Directive, and clarified under what conditions the operators of an unlicensed online platform are potentially liable for copyright infringement. The operators of a platform that makes available to the public third-party uploaded copyright content and provides functions such as indexing, categorization, deletion, and filtering of content may be liable for copyright infringement, jointly with the users. For a finding of liability it is not required that the operators possess actual knowledge of the infringing character of the content uploaded by users.

The Pirate Bay—This reference for a preliminary ruling from the Dutch Supreme Court arose in the context of litigation between Dutch anti-piracy foundation BREIN and two internet access providers regarding the application, by the former, for an order that would require the latter to block access for their customers to the website of The Pirate Bay. An engine for peer-to-peer (P2P) file-sharing, The Pirate Bay does not host any protected works. However, it operates a system by means of which metadata on protected works which is present on the users' computers is indexed and categorized for users, so that the users can trace, upload, and download the protected works on the basis thereof. It is estimated that the near totality (90–95 per cent) of the files shared on the network of The Pirate Bay contain copyright works distributed unlawfully.[106] Despite several attempts to prevent access to The Pirate Bay, including blocking injunctions against ISPs in several jurisdictions, the platform—also by using different domain names— remains easily accessible.

The Dutch Supreme Court sought guidance from the CJEU on whether the operators of a website like The Pirate Bay are to be regarded as making acts of communication

---

[106] Opinion of Advocate General Maciej Szpunar in *Stichting Brein*, C-610/15, EU:C:2017:99, para 23.

to the public within the meaning of Article 3(1) of the InfoSoc Directive. To answer this question the CJEU noted that the right of communication to the public, on the one hand, has a preventive character and must be interpreted broadly and, on the other hand, requires an individual assessment that depends on the circumstances at issue.[107]

The CJEU judgment—The Court agreed with AG Szpunar that in the case at hand there would be no dispute that acts of communication to the public are being made,[108] and are directed to a 'public' (a 'new public').[109] The point was however to determine whether the platform operators could be responsible for them.

Who makes the act of communication?—Considering the first requirement in Article 3(1), ie the need for an 'act of communication', the Court acknowledged that the works made available to the users of The Pirate Bay are placed online on that platform not by the platform operators but by users. However, by making that platform available and managing the platform, its operators provide users with access to the works concerned. They can therefore be regarded as playing an essential role in making the works in question available. As regards the requirement of full knowledge of the relevant facts, this is satisfied by consideration of how the Pirate Bay operators index torrent files so as to allow users of the platform to locate those works and share them within the context of a P2P network. Without such intervention, it would not be possible, or it would be more difficult, for users to share the works.

The Court also dismissed the argument that the Pirate Bay operators could be regarded as providing mere physical facilities for enabling or making a communication, thus falling outside the scope of Article 3(1). The undertaking by the Pirate Bay operators of indexing, categorization, deletion, or filtering activities rules out any assimilation to the mere provision of facilities within the meaning of Recital 27. The making available and management of an online sharing platform must therefore be considered an act of communication for the purposes of Article 3(1).[110]

'New public'—Turning to the requirement that the communication at hand must be directed to a 'new public', ie a public not taken into account by the copyright holders when they authorized the initial communication, the CJEU concluded that this requirement is also met. The Court referred to the fact that the Pirate Bay operators were informed that their platform provides access to works published without authorization of the relevant rightholders.[111]

Type of knowledge required—However, the CJEU did not limit liability to situations of actual knowledge (as the AG had done): it also included constructive knowledge ('could not be unaware') and arguably more. In relation to constructive knowledge, the Court observed how the Pirate Bay operators

could not be unaware that this platform provides access to works published without the consent of the rightholders, given that, as expressly highlighted by the referring court, a very large number of torrent files on the online sharing platform [The Pirate Bay] relate to works published without the consent of the rightholders. In those circumstances, it must be held that there is communication to a 'new public'.[112]

Liability based on 'constructive' knowledge echoes—though the Court did not mention it—the reasoning in the decision in *L'Oréal and Others*, C-324/09, notably the part in which the CJEU suggested that the safe harbour within Article 14 of the E-commerce Directive would not apply to an information society service which is

---

[107] *Stichting Brein*, C-610/15, EU:C:2017:456, para 22.
[108] Ibid, para 35.   [109] Ibid, paras 40–44.
[110] Ibid, paras 36–39.   [111] Ibid, para 45.   [112] Ibid (emphasis added).

aware of facts or circumstances on the basis of which a diligent economic operator should have identified the illegality in question and acted in accordance with Article 14(1)(b) of the E-commerce Directive.[113]

Actual, constructive and ... presumed knowledge—The Court could have limited liability to situations of actual or constructive knowledge (as per the 'diligent economic operator' criterion). However, if this were the case, it would be difficult to understand the meaning of paragraphs 46 and 47 of the judgment, in which the CJEU referred to the profit-making intention of the defendants and seemingly linked that to a finding of prima facie liability:

[46] Furthermore, there can be no dispute that the making available and management of an on-line sharing platform, such as that at issue in the main proceedings, is carried out with the purpose of obtaining profit therefrom, it being clear from the observations submitted to the Court that that platform generates considerable advertising revenues.

[47] Therefore, it must be held that the making available and management of an online sharing platform, such as that at issue in the main proceedings, constitutes a 'communication to the public', within the meaning of Article 3(1) of Directive 2001/29.

Although it did not refer explicitly to it, the Court had *GS Media*, C-160/15, in mind (the Judge-Rapporteur was the same in both cases: Marko Ilešič), when it linked together the making available and management of an online sharing platform, the profit-making intention of their operators, and prima facie liability under Article 3(1). In particular, the relevant part of that judgment is paragraphs 47 to 54.

As in that case, in *Stichting Brein*, C-601/15, the CJEU implied that the operator of an online platform that does so 'with the purpose of obtaining profit therefrom' (paragraph 46 of *Stichting Brein*, C-610/15) can be expected to have undertaken all the necessary checks to ensure that the work concerned is not illegally published on the website to which those hyperlinks lead, so that it must be presumed that that posting has occurred with the full knowledge of the protected nature of that work and the possible lack of consent to publication on the internet by the copyright holder. In such circumstances, so far as that rebuttable presumption is not rebutted, the act of posting a hyperlink to a work which was illegally placed on the internet constitutes a 'communication to the public' within the meaning of Article 3(1) of the InfoSoc Directive (paragraph 51 of *GS Media*, C-160/15).

This interpretation finds support in two additional considerations. The first one is that the reasoning of the Court follows extensively *Stichting Brein*, C-527/15 (here too the Judge-Rapporteur was Ilešič). In particular, the Court referred with approval to paragraph 50 of that judgment, in which the CJEU had concluded that both the indispensable intervention of the defendant/user and its profit-making intention would lead to a finding of liability under Article 3(1) of the InfoSoc Directive. As already mentioned, in *Stichting Brein*, C-527/15, the CJEU confirmed the validity and application of the *GS Media* presumption of knowledge. The second consideration is that 'knowledge' must not be intended in a subjective sense, ie as actual awareness of third-party infringements by the platform operators, but rather—in line with earlier CJEU case law—as knowledge and acceptance of the possible consequences of one's own conduct.

Hence, it is not convincing to suggest that *Stichting Brein*, C-610/15, is silent regarding the treatment of situations in which the operators of an online platform that makes available third-party uploaded content have no actual knowledge of the

---

[113] *L'Oréal SA and Others*, C-324/09, EU:C:2011:474, para 120. See further, Rosati, 'The CJEU *Pirate Bay* judgment' 743–4. For a discussion of the nature of 'limitation' or 'exemption' of the safe harbour within Article 14 of the E-commerce Directive, see further E Rosati, 'Why a reform of hosting providers' safe harbour is unnecessary under EU copyright law' (2016) 38(11) EIPR 668, 671–2.

unlawful character of the content thus made available, but nonetheless pursue a profit. On the contrary, this decision follows the same reasoning as the earlier CJEU decisions in *GS Media*, C-160/15, and *Stichting Brein*, C-527/15: a profit-making intention on the side of the defendant may be sufficient to trigger a rebuttable presumption of knowledge, by the defendant, of the character—licensed or not—of the content communicated through its platform.[114]

2.4 National applications of CJEU case law

Through its case law the CJEU has developed its own construction of the right of communication to the public. While the Court's interpretative stance has been expansive, this has not been devoid of criticism or such that no uncertainties would arise. The cases of linking and platform liability are telling in this sense.

2.4.1 *Linking after* GS Media *before national courts*

Difficulties and resistance—With regard to linking, national applications demonstrate diverging approaches to the interpretation of relevant CJEU case law or resistance *tout court*. This has been particularly the case of the presumption of knowledge for for-profit link providers, as envisaged in *GS Media*, C-160/15: should the profit-making intention be referred to the act of linking as such (as the Athens Court of Appeal held in 2017[115]) or, rather, the context in which the link is provided?

Sweden—The first national court to apply this CJEU decision was the Attunda District Court (Sweden) in 2016.[116] In 2012 the claimant created a video that was subsequently uploaded by a third party on YouTube without her authorization. The defendant embedded the video on its own website in the context of an article describing the content of the incident portrayed in the video. In her action the claimant submitted that the defendant had infringed copyright in her video by both embedding it and publishing a frozen still of the video on its website. Considering whether the provision of an embedded link to content whose publication on a third-party site has not been authorized would amount to a copyright infringement, the Attunda court found that the *GS Media* presumption relates to the context in which the link is provided. In the case at issue it was apparent that the defendant's press publication had published the link to the claimant's YouTube video with the intention of pursuing a profit. According to the court, the defendant had not been able to demonstrate that it had no knowledge of the unlicensed character of the video embedded on its website. Hence, it was found to have infringed the claimant's copyright by linking to the YouTube video without the claimant's permission.

Germany—Following Sweden, still in 2016, it was the turn of the Regional Court of Hamburg (Germany) to provide a first application (by means of an interim decision[117]) of *GS Media*, C-160/15. In that case the German court reasoned along lines

---

[114] See, *contra*, C Angelopoulos, 'Communication to the public and accessory copyright infringement' (2017) 76(3) CLJ 496, 498.

[115] Court of Appeal of Athens, Decision No 1909/2017 (18th section), on which see T Chiou, 'Athens Court of Appeal applies CJEU *GS Media* linking decision and interprets 'profit-making intention' restrictively' (20 November 2017), The IPKat, available at <http://ipkitten.blogspot.com/2017/11/athens-court-of-appeal-applies-cjeu-gs.html> (last accessed 15 August 2018).

[116] Attunda Tingsrätt, *Jonsson v Les Éditions de l'Avenir SA*, FT 11052-15, 13 October 2016, on which see N Malovic and P Haddad, 'Swedish court finds that an embedded link to unlicensed content infringes copyright' (2017) 12(2) JIPLP 89.

[117] LG Hamburg, 310 O 402/16, on which see M Brüß, 'CJEU *GS Media* decision finds its first application in Germany' (9 December 2016), The 1709 Blog, available at <http://the1709blog.

similar to the Attunda court in Sweden, holding that the presumption of knowledge refers to for-profit contexts, rather than individual links provided with a profit-making intention.

Despite a similar approach being followed in the Czech Republic,[118] subsequent decisions in Germany have however taken a rather different direction. So, in its 2017 decision concerning copyright content displayed on Google Images by means of thumbnails,[119] Germany's Federal Court of Justice dismissed the action that the operator of a photography website had brought against Google and its search engine. The former operated a website that included a restricted (password-protected) area to which customers could only have access upon payment of a fee. Some of the photographs hosted in the restricted area were re-uploaded unlawfully by customers onto freely accessible websites. Relevant thumbnails were subsequently indexed on Google Images from such freely accessible sites. According to the claimant, by indexing and displaying thumbnails of the photographs to which it owns the copyright, Google had infringed its own exclusive right of communication to the public pursuant to the right of communication to the public within §15(2) UrhG.

GS Media **presumption inapplicable to search engines**—The Federal Court of Justice held that Google had not infringed the claimant's copyrights by displaying thumbnails of and links to photographs publicly available on the internet without the rightholder's consent. To reach this conclusion the court considered that in *GS Media*, C-160/15, the CJEU had stressed the importance of the internet to freedom of expression and of information: hyperlinks contribute to its sound operation as well as to the exchange of opinions and information in that network characterized by the availability of immense amounts of information. Although *GS Media*, C-160/15, envisages a presumption of knowledge for for-profit link providers, such a presumption would not apply to search engines and for links displayed by search engines, because of the particular importance of these subjects to the functioning of the internet. Accordingly, the provider of a search function cannot be expected to check the lawfulness of the images automatically retrieved from publicly accessible websites. An approach critical of CJEU linking case law may also be discerned in two further cases decided by German courts.

Framing not an act of communication to the public—In a case concerning liability of the operator of a product search engine, the Regional Court of Hamburg ruled that holding that the simple linking of a work hosted on a third-party site by way of 'framing' does not constitute an act of communication to the public.[120] The decision originated in the context of proceedings brought against the operator of a product search engine which listed furniture and home accessories for sale by the operator of a website on which it offered photos and products displayed by photographs (to which it owned the rights) depicting a pug dog named Loulou (see Figures 4.3 and 4.4). The claimant discovered that the defendant's website also displayed among the various results a listing for a cushion (available for sale on Amazon) that reproduced—without his permission—one of the photographs. He submitted that, by displaying this result, the defendant had made unauthorized acts of making available and communication to the public.

---

blogspot.com/2016/12/cjeu-gs-media-decision-finds-its-first.html> (last accessed 15 August 2018), and S Abrar, '*GS Media* finds its first application in Germany' (12 December 2016), The IPKat, available at <http://ipkitten.blogspot.com/2016/12/gs-media-finds-its-first-application-in.html> (last accessed 15 August 2018).

[118] District Court for Prague 4, 33 T 54/2016, on which see J Vivoda, 'After Sweden and Germany, *GS Media* finds its application in the Czech Republic' (6 February 2017), The IPKat, available at <http://ipkitten.blogspot.com/2017/02/after-sweden-and-germany-gs-media-finds.html> (last accessed 15 August 2018).

[119] Bundesgerichtshof, I ZR 11/16—*Preview III.*   [120] LG Hamburg, 308 O 151/17.

Figure 4.3 *Loulou* case 1/1: The claimant's work (source: LG Hamburg, 308 O 151/17)

Figure 4.4 *Loulou* case 1/2: The product listing linked to by the defendant (source: LG Hamburg, 308 O 151/17)

The Hamburg court dismissed the action, holding that the simple linking of a work hosted on a third-party site by way of 'framing' does not constitute an act of making available to the public within §19a UrhG. The only provision that might come into consideration would thus be the 'unnamed' right of communication to the public within §15(2) UrhG. To determine whether that would actually be the case, the court deemed it necessary to review relevant CJEU case law on Article 3(1) of the InfoSoc Directive. The court excluded that there would be a communication to the public in the case at issue. Although the requirement of the 'new public' was met, the relevant act would not take place with the indispensable intervention of the defendant. According to the court, the defendant in this case—although operating for a profit— had neither positive knowledge of the unlawfulness of the offer displayed through its search engine, nor could it have acquired knowledge of the offer's unlawfulness in a reasonable way.

Automated linking—The links displayed were created through a completely automated process and the relevant offers were not subject to any editing or other manual control. Hence, it could not be assumed that the defendant had knowledge that the offer at issue incorporated content that would infringe the claimant's rights. In addition, upon becoming aware of the unlawfulness of the listing, the defendant promptly removed it. Considering that the defendant's databank contains 50 million offers, it would be unreasonable to expect that every single link be checked beforehand. In the event of (several) completely automated processes, the *GS Media* presumption could not apply in relation to each and every link. Referring to the Opinion of AG Szpunar in *Stichting Brein*, C-610/15, the court concluded that holding otherwise would extend liability to every imaginable far-removed contribution due to negligible lack of knowledge and, therefore, on the basis of merely fictitious intention. This would be also contrary to Article 16 of the EU Charter.

Lack of knowledge excludes liability—The Regional Court of Hamburg also decided another case in 2017 in which issues of linking and copyright protection were at issue.[121] It held that there is no act of communication to the public within §§15(2) UrhG and 19a UrhG if a person who links to protected content without the relevant rightholder's permission is unaware that such content is unlawful. Even if the link provider has a profit-making intention, there should be no presumption that they had awareness that the content linked to was unlawful if they operate in a context in which it would be unreasonable to expect that checks be performed to ensure that the content linked to is (and remains) lawful. In the case at issue, the defendant's linking activities were performed algorithmically and, similarly to the other decision, also in this instance the infringing content (again a product carrying an unlicensed reproduction of an image of pug dog Loulou) linked to was available on Amazon.de (see Figures 4.5 and 4.6). The defendant had no actual awareness that the content linked to was unlawful, nor was its unlawful nature recognizable at the outset. A relevant aspect was also the fact that, to be able to offer products for sale on Amazon, merchants have to agree to the platform's terms of use, including declaring that they own the copyright to the images displayed.

---

[121] LG Hamburg, 310 O 117/17.

Figure 4.5 *Loulou* case 2/1: The claimant's work (source: LG Hamburg, 310 O 117/17)

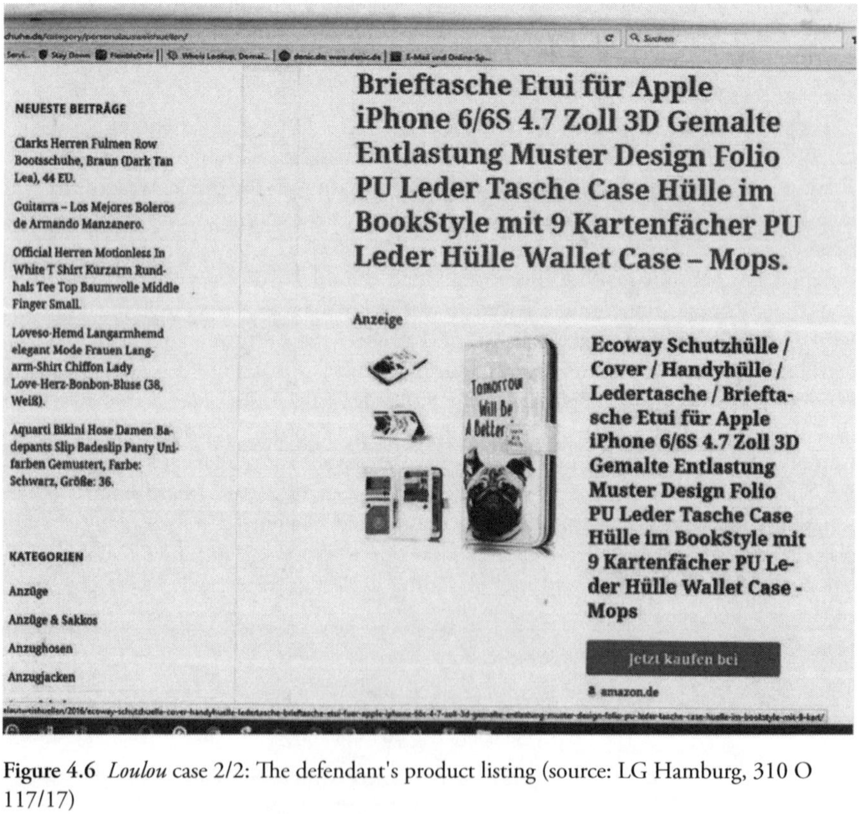

Figure 4.6 *Loulou* case 2/2: The defendant's product listing (source: LG Hamburg, 310 O 117/17)

GS Media presumption not generally applicable—In its decision the Hamburg court held that the *GS Media* presumption of knowledge cannot be considered as indistinctly applicable: instead, it should only be relevant in situations in which the link provider/defendant may be *expected* to carry out the necessary checks to determine the status—lawful or unlawful—of the content linked to. The court acknowledged that *GS Media*, C-160/15, mandates a generally applicable presumption for links posted out of profit. However, a conclusion of this kind would contradict what is stated at paragraph 34 of *GS Media*, C-160/15, itself, ie that the assessment of whether a link provider can be liable under Article 3(1) of the InfoSoc Directive must be individualized and take account of several complementary criteria that may, in different situations, be present to widely varying degrees. In a case like the one at issue, it would therefore be 'unreasonable' and 'economically unjustifiable' to expect that the defendant carry out such checks in relation to each and every element of content (automatically) linked to, including content hosted on a platform like Amazon. The defendant's business model—including the fact that the content is not 'incorporated' to look like the defendant's own content—is such that no specific searches for unlawfulness can be expected. Holding otherwise would not only be unreasonable, but also amount to an undue compression of the fundamental freedom to conduct a business under Article 16 of the EU Charter.

Clarity still needed—In the aftermath of the CJEU decision in *GS Media*, C-160/15, on the one hand, courts have adopted different approaches to the presumption of knowledge envisaged by the CJEU in its ruling and, on the other hand, the scope of application of CJEU case law has not been considered devoid of difficulties. This has been particularly the case of German courts: the decisions discussed earlier show how courts in that EU Member State, instead of holding the presumption rebutted in the specific instance considered (as is required under *GS Media*, C-160/15), held against its applicability *tout court,* on grounds of reasonableness and by placing significant emphasis on the fundamental rights dimension. Fears that the relationship between copyright protection and freedom to conduct a business might be unbalanced in favour of the former were acutely felt. This—together with considerations relating to the proper construction of the right of communication to the public, including the requirement of an individualized assessment—prompted the courts to depart from what a strict application of *GS Media*, C-160/15, would instead require.

2.4.2 *Platform liability after* Stichting Brein *before national courts*

Applicability of *Stichting Brein* to less egregious scenarios—With regard to platform liability, it is uncertain to what extent the conclusion achieved in *Stichting Brein*, C-610/15, may be applied to less egregious scenarios than The Pirate Bay. According to the CJEU, an 'intervention' for the purpose of determining what amounts to an act of communication merely requires, in fact, the doing of acts of indexing, categorization, deletion, or filtering of content. In addition, it is irrelevant whether such activities are carried out manually or automatically, for example, algorithmically: it is sufficient that a system is put in place to perform such activities. How many platforms would be caught within such a broad understanding of intervention as *incontournable*?

Austrian and German applications—National case law has begun emerging, although the issue remains controversial. This is also due to the fact that it is uncertain whether the safe harbour for hosting providers within Article 14 of the E-commerce Directive would be available (see further in what follows).[122]

A court in Austria (in the context of interim proceedings) recently ruled that YouTube makes acts of communication to the public and may be therefore liable, on a primary basis, for the making available of infringing user-uploaded content (UUC).[123] While recently the Regional Court of Hamburg ruled that the Usenet provider UseneXT would be liable if it promoted third-party unauthorized making available and sharing of protected content,[124] Germany's Federal Court of Justice in Germany is also expected to rule on whether YouTube might be regarded as primarily responsible (and liable) for acts of communication to the public.[125] The claimant in the latter case is a music producer who sued Google/YouTube over the unauthorized making available, on the defendants' platform, of videos containing musical works from the repertoire of a soprano. The claimant signed an exclusive contract with this singer in 2006, allowing him to exploit recordings of her performances. In 2008 unauthorized videos featuring such performances were made available on YouTube. Following a takedown request, these videos were removed from YouTube, but infringing material was made available once again shortly afterwards. In 2010 the first instance court sided with the claimant in respect of three songs, and dismissed the action for the remaining claims.[126] Both the producer and Google/YouTube appealed the decision and in 2015 the appellate court only partly sided with the producer. Most importantly, it rejected the idea that YouTube could be regarded as primarily liable for the making available of infringing content, although it found that liability would subsist under the 'Störerhaftung' doctrine (a form of accessory liability) under §97(1) UrhG.[127]

Primary and accessory liability—The decision in *Stichting Brein*, C-610/15, has also affected primary and accessory liability, by embracing an autonomous (EU) concept of liability through a process that, according to some commentators, was initiated as early as in *Svensson and Others*, C-466/12.[128] While the EU legislature has harmonized the conditions for primary liability, the existence of and conditions for a finding of liability as an accessory infringer have been left to the legal systems of individual Member States.[129] By introducing a knowledge requirement within the scope of

---

[122] For a discussion of selected national experiences (in the EU: France, Germany, the Netherlands, Poland, Spain, Sweden, and UK), see further the questionnaires in JP Quintais, *Global Online Piracy Study—Legal Background Report* (July 2018), available at <https://www.ivir.nl/publicaties/download/Global-Online-Piracy-Study-Legal-Background-Report.pdf> (last accessed 15 August 2018).

[123] Handelsgericht Wien, 11 Cg 65/14t – 56.　　[124] LG Hamburg, 308 O 314/16.

[125] Bundesgerichtshof, I ZR 140/15—*Haftung von YouTube für Urheberrechtsverletzungen*. [Update: in September 2018, the court decided to refer the case to the CJEU for guidance on whether a platform like YouTube could be deemed to be making acts of communication to the public: see <http://ipkitten.blogspot.com/2018/09/breaking-fcj-refers-case-regarding.html> (last accessed 28 October 2018); at the time of writing, the reference is still awaiting assignment of a case number.]

[126] LG Hamburg, 308 O 27/09.　　[127] OLG Hamburg, 5 U 175/10.

[128] A Ohly, 'The broad concept of "communication to the public" in recent CJEU judgments and the liability of intermediaries: primary, secondary or unitary liability?' (2018) 13(8) JIPLP 664, 670–1. In the same sense, see, also with regard to the impact on German law, JB Nordemann, 'Recent CJEU case law on communication to the public and its application in Germany: a new EU concept of liability' (2018) 13(9) JIPLP 744, 745; and, also with regard to UK law, N Cordell and B Potts, 'Communication to the public or accessory liability? Is the CJEU using communication to the public to harmonise accessory liability across the EU?' (2018) 40(5) EIPR 289, 293.

[129] GF Frosio, 'From horizontal to vertical: an intermediary liability earthquake in Europe' (2017) 12(7) JIPLP 565, 570, recalls that in the majority of EU Member States, accessory liability is subject to highly demanding conditions that are derived from miscellaneous doctrines of tort law, such as the doctrines of joint tortfeasance, authorization, inducement, common design, contributory liability, vicarious liability, or extra-contractual liability. See also M Leistner, 'Structural aspects of secondary

primary liability, the CJEU has blurred the distinction between what has been trad-itionally regarded as a strict liability tort (primary infringement) and liability informed by the defendant's subjective state of actual or constructive knowledge (accessory in-fringement).[130] All this is likely to result in practical uncertainties for those national jurisdictions with an accessory liability regime, notably liability by authorization.[131]

Availability of safe harbours—The decision in *Stichting Brein*, C-610/15, also raises the question whether a platform that is primarily liable for unauthorized acts of commu-nication to the public can nonetheless invoke the safe harbour regime available to hosting providers under Article 14 of the E-commerce Directive. With regard to the relation-ship between liability under the InfoSoc Directive and applicability of the E-commerce Directive safe harbours, while the former is without prejudice to the provisions of the latter (Recitals 16 and 20 of the InfoSoc Directive), confirmation that the operators of an online platform may be jointly liable with users for copyright infringement might indeed have an impact on the applicability of Articles 12 to 14 of the E-commerce Directive.

By proposing the adoption of the E-commerce Directive, the European Commission sought to clarify the responsibility of providers for transmitting and storing infor-mation at the request of third parties, that is when providers act as mere intermedi-aries. Although outside the scope of the present contribution, a similar trend towards a greater responsibilization of providers may also be found in recent decisions of the European Court of Human Rights (ECtHR), for example, *Delfi v Estonia*[132] and *Magyar Tartalomszolgáltatók v Hungary*,[133] which suggest that in certain situations the sole availability of a notice-and-takedown system might be insufficient.

The insulation[134] provided by the safe harbour regime does not apply to providers that go beyond a passive role of intermediary. This means that a provider that was found liable for the doing of unauthorized acts of communication to the public would also likely be regarded as playing an 'active role' (in the sense clarified by the CJEU in *L'Oréal and Others*, C-324/09) and would be, as such, ineligible for the protection offered under Article 14 of the E-commerce Directive.[135] This conclusion, which re-mains controversial,[136] is supported by both textual references to the wording of the

---

(provider) liability in Europe' (2014) 9(1) JIPLP 75, 87–90, addressing the question whether common principles of accessory liability may be discerned.

[130] C Angelopoulos, 'CJEU decision on *Ziggo*: The Pirate Bay communicates works to the public' (30 June 2017), Kluwer Copyright Blog, available at <http://copyrightblog.kluweriplaw.com/2017/06/30/cjeu-decision-ziggo-pirate-bay-communicates-works-public/> (last accessed 15 August 2018).

[131] See GB Dinwoodie, 'A comparative analysis of the secondary liability of online service providers' in GB Dinwoodie (ed), *Secondary Liability of Internet Service Providers* (Springer:2017), 8, noting that the concept of 'authorization' in this context is such as to establish 'an act of *nominally* primary liability that clearly maps in substance to conventional forms of secondary or joint tortfeasor liability'.

[132] *Delfi AS v Estonia*, Application No 64569/09, 16 June 2015.

[133] *Magyar Tartalomszolgáltatók Egyesülete and Index.hu Zrt v Hungary*, Application No 22947/13, 2 February 2016.

[134] J Riordan, *The Liability of Internet Intermediaries* (OUP:2016), §12.11.

[135] In the same sense, see also JB Nordemann, *Liability of Online Service Providers for Copyrighted Content—Regulatory Action Needed?* (2018) Directorate General for Internal Policies—Policy Department A: Economic and Scientific Policy, IP/A/IMCO/2017-08 - PE 614.207, 23.

[136] Arguing that the safe harbour protection would be available in cases of primary and ac-cessory infringements alike, see M Husovec, *Injunctions against Intermediaries in the European Union: Accountable but not Liable?* (CUP:2017), 56, also referring for support to *Papasavvas*, C-291/13, EU:C:2014:2209, and *L'Oréal and Others*, C-324/09, EU:C:2011:474; C Angelopoulos, *European Intermediary Liability in Copyright: A Tort-based Analysis* (Wolters Kluwer:2017), 68; and Riordan, *The Liability of Internet Intermediaries* §12.11, §§12.01, and 12.37.

E-commerce Directive and CJEU case law.[137] In *Google France and Google*, C-236/08 to C-238/08, the CJEU held that the exemptions from liability established in the E-commerce Directive cover only cases in which the activity of the information society service provider is 'of a mere technical, automatic and passive nature', which implies that that service provider 'has neither knowledge of nor control over the information which is transmitted or stored'.[138]

Further clarity on this point is required. A possible solution may be however to interpret the presumption imposed by the CJEU in *GS Media*, C-160/15, as part of a broader obligation to conform to the behaviour of a 'diligent economic operator'. In this sense, operators of platforms with a profit-making intention would have an *ex ante* reasonable duty of care and be subject to an *ex post* notice-and-takedown system,[139] which would also include an obligation to prevent infringements of the same kind, for example, by means of re-uploads of the same content. Albeit in the different context of intermediary injunctions, the CJEU has already clarified that requiring a provider to take measures which contribute, not just to bringing to an end existing infringements, but also preventing further infringements of that kind are compatible with Article 15(1) of the E-commerce Directive as long as the relevant order is effective, proportionate, dissuasive, and does not create barriers to legitimate trade.[140]

3. The Right of Distribution and Its Exhaustion

Content of the right—Also with regard to the construction of the right of distribution within Article 4 of the InfoSoc Directive, the CJEU has adopted an expansive interpretation of the scope of protection. The first paragraph of that provision states that:

Member States shall provide for authors, in respect of the original of their works or of copies thereof, the exclusive right to authorise or prohibit any form of distribution to the public by sale or otherwise.

Unlike the right of communication to the public, the right of distribution is subject to exhaustion following the first lawful sale or other transfer of ownership of the original or copies of the work. Article 4(2) provides in fact that:

[t]he distribution right shall not be exhausted within the Community in respect of the original or copies of the work, except where the first sale or other transfer of ownership in the Community of that object is made by the rightholder or with his consent.

With particular regard to exhaustion, the question that has arisen is whether this principle applies indistinctly to tangible and intangible (digital) copies of a work. So far, the CJEU has not provided a specific response with regard to the InfoSoc Directive, but has answered this question in the affirmative in *UsedSoft*, C-128/11, in relation to the Software Directive. The reasoning in that ruling is yet another instance of CJEU activism, which—as will be discussed further in Section 3.3—appears justified by internal market concerns, rather than a rigorous interpretation of legislative provisions.

---

[137] *L'Oréal and Others*, C-324/09, EU:C:2011:474, para 113, referring to *Google France and Google*, C-236/08 to C-238/08, EU:C:2010:159, paras 114 and 120.
[138] *Google France and Google*, C-236/08 to C-238/08, EU:C:2010:159, para 113.
[139] In this sense, M Leistner, 'Closing the book on the hyperlinks: brief outline of the CJEU's case law and proposal for European legislative reform' (2017) 39(6) EIPR 327, 331.
[140] *L'Oréal and Others*, C-324/09, EU:C:2011:474, paras 139 and 144.

3.1 The scope of the right of distribution

Concept of distribution—The Court has had the opportunity to tackle the scope of the right under Article 4 of the InfoSoc Directive in a number of rulings.[141] Similarly to concepts relevant to other economic rights, the InfoSoc Directive does not define 'distribution'. However, as the Court explained in *Peek & Cloppenburg*, C-456/06, reference should be made to the WIPO Internet Treaties. It follows from Article 6(1) of the WIPO Copyright Treaty and Articles 8 and 12 of the WIPO Performances and Phonograms Treaty that the right of distribution relates to the exclusive right of authorizing the making available to the public of the original and copies of a work through sale or 'other transfer of ownership'. Hence, the right under Article 4(1) of the InfoSoc Directive should be intended as encompassing forms of distribution which entail a transfer of ownership.[142] Furthermore, as the InfoSoc Directive does not make any reference to the laws of EU Member States, 'distribution' must be intended as an autonomous concept of EU law and, as such, cannot be contingent on the legislation applicable to transactions in which a distribution takes place.[143]

Inclusion of preparatory acts—In both *Donner*, C-5/11, and *Blomqvist*, C-98/13, the CJEU held that distribution to the public is characterized by a series of acts going, *at the very least*, from the conclusion of a contract of sale to the performance thereof by delivery to a member of the public.[144] The CJEU had the opportunity to apply this conclusion expansively in *Dimensione Direct Sales and Labianca*, C-516/13: in that ruling, in fact, the Court reached the conclusion that the holder of the right of distribution is entitled to control not just the actual distribution of the original or copies of a protected work, but also preparatory acts, including repressing third-party unauthorized advertisements for sale of copyright works or works protected by related rights.

Dimensione Direct Sales and Labianca—The ruling in *Dimensione Direct Sales and Labianca*, C-516/13, followed a reference from Germany's Federal Court of Justice in the context of litigation brought by a company trading in furniture against another company in relation to the online advertisement, by the latter, for sale in Germany of items that would infringe copyright in furniture to which the former owned the copyright. There was no evidence of actual sales of the infringing products, so the background in this case differed from *Peek & Cloppenburg*, C-456/06; *Donner*, C-5/11; and *Blomqvist*, C-98/13, in which actual acts of distribution had taken place. The German court asked the CJEU to clarify whether the scope of the right of distribution extends to activities like those of the defendant in the national proceedings.

The CJEU substantially followed the Opinion of AG Cruz Villalón, especially his view that the case at issue would differ from previous references for a preliminary ruling.[145] Having recalled that the concept of 'distribution' is an autonomous concept of EU law and that it should be read in light of Article 6(1) of the WIPO Copyright Treaty, the Court turned to its earlier decisions. It focused in particular on the phrase 'at the very least' used in *Donner*, C-5/11, and *Blomqvist*, C-98/13, and the idea that

---

[141] They are (in chronological order): *Laserdisken*, C-479/04, EU:C:2006:549; *Peek & Cloppenburg*, C-456/06, EU:C:2008:232; *Donner*, C-5/11, EU:C:2012:370; *Blomqvist*, C-98/13, EU:C:2014:55; *Art & Allposters International*, C-419/13, EU:C:2015:27; and *Dimensione Direct Sales and Labianca*, C-516/13, EU:C:2015:315.

[142] *Peek & Cloppenburg*, C-456/06, EU:C:2008:232, paras 29–33. In the same sense, see *Donner*, C-5/11, EU:C:2012:370, paras 23–24.

[143] *Donner*, C-5/11, EU:C:2012:370, para 25.

[144] Ibid, para 26; *Blomqvist*, C-98/13, EU:C:2014:55, para 28.

[145] Opinion of Advocate General Pedro Cruz Villalón in *Dimensione Direct Sales and Labianca*, C-516/13, EU:C:2014:2415, paras 1 and 32.

distribution to the public is characterized by a series of acts going, *at the very least*, from the conclusion of a contract of sale to the performance thereof by delivery to a member of the public. According to the Court this phrase means that it is not excluded that acts or steps that are preparatory to the conclusion of a contract of sale may also fall within the concept of distribution and be reserved, exclusively, to the copyright owner.

To strengthen this conclusion, the CJEU turned to contract law. Distribution to the public must be considered proven where a contract of sale and dispatch has been concluded, and the same is true of an offer of a contract of sale which binds its author. In fact, such an offer constitutes, by its very nature, a preparatory act to a sale. An invitation to submit an offer, or a non-binding advertisement for a protected object, also falls under the series of acts made with the objective of making a sale of that object. It is irrelevant—for the sake of establishing an infringement of the right of distribution—that the transfer of ownership of the protected work or a copy does not follow from the advertising at issue. This conclusion is also consistent with the objectives of the InfoSoc Directive (Recitals 9 to 11), ie that copyright harmonization must take as a basis a high level of protection, authors have to receive an appropriate reward for the use of their work, and the system for the protection of copyright must be rigorous and effective.[146]

3.2 The scope of the right: digital exhaustion

Exhaustion under the Software Directive—The CJEU has been asked explicitly about the application of the doctrine of exhaustion in the context of computer programs under Article 4(2) of the Software Directive, which so provides:

> The first sale in the Community of a copy of a program by the rightholder or with his consent shall exhaust the distribution right within the Community of that copy, with the exception of the right to control further rental of the program or a copy thereof.

Exhaustion under the InfoSoc Directive—The wording of this provision is substantially identical to Article 4(2) of the InfoSoc Directive. However, attempts to extend analogically the outcome in *UsedSoft*, C-128/11, (see further Section 3.3) to subject matter protected under the InfoSoc Directive prove challenging, in that exhaustion within the broader context and wording of the Software and InfoSoc Directive may differ.

First, Recital 28 in the preamble to the InfoSoc Directive links the right within Article 4 of the InfoSoc Directive to the 'right to control distribution of the work incorporated in a *tangible* article' (emphasis added). Second, Recital 29 in the preamble to the same directive clarifies that '[t]he question of exhaustion does not arise in the case of services and on-line services in particular'. In relation to this Recital, in its follow-up to the 1995 Green Paper, the EU Commission noted how 'a large consensus exists that no exhaustion of rights occurs in respect of works and other subject matter exploited on-line, as this qualifies as a service'.[147] Third, in relation to the right of communication/making available to the public, Article 3(3) of the InfoSoc Directive rules out that this right be subject to exhaustion. Fourth, it should be recalled once again that, by adopting the InfoSoc Directive, the EU legislature transposed into the EU legal order the WIPO Internet Treaties. The agreed statements to Article 6 of the

---

[146] *Dimensione Direct Sales and Labianca*, C-516/13, EU:C:2015:315, paras 25–34.

[147] EU Commission, *Communication from the Commission—Follow-up to the Green Paper on copyright and related rights in the information society*, COM(96) 568 final, 20 November 1996, Chapter 2, §4. See further (and critically), S Karapapa, 'Reconstructing copyright exhaustion in the online world' (2014) 2014/4 IPQ 307, 309–11.

WIPO Copyright Treaty provide that the expressions 'copies' and 'original and copies' in the context of the right of distribution exclusively refer to fixed copies that may be put into circulation as tangible objects. Finally, since its early case law, the CJEU has been careful in drawing a distinction between the right of distribution, which would be subject to exhaustion, and other rights for which no exhaustion would occur. For instance, in *Coditel*, C-62/79, the Court did not find that requiring payment of a fee for each public performance of a film would be contrary to EU law.[148] A similar distinction between the consequences of the first sale of a copyright work or a copy thereof for the exhaustion of the right of distribution and other economic rights was also made in *Warner Brothers and Metronome Video*, C-158/86, and *Tournier*, C-395/87.[149]

3.3 The *UsedSoft* decision

Digital exhaustion under the Software Directive—The ruling in *UsedSoft*, C-128/11, originated as a reference from Germany's Federal Court of Justice. That court sought clarification regarding the conditions that must be satisfied so that the authorized downloading from the internet of a copy of a computer program gives rise to exhaustion of the right of distribution of that copy under Article 4(2) of the Software Directive. The CJEU responded that this is the case if the contractual relationship between the copyright holder and its customer may be regarded as a (lawful) 'first sale'.

Notion of 'first sale'—Having defined the notion of 'sale' as 'an agreement by which a person, in return for payment, transfers to another person his rights of ownership in an item of tangible or intangible property belonging to him',[150] the Court held that even a licence agreement—including the one at issue in the background national proceedings—might be regarded as a sale for the sake of Article 4(2). This is the case if the copyright holder who has authorized, even free of charge, the downloading of that copy from the internet onto a data carrier has also conferred, in return for payment of a fee intended to enable him to obtain a remuneration corresponding to the economic value of the copy of the work of which he is the proprietor, a right to use that copy for an unlimited period. Thus, the Court assimilated the downloading of the copy of a computer program onto a lawful acquirer's hard disk or computer system as delivery into a material medium.[151]

Implications of the ruling for subject matter other than software—By focusing on the requirement that a copy of protected subject matter be delivered into a material medium, the CJEU might have ruled out that the same outcome is possible under the InfoSoc Directive. The Court dealt in fact with parallel provisions in the InfoSoc Directive, notably Article 4 and Recitals 28 and 29 in the preamble thereof, to discuss the possibility of applying them analogically in respect of the Software Directive, and thus exclude exhaustion in respect of intangible copies of a computer program.[152] Although identical concepts used in the Software and InfoSoc Directives must in principle have the same meaning,[153] the Court concluded in the negative on

---

[148] *Coditel*, C-62/79, EU:C:1980:84, para 12.

[149] T Cook, 'Exhaustion—a casualty of the borderless digital era', in L Bently, U Suthersanen, and P Torremans (eds), *Global Copyright—Three Hundred Years since the Statute of Anne, from 1709 to Cyberspace* (Edward Elgar:2010), 357–9.

[150] *UsedSoft*, C-128/11, EU:C:2012:407, para 42.

[151] On this particular aspect, see further RM Hilty, K Köklü, and F Hafenbrädl, 'Software agreements: stocktaking and outlook - lessons from the *UsedSoft v. Oracle* case from a comparative law perspective' (2013) 44(3) IIC 263, 273.

[152] *UsedSoft*, C-128/11, EU:C:2012:407, paras 53–54.   [153] Ibid, para 60.

this point, thus leaving room for a different interpretation of the provisions in these directives.[154]

In *UsedSoft*, C-128/09, by taking into account the literal wording of the Software Directive, which does not make any distinction between tangible and intangible copies of a computer program, together with the *lex specialis* character of this directive[155] (which the Court later reaffirmed in *Nintendo and Others*, C-355/12,[156] in relation to the subject matter qualification of videogames), which protects 'the expression in any form of a computer program',[157] the CJEU was in a position to confirm the existence of digital exhaustion under this piece of EU legislation. The Court subsequently confirmed the validity of the outcome achieved in *UsedSoft*, C-128/11, in its decision in *Ranks and Vasiļevičs*, C-166/15, however excluding that exhaustion would apply to back-up copies of a computer program.[158]

Internal market concerns—To justify the particular outcome achieved in *UsedSoft*, C-128/11, the Court stressed the specific internal market rationale of exhaustion in the EU context, which is that of avoiding the partitioning of markets, thus limiting any restrictions of the distribution of protected works to what is necessary to safeguard the specific subject matter of the intellectual property concerned. In the Court's view, restricting the resale of copies of computer programs downloaded from the internet, by means of an extended control over such copies, would go beyond what is necessary to safeguard protection of copyright, which is aimed at guaranteeing an appropriate—not the highest possible—remuneration,[159] and the enjoyment of the right of distribution.[160] The decision in *UsedSoft*, C-128/11, is therefore justifiable from an internal market perspective, but in reaching it the Court allowed the re-qualification of contractual relationships (so that a licence can be regarded as a sale), and did not rely on any particular wording of the Software Directive. Overall, it was the peculiar role of exhaustion in the EU intellectual property context that justified the particular outcome achieved in this preliminary ruling (on the rationale of exhaustion in EU law, see further Chapter 7, Section 2).

3.4 Digital exhaustion also under the InfoSoc Directive?

National case law on digital exhaustion—As mentioned, the CJEU has not yet had the chance to address specifically whether and to what extent the conclusion reached in *UsedSoft*, C-128/11, might be extended to works and subject matter protected under the InfoSoc Directive. In the aftermath of that decision, certain national courts have attempted to tackle its implications with reference to works other than computer programs, with diverging outcomes. For instance, in Germany in 2014 the Court of

---

[154] In this sense also L Bently, B Sherman, D Gangjee, and P Johnson, *Intellectual Property Law* (OUP:2018), 5th edn, 152.

[155] *UsedSoft*, C-128/11, EU:C:2012:407, paras 55–56.

[156] *Nintendo and Others* C-355/12, EU:C:2014:25, para 23.

[157] *UsedSoft*, C-128/11, EU:C:2012:407, para 57.

[158] *Ranks and Vasiļevičs*, C-166/15, EU:C:2016:762, paras 43–44.

[159] Speaking of 'appropriate remuneration', see also: *Football Association Premier League and Others*, C-403/08 and C-429/08, para 108 (on which see VL Benabou, 'Digital exhaustion of copyright in the EU or shall we cease being so schizophrenic?', in Stamatoudi (ed), *New Developments* 366–9); and *Renckhoff*, C-161/17, EU:C:2018:634, paras 18 and 34.

[160] *UsedSoft*, C-128/11, EU:C:2012:407, paras 62–63. See also C Sganga and S Scalzini, 'From abuse of right to European copyright misuse: a new doctrine for EU copyright law' (2017) 48(4) IIC 405, 424.

Appeal of Hamm excluded that the right of distribution under the InfoSoc Directive, as transposed into German law, could be exhausted in the case of audiobooks.[161] Taking a different view, in that same year the District Court of Amsterdam concluded that the right of distribution would be exhausted following the first lawful sale of copies of e-books.[162] The decision of the Amsterdam court was appealed to the Court of The Hague. This court held that the provider of second-hand e-books, Tom Kabinet, would not be liable for unauthorized acts of communication to the public under the Dutch equivalent of Article 3(1) of the InfoSoc Directive. However, it is unclear whether it could invoke the digital exhaustion of the right of distribution in relation to its e-book trade. Hence, the court in The Hague decided to seek guidance from the CJEU, as will be explained further in Section 3.5.[163]

Until the CJEU has the opportunity to address the specific question of exhaustion under the InfoSoc Directive as applied to works in digital format or digital copies thereof, one may only speculate whether *UsedSoft*, C-128/11, has significance beyond the narrow realm of the Software Directive. Some indirect guidance may already be inferred from the decisions in *Art & Allposters International*, C-419/13, and *Vereniging Openbare Bibliotheken*, C-174/15.

Art & Allposters International—The reference in *Art & Allposters International*, C-419/13, was made in the context of proceedings between a Dutch collecting society and a company making and marketing posters and canvas. They concerned the use of artistic works to which the claimant administered relevant copyrights. More specifically, the case considered the making and selling, by the defendant, of canvas realized by transferring—thanks to a chemical process—the images reproduced in posters that it had lawfully acquired and their subsequent commercialization. The litigation eventually reached the Dutch Supreme Court, which decided to stay the proceedings and ask the CJEU whether—among other things—Article 4 of the InfoSoc Directive governs the answer to the question whether the right of distribution of the copyright holder may be exercised with regard to the reproduction of a copyright work which has been sold and delivered within the EEA by or with the consent of the rightholder, in the case where that reproduction had subsequently undergone an alteration in respect of its form and is again brought into circulation in that form.

Corpus mysticum **and** *corpus mechanicum*—From its facts, it is apparent that this case does not have any digital component. Yet what is of interest is the dichotomy between a work and its *tangible* support. The CJEU relied on that in order to tackle the issue of exhaustion. In his Opinion, AG Cruz Villalón had held the view that the right of distribution may only be exhausted in relation to the tangible support (*corpus mechanicum*) of a work, not also the work itself (*corpus mysticum*).[164] The AG suggested that, not only can there be only analogue exhaustion under the InfoSoc Directive, but exhaustion is to be interpreted strictly. The case pending before the Dutch Supreme Court would not be one in which exhaustion comes into consideration, in that the alteration undertaken by the defendant was particularly relevant and concerned the same support used for the original artworks.

---

[161] OLG Hamm, 22 U 60/13.

[162] Rechtbank Amsterdam, C/13/567567/KG ZA 14-795 SP/MV, NL:RBAMS:2014:4360.

[163] See further M Savič, 'The legality of resale of digital content after *UsedSoft* in subsequent German and CJEU case law' (2015) 37(7) EIPR 414, in particular 416–19 and 420–3, and P Mezei, 'Digital first sale doctrine *ante portas*' (2015) 6(2) JIPITEC 23, 38.

[164] Opinion of Advocate General Pedro Cruz Villalón in *Art & Allposters International*, C-419/13, EU:C:2014:2214, para 67.

The CJEU agreed with the AG and justified its decision by means of both a literal and teleological interpretation of the relevant applicable provisions. The Court identified the purpose of the right of distribution within Article 4 of the InfoSoc Directive, this being only to encompass a work or a tangible copy thereof. This would be because Article 4(2) refers to the first sale or other transfer of ownership of 'that object'.[165] According to the CJEU this conclusion could be drawn from Recital 28, in the sense that the EU legislature, by using the terms 'tangible article' and 'that object', intended to give authors control over the initial marketing in the EU of each tangible object incorporating their intellectual creation.[166] As such, exhaustion of the right of distribution would only apply to the tangible copy of a work. This interpretation would be supported by international law, notably the WIPO Copyright Treaty. The CJEU thus concluded that 'exhaustion of the distribution right applies to the tangible object into which a protected work or its copy is incorporated if it has been placed onto the market with the copyright holder's consent'.[167] Thus, exhaustion does not apply to the alteration of an existing object that has been lawfully sold or transferred if the object in question, because of those alterations, is to be regarded as a new object.[168]

Difficulties with subject matter in immaterial format—By insisting on the dichotomy between a work and its physical embodiment,[169] this ruling questions whether for digital copies it is possible to identify a tangible support at all. This also prompts one to wonder whether in certain, dematerialized contexts digital copies may be classified as services, rather than goods, so that the exclusion in Recital 29 would apply in a straightforward fashion. Although not a case involving interpretation of the InfoSoc Directive, but rather interpretation of Council Directive 2006/112 on the common system of value added tax (the VAT Directive)[170] as applied to e-books, this is the conclusion that the CJEU achieved in its decision in *Commission v France*.[171] For the purpose of Article 98(2) of the VAT Directive, an e-book is not a good, but rather an 'electronically supplied service' within the meaning of the second subparagraph of Article 98(2) of that directive.[172]

Vereniging Openbare Bibliotheken—In *Vereniging Openbare Bibliotheken*, C-174/15, both AG Szpunar and the CJEU dismissed the relevance of exhaustion to the topic of the questions referred. Yet, the resulting judgment refers once again to the notion of tangible support in connection with the issue of exhaustion. The reference primarily concerned the Rental and Lending Rights Directive, notably whether libraries may lend electronic copies of works in their collections (e-lending), but also included a question regarding the possibility of digital exhaustion under the InfoSoc Directive.

In his Opinion, AG Szpunar did not undertake a specific discussion of digital exhaustion, in that he considered that this would be distinct from and not relevant to the

---

[165] *Art & Allposters International*, C-419/13, EU:C:2015:27, para 34.
[166] Ibid, para 37.   [167] Ibid, para 40.
[168] This approach is considered particularly problematic by T Headdon, 'The *Allposters* problem: reproduction, alteration and the misappropriation of value' (2018) 40(8) EIPR 501, 503, who notes how it raises a profoundly difficult question of a more ontological nature: at what point does an alteration give rise to a new object?
[169] This is the case also at the national level: in relation to UK copyright, see YH Lee, 'The persistence of the text: the concept of the work in copyright law—Part 2' (2018) 2018/2 IPQ 107, in particular 127–30.
[170] Council Directive 2006/112/EC of 28 November 2006 on the common system of value added tax, OJ L 347, 11 December 2006, 1–118.
[171] *Commission v France*, C-479/13, EU:C:2015:141.
[172] See further E Rosati, 'Online copyright exhaustion in a post-*Allposters* world' (2015) 10(9) JIPLP 673, 677.

question of whether e-lending falls within the scope of the Rental and Lending Rights Directive. Nonetheless, he suggested that there are no particularly strong reasons why digital copies should be treated differently from analogue ones, at least under the Rental and Lending Rights Directive.[173] Furthermore, the AG did note that *UsedSoft*, C-128/11, has been the only case in which the Court has interpreted copyright concepts in the digital context, including the notion of 'copy': 'According to a rigorous interpretation of the principle of terminological coherence, the term «copy» employed both in Directive 2001/29 and Directive 2006/115 should be intended in the sense of including digital copies devoid of physical support.' In the view of the AG, the decision *Art & Allposters International*, C-419/13, neither re-opens nor limits in any way the conclusions arising from the decision in *UsedSoft*, C-128/11.[174]

The Court did not address directly the issue of digital exhaustion. However, the judgment takes a rather different approach from the AG Opinion, in the sense that the Court reasoned along lines similar to those in *Art & Allposters International*, C-419/13, when it suggested that exhaustion relates to the 'physical medium' of a work. More specifically, in contrasting the concepts of 'rental' and 'distribution', the Court noted that:

> forms of exploitation of a protected work, such as public lending, are different in nature from a sale or any other lawful form of distribution, since the lending right remains one of the prerogatives of the author notwithstanding the sale of the *physical medium* containing the work. Consequently, the lending right is not exhausted by the sale or any other act of distribution, whereas the distribution right may be exhausted, but only and specifically upon the first sale in the European Union by the rightholder or with his consent.[175]

this part of the judgment confirms the interpretation that the concept of copy, to which exhaustion is attached, is to be intended as referring to the tangible copy of a work.[176]

3.5 Conclusion on the right of distribution and a new CJEU referral

Scope of the right and its exhaustion—Through its case law on the right of distribution two trends have emerged. On the one hand, the Court has employed the principle of high level of protection, in parallel with the need to interpret EU law provisions in

---

[173] Opinion of Advocate General Maciej Szpunar in *Vereniging Openbare Bibliotheken*, C-174/15, EU:C:2016:459, paras 31 and 44 in particular.

[174] Ibid, para 54.

[175] *Vereniging Openbare Bibliotheken*, C-174/15, EU:C:2016:856, para 59 (emphasis added).

[176] This is the conclusion that I reached in Rosati, 'Online copyright exhaustion' 681. In this sense, see also E Linklater, '*UsedSoft* and the Big Bang theory: is the e-exhaustion meteor about to strike?' 5(1) JIPITEC 12, 16–17, and M Savič, 'The CJEU *Allposters* case: beginning of the end of digital exhaustion?' (2015) 37(6) EIPR 378, 380–1. Cf however Hilty, Köklü, and Hafenbrädl, 'Software agreements' 284 considering that the economic considerations undertaken in *UsedSoft*, C-128/11, might also become relevant for works other than software and a broader applicability of that CJEU decision is not precluded a priori. In the same sense, see also P Günther, 'The principle of exhaustion and the resale of digital music in Europe: a comparative analysis of the *UsedSoft GmbH v. Oracle International Corp.* and *Capitol Records, LLC v. ReDigi, Inc.* cases' (2014) 2014/3 NIR 205, 216–17, and P Mysoor, 'Exhaustion, non-exhaustion and implied licence' (2018) 49(6) IIC 656, 677–680, holding the view that the conclusions in *UsedSoft*, C-128/11, might extend to copyright works other than software. Finally, see L Oprysk, R Matulevičius, and A Kelli, 'Development of a secondary market for e-books—The case of Amazon' (2017) 8(2) JIPITEC 128, 131, holding that whether digital exhaustion is allowed for e-books is uncertain and discussing the challenges for the establishment of secondary markets for e-books.

light of corresponding provisions of international law, in order to establish a broad understanding of the right of distribution. On the other hand, internal market concerns have been decisive in leading to the outcome achieved in *UsedSoft*, C-128/11, with regard to digital exhaustion as applied to computer programs. As the discussion around digital exhaustion in the context of the InfoSoc Directive suggests, such trends may eventually lead to diverging outcomes. In this sense, the pending reference in *Nederlands Uitgeversverbond and Groep Algemene Uitgevers*, C-263/18, will serve to determine whether and to what extent the high level of protection in the field of copyright may be reconciled with the internal market-building rationale underlying exhaustion of the right of distribution.

Nederlands Uitgeversverbond and Groep Algemene Uitgevers (**the** *Tom Kabinet* **case**)—This referral has been made in the context of long-standing litigation regarding the activities of Tom Kabinet, a Dutch business that trades in second-hand e-books (<https://www.tomkabinet.nl/>). Upon launching its own website, Tom Kabinet sent letters to publishers explaining its commercial initiative and inviting them—unsuccessfully—to support it. Two organizations representing publishers (Nederlandse Uitgeversverbond and Groep Algemene Uitgevers) instead initiated proceedings for copyright infringement against it.

In its 2014 decision the Court of First Instance of Amsterdam held[177] that there was no evidence of bad faith on the side of Tom Kabinet, and there was also uncertainty surrounding the applicability of the principle of exhaustion to subject matter like literary works in digital format. The decision was appealed, and in 2017 the Court of The Hague held that Tom Kabinet would not liable for unauthorized acts of communication to the public under the Dutch equivalent of Article 3(1) of the InfoSoc Directive.[178] However, it deemed it unclear whether it could also invoke the digital exhaustion of the right of distribution in relation to its e-book trade and, should exhaustion apply, whether acts of reproduction by subsequent users of the copy of the e-book purchased from time to time could be regarded as lawful in light of the exhausted right of distribution. In 2018 the Court of The Hague finalized its questions for the CJEU. The referral seeks clarification on the meaning of 'any form of distribution to the public of the original of a work or a copy thereof by sale or otherwise' in Article 4(1) of the InfoSoc Directive, in particular whether it encompasses the making available remotely by means of downloading for use for an unlimited period of time of an e-book by paying a price that the copyright holder receives as remuneration and which corresponds to the economic value of that copy of the work.

Should the answer to this be in the affirmative, then the other question is whether the right of distribution is exhausted within the meaning of Article 4(2) of the InfoSoc Directive, also following the remote downloading of an e-book for use for an unlimited period by paying a price which the copyright holder receives as remuneration and which corresponds to the economic value of that copy of a work. The referral also asks about the treatment of acts of reproduction in relation to copies in respect of which the right of distribution has been exhausted, and whether Article 5 of the InfoSoc Directive is to be interpreted as meaning that the copyright owner cannot oppose the acts of reproduction in relation to a lawfully obtained copy in respect of transfers between subsequent purchasers and in relation to which the right of distribution has been exhausted.

At the time of writing, the case is pending before the CJEU.

---

[177] Rechtbank Amsterdam, C/13/567567/KG ZA 14-795 SP/MV, NL:RBAMS:2014:4360.
[178] Rechtbank Den Haag, C/09/492558/HA ZA 15-827, NL:RBDHA:2017:7543.

Conclusion

In its case law on economic rights harmonized under the InfoSoc Directive, the CJEU has achieved similar outcomes, in the sense that the interpretation and construction of the scope of protection has been informed by the overarching objective of guaranteeing a 'high level of protection', which is one of the objectives underlying adoption of that directive. In this sense, the trends detected in the Data-Based Case Law (DBCL) analysis in Chapter 2, Section 3 are reflected in the activity of the Court and its expansive approach to the construction of the economic rights harmonized at the EU level.

5

The Construction of Exceptions and Limitations in the InfoSoc Directive

Introduction

Focus of this chapter—In parallel with harmonization of the scope of the exclusive rights available to holders of copyright and related rights, the EU legislature has also undertaken the harmonization of relevant exceptions and limitations. While a number of EU directives contain provisions devoted to exceptions and limitations, this chapter only considers exceptions and limitations under the InfoSoc Directive.

Economic rights and their exceptions and limitations—Exceptions and limitations are related, though in an inverse manner, to economic rights: the broader the scope of the latter, the narrower is the scope of the former. In the case of CJEU jurisprudence, this statement is particularly true if one considers that the need to fulfil one of the principal objectives of the InfoSoc Directive, ie ensuring a high level of protection, has been key to interpreting—as a result—exceptions and limitations 'strictly'. However, exceptions and limitations should not be considered as dichotomic to rightholders' control over the making of restricted acts. In fact, copyright protection is not absolute, and must be balanced with other rights and interests. This aspect has been increasingly relied upon by the Court, which has often referred to the need for a fair balance of rights and interests, and stressed the importance of guaranteeing the effectiveness of exceptions and limitations (see Chapter 2, Section 2.3)

In addition, reference by the Court to the need to interpret concepts in exceptions and limitations that do not refer to the individual laws of EU Member States as autonomous concepts of EU law, which must be given uniform interpretation and application throughout the EU (see Chapter 2, Section 2.2), has served the goal of increasing homogeneity of copyright laws, also from an internal market-building perspective. In this way—and together with the de facto application of EU preemption (see Chapter 3, Section 4)—the CJEU has been able to overcome, at least to a certain extent, the formally weak harmonizing force of Article 5 of the InfoSoc Directive.[1]

Exceptions and limitations in the InfoSoc Directive—With the exclusion of temporary copies (Article 5(1)), exceptions and limitations are *optional* for EU Member States to implement. All exceptions and limitations are subject to the three-step test contained in Article 5(5): they shall only be applied in certain special cases, which do not conflict with a normal exploitation of the work or other subject matter, and do not unreasonably prejudice the legitimate interests of the rightholder.

The (formal) harmonization of exceptions and limitations may be regarded as limited *also* because the directive itself states that their actual degree of harmonization should be based on their impact on the smooth functioning of the internal market, taking into account the different legal traditions in the various Member States.[2] It is

---

[1] In a similar sense, see also R Xalabarder, 'The role of the CJEU in harmonizing EU copyright law' (2016) 47(6) IIC 635, 638.
[2] InfoSoc Directive, Recital 31.

essentially for this reason that the Directive includes a 'grandfather clause' in Article 5(3)(o), which allows Member States to retain existing (at the time of the adoption of the InfoSoc Directive) exceptions and limitations for uses of protected subject matter 'in certain other cases of minor importance'. Such uses shall be allowed insofar as they only concern analogue uses and do not affect the functioning of the internal market, without prejudice to the other exceptions and limitations harmonized by the remaining provisions in Article 5.[3]

Criticisms of Article 5—Over time, several commentators have criticized the relatively weak harmonizing force of Article 5 of the InfoSoc Directive, with some even labelling the directive as 'a total failure, in terms of harmonization'.[4] Since the adoption of the InfoSoc Directive, not only have some exceptions and limitations not been adopted in certain Member States,[5] but also—and more seriously—national exceptions and limitations have been designed in such a way as to have diverging scope across the EU. The language employed by national legislatures, in fact, may not correspond to the language in the relevant exception or limitation at the EU level, or even provide for different conditions than the ones established at the EU level.

Yet, the CJEU has attempted—especially in more recent times—to remedy the material lack of a harmonized framework. On the one hand, as explained in Chapter 3, the CJEU has had the opportunity to preempt certain diverging national approaches. On the other hand, as it will be explained further later by means of selected examples, similarly to the case of economic rights, the Court has carried out its own construction of relevant concepts in exceptions and limitations, by means of a purpose-driven approach to the text of the directive. In all this, the CJEU has also increasingly relied on the three-step test to define the scope of exceptions and limitations, and also mandated it as a tool directly binding national legislatures and courts alike. The cases of parody, quotation, and private copying will be used as instances of this approach. Relevant case law developments show how the Court has construed relevant concepts as autonomous within EU law, while trying to define relevant scope and boundaries thereof.

1. Parody as an Autonomous Concept of EU Law and the Limited Freedom of EU Member States

Deckmyn and Vrijheidsfonds—Article 5(3)(k) of the InfoSoc Directive allows Member States to introduce into their own legal systems an exception or limitation to the rights of reproduction, communication/making available to the public, and distribution to

---

[3] M van Eechoud, PB Hungeholtz, S van Gompel, L Guibault, and N Helberger, *Harmonizing European Copyright Law—The Challenges of Better Lawmaking* (Wolters Kluwer:2009), 103. See also C Geiger and F Schönherr, 'Limitations to copyright in the digital age', in A Savin and J Trzaskowski (eds), *Research Handbook on EU Internet Law* (Edward Elgar:2014), 114–15.

[4] PB Hugenholtz, 'Why the Copyright Directive is unimportant, and possibly invalid' (2000) 22(11) EIPR 499, 501. In the same sense, see MC Janssens 'The issue of exceptions: reshaping the keys to the gates in the territory of literary, musical and artistic creation', in E Derclaye (ed), *Research Handbook on the Future of EU Copyright* (Edward Elgar:2009), 332, and bibliography cited in it. For similar criticisms of the directive expressed at the proposal stage with particular regard to exceptions and limitations, see M Hart 'The proposed directive for copyright in the information society: nice rights, shame about the exceptions' (1998) 20(5) EIPR 169, 169–70, and T Heide, 'The approach to innovation under the proposed Copyright Directive: time for mandatory exceptions?' (2000) 2000/3 IPQ 215, 219–22.

[5] For an overview of the various exceptions and limitations adopted by the individual Member States, see <http://copyrightexceptions.eu> (last accessed 15 August 2018).

Figure 5.1 *Deckmyn and Vrijheidsfonds* case: The original work (L) and its alleged parody (R)

allow the use of works for the purpose of caricature, parody, or pastiche. The CJEU had the opportunity to clarify the scope of this exception in its 2014 decision in *Deckmyn and Vrijheidsfonds*, C-201/13. Even if a parody may be regarded as involving an adaptation (the right of adaptation has not been generally harmonized at the EU level[6]), the broad scope of the right of reproduction as provided in, for example, *Infopaq International*, C-5/08 (on which see Chapter 4, Section 1) would be engaged in the making of a parody of a copyright work.[7]

Deckmyn and Vrijheidsfonds, C-201/13, was a reference for a preliminary ruling from the Brussels Court of Appeal (Belgium), made in the context of proceedings concerning the cover of a calendar distributed by a Flemish nationalist political party during a public event in early 2011. The calendar cover reproduced a modified version of the cover to a 1961 comic book of the popular *Suske en Wiske* series by Willy Vandersteen, *De Wilde Weldoener* ('The Compulsive Benefactor'). The original drawing depicts one of the comic book's main characters wearing a white tunic and throwing coins to people who are trying to pick them up. In the drawing used for the calendar cover, the Mayor of the City of Ghent replaces the original character and people wearing veils and people of colour replace the people picking up the coins (see Figure 5.1).

Further to proceedings for copyright infringement initiated by the Vandersteen estate, the political party claimed that no liability could be established, in that the parody

---

[6] Express harmonization has only occurred in relation to software (Article 4(1)(b) of the Software Directive) and databases (Article 5(b) of the Database Directive).
[7] See further E Rosati, 'Copyright in the EU: in search of (in)flexibilities' (2014) 9(7) JIPLP 585, 596–7, and E Rosati, 'The right of adaptation has not been generally harmonised at the EU level: true or false?' (1 May 2014) The IPKat, available at <http://ipkitten.blogspot.com/2014/05/the-right-of-adaptation-has-not-been.html> (last accessed 15 August 2018). With specific regard to parodies, see D Jongsma, 'Parody after *Deckmyn*—a comparative overview of the approach to parody under copyright law in Belgium, France, Germany and the Netherlands' (2017) 48(6) IIC 652, 666–70.

defence under Belgian law would be applicable. The Brussels Court of First Instance issued an injunction against the defendants, who appealed to the Brussels Court Appeal. This court made a reference for a preliminary ruling to the CJEU, seeking guidance regarding both the understanding of the concept of 'parody' and the characteristics that a work must possess to be considered as such.

Parody as an autonomous concept of EU law—The CJEU noted that Article 5(3) (k) does not contain any reference to national laws. The concept of 'parody' is therefore an autonomous concept of EU law which must be interpreted uniformly throughout the EU, having regard to the context of the provision and the objective pursued by the legislation in question. This conclusion follows from the need for uniform application of EU law and from the principle of equality.[8]

Characteristics—The concept of parody must thus be understood according to its usual meaning in everyday language, and has just two essential characteristics: first, to evoke an existing work while being noticeably different from it and, second, to constitute an expression of humour or mockery. According to the CJEU there are no other requirements, not even that a parody must be sufficiently original (as AG Cruz Villalón had instead suggested[9]). This is because such additional requirements are found neither in the usual meaning of 'parody' in everyday language nor the wording of Article 5(3) (k) of the InfoSoc Directive. To state otherwise would mean unduly compressing the scope of the exception or limitation for parody. This would be both against Recital 3 in the preamble to this directive, which requires compliance with—amongst others—the protection of intellectual property and freedom of expression (parody being a way to exert such freedom), and subsequent Recital 31, which states that exceptions and limitations must strike a 'fair balance' between the rights and interests of authors on the one hand, and the rights of users of protected subject matter on the other. EU Member States cannot add additional requirements for the availability of the national parody exception, beyond the requirements set at the EU level.

Humorous 'intent' or 'effect'?—As mentioned, one of the characteristics of a parody is that it must constitute an expression of humour or mockery. The Court did not clarify whether this requirement is fulfilled when an alleged parody pursues a humorous intent, or whether it is also required that it achieves it (as the AG had suggested in his Opinion[10]).

As discussed more at length elsewhere,[11] if the test was 'intent', then the exception under Article 5(3)(k) of the InfoSoc Directive would be broader than if a humorous 'effect' was also required. Above all, requiring just intent would be more compliant with the need to safeguard parody as a means to exercise freedom of expression. In relation to Article 10 ECHR, which guarantees freedom of expression to 'everyone',[12] the ECtHR has consistently held that freedom of expression constitutes one of the essential foundations of a democratic society and one of the basic conditions for its progress

---

[8] *Deckmyn and Vrijheidsfonds*, C-201/13, EU:C:2014:2132, paras 14–15. Based on the AG Opinion (Opinion of Advocate General Pedro Cruz Villalón in *Deckmyn and Vrijheidsfonds*, C-201/13, EU:C:2014:458, para 46), according to S Jacques, *The Parody Exception in Copyright Law* (forthcoming:OUP), chapter 1, §1.1, the CJEU too considered parody as a multivalent concept which includes forms of pastiche and caricature.

[9] *Deckmyn and Vrijheidsfonds*, C-201/13, EU:C:2014:2132, paras 57–58.

[10] Opinion of Advocate General Pedro Cruz Villalón in *Deckmyn and Vrijheidsfonds*, C-201/13, EU:C:2014:458, para 67.

[11] E Rosati, 'Just a laughing matter? Why the decision in *Deckmyn* is broader than parody' (2015) 52(2) CMLRev 511, 516–20.

[12] *Fredrik Neji and Peter Sunde Kolmisoppi v Sweden*, Application No 40397/12, 19 February 2013, referring to *Autronic AG v Switzerland*, Application No 12726/87, 22 March 1990, para 47.

and for each individual's self-fulfilment. Subject to the limitations within Article 10 ECHR, it is applicable not only to information or ideas that are favourably received or regarded as inoffensive or as a matter of indifference, but also to those that offend, shock, or disturb. Such are the demands of pluralism, tolerance, and broadmindedness without which there is no 'democratic society'.[13]

If the test, instead, was 'effect', it is unclear from what perspective this requirement would need to be considered: would the parody have to be an expression of humour or mockery in the opinion of the judge who has been requested to decide a certain case? Or would it rather have to be so according to the standards of that particular Member State? Another option could be that the humorous effect is to be assessed against the standards of the 'society' (possibly to be intended as the European/EU society) invoked by the AG in his Opinion.[14] However, if this was the case, one might wonder how a parody that is closely bound to the specific reality of a certain Member State (as was the case in *Deckmyn and Vrijheidsfonds*, C-201/13) could qualify for protection under the parody exception. This would be because the European/EU society could fail to recognize the humorous nature (intent or effect) of country- or sector-specific parodies.

The difficulties, which would arise should a humorous effect be required, lead to the conclusion that the correct test under *Deckmyn and Vrijheidsfonds*, C-201/13, is that of a humorous 'intent'. This conclusion is also one that best complies with Article 10 ECHR jurisprudence, in particular the universal nature of freedom of expression and the need to avoid unduly compressing the enjoyment and exercise of this human right.

Limitations—In any case, it follows from Recital 31 that freedom of parody, as an expression of one's own opinion, is not unlimited. Despite the broad understanding of freedom of expression in ECtHR jurisprudence, a parody that conveys a message that is discriminatory/racist is not eligible for protection under Article 5(3)(k) of the InfoSoc Directive. Stating otherwise would contradict the requirement for a fair balance between the rights and interests of the author of the parodied work and the rights of the parodist. In these instances the person who holds the rights to a work has a legitimate interest in ensuring that the work protected by copyright is not associated with the message conveyed by its parody.[15] This is the most ambiguous part of the decision. The reason is that the Court failed to elaborate at any particular length on what legal grounds a copyright holder could object to a parody of this kind.[16] As discussed further elsewhere, the legitimate interest referred to by the Court might be enforced in national proceedings by relying on national (unharmonized) moral rights legislation and, in particular, the right of integrity available under individual EU Member States' laws.[17]

Parody in the internal market—Despite its shortcomings, the judgment is noteworthy because it shows how the Court's attempt to define an EU parody concept is essentially informed by an internal market rationale. Following the clarification that the conclusion that parody is an autonomous concept of EU law is not invalidated by the optional nature of the exception in Article 5(3)(k), the Court stressed that this would be so because:

---

[13] *Sekmadienis v Lithuania*, Application No 69317/14, 30 January 2018, para 70.
[14] Opinion of Advocate General Pedro Cruz Villalón in *Deckmyn and Vrijheidsfonds*, C-201/13, EU:C:2014:458, paras 83 and 87.
[15] *Deckmyn and Vrijheidsfonds*, C-201/13, EU:C:2014:2132, para 31.
[16] E Rosati, 'Just a laughing matter? Why the decision in *Deckmyn* is broader than parody' (2015) 52(2) CMLRev 511, 516–20.
[17] Ibid, 523–8.

[a]n interpretation according to which Member States that have introduced that exception are free to determine the limits in an unharmonised manner, which may vary from one Member State to another, would be incompatible with the objective of that directive.[18]

Besides *Padawan*, C-467/08, and *ACI Adam*, C-435/12, this approach echoes the one that the Court had already adopted, for example, in *DR and TV2 Danmark*, C-510/10. That case related to the exception or limitation for ephemeral recordings within Article 5(3)(n) of the InfoSoc Directive. An interpretation according to which Member States that, exercising the option afforded to them by European Union law, have introduced an exception within Article 5, are free to determine, in an unharmonized manner, the limits thereof would be contrary to the objective of that directive. Said objective is to achieve a uniform interpretation of the concepts contained in the InfoSoc Directive. That would be so because the limits of that exception would vary from one Member State to another and would therefore give rise to potential inconsistencies.[19] This reasoning does indeed echo the one in the earlier decision *Padawan*, C-467/08. In discussing private copying within Article 5(2)(b) of the InfoSoc Directive, the CJEU held in fact that, although it is open to the Member States to introduce a private copying exception to the exclusive right of reproduction, those Member States which make use of that option must provide for the payment of fair compensation to authors affected by the application of that exception: an interpretation according to which Member States that have introduced an identical exception of that kind are free to determine the limits in an inconsistent and un-harmonized manner, which may vary from one Member State to another, would be incompatible with the harmonizing objective underlying adoption of the InfoSoc Directive.[20]

The idea that Article 5 of the InfoSoc Directive would allow flexible national interpretations of the exceptions and limitations contained therein is not correct. This approach has however been considered favourably by a number of AGs over time. For instance, in her Opinion in *Padawan*, C-467/08, AG Trstenjak held the view that Article 5 'allows the Member States considerable flexibility in the transposition of the directive'.[21] AG Trstenjak elaborated further upon this in her subsequent Opinion in *Painer*, C-145/10, in which she stated that, subject to a number of requirements (including the three-step test in Article 5(5)), '[i]f the Member States are able to decide whether to provide for one of the constraints … they are also able, according to the principle of *qui potest majus, potest et minus*, to decide in principle how to organise such a constraint'.[22] This conclusion was also shared by AG Eleanor Sharpston in her Opinion in *VG Wort*, C-457/11, in which she stated that '[t]he optional nature of the exceptions or limitations gives Member States a certain freedom of action in this area, which is reflected in the preamble to the Directive, particularly in recitals 34, 36 to 40, 51 and 52'.[23]

Harmonization and fundamental rights—The ruling in *Deckmyn and Vrijheidsfonds*, C-201/13, further confirms that tolerating divergences at the national level in areas that have been formally harmonized would result—as has indeed been the case—in barriers to the free movement of goods and services based on or incorporating copyright works

---

[18] *Deckmyn and Vrijheidsfonds*, C-201/13, EU:C:2014:2132, para 16, referring to *Padawan*, EU:C:2010:620, para 36, and *ACI Adam and Others*, C-435/12, EU:C:2014:254, para 49.

[19] *DR and TV2 Danmark*, C-510/10, EU:C:2012:244, paras 35–36.

[20] *Padawan*, C-467/08, EU:C:2010:620, para 36.

[21] Opinion of Advocate General Verica Trstenjak in *Padawan*, C-467/08, EU:C:2010:264, para 43.

[22] Opinion of Advocate General Verica Trstenjak in *Painer*, C-145/10, EU:C:2011:239, para 148.

[23] Opinion of Advocate General Eleanor Sharpston in *VG Wort*, C-457/11, EU:C:2013:34, para 35.

and protected subject matter. In all this, however, respect of the object of a 'high level of protection' should not be intended as absolute: rather, the need to balance the rights of copyright holders with third-party rights and freedoms (in *Eugen Ulmer*, C-117/13, the CJEU reached the point of referring to exceptions and limitations as 'rights'[24]) is a requirement under both EU copyright law and the EU Charter's fundamental rights.[25]

2. An EU Quotation Exception

Similar to other exceptions and limitations, in relation to quotation within Article 5(3) (d) of the InfoSoc Directive the CJEU envisaged a EU-wide approach in its decision in *Painer*, C-145/10.

Quotation in international and EU laws: an exception or a right?—An aspect to note at the outset is the peculiar relationship between the EU approach to quotation, ie that of an optional exception or limitation for EU Member States to introduce into their own legal system, and what some commentators have indicated as a mandatory right of quotation or even mandatory fair use (admittedly narrower than the fair use doctrine under US copyright law,[26] but nonetheless such as to admit quotations of entire works[27]) at the international level. Article 10(1) of the Berne Convention generously[28] states that:

[i]t *shall* be permissible to make quotations from a work which has already been lawfully made available to the public, provided that their making is compatible with fair practice, and their extent does not exceed that justified by the purpose, including quotations from newspaper articles and periodicals in the form of press summaries. (emphasis added)

It has been argued that, by using the modal verb 'shall' (the French version uses even stronger language, by stating 'Sont licites les citations tirées d'une œuvre'), the Berne Convention imposes on members of the Berne Union an obligation to introduce a quotation 'right'.[29] However, it is unlikely that individual EU Member States may bypass the optional character of the defence in the InfoSoc Directive and refer directly to the Berne Convention. By adopting the InfoSoc Directive, in fact, the EU deprived Member States of their competence to implement the relevant provisions of the Berne Convention. As such, individual EU Member States cannot give effect to Article 10(1)

---

[24] *Eugen Ulmer*, C-117/13, EU:C:2014:2196, para 39.
[25] See further European Copyright Society, *Limitations and exceptions as key elements of the legal framework for copyright in the European Union – Opinion on the Judgment of the CJEU in Case C201/13 Deckmyn* (20 October 2014), available at <https://europeancopyrightsocietydotorg.files.wordpress.com/2015/12/deckmyn-opinion-final-with-signatures.pdf> (last accessed 15 August 2018), §IV.
[26] L Bently and T Aplin, *Whatever became of global mandatory fair use? A case study in dysfunctional pluralism* (2018) University of Cambridge Faculty of Law Research Paper No 34/2018, §1 (forthcoming in S Frankel (ed), *Is Intellectual Property Pluralism Functional?* (Edward Elgar:2018)).
[27] T Aplin and L Bently, *Displacing the dominance of the three-step test: the role of global, mandatory fair use* (2018) University of Cambridge Faculty of Law Research Paper No 33/2018, 6 (forthcoming in WL Ng, H Sun, and S Balganesh (eds), *Comparative Aspects of Limitations and Exceptions in Copyright Law* (CUP:2018)).
[28] S Ricketson 'The boundaries of copyright: its proper limitations and exceptions: international conventions and treaties' (1991) 1991/1 IPQ 56, 64, speaks in fact of 'reasonably generous boundaries' in relation to the scope of Article 10(1) of the Berne Convention.
[29] H Cohen Jeroham, 'Restrictions on copyright and their abuse' (2005) 27(10) EIPR 359, 360; S von Lewinski, *International Copyright Law and Policy* (OUP:2008), §5.163; P Goldstein and B Hugenholtz, *International Copyright. Principles, Law, and Practice* (2013:OUP), 3rd edn, 391. *Contra* M Ficsor, *The Law of Copyright and the Internet: The 1996 WIPO Treaties, their Interpretation and Implementation* (OUP:2002), §5.11.

of the Berne Convention without also complying with the InfoSoc Directive and its Article 5.

Luksan—This conclusion is in line with both the literal wording of the InfoSoc Directive and—by analogy—CJEU case law, notably the 2012 decision in *Luksan*, C-277/10. In that reference for a preliminary ruling the Court considered whether Austrian legislation which provided that all exclusive exploitation rights in a film vested in its producer and not also its principal director (as is instead the case under EU copyright) would be compatible with EU law. The Austrian government had relied on Article 14*bis*(a) of the Berne Convention to argue that copyright ownership in a cinematographic work is a matter for legislation in the country where protection is sought. The CJEU, however, refused to endorse such an interpretation. It held that, in providing that the principal director of a cinematographic work is to be considered its author or one of the authors, the EU legislature exercised EU competence in the field of intellectual property. In those circumstances, the Member States are no longer competent to adopt provisions compromising that European Union legislature. Accordingly, they can no longer rely on the power granted by Article 14*bis* of the Berne Convention.[30]

The InfoSoc Directive—In any case, even assuming the mandatory character of the Berne provision, national legislatures (including the EU legislature) should remain free to prescribe the relevant conditions for their exercise.[31] In the first place, such limits derive from the system of the InfoSoc Directive. Article 5(3)(d) allows quotations for purposes such as (but not limited to) criticism or review insofar as: first, they relate to a work or other subject matter which has already been lawfully made available to the public; second, unless this turns out to be impossible, the source (including the author's name) is indicated; and, third, their use is in accordance with fair practice, and to the extent required by the specific purpose. The overarching, horizontal, threshold imposed by the three-step test is also applicable.

Painer—In addition to the formal limits, the CJEU has added further ones in its decision in *Painer*, C-145/10, and, in doing so, questioned certain diverging approaches seen at the level of national legislation. This case arose as a reference for a preliminary ruling from the Vienna Commercial Court (Austria) made in the context of proceedings between a freelance photographer and a number of German and Austrian press publishers over unauthorized publication of a number of photographs—as well as a photo-fit—that the claimant had taken. The Austrian court sought guidance from the CJEU on a number of issues, including the conditions of applicability of Article 5(3)(d) of the InfoSoc Directive.

In its analysis the CJEU held that the defence in Article 5(3)(d) has a material scope comparable to that of Article 10(1) of the Berne Convention.[32] Article 5(3)(d) aims at striking a fair balance between the right to freedom of expression of users of a work or other protected subject matter and exclusive rights. It does so by favouring the exercise of the user's right to freedom of expression over the interest of the author in being able to prevent the reproduction of extracts from a work which has already been lawfully made available to the public, whilst ensuring that the author has the right, in principle, to have their name indicated.[33]

Requirements of quotation—The most interesting part of the Court's assessment of Article 5(3)(d) is probably when it held that this exception intends 'to preclude the

---

[30] *Luksan*, C-277/10, EU:C:2012:65, para 64.
[31] Goldstein and Hugenholtz, *International Copyright* 392.
[32] *Painer*, C-145/10, EU:C:2011:798, para 127.   [33] Ibid, paras 134–135.

exclusive right of reproduction conferred on authors from preventing the publication, by means of quotation *accompanied by comments or criticism,* of extracts from a work already available to the public'.[34] The CJEU also stated that the meaning of 'provided that they relate to a work or other subject matter which has already been lawfully made available to the public' in Article 5(3)(d) means that whether the quotation is made as part of a work protected by copyright or, on the other hand, as part of a subject matter not protected by copyright, is irrelevant.[35] The Court implicitly noted the incompatibility with EU law of those Member States' quotation defences that envisage requirements for the availability of the defence that do not have a corresponding provision in the text of the directive. Thus, national defences that allow quotations insofar as they are justified by the critical, polemic, educational, scientific, or informational character of the work in which they are *incorporated* (this is, for example, the case of France[36]) are unduly restrictive in light of EU law.

However, it should also be highlighted how Article 5(3)(d) does not mandate—as the CJEU did—that the quotation be necessarily accompanied by comment or criticism. In *Painer*, C-145/10, the CJEU took a different direction from that which it later did in, for example, *Deckmyn and Vrijheidsfonds*, C-201/13. While in the latter the Court was wary of the risks of adding requirements other than those envisaged at the level of the InfoSoc Directive for parodies, the same cannot be said in relation to quotation.

National experiences—Further to *Painer*, C-145/10, to be compatible with EU law, a quotation must be justified in light of accompanying comments or criticism. While the latter requirement, which, for example, is also envisaged in the relevant Italian quotation exception,[37] may be considered an (implicit) expression of compliance with the three-step test, it also informs the interpretation of certain national exceptions that do not require quotations to be for any particular purposes. This is for instance the case of the UK (on which see further Chapter 7, Section 5.1) which in 2014 introduced a defence, framed within fair dealing, allowing the use of a quotation from a work (whether for criticism or review or *otherwise*) provided that: (a) the work has been made available to the public; (b) the use of the quotation is fair dealing with the work; (c) the extent of the quotation is no more than is required by the specific purpose for which it is used; and (d) the quotation is accompanied by a sufficient acknowledgement (unless this would be impossible for reasons of practicality or otherwise). As of today the defence (and its scope) is yet to be tested in court.

---

[34]   Ibid, para 120 (emphasis added).   [35]   Ibid, para 136.
[36]   Article L-122-5(3)(a) CPI states that quotations are allowed insofar as they clearly indicate the name of the author and the source, and are justified by the critical, polemic, educational, scientific, or informational character of the work in which they are incorporated ('Sous réserve que soient indiqués clairement le nom de l'auteur et la source ... Les analyses et courtes citations justifiées par le caractère critique, polémique, pédagogique, scientifique ou d'information de l'oeuvre à laquelle elles sont incorporées'). According to V Benabou, 'Retour sur dix ans de jurisprudence de la Cour de Justice de l'Union Européenne en matière de propriété littéraire et artistique' (2012) 43 Propriétés Intellectuelles 140, 148, and E Derclaye, 'The Court of Justice copyright case law: quo vadis?' (2014) 36(11) EIPR 716, 718, the CJEU decision in *Painer*, C-145/10 has de facto abolished the rule that a quotation must be attached to another work or subject matter.
[37]   Article 70(1) of the Italian Copyright Act allows quotations if they are made for purposes of criticism or discussion, within the limits justified by such purposes and insofar as they do not compete with the economic exploitation of the work ('Il riassunto, la citazione o la riproduzione di brani o di parti di opera e la loro comunicazione al pubblico sono liberi se effettuati per uso di critica o di discussione, nei limiti giustificati da tali fini e purché non costituiscano concorrenza all'utilizzazione economica dell'opera; se effettuati a fini di insegnamento o di ricerca scientifica l'utilizzo deve inoltre avvenire per finalità illustrative e per fini non commerciali.')

Even more liberal are the approaches of Ireland, Belgium, Denmark, Sweden, and Germany. Section 52(4) of the Irish Copyright Act states that 'copyright in a work which has been lawfully made available to the public is not infringed by the use of quotations or extracts from the work, where such use does not prejudice the interests of the owner of the copyright in that work and such use is accompanied by a sufficient acknowledgement'. Article XI of the Belgian Code de Droit Économique, Article 22 of the Danish Copyright Act, and section 22 of the Swedish Copyright Act allow anyone, in accordance with proper usage and to the extent necessary for the purpose, to quote from works which have been made available to the public. Similarly, §51 of the German Copyright Act (Urheberrechtsgesetz, UrhG) allows the reproduction, distribution and communication to the public of a published work for the purpose of quotation, so far as such use is justified to that extent by the particular purpose.

3. The EU Private Copying System

Article 5(2)(b) of the InfoSoc Directive—The provision in Article 5(2)(b) of the InfoSoc Directive is one that has given rise to, on the one hand, heterogeneous approaches at the level of individual EU Member States and, on the other hand and as a result, uncertainties regarding their compatibility with the EU private copying system. Such uncertainties have translated to a significant number of CJEU preliminary rulings.[38]

There is little doubt that all this is due to what—on the surface of it—is a relatively weak harmonizing force of the InfoSoc Directive in respect of private copying. Article 5(2)(b) reads as follows:

Member States may provide for exceptions or limitations to the reproduction right provided for in Article 2 ... (b) in respect of reproductions on any medium made by a natural person for private use and for ends that are neither directly nor indirectly commercial, on condition that the rightholders receive fair compensation which takes account of the application or non-application of technological measures referred to in Article 6 to the work or subject matter concerned.

The provision does not add much as regards how the requirement of 'fair compensation' is to be intended. The only (limited) guidance is provided by Recital 35 in the preamble to the directive, which states that, when determining the form, detailed arrangements, and possible level of such fair compensation, account should be taken of the particular circumstances of each case. When evaluating these circumstances, a valuable criterion would be the possible harm to the rightholders as resulting from the act in question. Recital 35 provides further guidance:

- It excludes that payment may be due in cases where rightholders have already received payment in some other form, for instance as part of a licence fee.

- It considers that the level of fair compensation should take full account of the degree of use of technological protection measures, like those within Article 6

---

[38] They are (in chronological order): *Padawan*, C-467/08, EU:C:2010:620; *Stichting de Thuiskopie*, C-462/09, EU:C:2011:397; *Luksan*, C-277/10, EU:C:2012:65; *VG Wort*, C-457/11, EU:C:2013:426; *Amazon.com International Sales and Others*, C-521/11, EU:C:2013:515; *ACI Adam and Others*, C-435/12, EU:C:2014:254; *Copydan Båndkopi*, C-463/12, EU:C:2015:144; *Hewlett-Packard Belgium*, C-572/13, EU:C:2015:750; *Austro-Mechana*, C-572/14, EU:C:2016:286; *EGEDA and Others*, C-470/14, EU:C:2016:418; *Microsoft Mobile Sales International and Others*, C-110/15, EU:C:2016:717; and *VCAST*, C-265/16, EU:C:2017:913.

of the directive. In this respect, Recital 39 adds that exceptions or limitations should not inhibit the use of technological measures or their enforcement against circumvention.

- Importantly, it excludes that payment of a fair compensation may be due in certain situations where the prejudice to the rightholder is minimal.

Fragmented approaches to private copying—It is challenging to identify a common model for a European private copying exception. In this regard, it may be worth recalling that in 2011 EU Commissioner for Internal Market and Services, Michel Barnier, asked António Vitorino, previously EU Commissioner for Justice and Home Affairs, to preside over a stakeholder dialogue on private copying and reprography levies, and formulate a number of recommendations. In 2013, Vitorino presented his recommendations, highlighting how the different approaches to imposing and administering private copying and reprography levies had been a source of friction with internal market principles concerning the free movement of goods and services. Although he remained of the view that levies would retain their relevance in the foreseeable future, greater consistency, effectiveness, and legitimacy of the levy systems should be pursued.[39] The fragmented state of the private copying exception across the EU has also been acknowledged by the CJEU. In its decision in *Microsoft Mobile Sales International and Others*, C-110/15, the Court stated that:

[i]nasmuch as Directive 2001/29 does not expressly address the various elements of the fair compensation system, the Member States enjoy broad discretion in determining who is to pay that compensation. The same is true of the form, detailed arrangements and possible level of such compensation.[40]

In respect of the challenges presented by the EU framework it may be worth discussing the recent experience of the UK, which managed to introduce a private copying exception into its own law only in 2014. Although the attempt succeeded, the resulting defence was short-lived and was quashed in 2015.

3.1 The case of the UK

Private copying without a levy system—When discussing the introduction of a private copying exception into UK copyright law, the UK government was sceptical regarding the opportunity of envisaging a levy system, and ultimately decided against its introduction into that country's law.[41] Discussing the forthcoming introduction of section 28B into the CDPA (which eventually took place in 2014), the government noted that the UK exception for 'personal copies for private use' would be narrower than corresponding exceptions in other EU Member States. This would be so because the UK provision would not allow the transfer or sharing of the copies being made, ie a 'household' exception, or the making of copies from sources that one does not own, for example, rented copies, broadcasts, or on-demand services. Furthermore, it would not prevent copyright owners from using technological protection measures or licensing

---

[39] A Vitorino, *Recommendations Resulting from the Mediation on Private Copying and Reprography Levies* (2013), available at <http://ec.europa.eu/internal_market/copyright/docs/levy_reform/130131_levies-vitorino-recommendations_en.pdf> (last accessed 15 August 2018), 3.

[40] *Microsoft Mobile Sales International and Others*, C-110/15, para 27.

[41] See further B Hazucha, 'Private copying and harm to authors - compensation versus remuneration' (2017) 133(Apr) LQR 269, 273–5.

additional services, including cloud services which allow shared access to content.[42] Because of its narrow scope, the UK government decided against the introduction of private copying levies, considering that UK consumers would not tolerate them. Overall, the UK government viewed levies as 'inefficient, bureaucratic and unfair, and [such as to] disadvantage people who pay for content'.[43]

Recital 35 of the InfoSoc Directive—To this end, it relied upon the *de minimis* rule within Recital 35 in the preamble to the InfoSoc Directive, arguing that EU Member States are free not to provide compensation where a private copying limitation is likely to cause minimal or no harm, or where appropriate payment has already been made.[44] The only relevant 'harm' that would, in principle, need to be compensated for is the risk to rightholders of lost, duplicate sales. In the view of the UK Secretary of State, there was no automatic correlation between the wish to copy and lost sales; if the former was constrained, the latter would not necessarily occur. As such, if a limited exception to copyright were introduced, this would not impact upon duplicate sales. In addition, sellers of content already price-in to the initial sale price—whether fully or in part—the fact that consumers treat content that they purchase as fair game when it comes to copying for personal use (pricing-in principle).

Judicial review of section 28B—Further to an application for judicial review filed by the British Academy of Songwriters, Composers, and Authors (BASCA), the Musicians' Union, and UK Music, which submitted that lack of compensation would render the UK exception incompatible with EU law, in 2015 the High Court of England and Wales quashed section 28B CDPA.[45] While accepting claimants' application, in an initial judgment the court did not expressly rule on the actual compliance of the UK exception for personal copies for private use with EU law, and did not exclude making a reference for a preliminary ruling to the CJEU on issues of compatibility of section 28B with the InfoSoc Directive. Its view of section 28B was that the UK government had failed to provide adequate evidence as to the fact that no compensation was required because the harm to rightholders would be minimal.

After both the claimants and the Secretary of State accepted that the best course of action would be to invalidate the exception, in a follow-up ruling the High Court decided not to seek guidance from the CJEU, and invalidated the entirety of the Regulations that had introduced the defence for personal copies for private use and all of the rights and obligations contained therein. The court also addressed—admittedly unsatisfactorily—the temporal effect of the quashing of the Regulations, ie whether this should only have prospective effect (*ex nunc*), or also retrospective effect (*ex tunc*). In fact, the court declined to make any ruling as to whether or not the Regulations should be void *ex tunc*. This was on consideration that a declaration to this effect would raise

---

[42] For a discussion of the scope of the now defunct UK exception, see A Cameron, 'Copyright exceptions for the digital age: new rights of private copying, parody and quotation (2014) 9(12) JIPLP 1002, 1003; K Grisse and S Koroch, 'The British private copying exception and its compatibility with the Information Society Directive' (2015) 10(7) JIPLP 562, 563–4.

[43] Lords Hansard text of 29 July 2014, Column 1517, available at <https://publications.parliament.uk/pa/ld201415/ldhansrd/text/140729-0001.htm#14072947000224> (last accessed 15 August 2018).

[44] Also in support of the introduction of section 28B CDPA, see L Bently and Others, *Draft Statutory Instruments on Exceptions to Copyright* (6 June 2014), available at <http://www.create.ac.uk/wpcontent/uploads/2014/03/Scrutiny-Committee-Profs-letter-June2014.pdf> (last accessed 15 August 2018).

[45] *British Academy of Songwriters, Composers and Authors and Others, R (on the Application of) v Secretary of State for Business, Innovation And Skills* [2015] EWHC 1723 (Admin) (19 June 2015).

potentially complex and far reaching issues which it is appropriate to address in the circumstances of private law litigation between a specific rightholder and an alleged infringer. It will be for a defendant in future proceedings to explore and raise this issue, including whether the effect of the fact that they relied at the time upon Section 28B creates some species of estoppel, legitimate expectation or fair use defence in private law and whether, if such exists, this goes to the cause of action or the remedy or both.[46]

Since the 2015 decisions, the UK government has not attempted to re-introduce a defence for the making of private copies into UK law.[47]

3.2 CJEU case law on selected issues relating to private copying: towards greater uniformity?

Since the adoption of the InfoSoc Directive the CJEU has been asked to clarify on multiple occasions the requirements of the EU system of private copying and, in doing so, indirectly assess the compatibility (or lack thereof) with EU law of various EU Member States' systems of private copying and fair compensation. This has been the case, for instance, of both the scope of the private copying exception and the notion of fair compensation. With particular regard to the latter, the CJEU has addressed issues such as responsibility for its payment, funding of fair compensation, and its beneficiaries. In doing so, the Court has contributed to the creation—given the thin framework established by the InfoSoc Directive—of a more homogeneous system of private copying across the EU.

3.2.1 *Strict interpretation applied to private copying: lawful access to the work*

With regard to the scope of the private copying exception, in its case law the CJEU has been consistent in stressing that its availability is subject to the prior, lawful, access to the work that is being reproduced. In particular, the CJEU has clarified this point—which is an application of the principle of strict interpretation of exceptions and limitations (on which see Chapter 2, Section 2.11)—in its judgments in *ACI Adam and Others*, C-435/12, and *VCAST*, C-265/16.

The three-step test—In the former, the Court held that Article 5(2)(b) of the InfoSoc Directive, read in conjunction with the three-step test in Article 5(5) (on which see further Section 4), must be interpreted as precluding national legislations that do not distinguish the situation in which the source from which a reproduction for private use is made is lawful from that in which that source is unlawful. As AG Cruz Villalón had observed in his Opinion, although in some Member States (eg, Denmark, Germany, Spain, Italy, Portugal) the law already excludes applicability of the relevant national private copying exception to reproductions from unlawful sources, and some

---

[46] *British Academy of Songwriters, Composers and Authors Musicians' Union and Others, R (on the Application of) v Secretary of State for Business, Innovation and Skills and Another* [2015] EWHC 2041 (Admin) (17 July 2015), para 19. See however E Steyn, 'Private copying: unlawful once again' (2015) 21(7) CTLR 212, 214, noting that it is unlikely that rightholders would seek to enforce their rights in relation to the relatively short period from when section 28B came into force until it was quashed.

[47] See J Smith and H Newton, 'A pause in private copying: judicial review holds the UK private copying exception to be unlawful because there was no evidence to support the decision not to provide compensation to rights holders' (2015) 37(10) EIPR 667, 669, highlighting how, given the number of referrals to the CJEU on national compensation schemes, drafting such a compensation scheme anew might be akin to trying to hit a moving target.

national judges (eg in France[48]) have interpreted the scope of this exception in the sense of excluding its applicability to reproductions from unlawful sources (as it was instead the case of the Netherlands at the time of the referral), whether the private copying exception within Article 5(2)(b) of the InfoSoc Directive might only encompass reproductions from licensed sources was an issue on which the CJEU had not ruled yet.[49]

High level of protection and strict interpretation—The Court observed that Article 5(2)(b) does not address expressly the lawful or unlawful character of the source from which a reproduction may be made. However, when adopting the InfoSoc Directive, one of the objectives of the EU legislature was providing a high level of copyright protection. As a consequence, exceptions and limitations to exclusive rights must be interpreted strictly, and Member States must comply with the three-step test within Article 5(5) of this directive. In compliance with these standards—notably strict interpretation of exceptions and limitations—private copying must be understood as excluding reproductions from unlicensed sources. This conclusion is also compliant with Article 5(5): holding otherwise, ie accepting that reproductions for private uses may be made from an unlawful source, would in fact encourage the circulation of unlicensed works and inevitably reduce the volume of sales or of other lawful transactions relating to the protected works. This would be contrary to exceptions and limitations not being in conflict with a normal exploitation of the work and not unreasonably prejudicing the legitimate interests of rightholders.

Private copying in the cloud—A similar line of reasoning, which appears correct,[50] has been applied also in the context of cloud-based recording of unlawful streams in *VCAST*, C-265/16. This was a reference from the Turin Court of First Instance (Italy) asking about the application of private copying within Article 5(2)(b) of the InfoSoc Directive to cloud-based video-recording services. The background national proceedings concerned the lawfulness of a cloud-based recording service, provided by VCAST, that allowed its customers to make copies of terrestrial TV programme broadcasts including, among other things, those of the claimant, RTI. Importantly, the possibility to make such a recording was granted irrespective of whether customers could lawfully access the programmes terrestrially, ie offline. While for RTI programmes it was generally required that the user be on Italian territory, VCAST's service was not limited to persons who actually have access to programmes broadcast on Italian terrestrial television or even to persons who could theoretically access them.[51]

Under Italian law VCAST activity might be lawful, although the CJEU did not regard this as certain. Nonetheless, the Court deemed it helpful to base its analysis on the assumption that Italian private copying legislation would apply to VCAST's activities. Hence, the question became whether a national law of this kind would be compliant with Article 5(2)(b) of the InfoSoc Directive, read in combination with the three-step test in Article 5(5) therein. After recalling that exceptions and limitations should be

---

[48] Conseil d'État, *Syndicat de l'industrie de matériels audiovisuels*, No 298779/2008, FR:CE SSR:2008:298779.20080711.

[49] Opinion of Advocate General Pedro Cruz Villalón in *ACI Adam and Others*, C-435/12, EU:C:2014:1, para 3.

[50] Cf, however, JP Quintais, 'Private copying and downloading from unlawful sources' (2015) 46(1) IIC 66, 82–4, holding that in *ACI Adam*, C-435/12, the CJEU provided too narrow an interpretation of Article 5(2)(b) and (5) of the InfoSoc Directive, thus failing to provide a fair balance of competing rights and interests. Cf also K Frolova, 'Auteurswhat? Dutch copyright law not tolerated by the CJEU: *ACI Adam BV and Others v Stichting de Thuiskopie and Stichting Onderhandelingen Thuiskopie vergoeding* (C-435/12)' (2014) 36(1) EIPR 738, 741–2, discussing the difficulties associated with determining whether the source from which the reproduction is made is lawful or not.

[51] Opinion of Advocate General Maciej Szpunar in *VCAST*, C-265/16, EU:C:2017:649, para 37.

interpreted strictly, the Court confirmed the finding of the AG—which followed from the holding in *Padawan*, C-467/08—that for the private copying exception to apply it is not required that the beneficiary be the one who directly makes the copy of the copyright work at issue.

However, VCAST's activity was not about reproductions or, at least, was not just about reproductions. More fundamentally, in fact, VCAST did not only organize the recording of TV programmes for its customers but, instead, made them available to them in the first place. VCAST's activity should not be assessed exclusively under the binary distinction reproduction/private copying. It was also necessary to take into account the making available part and, with it, Article 3 of the InfoSoc Directive. The CJEU thus held that:

[39] [A]lthough the private copy exception means that the rightholder must abstain from exercising his exclusive right to authorise or prohibit private copies made by natural persons under the conditions provided for in Article 5(2)(b) of Directive 2001/29, the requirement for a strict interpretation of that exception implies that that rightholder is not deprived of his right to prohibit or authorise access to the works or the subject matter of which those same natural persons wish to make private copies.

[40] It follows from Article 3 of Directive 2001/29 that any communication to the public, including the making available of a protected work or subject matter, requires the rightholder's consent, given that, as is apparent from recital 23 of that directive, the right of communication of works to the public should be understood in a broad sense covering any transmission or retransmission of a work to the public by wire or wireless means, including broadcasting.[52]

The Court turned to the requirements for an act of communication (more appropriately in this case, making available) to the public, and referred extensively to *Reha Training*, C-117/15. It concluded that, without the rightholder's consent, the making of copies of works by means of a service such as that at issue in the background proceedings would undermine the rights of that rightholder. Accordingly, such a remote recording service would not fall within the scope of Article 5(2)(b).[53] This means that VCAST's service could not be provided without the prior authorization of the relevant rightholders, in that its activity would also amount to communication (making available) to the public within Article 3 of the InfoSoc Directive.

The outcome of the *VCAST*, C-265/16, case is not surprising, and highlights once again the absolute centrality of the right of communication/making available to the public, especially in the online environment. Whilst cloud-based video recording services per se are not to be regarded as unlawful, the CJEU decision sets precise boundaries for designing services that would be compatible with EU law.[54] The first condition, stressed in particular in the AG Opinion, is that users of a cloud-based recording service must have prior lawful access to the terrestrial programmes that they wish to record. The second condition is that the provider of a video-recording service may not elude the authorization of the relevant rightholders when what it wishes to provide is a service that allows the recording of content by making it *available for recording* in the first place. This might translate to a *probatio diabolica*, with the result of making the private copying exception unavailable in a situation like the one at issue in *VCAST*, C-265/16.[55]

---

[52] *VCAST*, C-265/16, EU:C:2017:913, paras 39–40.   [53] Ibid, paras 51–52.
[54] For a more problematic view of the judgment's implications, see S Stanley and AP Ringelhann, 'Casting doubt on the legality of remote recording services' (2018) 40(5) EIPR 333, 336–7.
[55] Also discussing the difficulties and legal uncertainties raised by the judgment, see JP Quintais and T Rendas, 'EU copyright law and the Cloud: *VCAST* and the intersection of private copying and

3.2.2 *The fair compensation requirement*

Autonomous concept of EU law—Through its case law, the CJEU has also tackled the notion of fair compensation. In its landmark ruling in *Padawan*, C-467/08, the CJEU clarified at the outset that—similarly to other notions that do not make reference to the national law of individual Member States, 'fair compensation' too is an autonomous concept of EU law (see further Chapter 2, Section 2.2). This entails that, if EU Member States have opted for the introduction of a private copying exception accompanied by a fair compensation requirement, they are not in a position to determine the limits thereof in an inconsistent and unharmonized manner. Holding otherwise would be incompatible with the objective of the InfoSoc Directive to harmonize certain aspects of the law on copyright and related rights in the information society and to ensure that competition in the internal market is not distorted as a result of Member States' different legislation. The EU legislature's aim of achieving the most uniform interpretation possible of the InfoSoc Directive may also be discerned from Recital 32 in the preamble thereto, which calls on the Member States to arrive at a coherent application of the exceptions to and limitations on the right of reproduction, with the aim of ensuring a functioning internal market.[56]

Notion of 'harm'—Besides it being an autonomous concept of EU law that requires uniform interpretation across the EU, the second feature is that fair compensation—and the level of such compensation—is linked to the presence of a harm caused to the holder of the right of reproduction. The Court has clarified this also by referring to the wording of Recitals 35 and 38 in the preamble to the InfoSoc Directive. The purpose of fair compensation is to compensate authors 'adequately' for the use made of their protected works without their authorization. In determining the due amount, account should be taken of the 'possible harm' suffered as a result of the act of reproduction at issue, although prejudice which is 'minimal' does not give rise to a payment obligation. Use of the term 'compensation' implies in fact that the scheme underlying the 'fair compensation' requirement is triggered by the existence of harm to the detriment of the rightholders, which gives rise, in principle, to the obligation to 'compensate' them:[57] the obligation to pay a fair compensation for the making of private copies does not arise in situations in which harm would be so minimal as to be regarded as non-existent.[58]

Responsibility for payment—The third feature of the fair compensation requirement is that responsibility for its payment lies with the subject causing the harm to the relevant rightholder. The CJEU first clarified this in *Padawan*, C-467/08, noting that a fair balance is to be struck between the rights and interests of the rightholders, who are to receive the fair compensation, on one hand, and those of the users of protected works, on the other.[59] The making of copies by natural persons acting in a private capacity is to be regarded as an act likely to cause harm to the author of the work concerned. Hence, 'in principle, it is for that person to make good the harm related to

---

communication to the public' (2018) 13(9) JIPLP 711, 718, and A Ross, '*Vcast Ltd v RTI SpA*—a cloudy judgment re network personal video recorders' (2018) 29(3) Ent L Rev 89, 90–1.

[56] *Padawan*, C-467/08, EU:C:2010:620, paras 33–37.   [57] Ibid, para 41.

[58] On the notion of 'minimal harm', see also *Copydan Båndkopi*, C-463/12, EU:C:2015:144, para 28; *Hewlett-Packard Belgium*, C-572/13, EU:C:2015:750, para 56. For a helpful thematic overview of CJEU case law and private copying levies, see AL Dias Pereira, 'Levies in EU copyright law: an overview of the CJEU's judgments on the fair compensation of private copying and reprography' (2017) 12(7) JIPLP 591, 593–600.

[59] *Padawan*, C-467/08, EU:C:2010:620, para 43.

that copying by financing the compensation which will be paid to the rightholder.'[60] However, there may be practical difficulties associated with identifying private users and obliging them to compensate rightholders for the harm caused to them. Also the harm which may arise from each private use, considered separately, may be minimal. Hence, it does not give rise to an obligation for payment. It is essentially in light of these considerations that the directive leaves to Member States the possibility of establishing a private copying levy for the purposes of financing fair compensation.[61]

Private copying levies—Levies are chargeable not to the private persons making the relevant acts of reproduction, but to those that have the digital reproduction equipment, devices, and media and that, on that basis, in law or in fact, make said equipment available to private users or who provide copying services for them. Under such a system, it is the subjects having that equipment that must provide the payment of the private copying levy.[62] Of course in a levy system users are not directly responsible for the payment of the fair compensation, and this would be contrary to what is required under Recital 31 in the preamble to the InfoSoc Directive. According to the CJEU this is not irremediable: first the making available of blank equipment, devices, and media is the factual precondition for the making of private copies; second, the producers of such equipment, devices, and media are in a position to pass on the private copying levy in the price charged to users.[63]

Technological measures—Finally, the CJEU has clarified that the possibility of applying technological measures under Article 6 of the InfoSoc Directive might render inapplicable the condition relating to fair compensation provided for by Article 5(2)(b) of that directive.[64]

This being the framework envisaged by the InfoSoc Directive and deciphered by the CJEU early on, uncertainties have remained at the national level regarding certain key aspects of the fair compensation requirement. This has prompted national courts to make additional references for a preliminary ruling to the CJEU. In the resulting judgments, further light has been shed on key issues such as funding of fair compensation and beneficiaries of fair compensation.

3.2.3 Financing of fair compensation

Padawan—The InfoSoc Directive, as such, does not explicitly clarify how the financing of fair compensation should be done. Nonetheless, linking such requirement to the harm caused to rightholders by the unlicensed acts of reproduction means that responsibility for such payment lies with those who cause such harm, ie natural persons who make copies for private use and for ends that are neither directly nor indirectly commercial. This approach has been clarified further by the CJEU, starting from the landmark decision in *Padawan*, C-467/08. As recalled in the preceding section, in that case the Court discussed the rationale of the levy system, and its origin within the practical difficulties of identifying private users and obliging them to compensate rightholders for the harm suffered, together with consideration of how harm caused by users considered in their isolation may be minimal and, as such, fall within the scope of the exemption envisaged in Recital 35. A levy system may be applied to producers of blank reproduction equipment, devices, and media, which are made available to users

---

[60] Ibid, para 45.
[61] Ibid, para 46. On the origins of the levy system in Europe, see S Karapapa, *Private Copying* (Routledge:2012), 120–4.
[62] Ibid.   [63] Ibid, para 48.   [64] *VG Wort*, C-457/11, EU:C:2013:426, para 59.

for the making of acts of reproduction. These subjects may pass on the levy in the price charged for such products or services, so that users, in their capacity as beneficiaries of the private copying limitation, ultimately pay the levy.

The need for a 'fair balance'—In any case, a system of private copying levies must comply with the 'fair balance' requirement within the InfoSoc Directive. This implies that an indiscriminate application of levies to all types of digital reproduction equipment, devices, and media would not comply with Article 5(2)(b) of the InfoSoc Directive.[65] It is required, in fact, that such devices and services are likely to cause harm to the rightholder. There must therefore be 'a necessary link between the application of the private copying levy to the digital reproduction equipment, devices and media and their use for private copying'.[66]

Multifunctional devices—This issue has resurfaced in connection with multifunctional devices such as mobile telephone memory cards. In *Copydan Båndkopi*, C-463/12, the CJEU built upon its earlier ruling in *Padawan*, C-467/08, and allowed the application of a private copying levy to such devices, provided that one of the functions of the media, be it merely an ancillary one, enables the operator to use them for that purpose. However, the question of whether the function is a main or an ancillary one and the relative importance of the medium's capacity to make copies are liable to affect the amount of fair compensation payable. Insofar as the prejudice to the rightholder may be regarded as minimal, the making available of such a function need not give rise to an obligation to pay fair compensation.[67]

Throughout the wealth of private copying references, the CJEU has also addressed a number of additional questions, including: whether it might be possible for a Member State to apply a levy indiscriminately; whether the levy system may be funded through a Member State's own general budget; whether exemption from payment of levies can be subjected to an agreement with a collecting society.

Indiscriminate application of levies—With regard to the question of whether a levy system may be applied indiscriminately, the CJEU addressed it in *Amazon.com International Sales and Others*, C-521/11, in the context of a reference for a preliminary ruling concerning the compatibility with EU law of Austrian legislation. This, among other things, provided that a private copying levy would be charged in respect of any recording media capable of reproducing copyright works or works protected by related rights, irrespective of whether the media would be marketed to intermediaries, natural or legal persons for use other than for private purposes, or natural persons for use for private purposes. The CJEU answered that EU law does not preclude legislation, like the statute at issue, that indiscriminately applies a private copying levy on the first placing on the market in its territory, for commercial purposes and for consideration, of recording media suitable for reproduction, if at the same time such legislation envisages a right to reimbursement—which must be effective[68]—of the levies paid in the event that the final use of those media does not meet the criteria set out in Article 5(2)(b) of the InfoSoc Directive.

Financing through a Member State's general budget—Turning to the question of whether a levy system may be funded through a Member State's own general budget, the CJEU addressed this point in *EGEDA and Others*, C-470/14, in the context of a reference for a preliminary ruling concerning the compatibility with EU law of Spanish legislation. In his Opinion in that case, AG Szpunar held that a system of this

---

[65] *Padawan*, C-467/08, EU:C:2010:620, para 53.   [66] Ibid, para 52.
[67] *Copydan Båndkopi*, C-463/12, EU:C:2015:144, para 29.
[68] *Amazon.com International Sales and Others*, C-521/11, EU:C:2013:515, para 31.

kind would not be necessarily incompatible with EU law. This would be so for two reasons: first, the InfoSoc Directive is silent as regards how fair compensation is to be funded; second, earlier CJEU decisions, including the one in *Padawan*, C-467/08, may not be read in the sense of considering fair compensation funded through a state budget incompatible with the InfoSoc Directive.[69] The AG also added that techno-logical evolution is such that discourse around fair compensation for private copying should not crystallize around the topic of levies.[70]

In its judgment, the CJEU departed from the Opinion of AG Szpunar. First, it ob-served that—in light of Recitals 35 and 38 in the preamble to the InfoSoc Directive—the possibility for Member States to introduce a private copying exception is linked to the contextual introduction of a fair compensation scheme. This is 'triggered by the existence of harm caused to rightholders, which gives rise, in principle, to the ob-ligation to "compensate" them'.[71] Furthermore the provision of a fair compensation scheme imposes on Member States an obligation to achieve a certain result, this being to guarantee that the fair compensation intended to compensate rightholders is actu-ally recovered. The InfoSoc Directive leaves Member States a significant freedom as to how this result is to be achieved. This includes determining who has to pay that fair compensation, in what form, in what amount, etc.[72] In principle, nothing precludes the establishment of a fair compensation scheme financed by the general state budget of a Member State in lieu of a levy system. However, it is ultimately the persons who reproduce the protected works or subject matter without the prior authorization of the rightholder concerned, and who therefore cause harm to them, who have to make good that harm by financing the fair compensation provided for that purpose. This would not be the case of a scheme—like the Spanish one—financed by the generality of taxpayers. Indeed, 'such a scheme for financing the fair compensation from the General State Budget of the Member State concerned is not such as to guarantee that the cost of that compensation is ultimately borne solely by the users of private copies.'[73] The Court thus concluded that Article 5(2)(b) of the InfoSoc Directive precludes a fair compensation scheme financed from the general state budget in such a way that it is not possible to ensure that the cost of that compensation is borne by the users of private copies.

Exemption from payment—With regard to the issue whether exemption from the payment of levies may be subjected to a prior agreement with a collecting society, the CJEU addressed this point in *Microsoft Mobile Sales International and Others*, C-110/15. In that case, the Court had to consider the compatibility with EU law of Italian legislation, which provided for a requirement of this kind. To answer this question, the Court noted that the two principles that would guide the response would be: first, that levy must not be applied to the supply of reproduction equipment, devices, and media to persons other than natural persons for purposes clearly unrelated to private copying;[74] second, that there must be an effective right of reimbursement which allows for the repayment of the levy unduly paid.[75] The Court concluded that Article 5(2)(b) precludes national legislation like the one in place in Italy at the time of the referral.

---

[69] Opinion of Advocate General Maciej Szpunar in *EGEDA and Others*, C-470/14, EU:C:2016:24, paras 29–32.

[70] Ibid, para 47.   [71] *EGEDA and Others*, C-470/14, EU:C:2016:418, para 19.

[72] Ibid, paras 21–23.   [73] Ibid, para 41.

[74] *Microsoft Mobile Sales International and Others*, C-110/15, EU:C:2016:717, para 36, referring to *Copydan Båndkopi*, C-463/12, EU:C:2015:144, para 47, and the case law cited therein.

[75] *Microsoft Mobile Sales International and Others*, C-110/15, EU:C:2016:717, para 37, recalling *Amazon.com International Sales and Others*, C-521/11, EU:C:2013:515, para 36, and *Copydan Båndkopi*, C-463/12, EU:C:2015:144, para 52.

3.2.4 Beneficiaries of the fair compensation

The CJEU has not only tackled issues relating to financing of fair compensation and responsibility for its payment, but also addressed who the beneficiary of such payment should be. The CJEU has had the opportunity to tackle this issue on two occasions: *Luksan*, C-277/10, and *Hewlett-Packard Belgium*, C-572/13.

Luksan—This was a reference for a preliminary ruling from the Vienna Commercial Court (Austria) asking, among other things, whether the right to fair compensation for private copying vests by operation of law, directly and originally, in the principal director of a cinematographic work, in his capacity as author or co-author thereof. To answer this question, the CJEU deemed it necessary to determine, first, whom the InfoSoc Directive would regard as the holders of the right of reproduction within Article 2 therein, of which private copying represents a limitation. It highlighted that, among other things, such a right belongs to authors in respect of their works and producers in respect of the first fixation of films:

> It follows that both the principal director, in his capacity as author of the cinematographic work, and the producer, as the person responsible for the investment necessary for the production of that work, must be regarded as being the holders, by operation of law, of the reproduction right.[76]

The implication is that the director of a cinematographic work is entitled to receive fair compensation within the meaning of Article 5(2)(b) of the InfoSoc Directive.[77]

Rationale of fair compensation requirement—The CJEU also addressed whether a national law (like the Austrian one) may envisage a presumption of transfer, in favour of the producer of a cinematographic work, of the remuneration rights vesting in the principal director of that work, including the fair compensation requirement for private copying. It answered in the negative, considering both *whom* the directive acknowledges as holders of the right of reproduction[78] and the language of Article 5(2)(b). The latter allowed the Court to conclude that in the Member States which have decided to establish the private copying exception, the rightholders concerned must, in return, receive payment of fair compensation. The wording of the provision is clear: the EU legislature did not wish to allow the persons concerned to be able to waive payment of the compensation owed to them.[79] The rationale of the fair compensation requirement is such that, as the Court reiterated, Member States are under an obligation to ensure that the fair compensation intended to compensate the rightholders harmed for the prejudice sustained is actually recovered.[80]

Hewlett-Packard Belgium—This approach was consistently (and correctly) followed in the subsequent judgment in *Hewlett-Packard Belgium*, C-572/13. This ruling originated as a reference from the Brussels Court of Appeal (Belgium) asking, among other things, whether Member States may allocate *ab initio* part (half in the specific case of Belgium) of the fair compensation due to rightholders to the publishers of works created by authors, the publishers being under no obligation to ensure that the authors benefit, even indirectly, from some of the compensation of which they have been deprived.

Publishers as beneficiaries of fair compensation—The CJEU answered this question in the negative, holding that publishers are not among the reproduction rightholders listed in Article 2 of the InfoSoc Directive. It then recalled how the rationale of the

---

[76] *Luksan*, C-277/10, EU:C:2012:65, para 91.   [77] Ibid, para 94.
[78] Ibid, paras 90–91.   [79] Ibid, para 100.
[80] Ibid, para 106, referring to *Stichting de Thuiskopie*, C-462/09, EU:C:2011:397, para 34.

fair compensation requirement is compensating the harm suffered by rightholders as a result of the unauthorized reproduction of their works and protected subject matter. Not only are publishers excluded from the list of exclusive reproduction rightholders pursuant to Article 2 of the InfoSoc Directive, but they are not subject to any harm for the purpose of those limitations either. As such, the rationale underlying the fair compensation requirement would not justify the allocation of part of such compensation to them.[81] As it will be explained further in Chapter 8, Section 3, the outcome of the reference in *Hewlett-Packard Belgium*, C-572/13, has been regarded as undermining the activity of publishers, with the result that legislation has been proposed to remedy such a situation and—substantially—expunge the CJEU ruling in this case.

4. The Three-Step Test

Origin of the InfoSoc three-step test—Article 5(5) of the InfoSoc Directive requires that the exceptions and limitations provided for in preceding paragraphs of that provision shall only be applied in certain special cases which do not conflict with a normal exploitation of the work or other subject matter and do not unreasonably prejudice the legitimate interests of the rightholder. Despite precedents in the Berne Convention (Article 9(2)) and the Agreement on Trade-Related Aspects of Intellectual Property Rights (TRIPS, Article 13), the InfoSoc three-step test is derived from the one contained in the WIPO Internet Treaties (Article 10 of WIPO Copyright Treaty and Article 16(2) of the WIPO Phonograms and Performances Treaty), which the EU legislature implemented into the EU legal order by adopting the InfoSoc Directive.[82]

Before the InfoSoc Directive was adopted, other copyright directives were designed to include references to the international three-step test: Article 6(3) of the 1991 Software Directive (now Article 6(3) of the Software Directive) states that the provisions of that article may not be interpreted in such a way as to allow its application to be used in a manner which unreasonably prejudices the rightholder's legitimate interests or conflicts with a normal exploitation of the computer program. In a similar sense, Article 6(3) of the Database Directive provides that, in accordance with the Berne Convention (which only refers to the three-step test in relation to exceptions to the right of reproduction), exceptions to restricted acts done in relation to databases may not be interpreted in such a way as to allow uses of a protected database which unreasonably prejudice the rightholder's legitimate interests or conflict with its normal exploitation.

Addressees of the three-step test—Besides the issue of whether it is the presence of the three-step test that requires exceptions and limitations to be strictly interpreted (on the CJEU's approach to this matter, see Chapter 2, Section 2.11), another question that has arisen is that of the addressees of the InfoSoc three-step test: is it just national legislatures which have to comply with it when transposing relevant exceptions and limitations into their own legal regimes, or also courts when interpreting the

---

[81] *Hewlett-Packard Belgium*, C-572/13, EU:C:2015:750, paras 44–49. Prior to the CJEU judgment, the European Copyright Society too had called on the Court to apply the author principle: European Copyright Society, *Opinion on the reference to the CJEU in Case C-572/13 Hewlett-Packard Belgium SPRL v. Reprobel SCRL* (5 September 2015), available at <https://europeancopyrightsociety.org/opinion-on-reprobel/> (last accessed 15 August 2018).

[82] See, however, with regard to the proposal for what would eventually become the InfoSoc Directive, T Heide, 'The Berne three-step test and the proposed Copyright Directive' (1999) 21(3) EIPR 105, 107–9.

scope of relevant exceptions—whether at the national or EU level? Neither the text of the directive nor the relevant *travaux préparatoires* provide an explicit answer.[83] Some commentators thus believe that Article 5(5) does not provide 'grounds which can be raised in the course of private litigation',[84] and that only national legislatures are to be regarded as the addressees of the InfoSoc three-step test.[85]

However, there are indications—at the level of both the CJEU and national courts—that the InfoSoc three-step test should not be intended as limited to national legislatures when implementing relevant provisions contained in Article 5 of this directive in their own legal systems. As explained more at length elsewhere,[86] CJEU case law on Article 5(5) suggests in fact that:

- It is not intended to affect the substantive content of the exceptions contained in Articles 5(1)–(4), and cannot therefore extend their scope;[87]
- If acts clearly fall within one of those exceptions, they satisfy Article 5(5);[88]
- In any case Article 5 exceptions must be construed in light of Article 5(5);[89]
- Although Article 5(5) takes effect only at the time that the exceptions are applied by the Member States;[90] the acts of the defendant in question must satisfy the requirements of Article 5(5).[91]

Stichting Brein—The recent judgment in *Stichting Brein*, C-527/15, is an enlightening application of these principles. One of the questions referred by the District Court of Central Netherlands was whether the making of a temporary reproduction by an end user during the streaming of a copyright work from a website where that copyright-protected work is offered without the authorization of the rightholder(s) would fall within the scope of the temporary copies exemption within Article 5(1) of the InfoSoc Directive. The CJEU answered in the negative, stating that such a question must be answered in light of both the conditions set in Article 5(1) of the InfoSoc Directive and the three-step test in Article 5(5). Agreeing with the Opinion of AG Campos

---

[83] J Griffiths, 'The "three-step test" in European copyright law—problems and solutions' (2009) 2009/4 IPQ 428, 431; MRF Senftleben, *Copyright, Limitations, and the Three-Step Test. An Analysis of the Three-Step Test in International and EC Copyright Law* (Kluwer Law International:2004), 279; and L Guibault, G Westkamp, and T Rieber-Mohn, *Study on the implementation and effect in Member States' laws of Directive 2001/29/EC on the harmonisation of certain aspects of copyright and related rights in the Information Society* (2012), Amsterdam Law School Research Paper No 2012-28, 57.

[84] W Cornish, D Llewelyn, and T Aplin, *Intellectual Property: Patents, Copyright, Trade Marks and Allied Rights* (Sweet & Maxwell:2013), 8th edn, §12.37.

[85] C Geiger, 'From Berne to national law, via the Copyright Directive: the dangerous mutations of the three-step test' (2007) 29(12) EIPR 486, 488

[86] R Arnold and E Rosati, 'Are national courts the addressees of the InfoSoc three-step test?' (2015) 10(10) JIPLP 741, 744–7.

[87] *ACI Adam and Others*, C-435/12, EU:C:2014:254, para 26; *Eugen Ulmer*, C-117/13, EU:C:2014:2196, para 47; *Copydan Båndkopi*, C-463/12, EU:C:2015:144, para 90.

[88] *Infopaq International*, C-302/10, EU:C:2012:16, paras 55–57.

[89] *Infopaq International*, C-5/08, EU:C:2009:465, para 58; *OSA*, C-351/12, EU:C:2014:110, para 40; *Eugen Ulmer*, C-117/13, EU:C:2014:2196, para 47; *Stichting Brein*, C-527/15, EU:C:2017:300, para 63. In the same sense (in relation to Article 10(3) of the Rental and Lending Rights Directive), see also *Phonographic Performance (Ireland)*, C-162/10, EU:C:2012:141.

[90] *Stichting de Thuiskopie*, C-462/09, EU:C:2011:397, paras 21–22 and 33; *Painer*, C-145/10, EU:C:2011:798, paras 101 and 104–110; *ACI Adam and Others*, C-435/12, EU:C:2014:254, para 25.

[91] *Football Association Premier League and Others*, C-403/08 and C-429/08, EU:C:2011:631, paras 180–181; *Public Relations Consultants Association*, C-360/13, EU:C:2014:1195, paras 53–63; *Eugen Ulmer*, C-117/13, EU:C:2014:2196, paras 52 and 56; *Stichting Brein*, C-527/15, EU:C:2017:300, paras 65–66 and 69–71.

Sánchez-Bordona,[92] the Court held that unauthorized streaming services usually result in a diminution of lawful transactions relating to the protected works, which would cause unreasonable prejudice to copyright holders. Hence, those acts do not satisfy the conditions set out in Article 5(1) and (5) of the InfoSoc Directive.[93]

4.1 The three-step test before national courts

Also national courts have discussed and made direct application of the InfoSoc three-step test, irrespective of whether the language of the three-step test has been transposed into national law.[94] In what follows, three examples are provided from jurisdictions (Italy, Sweden, and the UK, respectively) that have traditionally been part of different copyright traditions and adopted diverging approaches towards the transposition of the language of Article 5(5) of the InfoSoc Directive into their own legal systems.[95]

Italy—Italian copyright law contains an express reference to the three-step test. Article 71-*nonies* of the Italian Copyright Act provides that all exceptions and limitations shall neither be in conflict with a normal exploitation of works or other subject matter, nor shall they unreasonably prejudice the legitimate interests of the rightholder. A recent application of the three-step test was made in a case decided by the Rome Court of First Instance[96] concerning applicability of copyright exceptions for news reporting and criticism/review (Articles 65 and 70 of the Italian Copyright Act, respectively) to the reproduction and making available on a newspaper's website of extracts of TV programmes having the character of pure entertainment. The Rome court noted how the exceptions in Articles 65 and 70 of the Italian Copyright Act have an exceptional and special character compared to the principle according to which the author has the exclusive right to exploit economically their work, and would not be applicable—due to their language and scope—to the case at issue. As such, these provisions must only be applied in the cases expressly provided for by the law and as long as they are justified in protecting interests that are recognized by the Italian Constitution, for example, freedom of expression/information within Article 21 therein, and have an equal—if not superior—rank to copyright protection. The court also recalled that in *ACI Adam*, C-435/12, the CJEU suggested that copyright exceptions must be applied by courts in compliance with the three-step test in Article 5(5) of the InfoSoc Directive.

Sweden—Sweden is a Member State that has not directly transposed the language of the three-step test into its own law. Yet, this did not prevent the Swedish Supreme Court from applying directly the substance of Article 5(5) of the InfoSoc Directive when deciding a case concerning 'freedom of panorama' under section 24(1) of the Swedish Act.[97] This provision states:

---

[92] Opinion of Advocate General Manuel Campos Sánchez-Bordona in *Stichting Brein*, C-527/15, EU:C:2016:938, in particular paras 80–81.

[93] *Stichting Brein*, C-527/15, EU:C:2017:300, paras 70–71.

[94] Guibault, Westkamp, and Rieber-Mohn, *Study on the implementation and effect in Member States' laws of Directive 2001/29/EC* §2.3.3.

[95] With regard to more or less restrictive applications of the three-step test in France, the Netherlands, Belgium, Germany, Switzerland, and Spain, see Griffiths, 'The "three-step test"' 433–40, and, with regard to France, also C Geiger, 'The three-step test, a threat to a balanced copyright law?' (2006) 37(6) IIC 683, 684–7.

[96] Tribunale di Roma, decision 18413/2016, *RTI—Reti Televisive Italiane v Gruppo Editoriale L'Espresso*.

[97] Högsta domstolen, *Bildupphovsrätt i Sverige v Wikimedia Sverige*, Ö 849-15, 4 April 2016.

Works of fine art may be reproduced in pictorial form

1. if they are permanently located outdoors on, or at, a public place
2. if the purpose is to advertise an exhibition or a sale of the works of fine art but only to the extent necessary for the promotion of the exhibition or the sale or
3. if they form part of a collection, in catalogues, however not in digital form.[98]

In 2016, the Supreme Court ruled that this provision does not go as far as allowing an online publicly accessible database to make photographs of artworks located permanently outdoors or in public spaces available to the public. Whether the objective pursued is commercial or not is irrelevant. The Supreme Court also clarified that the provisions in the Swedish Copyright Act should be read in light of the InfoSoc Directive, which mandates a high level of protection of copyright—'especially in the digital environment'—and also seeks to balance the rights of authors with the public interest in accessing and using works. With regard to the system of exceptions and limitations in Article 5 of the InfoSoc Directive, the Supreme Court recalled how this contains an exhaustive list of optional exceptions and limitations that Member States may adopt into their own legal systems. The court also noted how the three-step test in Article 5(5) mandates that exceptions and limitations be applied: (1) in certain special cases; (2) which do not conflict with a normal exploitation of the work or other subject matter; and (3) do not unreasonably prejudice the legitimate interests of the rightholder.

The Swedish court applied directly the three-step test to interpret the scope of Article 24(1) of the Swedish Copyright Act. It considered the individual steps in the three-step test, and held that: 'certain special cases' means that the exception at hand must be clearly defined and precise in scope; as regards the 'normal exploitation' of the work, this should take into consideration not only current uses of a work, but also the uses that could become possible thanks to technological advancement; as to the notion of 'legitimate interests', these should be assessed in light of whether a restriction in copyright exclusive rights would be justified to safeguard a stronger general interest. As such, it is a proportionality assessment.

Following these remarks, the Supreme Court considered the rationale and wording of Article 24(1) of the Swedish Copyright Act. It held that this provision is rooted within the public interest to reproduce freely subject matter placed outdoors or in public spaces. The term 'image' means that the artwork at issue may be reproduced by painting, drawing, photograph, or other two-dimensional technique. The exception would also apply if the artwork at hand were the main subject of such reproduction (eg a postcard). Unlike other Nordic countries, the Swedish legislature decided not to distinguish between commercial and non-commercial uses of this type of image.

The Supreme Court held that Article 24(1) and the notion of 'image' therein should be interpreted in light of the three-step test in Article 5(5) of the InfoSoc Directive. It noted how analogue dissemination of images of artworks might not be particularly prejudicial to relevant rightholders. However, things are different when it comes to online dissemination by means of a publicly accessible database. The making available of images of artworks through publicly accessible online databases would unreasonably prejudice the rightholders' legitimate interests, in that it would deprive them of potential revenue streams arising from the exploitation of such dissemination channels.

---

[98] The translation from Swedish is the one found at <http://www.wipo.int/edocs/lexdocs/laws/en/se/se124en.pdf> (last accessed 15 August 2018).

To this end, the public interest underlying the non-profit and open nature of the defendant's database would not offset the prejudice caused to rightholders.

UK—The UK is also a Member State that has not transposed the language of the three-step test into its own law. At the time of implementing the InfoSoc Directive into its own legal system, the UK government held the view that relevant copyright exceptions already complied with Article 5(5).[99] This has however resulted in very little consideration of the three-step test in UK case law. Only the decisions in *Forensic Telecommunications Services v Chief Constable of West Yorkshire*[100] (2011) and *England and Wales Cricket Board v Tixdaq* (2016) provide some meaningful considerations thereof. In particular, the latter was a case concerning whether the unauthorized re-production and making available of short extracts of television broadcasts of cricket matches would amount to a copyright infringement or whether, instead and among other things, the defence of fair dealing for the purpose of reporting current events within section 30(2) CDPA would apply.

The High Court of England and Wales ruled against the defendants, holding that their conduct could not be regarded as fair dealing within such provision. In reaching its conclusion, the court also addressed the individual steps in the three-step test. In particular, it noted that 'conflict with a normal exploitation of the work or other subject matter' refers to exploitation of the work by the copyright owner, whether directly or through licensees. This requires:

> consideration of potential future ways in which the copyright owner may extract value from the work as well as the ways in which the copyright owner currently does so. On the other hand, it also embraces normative considerations ie the extent to which the copyright owner should be able to control exploitation of the kind in question having regard to countervailing interests such as freedom of speech.[101]

Considering the third step (that the exception at hand must not 'unreasonably prejudice the legitimate interests of the rightholder'), the court found that:

> [a]lthough this is often treated as a separate and additional requirement to the second step, it has also been forcefully argued that it qualifies the second step. In other words, it indicates that it is not sufficient for an exception not to apply that there is some conflict with the copyright owner's legitimate interests, including the copyright owner's normal exploitation of the work. Rather, the exception can apply unless those interests are unreasonably prejudiced. This requires consideration of proportionality, and a balance to be struck between the copyright owners' legitimate interests and the countervailing interests served by the exception.[102]

Role of the InfoSoc three-step test—In conclusion, as both CJEU and national case law demonstrates, the three-step test in Article 5(5) of the InfoSoc Directive informs the interpretation of Article 5 exceptions, their implementation, as well as the application of resulting national provisions. In this sense, even if a certain national law does not incorporate the language of the three-step test, this should not be intended as precluding the parties to judicial proceedings from invoking it before a national court.[103]

---

[99] Arnold and Rosati, 'Are national courts?' 743.
[100] *Forensic Telecommunications Services Ltd v West Yorkshire Police and Another* [2011] EWHC 2892 (Ch) (9 November 2011).
[101] *England and Wales Cricket Board Ltd and Another v Tixdaq Ltd and Another* [2016] EWHC 575 (Ch) (18 March 2016), para 91.
[102] Ibid, para 92.
[103] *Contra*, H Cohen Jehoram, 'Is there a hidden agenda behind the general non-implementation of the EU three-step test?' (2009) 31(8) EIPR 408, 409.

Conclusion

This chapter has focused on a number of selected aspects relating to exceptions and limitations within Article 5 of the InfoSoc Directive. It has provided an illustration of how the CJEU, by relying on certain key standards, has shaped a harmonized approach in this area of copyright, by strengthening the effects of Article 5 through an expansive reading of its competence as interpreter of EU law. The result has been, on the one hand, the development of a number of EU concepts that have increased uniformity of approaches across the EU and, on the other hand, the awareness that Member States' transpositions efforts have not always been consistent with the harmonization objectives pursued by the EU legislature. Also, clarification of the role of the three-step test by the Court, as being aimed not just at national legislatures but also courts in individual EU Member States, should be seen as an expression of such a harmonizing effort.

6

Enforcement of Copyright

Introduction

Moving from a rather vague and potentially ambiguous legislative framework, the CJEU has also had the opportunity to develop a substantial body of case law on the enforcement of copyright (and, more generally, intellectual property rights). Among other things, the Court has been asked on a number of occasions to clarify the law on a particular type of remedy, this being injunctions against intermediaries. CJEU case law has also touched upon other issues of enforcement, including costs and damages, as well as private international law issues, including applicable law (to a limited extent) and jurisdiction in copyright proceedings. The resulting enforcement framework owes most to CJEU interpretative efforts, rather than the wording of legislative provisions considered in their isolation.

1. Intermediary Injunctions: The Legislative Framework

Safe harbours and prohibition of general monitoring obligations—EU law provides that, in principle and insofar as certain conditions are satisfied, information society service providers are not liable for infringements committed by users of their services. Inspired in part by relevant provisions in the US Digital Millennium Copyright Act 1998, Articles 12, 13, and 14 of the E-commerce Directive set out 'safe harbours' for, respectively, mere conduit, caching, and hosting providers.

Article 15 of the same directive prohibits Member States from imposing on information society service providers, when providing the services covered by Articles 12, 13, and 14 therein, a general obligation to monitor the information which they transmit or store, or a general obligation actively to seek facts or circumstances indicating illegal activity:

1. Member States shall not impose a general obligation on providers, when providing the services covered by Articles 12, 13 and 14, to monitor the information which they transmit or store, nor a general obligation actively to seek facts or circumstances indicating illegal activity.
2. Member States may establish obligations for information society service providers promptly to inform the competent public authorities of alleged illegal activities undertaken or information provided by recipients of their service or obligations to communicate to the competent authorities, at their request, information enabling the identification of recipients of their service with whom they have storage agreements.

Injunctions against intermediaries—While being without prejudice to the provisions of the E-commerce Directive (Recitals 16 and 20 of the InfoSoc Directive), Article 8(3) the InfoSoc Directive sets an obligation for EU Member States to ensure that 'rightholders are in a position to apply for an injunction against intermediaries whose services are used by a third party to infringe a copyright or related right'. A provision to the same effect is available for intellectual property rights other than copyright in the third sentence of Article 11 of the Enforcement Directive, which also contains general principles on intermediary injunctions. Article 3 of the Enforcement Directive states in fact that measures, procedures, and remedies necessary to ensure the enforcement of the intellectual property rights shall be 'fair and equitable and shall not be unnecessarily complicated or costly, or entail unreasonable time-limits or unwarranted delays'. It mandates that '[t]hose measures, procedures and remedies shall also be effective, proportionate and dissuasive and shall be applied in such a manner as to avoid the creation of barriers to legitimate trade and to provide for safeguards against their abuse'.

The reason why intermediaries should be involved in the enforcement process through injunctions against them—and why this proves particularly helpful in the online context—is explained by Recital 59 in the preamble to the InfoSoc Directive:

In the digital environment, in particular, the services of intermediaries may increasingly be used by third parties for infringing activities. In many cases such intermediaries are *best placed* to bring such infringing activities to an end. (emphasis added)

The possibility for rightholders to seek an injunction against an intermediary is without prejudice to other available sanctions and remedies, and is irrespective of any liability of the intermediary targeted by the injunction. Similarly to other intellectual property rights (Recital 23 in the preamble to the Enforcement Directive), for copyright intermediary injunctions too, the relevant conditions and modalities are left to the national law of the Member States (Recital 59 in the preamble to the InfoSoc Directive).

Fundamental rights—When envisaging enforcement measures, one should not overlook that an appropriate balance must be struck between different rights and interests, notably those rights that the EU Charter (which, as already mentioned, has the value of primary source of EU law) recognizes as fundamental rights. They are, in particular:

- The protection of intellectual property within the fundamental right to property (Article 17(2));
- Freedom to conduct a business, especially on the side of an intermediary targeted by an injunction (Article 16);
- Freedom of internet users to access and exchange information as part of their freedom of expression and information (Article 11), and the respect of their private life (Article 7) and personal data (Article 8).

1.1 Intermediary injunctions: the standards established through CJEU case law

Despite a rich but not particularly detailed legislative framework, the task of filling its gaps has been undertaken by the CJEU. Through a number of decisions—notably those (in chronological order) in *L'Oréal and Others*, C-324/09 (2011), *Scarlet Extended*, C-70/10 (2011), *SABAM*, C-360/10 (2011), *UPC Telekabel Wien*, C-314/12 (2014), *Mc Fadden*, C-484/14 (2016), *Tommy Hilfiger*, C-494/15 (2016), and *Stichting Brein*, C-610/15 (2017)—the CJEU has provided five key standards.[1] They are:

i. The notion of 'intermediary' is broad;
ii. Injunctions may be aimed at repressing existing infringements and preventing further infringements;

---

[1] The analysis which follows builds upon E Rosati, 'Intermediary IP injunctions in the EU and UK experiences: when less (harmonization) is more?' (2017) 12(4) JIPLP 338, 339–42.

iii. Injunctions must comply with various legislative sources and standards;
iv. Blocking injunctions are allowed under EU law;
v. An intermediary may be primarily (directly) liable together with users of its services.

The meaning and content of these standards is explained in the following sections.

1.1.1 The notion of 'intermediary' is broad

In light of relevant CJEU case law, the notion of 'intermediary' itself is both loose and broad: for an economic operator to be considered as an 'intermediary' it is sufficient that they provide—even among other things—a service capable of being used by one or more other persons in order to infringe one or more intellectual property rights.

Mc Fadden—In *Mc Fadden*, C-484/14, the CJEU had been asked to clarify whether a service consisting of the making available to the general public of an open wireless communication network free of charge could be regarded as an 'information society service' within the meaning of Article 12(1) of the E-commerce Directive. By means of a combined reading of relevant provisions in Directive 98/48,[2] Article 57 TFEU, and the E-commerce Directive, the CJEU concluded that the economic nature of a service provided, even free of charge, may be inferred from factors other than the fact that the service is paid for by those for whom it is performed,[3] for example, by the fact that its free nature is justified by the purpose of advertising goods sold and services provided by that service provider.[4] In any case, qualification as an information society service and eligibility for the safe harbour protection would not shield the intermediary at issue from certain monetary claims.[5]

Tommy Hilfiger—In *Tommy Hilfiger*, C-494/15, the CJEU had been asked to consider whether a tenant of market halls who sublets the various sales points situated in those halls to market traders, some of whom use their pitches in order to sell counterfeit goods of branded products, falls within the concept of 'an intermediary whose services are being used by a third party to infringe an intellectual property right' within the meaning of the third sentence in Article 11 of the Enforcement Directive and, if so, whether they are subject to the measures envisaged by that provision. Recalling its earlier judgment in *UPC Telekabel Wien*, C-314/12,[6] the CJEU noted that for an economic operator to fall within the classification of 'intermediary' it is sufficient that they provide—even among other things—a service capable of being used by one or more other persons in order to infringe one or more intellectual property rights. The Court concluded that injunctions ordered pursuant to the third sentence in Article 11 of the Enforcement Directive are also available against operators of physical marketplaces and, while Member States are free to determine the conditions to be met and the procedure to be followed for injunctions in these

---

[2] Directive 98/48/EC of the European Parliament and of the Council of 20 July 1998 amending Directive 98/34/EC laying down a procedure for the provision of information in the field of technical standards and regulations, OJ L 217, 5 August 1998, 18–26.
[3] *Mc Fadden*, C-484/14, EU:C:2016:689, para 41, referring to *Papasavvas and Others*, C-291/13, EU:C:2014:2209, paras 28–29.
[4] *Mc Fadden*, C-484/14, EU:C:2016:689, para 42.
[5] Ibid, paras 72–79. For a criticism of this conclusion, see M Husovec, 'Holey cap! CJEU drills (yet) another hole in the e-Commerce Directive's safe harbours' (2017) 12(2) JIPLP 115, 118–20.
[6] *UPC Telekabel Wien*, C-314/12, EU:C:2014:192, paras 32 and 35.

cases, the principles set out in Article 3 of the Enforcement Directive would also be applicable to such situations.[7]

Notion of 'intermediary'—Despite the Court's attempts at clarifying the notion of 'intermediary', doubts remain as to the requirements for such a classification in the context of injunctive relief. According to some commentators, the fact that Article 8(3) of the InfoSoc Directive and the third sentence of Article 11 of the Enforcement Directive refer to the use of the services in question by a third party to infringe copyright/an intellectual property right means that it need not necessarily be the *infringer* itself that (directly) uses the services. In any case, not just *any* third-party service provider is included: in light of its ordinary meaning, the word 'intermediary' implies the need for an intermediation relationship between the infringer (primary or secondary) and the intermediary's customers.[8] In *LSG-Gesellschaft zur Wahrnehmung von Leistungsschutzrechten*, C-557/07, the CJEU considered that access providers which merely provide users with internet access, without offering other services or exercising any control—whether de jure or de facto—over the services which users make use of, must be regarded as 'intermediaries' within the meaning of Article 8(3) of the InfoSoc Directive.[9] The overarching criterion and limit remain in any case the ability of the intermediary at issue to put an end to the infringement.[10]

1.1.2 Injunctions may be aimed at repressing existing infringements and preventing further infringements

L'Oréal and Others—This is a standard that the CJEU clarified in its landmark decision in *L'Oréal and Others*, C-324/09, in relation to injunctions under the third sentence in Article 11 of the Enforcement Directive. Among other things, the referring court had asked the CJEU whether this provision allows injunctions aimed not just at repressing existing infringements of intellectual property rights, but also preventing future infringements of those rights.

Features of injunctions under third sentence of Article 11—The CJEU clarified at the outset how the injunctions referred to in the third sentence of Article 11 differ from those referred to in the first sentence of that provision: while the latter directly target infringers and seek to prohibit the continuation of an infringement, the former relate to the 'more complex' situation of intermediaries whose services are used by third parties to infringe. Also taking into account the overall objective of the Enforcement Directive, this being to ensure an effective protection of intellectual property rights,[11] alongside the provision in Article 18 of the E-commerce Directive and Recital 24 in the preamble to the Enforcement Directive, the Court concluded—contrary to the more limited view expressed by AG Jääskinen in his Opinion[12]—that the jurisdiction conferred by the third sentence in Article 11 of the Enforcement Directive allows

---

[7] *Tommy Hilfiger*, C-494/15, EU:C:2016:528, paras 23, 32, and 36.

[8] FG Wilman, 'A decade of private enforcement of intellectual property rights under IPR Enforcement Directive 2004/48: where do we stand (and where might we go)?' (2017) 42(4) EL Rev 509, 521.

[9] *LSG-Gesellschaft zur Wahrnehmung von Leistungsschutzrechten*, C-557/07, EU:C:2009:107, para 43.

[10] M Husovec and M Peguera, 'Much ado about little—privately litigated internet disconnection injunctions' (2015) 46(1) IIC 10, 13.

[11] *L'Oréal and Others*, C-324/09, EU:C:2011:474, paras 128–129 and 131, referring to *Promusicae*, C-275/06, EU:C:2008:54, para 43.

[12] Opinion of Advocate General Niilo Jääskinen in *L'Oréal SA and Others*, C-324/09, EU:C:2010:757, paras 175 and 181.

national courts to order an intermediary to take measures that contribute not only to the termination of infringements committed through its services, but also preventing further infringements.[13] This conclusion is in line with the overall framework established by the E-commerce Directive: Articles 12(3) (in relation to mere conduit providers), 13(2) (in relation to caching providers), and 14(3) clarify in fact that a court or administrative authority, in accordance with Member States' legal systems, may require the service provider at issue to terminate or *prevent* an infringement.

Preventive and voluntary filtering—Following *L'Oréal and Others*, C-324/09, some commentators have discussed the opportunity for intermediaries to consider preventive action to avoid being subject to an injunction in the future.[14] This is something that the High Court of England and Wales also tackled in the context of the first application for a trade mark blocking injunction in that country, *Cartier v BskyB* (see further Chapter 7, Section 6.2). There, the court recalled that the stance in Recital 59 in the preamble to the InfoSoc Directive postulates that the economic logic of granting injunctions against intermediaries such as ISPs is that they are the 'lowest cost avoiders' of infringement. Accordingly, 'it is economically more efficient to require intermediaries to take action to prevent infringement occurring via their services than it is to require rightholders to take action directly against infringers'.[15] Overall, this would support the idea that voluntary implementation by intermediaries of filtering systems would have its own advantages.[16]

1.1.3 Injunctions must comply with various legislative sources and standards

In *L'Oréal and Others*, C-324/09, the CJEU also recalled that the conditions to be met and the procedures to be followed when issuing an injunction against an intermediary are a matter for national law. In any case, domestic rules must be designed in such a way that the objective pursued by the Enforcement Directive may be achieved, including ensuring—as Article 3(2) mandates—that the measures concerned are effective and proportionate (these being also general principles of EU law, as discussed further in Chapter 2, Sections 2.3 and 2.4), as well as dissuasive.[17]

Filtering in *Scarlet Extended* and *SABAM*—The CJEU considered the interplay between intermediary injunctions, Article 15 of the E-commerce Directive, and fundamental rights in its twin decisions in *Scarlet Extended*, C-70/10, and *SABAM*, C-360/10, albeit to a more limited extent than AG Cruz Villalón had done in his Opinion in the former case.[18] Both references for a preliminary ruling from Belgium (the Brussels

---

[13] *L'Oréal and Others*, C-324/09, EU:C:2011:474, paras 131–134. According to E Bonadio, 'Trade marks in online marketplaces: the CJEU's stance in *L'Oreal v eBay*' (2012) 18(2) CTLR 37, 41, this conclusion goes beyond a literal interpretation of Article 11 of the Enforcement Directive, but holding otherwise would have been at odds with both Recital 24 and Article 3(2) therein. In a similar sense, see T Headdon, 'Beyond liability: on the availability and scope of injunctions against online intermediaries after *L'Oreal v Ebay*' (2012) 34(3) EIPR 137, 138.

[14] F Rizzuto, 'The liability of online intermediary service providers for infringements of intellectual property rights' (2012) 18(1) CTLR 4, 11.

[15] *Cartier International AG and Others v British Sky Broadcasting Ltd and Others* [2014] EWHC 3354 (Ch) (17 October 2014), para 251.

[16] For a (critical) discussion of intermediaries' proactive enforcement measures, see N Elkin-Koren, 'After twenty years: revisiting copyright liability of online intermediaries', in S Frankel and D Gervais (eds), *The Evolution and Equilibrium of Copyright in the Digital Age* (CUP:2014), 45–8.

[17] *L'Oréal and Others*, C-324/09, EU:C:2011:474, paras 135 and 137.

[18] In his Opinion, the AG had in fact discussed fundamental rights extensively, also including references to ECtHR case law: Opinion of Advocate General Pedro Cruz Villalón in *Scarlet Extended*,

Court of Appeal and the Brussels Court of First Instance, respectively), these cases required the CJEU to consider whether an intermediary (an access provider and a social networking site, respectively) could be the addressee of an injunction that would require it to introduce a system for filtering:

- all electronic communications passing via its services;
- which would apply indiscriminately to all its customers;
- as a preventive measure;
- exclusively at its expense; *and*
- for an unlimited period.

The CJEU answered in the negative, noting how preventative monitoring *of this particular kind* would be incompatible—among other things—with Article 15 of the E-commerce Directive, in that it would require active observation of all electronic communications conducted on the network of the intermediary concerned and, consequently, would encompass all information to be transmitted and all customers using that network (see also further Chapter 8, Section 1.3).[19] The CJEU also held that, while the protection of intellectual property is enshrined in Article 17(2) of the EU Charter, other fundamental rights must be also considered,[20] including intermediaries' freedom to conduct a business as per Article 16 of the Charter[21] and their customers' right to protection of their personal data (Article 8 of the Charter) and their freedom to receive or impart information (Article 11 of the EU Charter).[22] With particular regard to intermediaries' freedom to conduct a business, the CJEU noted how a filtering system like the one at issue in the national background proceedings would require the installation of a complicated, costly, permanent computer system at the expense of the intermediary concerned, which would also be contrary to the conditions laid down in Article 3(1) of the Enforcement Directive.[23] Overall, the twin judgments in *Scarlet Extended*, C-70/10, and *SABAM*, C-360/10, make it clear that the fundamental rights discourse is central to the assessment of intermediary liability and relevant remedies,[24] although some commentators have considered Article 16 of the EU Charter to provide limited assistance to intermediaries in this specific context.[25]

C-70/10, EU:C:2011:25. For a criticism of the limited engagement of the CJEU with fundamental rights aspects, see further S Kulk and F Zuiderveen Borgesius, 'Filtering for copyright enforcement in Europe after the *Sabam* cases' (2012) 34(11) EIPR 791, 794–5. However, as noted by E Psychogiopoulou, 'Copyright enforcement, human rights protection and the responsibilities of internet service providers after *Scarlet*' (2012) 34(8) EIPR 552, 554–5, the Court's cautious language might be explained by the technical uncertainty surrounding the introduction of the filtering system, and the fact that no detailed information regarding the technical specificities thereof had been provided by the referring court.

[19] *Scarlet Extended*, C-70/10, EU:C:2011:771, para 39. In the same sense, *SABAM*, C-360/10, EU:C:2012:85, para 38.
[20] *Scarlet Extended*, C-70/10, EU:C:2011:771, para 44, recalling *Promusicae*, C-275/06, EU:C:2008:54, paras 62–68. In the same sense, *SABAM*, C-360/10, EU:C:2012:85, para 43.
[21] Ibid, para 46. In the same sense, *SABAM*, C-360/10, EU:C:2012:85, para 44.
[22] Ibid, para 50. In the same sense, *SABAM*, C-360/10, EU:C:2012:85, para 48.
[23] Ibid, para 48. In the same sense, *SABAM*, C-360/10, EU:C:2012:85, para 46.
[24] C Angelopoulos, 'Are blocking injunctions against ISPs allowed in Europe? Copyright enforcement in the post-*Telekabel* EU legal landscape' (2014) 9(10) JIPLP 812, 814.
[25] KT O'Sullivan, 'Enforcing copyright online: internet service provider obligations and the European Charter of Human Rights' (2014) 36(9) EIPR 577, 581–2.

1.1.4 Blocking injunctions are allowed under EU law

UPC Telekabel Wien—In *UPC Telekabel Wien*, C-314/12, the CJEU had been asked to clarify whether a particular type of intermediary injunction, consisting of an order to an access provider to block access for its customers to a certain website where un-licensed copyright content is available, ie a blocking injunction, would be compatible with the fundamental rights recognized by EU law. In this sense, the question was also whether relevant provisions under EU law, ie Article 8(3) of the InfoSoc Directive and Article 11 of the Enforcement Directive, provide an adequate legislative basis for web-site blocking orders.[26]

Need for a fair balance—Answering in the affirmative, the CJEU recalled that, where several fundamental rights are at issue, a fair balance must be struck between them, and both the proportionality[27] and effectiveness[28] of the resulting measure must be guaranteed. In the case at hand, the fundamental rights to consider would be: copy-right and rights related to copyright, which are protected under Article 17(2) of the Charter; freedom to conduct a business, which economic agents such as online inter-mediaries enjoy under Article 16 of the Charter; and the freedom of information of internet users, whose protection is ensured by Article 11 of the Charter.

The CJEU acknowledged that, on the one hand, a blocking injunction would com-press an intermediary's freedom to conduct a business but, on the other hand, an injunction of this kind would not infringe the very substance of such freedom. This would be so for two principal reasons. First, a blocking order would leave its addressee free to determine the specific measures to be taken in order to achieve the result sought. In his Opinion, AG Cruz Villalón had instead expressed the view that a mere outcome prohibition not specifying the measures that the addressee of a blocking injunction must take would be incompatible with EU fundamental rights.[29] The second point is that an intermediary could avoid liability by proving that it had taken all reasonable measures.[30]

In any case, while an intermediary must adopt measures that are sufficiently ef-fective to ensure genuine protection of copyright,[31] such measures must also be strictly

---

[26] Answering in the affirmative, see R Arnold, 'Website-blocking injunctions: the question of legis-lative basis' (2015) 37(10) EIPR 623, 630.

[27] Cf P Savola, 'Proportionality of website blocking: internet connectivity providers as copyright enforcers' (2014) 5(2) JIPITEC 116, 126, noting how proportionality has been considered in national case law, though often in a summary fashion.

[28] Economic studies on the effectiveness of website blocking have been conducted: see eg J Poort, J Leenheer, J der Ham, and C Dumitru, 'Baywatch: two approaches to measure the effects of blocking access to the Pirate Bay' (2014) 38(4) Telecom Policy 383 (arguing for the limited efficacy of blocking of The Pirate Bay in the Netherlands), and B Danaher, MD Smith, and R Telang, 'Copyright enforce-ment in the digital age: empirical evidence and policy implications' (2017) 60(2) Communications of the ACM 68 (finding that blocking access to multiple sites would decrease consumption of unlawful content and lead consumers to switch to licensed alternatives). For a legal (critical) discussion of web-site blocking's effectiveness, see A Lodder and P Polter, 'ISP blocking and filtering: on the shallow justification in case law regarding effectiveness of measures' (2017) 8(2) EJLT, available at <http://ejlt.org/article/view/517/764> (last accessed 15 August 2018). Finally, suggesting that the effectiveness of enforcement is positively related to the availability and affordability of lawful alternatives, see W Page, *Adventures in The Netherlands—Spotify, Piracy and the Dutch Experience* (2013), available at <https://www.musicbusinessworldwide.com/files/2014/12/Will-Page-2013-Adventures-in-the-Netherlands-Final.pdf> (last accessed 15 August 2018); M van der Ende, M Hageraats, J Poort, J Quintais, and A Yagafarova, *Global Online Piracy Study* (July 2018), available at <https://www.ivir.nl/publicaties/download/Global-Online-Piracy-Study.pdf> (last accessed 15 August 2018), 14–15.

[29] Opinion of Advocate General Pedro Cruz Villalón in *UPC Telekabel Wien*, C-314/12, EU:C:2013:781, paras 84–90.

[30] *UPC Telekabel Wien*, C-314/12, EU:C:2014:192, paras 46–47 and 50–53.

[31] Ibid, para 62.

targeted, in the sense that they must serve to bring third-party infringements to an end without thereby affecting internet users who are using the provider's services to access information lawfully.[32] In this sense, the duty to strike an appropriate balance between conflicting rights and interests is on the intermediary targeted by the injunction.[33]

Availability of blocking injunctions in the EU—It should be noted that, despite the EU legislative framework and the development of CJEU case law, the availability of blocking injunctions has remained controversial for a long time in the EU, including in individual Member States like Sweden,[34] Germany,[35] and the Netherlands,[36] and also due to the fact that website blocking would result in disabling access to information publicly available online. It is essentially in light of such potential issues that some commentators have emphasized the importance of considering fundamental rights, including procedural rights under Article 47 of the EU Charter. So far, this provision has not received particularly detailed attention in the context of injunctive relief. Yet, the requirement of effective judicial protection underlies the whole process of application for an injunction against an intermediary, and might serve to ensure both effective enforcement of intellectual property rights and the rights of those against whom the resulting relief would take effect.[37]

1.1.5 An intermediary may be primarily (directly) liable together with users of its services

The final standard, which the CJEU has adopted in the context of a reference also concerning the availability of intermediary injunctions (*Stichting Brein*, C-610/15) serves to demonstrate that—when we speak of intermediaries—we should not (or perhaps, no longer) think about them solely as addressees of injunctions or as subjects that might lose (if the relevant conditions are satisfied) their safe harbour protection, but also as subjects that—in certain contexts—might be directly liable for the infringement of third-party intellectual property rights.

Stichting Brein (*The Pirate Bay* case)—The referral in *Stichting Brein*, C-610/15 from the Dutch Supreme Court was made in the context of litigation between a Dutch

---

[32] Ibid, para 56.

[33] C Angelopoulos and S Smet, 'Notice-and-fair-balance: how to reach a compromise between fundamental rights in European intermediary liability' (2016) 8(2) JML 266, 281. See also A Kuczerawy, 'The power of positive thinking—Intermediary liability and the effective enjoyment of the right to freedom of expression' (2017) 8(2) JIPITEC 226, 232–3, from the perspective of positive obligations imposed by the EU Charter.

[34] The first blocking injunction in this Member State was only issued recently: Svea Hovrätt—Patent- och marknadsöverdomstolen, *Universal Music AB v B2 Bredband AB*, PMT 11706-15, 13 February 2017. See further N Malovic, 'Online copyright enforcement in Sweden: the first blocking injunction' (2017) 28(5) Ent LR 171, 173.

[35] The first blocking injunction in this Member State was only issued recently: Bundesgerichtshof, I ZR 174/14—*Goldesel*. See further M Schaefer, 'ISP liability for blocking access to third-party infringing content' (2016) 38(10) EIPR 633, 634–6.

[36] In this country blocking of The Pirate Bay has been at the centre of long-running controversy which, at the time of writing is not yet over. In June 2018 the Dutch Supreme Court asked the Amsterdam Court of Appeal to review the blocking order issued against local ISPs to block access to The Pirate Bay (Hoge Raad, 14/02399, NL:HR:2018:1046). For the time being the interim blocking injunction secured by BREIN in 2017 remains in place (Rechtbank Den Haag, C/09/535341/KG ZA 17-891, NL:RBDHA:2017:10789). The CJEU referral in *Stichting Brein*, C-610/15, originated from an application for a blocking injunction against local ISPs to block access to The Pirate Bay.

[37] SL Kaléda, 'The role of the principle of effective judicial protection in relation to website blocking injunctions' (2017) 8(3) JIPITEC 216, 218–19. See also Husovec and Peguera, 'Much ado about little' 27–9.

anti-piracy foundation and two internet access providers over the application, by the former, for an order that would require the latter to block access for their customers to the website of The Pirate Bay. An engine for P2P file-sharing, as discussed at greater length in Chapter 4, Section 2.3, The Pirate Bay does not host any protected works. However, it operates a system by means of which metadata on protected works which is present on the users' computers is indexed and categorized for users, so that the users may trace, upload, and download the protected works on the basis thereof. It is estimated that the near totality (90 to 95 per cent) of the files shared on the network of The Pirate Bay contain copyright works distributed unlawfully.[38]

Upheld at first instance, the application of Stichting Brein (now BREIN) was dismissed on appeal. This was based on the consideration that it would be the users of The Pirate Bay—rather than the platform operators—who would be responsible for copyright infringements. In addition, the blocking order sought was found to be disproportionate to the aim pursued, this being effective copyright protection. The decision was appealed to the Supreme Court, which decided to stay the proceedings and seek guidance from the CJEU on whether the operators of a website like The Pirate Bay are to be regarded as doing acts of communication to the public within the meaning of Article 3(1) of the InfoSoc Directive. The CJEU answered in the affirmative.

Applicability to other scenarios—This ruling has potentially begun a new chapter on the topic of intermediary liability (and also injunctions), the relevant implications of which need to be worked out fully. Whilst it is true that the CJEU case concerned a rather 'rogue' platform (The Pirate Bay), are the considerations made in that decision more broadly applicable? This, at the judicial level, remains still to be fully explored (see Chapter 4, Section 2.4.2). However, at the policy and legislative levels—notably in the context of the 'value gap' proposal—it is assumed that certain providers that give access to third-party content uploaded by users of their services without a licence from relevant rightholders would indeed be potentially liable for unauthorized acts of communication to the public (see further Chapter 8, Sections 1, 5.1, and 6.1).

2. Costs and Damages

The Enforcement Directive sets rules that are generally applicable to the enforcement of all intellectual property rights, including copyright. With specific regard to the latter, the CJEU has had the opportunity to clarify a number of aspects, including costs and damages.

Notion of 'reasonable and proportionate legal costs'—Article 14 of the directive requires Member States to ensure that reasonable and proportionate legal costs and other expenses incurred by the successful party shall, as a general rule, be borne by the unsuccessful party, unless equity requires otherwise. In *United Video Properties*, C-57/15 (whose national background proceedings related to patent infringement), the Court had been asked to clarify the meaning of 'reasonable and proportionate legal costs and other expenses' in that provision. The CJEU considered whether EU law would prevent national legislation (like the one in place in the EU Member State of the referral, Belgium) which provides that the unsuccessful party is to be ordered to pay the legal costs incurred by the successful party. In a context of this kind, the courts responsible for issuing that order might take into account features specific to the case at hand, and

---

[38] Opinion of Advocate General Maciej Szpunar in *Stichting Brein*, C-610/15, EU:C:2017:99, para 23.

apply a flat-rate scheme setting out an absolute reimbursement ceiling in respect of costs for the assistance of a lawyer.

Flat-rate reimbursement schemes—In this regard, the CJEU noted that the concept of 'legal costs' to be reimbursed includes, amongst others, a lawyer's fees. The provision of a flat-rate scheme might be considered contrary to the objective (Recital 17) that the measures, procedures, and remedies set out in that directive be determined in each case in such a manner as to take due account of the specific characteristics of that case. However, Article 14 also requires Member States to ensure the reimbursement only of 'reasonable' legal costs and Article 3(1) mandates that the procedures laid down by the Member States must not be unnecessarily costly. The provision of a flat-rate reimbursement scheme of a lawyer's fees could in principle be justified in light of the standard of reasonableness of the costs to be reimbursed. However, the requirement that the unsuccessful party must bear 'reasonable' legal costs cannot justify, for the purposes of the implementation of Article 14, legislation imposing a flat-rate significantly below the average rate actually charged for the services of a lawyer in that Member State, in that this would be incompatible with Article 3(2) and the requirement that procedures and remedies must be dissuasive, as well as the objective of the Enforcement Directive (Recital 10) to guarantee a high level of protection,[39] also in light of Article 17(2) of the EU Charter (Recital 32).[40] Article 14 also sets a requirement of proportionality:

If the requirement of proportionality does not imply that the unsuccessful party must necessarily reimburse the entirety of the costs incurred by the other party, it does however mean that the successful party should have the right to reimbursement of, at the very least, a significant and appropriate part of the reasonable costs actually incurred by that party.[41]

Hence, national legislation that provides for a flat-rate scheme for the reimbursement of a lawyer's fees must ensure, on the one hand, that that limit reflects the reality of the rates charged for the services of a lawyer in the field of intellectual property, and, on the other, that, at the very least, a significant and appropriate part of the reasonable costs actually incurred by the successful party are borne by the unsuccessful party.

Costs of technical advisers—In *United Video Properties*, C-57/15, the Court also considered whether Article 14 precludes national rules that provide that reimbursement of the costs of a technical adviser is only possible in the case of fault of the unsuccessful party. According to the Court, the answer to this question depends on the link between those costs and the judicial procedure concerned: those costs fall within the notion of 'other expenses' under Article 14 if such a link is direct and close.[42]

Appropriateness of damages awarded—In relation to damages for infringement of intellectual property rights, Article 13 of the Enforcement Directive mandates Member States to ensure that the competent judicial authorities 'order the infringer who knowingly, or with reasonable grounds to know, engaged in an infringing activity, to pay the rightholder damages *appropriate to the actual prejudice* suffered by him/her as a result of the infringement.' (emphasis added). That provision does not really clarify the subjective element required in the infringer's conduct in order to seek compensation for damages. However, damages are due when the defendant 'knowingly, or with reasonable grounds to know' engaged in infringing activity. This requires demonstration

---

[39] See also *Liffers*, C-99/15, EU:C:2016:173, para 21.

[40] Also stressing how the Enforcement Directive respects the fundamental rights and observes the principles recognized by the EU Charter while seeking to ensure full respect for intellectual property, in accordance with Article 17(2) of the EU Charter, see *Coty Germany*, C-580/13, EU:C:2015:485, para 31.

[41] *United Video Properties*, C-57/15, EU:C:2016:611, para 29.   [42] Ibid, para 38.

that, at the very least, the infringer was at fault. According to some commentators, this would entail comparing the conduct of the alleged infringer with that of a reasonably circumspect and diligent party in the same set of circumstances.[43]

Elements to consider—Article 13 requires judicial authorities to either: (a) take into account aspects such as the negative economic consequences, including lost profits, which the injured party has suffered, any unfair profits made by the infringer and, in appropriate cases, elements other than economic factors, such as the moral prejudice caused to the rightholder by the infringement; or—in appropriate cases—(b) set the damages as a lump sum on the basis of elements such as at least the amount of royalties or fees which would have been due if the infringer had requested authorization to use the intellectual property right in question. With regard to (a), the Court has clarified that compensation is not limited to the material damage suffered, but may also include compensation of the moral prejudice suffered.[44] Turning to (b), a question that has arisen is how far the amount of damages as a predetermined lump sum can go, especially considering that Recital 26 in the preamble to the Enforcement Directive states that (b) is not aimed at introducing an obligation for Member States to provide for punitive damages but, more simply, to allow for compensation to be based on an objective criterion while taking account of the expenses incurred by the rightholder, eg, the costs of identification and research.

Stowarzyszenie Oławska Telewizja Kablowa—In *Stowarzyszenie Oławska Telewizja Kablowa*, C-367/15, the Polish Supreme Court had asked the CJEU whether it would be incompatible with Article 13 of the Enforcement Directive to award as damages a lump sum corresponding to twice or three times the amount of the appropriate fee. The CJEU answered in the negative, holding that 'the fact that Directive 2004/48 does not entail an obligation on the Member States to provide for "punitive" damages cannot be interpreted as a prohibition on introducing such a measure'.[45] Having recalled both Recitals 3 and 10 in the preamble to the Enforcement Directive, the Court referred to its earlier decision in *Hansson*, C-481/14,[46] and stated that the Enforcement Directive 'lays down a minimum standard concerning the enforcement of intellectual property rights and does not prevent the Member States from laying down measures that are more protective'.[47] It concluded that the Enforcement Directive does not preclude national legislation, which provides that the holder of economic rights of copyright that have been infringed may require the person who has infringed those rights to compensate for the loss caused by payment of a sum corresponding to twice the amount of a hypothetical royalty.[48] It follows that EU law does not prevent individual Member States from allowing damage awards with a punitive component.[49]

Limited harmonization—Overall, while the judgments discussed in this section provide some clarity when interpreting relevant provisions in the Enforcement Directive, they are also a demonstration of the relatively weak harmonizing force of the Enforcement Directive. All this being so, despite that—at the time of its adoption—the

---

[43] FG Wilman, 'A decade of private enforcement' 524.
[44] *Liffers*, C-99/15, EU:C:2016:173, para 27.
[45] *Stowarzyszenie Oławska Telewizja Kablowa*, C-367/15, EU:C:2017:36, para 28.
[46] *Hansson*, C-481/14, EU:C:2016:419, paras 36 and 40.
[47] *Stowarzyszenie Oławska Telewizja Kablowa*, C-367/15, EU:C:2017:36, para 23.
[48] Ibid, para 25.
[49] Cf, critically, regarding the admissibility of punitive damages in the aftermath of this judgment, M Schweizer, 'The Enforcement Directive permits punitive damages—or does it?' (24 February 2017) The IPKat, available at <http://ipkitten.blogspot.com/2017/02/the-enforcement-directive-permits.html> (last accessed 15 August 2018).

EU legislature stressed how disparities between the systems of the Member States as regards the means of enforcing intellectual property rights are prejudicial to the proper functioning of the internal market, make it impossible to ensure that intellectual property rights enjoy an equivalent level of protection throughout the EU (Recital 8), and also lead to a weakening of substantive intellectual property rights (Recital 9).[50]

3. Law Applicable in International Online Infringement Cases

Rome II Regulation—When it comes to disputes with international elements, lacking specific agreements between the parties, determination of the applicable law is a matter of international law. At the EU level, the relevant provisions are those contained in Regulation 864/2007[51] (Rome II Regulation). The specific rule relating to an unregistered and territorial intellectual property right (as is copyright) is the one contained in Article 8(1):

The law applicable to a non-contractual obligation arising from an infringement of an intellectual property right shall be the law of the country for which protection is claimed.

The CJEU has not yet had the chance to clarify directly how such a criterion is to be interpreted and applied in the context of an action for copyright infringement occurring on the internet, in which the infringement may be ubiquitous and several *leges loci protectionis* might be applicable due to the territoriality of copyright laws.[52] In the specific context of databases and the *sui generis* (database) right within Article 7 of the Database Directive, the CJEU has however envisaged a targeting approach.

Football Dataco and Others—In *Football Dataco and Others*, C-173/11, the Court had been asked to consider whether Article 7 of that directive must be interpreted as meaning that the sending by one person, by means of a web server located in Member State A, of data previously uploaded by that person from a database protected by the *sui generis* right under that directive to the computer of another person located in Member State B, at that person's request, for the purpose of storage in that computer's memory and display on its screen, constitutes an act of extraction or re-utilization of the data by the person sending it. If so, must that act be regarded as taking place in Member State A, in Member State B, or in both those States?

Lex loci protectionis **and targeting**—In order to answer these questions, the CJEU referred, among other things, to Article 8(1) of the Rome II Regulation. It noted how that provision requires, at the outset, to determine whether such acts took place in the Member State in which protection is claimed (*lex loci protectionis*).[53] For complex acts that involve a series of operations (as is the case of re-utilization of the content of a database), different Member States' territories might be involved.[54] The mere fact that the website containing the data in question is accessible in a particular national territory is not a sufficient basis for concluding that the operator of the website is

---

[50] See *Diageo Brands*, C-681/13, EU:C:2015:471, para 71.

[51] Regulation (EC) No 864/2007 of the European Parliament and of the Council of 11 July 2007 on the law applicable to non-contractual obligations (Rome II), OJ L 199, 31 July 2007, 40–9.

[52] See A Ohly, 'Choice of law in the digital environment – Problems and possible solutions', in J Drexl and A Kur (eds), *Intellectual Property and Private International Law—Heading for the Future* (Hart:2005), 243–4.

[53] *Football Dataco and Others*, C-173/11, EU:C:2012:642, para 32.   [54] Ibid, para 34.

performing an act of re-utilization caught by the national law applicable in that territory concerning protection by the *sui generis* right:[55]

> If the mere fact of being accessible were sufficient for it to be concluded that there was an act of re-utilisation, websites and data which, although obviously targeted at persons outside the territory of the Member State concerned, were nevertheless technically accessible in that State would wrongly be subject to the application of the relevant law of that State.[56]

Some national courts consider it a well-established principle that targeting remains the criterion to employ to determine whether that Member State's copyright law would apply: in particular, and despite the fact that the question of whether a website is targeted to a particular country is a multi-factorial one which depends on all the circumstances,[57] where a communication to the public which originates outside the territory of a Member State is received inside that Member State, the act will be treated as occurring within that territory if the communication is targeted at the public in that Member State.[58]

Also employing the targeting criterion, however, there might be the risk that multiple laws would apply to the infringement at issue. A possible solution might be to follow a ubiquitous infringement rule that could be modelled in accordance with the Max Planck CLIP Principles[59] and that would allow the court seized to decide on remedies for infringing conduct which also occurred outside the EU Member State where the court has its seat.[60]

4. International Jurisdiction in Online Infringement Cases

Brussels I Regulation recast—An area in which the CJEU has had a more direct influence, also due to the number of referrals,[61] is the interpretation of private international law rules concerning jurisdiction in online infringement cases. The relevant provisions are contained in Articles 4 and 7(2) of the Brussels I Regulation recast, formerly Articles 2 and 5(3), respectively, of the Brussels I Regulation. The purpose of EU legislation is not to unify the procedural rules of the Member States, but rather to determine which court has jurisdiction in disputes concerning civil and commercial matters in relations between Member States and to facilitate the enforcement of judgments.[62] The general

---

[55] Ibid, para 36, referring by analogy to *Pammer*, C-585/08, EU:C:2010:740, para 69, and *L'Oréal and Others*, C-324/09, EU:C:2011:474, para 64.

[56] Ibid, para 37, referring by analogy to *L'Oréal and Others*, C-324/09, EU:C:2011:474, para 64.

[57] In this sense, with regard to UK law: *Omnibill (Pty) Ltd v Egpsxxx Ltd and Another* [2014] EWHC 3762 (IPEC) (17 November 2014), para 12, on which see, critically, K Frolova, 'The UK public is a titillating target: a case comment on *Omnibill v Egpsxx*' (2015) 37(6) EIPR 383, 387.

[58] See, with regard to UK law, *EMI Records Ltd and Others v British Sky Broadcasting Ltd and Others* [2013] EWHC 379 (Ch) (28 February 2013), para 38.

[59] European Max Planck Group on Conflict of Laws in Intellectual Property (CLIP), *Principles on Conflict of Laws in Intellectual Property* (2011), Article 3.603. See also the discussion in JJ Fawcett and P Torremans, *Intellectual Property and Private International Law* (OUP:2011), 2nd edn, §§17.26–17.29; J Koo, 'Enforcing the EU right of communication to the public', in P Torremans (ed), *Research Handbook on Copyright Law* (Edward Elgar:2017), 2nd edn, 198–9.

[60] In relation to designs, see the recent decision in *Nintendo*, C-24/16 and C-25/16, EU:C:2017:724, para 111.

[61] They are (in chronological order): *Pinckney*, C-170/12, EU:C:2013:635; *Hi Hotel HCF*, C-387/12, EU:C:2014:215; and *Hejduk*, C-441/13, EU:C:2015:28.

[62] In this sense, *Nothartová*, C-306/17, EU:C:2018:360, para 28, referring to *Hypoteční banka*, C-327/10, EU:C:2011:745, para 37.

rule in Article 4 of the Brussels I Regulation recast is that 'persons domiciled in a Member State shall, whatever their nationality, be sued in the courts of that Member State'. The special rule contained in Article 7(2) provides, as an alternative, that '[a] person domiciled in a Member State may be sued in another Member State ... in the courts for the place where the harmful event occurred or may occur'.

Notion of 'place of the harmful event'—While the general rule does not raise particular interpretative problems, determination of the *place of the harmful event* in the event of an infringement carried out via the internet may not be straightforward. Over time, Article 7(2) has received a fairly broad[63] and autonomous[64]—yet at times oscillating[65]—interpretation. Nonetheless, the CJEU has been consistent in holding that the place where the harmful event occurred or may occur is to be intended as either the place where the *damage* occurred or the place of the *event* giving rise to it, so that the defendant may be sued—at the option of the claimant—in the courts for either of those places.[66]

Pinckney—The CJEU was given for the first time the opportunity to apply the special rule of jurisdiction in an online copyright context in its 2013 decision in *Pinckney*, C-170/12. This referral was made in the context of proceedings between a UK national living in France and a company established in Austria, concerning a claim for damages resulting from the infringement of copyright of the former in a number of musical works. The claimant had discovered that those works had been reproduced without his consent on CDs pressed in Austria by the defendant, and then marketed by two UK companies through various internet websites accessible from his residence in Toulouse. He brought proceedings before the Toulouse Regional Court seeking compensation for the damages suffered on account of the infringement of his copyrights. The defendant unsuccessfully challenged the jurisdiction of the French courts. It thus appealed the decision at first instance, arguing that the only courts having jurisdiction were those of the place of the defendant's domicile (Austria), or the courts of the place where the damage was caused (United Kingdom). The Toulouse Court of Appeal agreed with the defendant. The copyright owner appealed to the French Court of Cassation, which decided to stay the proceedings and seek guidance from the CJEU.

Targeting rejected over accessibility but with limitations for damages—The reference concerned interpretation of the concept of place where the *damage* occurred, rather than place of the event giving rise to the damage. The CJEU rejected the approach indicated as preferable by AG Jääskinen in his Opinion, ie a targeting approach that would result in rooting jurisdiction with courts in the Member State at which the allegedly infringing act of the defendant is targeted.[67] This would not be correct because nothing in Article 7(2) Brussels I recast requires following a targeting approach.[68] The

---

[63] D Jerker and B Svantesson, *Private International Law and the Internet* (Wolters Kluwer:2012), 2nd edn, 257.

[64] T Kono and P Jurčys, 'General report' in T Kono (ed), *Intellectual Property and Private International Law* (Hart Publishing:2012), 53.

[65] Ibid, 53–4.

[66] *Bier*, 21-76, EU:C:1976:166, para 19; *Shevill*, C-68/93, EU:C:1995:61, paras 20–21; *Zuid-Chemie*, C-189/08, EU:C:2009:475, para 23; *eDate Advertising*, C-509/09 and C-161/10, EU:C:2011:685, para 41; *Wintersteiger*, C-523/10, EU:C:2012:220, para 19; *Melzer*, C-228/11, EU:C:2013:305, para 25; *Pinckney*, C-170/12, EU:C:2013:635, para 26; *Kainz*, C-45/13, EU:C:2014:7, para 23; *Hi Hotel HCF*, C-387/12, EU:C:2014:215, para 27; *Coty Germany (anciennement Coty Prestige Lancaster Group)*, C-360/12, EU:C:2014:1318, para 32; *Hejduk*, C-441/13, EU:C:2015:28, para 18.

[67] Opinion of Advocate General Niilo Jääskinen in *Pinckney*, C-170/12, EU:C:2013:400, paras 61–65.

[68] *Pinckney*, C-170/12, EU:C:2013:635, para 42.

CJEU concluded that jurisdiction within Article 7(2) Brussels I recast subsists also in relation to the courts located in the Member State in which the allegedly infringing content may be accessed, although in this case the court seized would be only competent to adjudicate on the damages which occurred on that specific territory.[69]

Hi Hotel HCF—The CJEU confirmed accessibility as a valid criterion to establish jurisdiction pursuant to Article 7(2) Brussels I recast in *Hi Hotel HCF*, C-387/12. This reference from the German Federal Court of Justice was made in the context of litigation between a photographer and a hotel chain. The former had been commissioned to take a number of photographs of Hi Hotel rooms in Nice (France), and granted Hi Hotel the right to use them in advertising brochures and on its website. He subsequently noticed in a bookshop in Cologne (Germany) an illustrated book on interior architecture published by a German publisher, containing reproductions of some of his photographs. He successfully sued Hi Hotel (established in France) for copyright infringement before a German court. The subsequent appeal brought by Hi Hotel was dismissed. The Federal Court of Justice decided to stay the proceedings and seek guidance from the CJEU as to whether German courts would have jurisdiction. The CJEU confirmed that the place giving rise to the damage within that provision cannot be considered as conferring jurisdiction on courts located in a Member State in which the alleged infringer has not acted. However, jurisdiction could subsist on the basis of the place where the alleged damage occurs. In such an instance, the court would only have jurisdiction to rule on the damage caused in the territory of the Member State where it has its seat.[70]

Hejduk—In his Opinion in the subsequent referral in *Hejduk*, C-441/13, AG Cruz Villalón highlighted the potential shortcomings of the accessibility criterion, and advised (unsuccessfully) the CJEU to employ the causal event criterion that the Court itself had rejected in *Hi Hotel HCF*, C-387/12.[71] This referral was made in the context of proceedings for copyright infringement that an Austrian resident and professional photographer had brought before the Vienna Court of First Instance (Austria) against a company established in Germany. The proceedings concerned unauthorized publication of protected works of the claimant on the defendant's website for viewing and downloading. The defendant objected to the jurisdiction of Austrian courts: since it was established in Germany and its webpage used a .de top level domain, the competence to hear this case would lie with German courts. The Vienna court asked the CJEU whether Article 7(2) of the Brussels I Regulation recast provides that jurisdiction subsists for courts situated alternatively in the Member State in which the alleged perpetrator of the infringement is established or that at which the website, according to its content, is directed.

Delocalized damage—In his Opinion, AG Cruz Villalón noted at the outset how the factual background made this case different from *Pinckney*, C-170/12, notably because the works at issue were not offered for sale.[72] As such, localizing the damage would prove challenging. Although the Austrian court only referred to two possible linking factors (these being the defendant's domicile and the Member State at which the website's content is directed), in his analysis the AG also explored further possibilities.

---

[69] Ibid, paras 44–47. For a critical assessment of the ruling in its immediate aftermath, see M Husovec, 'European Union: comment on *Pinckney*' (2014) 45(3) IIC 370, 372–4.
[70] *Hi Hotel HCF*, C-387/12, EU:C:2014:215, para 31, recalling *Melzer*, C-228/11, EU:C:2013:305, para 40.
[71] Opinion of Advocate General Cruz Villalón in *Hejduk*, C-441/13, EU:C:2014:2212, para 27.
[72] Ibid, paras 2–3.

After reviewing the centre of interest criterion (which the CJEU adopted in *Shevill*, C-68/93,[73] and *eDate Advertising*, C-509/09 and C-161/10,[74] but rejected in relation to national trade marks in *Wintersteiger*, C-523/10),[75] the AG addressed the targeting criterion (referred to in the Opinion as a 'focalisation criterion'). He noted how the CJEU adopted it in *L'Oréal and Others*, C-324/09, but subsequently rejected it in *Pinckney*, C-170/12, on grounds that Article 7(2) of the Brussels I Regulation recast does not require that the activity concerned be targeted at the Member State in which the court seized is situated. According to the AG, the CJEU stance in *Pinckney* should be read as 'rul[ing] out in principle the possibility of extending the focalization criterion to cases of non-contractual damages based on infringements of intellectual property rights'.[76]

The AG also dismissed the accessibility criterion (referred to in the Opinion as the 'territoriality criterion') adopted in *Pinckney*, C-170/12. He agreed with the EU Commission that had noted in its intervention how limitations on damages (only those suffered on the territory of the EU Member State in which the court seized is situated) might prove ineffective in a case like the one at hand. Not only would it be difficult for the defendant having potentially to face actions in multiple Member States, but also the claimant would have no real benefits from seeking limited damages in more jurisdictions.[77] The AG concluded that to comply with the objectives of Article 7(2), notably the sound administration of justice,[78] in cases where delocalized damage occurs on the internet the best option is to exclude the possibility of suing in the courts of the State where the damage occurred and limit jurisdiction, at least that based on Article 7(2), to that of the courts of the State where the event giving rise to the damage occurred. In any case, this option would not exclude the jurisdiction of the courts of the Member State where the defendant is domiciled. Although in the majority of cases both criteria would lead to the same court, this might not always be so.[79]

Confirmation of accessibility criterion and limited damages—The CJEU did not follow the approach suggested by AG Cruz Villalón. Instead, it confirmed the possibility for one to sue *also* before the courts of the Member State in which the damage occurred. The Court also stated that the causal event, which is defined as the event giving rise to the alleged damage, would not attribute jurisdiction to the court seized.[80] Where the alleged tort consisted in the online infringement of an intellectual property right (copyright), 'the activation of the process for the technical display of the photographs on that website must be regarded as the causal event. The event giving rise to a possible infringement of copyright therefore lies in the actions of the owner of that site.'[81] In a case like the one at hand, the acts or omissions liable to constitute such an infringement could be localized only at the place where the defendant had its seat, since that is where the company took and implemented the decision to place the allegedly infringing reproductions online on a particular website.[82]

Potential issues with accessibility as a jurisdiction criterion—In his Opinion in *Pinckney*, C-170/12, AG Jääskinen warned against the potential risks associated with the adoption of an accessibility criterion to establish jurisdiction, in lieu of a targeting approach, particularly with regard to forum shopping and ultimately 'a multiplication

---

[73] *Shevill*, C-68/93, EU:C:1995:61, paras 30–33.
[74] *eDate Advertising and Others,* EU:C:2011:685, para 48.
[75] *Wintersteiger*, C-523/10, EU:C:2012:220.
[76] Opinion of Advocate General Cruz Villalón in *Hejduk*, C-441/13, EU:C:2014:2212, para 31.
[77] Ibid, para 40.   [78] Ibid, para 42.   [79] Ibid, para 45.
[80] *Hejduk*, C-441/13, EU:C:2015:28, paras 23–26.
[81] Ibid, para 24, referring to *Wintersteiger*, C-523/10, EU:C:2012:220, paras 34–35.
[82] Ibid, para 25.

of courts'.[83] Besides issues arising from limitations in damages, adopting accessibility as a criterion to establish jurisdiction might also facilitate a deep-pocketed claimant to sue—if not harass altogether—the defendant before a multiplicity of courts, possibly with the objective of pushing them into a settlement.[84]

Above all, this approach might have the effect of conferring jurisdiction over non-existent torts (and damages). This is because the issue of competence would not really depend on the merits of the underlying cause of action. The result might be that a national court is compelled to accept jurisdiction on the basis that the allegedly infringing content can be accessed in that territory, to conclude eventually that there is no infringement of relevant rights because the website at issue is not targeted at that territory.[85] It is essentially to avoid the materialization of risks of this kind that, in the online context, jurisdiction rooted within an accessibility criterion would need to be matched with a targeting approach to determine the law applicable to the substance of the dispute at issue.[86] Nonetheless, in a situation like the one in *Hejduk*, C-441/13, that is, one in which the damage is delocalized, the application of a targeting approach might prove challenging.[87]

Conclusion

At the policy and legislative levels, harmonization of certain issues that relate to the enforcement of copyright and, more generally, intellectual property rights, was deemed necessary on consideration of the fragmentation that different approaches at the level of individual EU Member States would cause from an internal market perspective. This chapter has focused on a selected group of enforcement tools in which CJEU action has been decisive. This has been particularly the case of injunctions against intermediaries. The interpretative efforts of the Court have also been decisive in clarifying a number of other aspects, including issues of costs and damages, and the interpretation of private international law rules in cross-border contexts in relation to online copyright infringements. Overall, the Court's interpretation of legislative provisions has been informed by the overarching goal of ensuring a high level of intellectual property protection and also, yet with greater difficulties, balancing opposing rights and interests in line with what EU legislation requires.

---

[83] Opinion of Advocate General Niilo Jääskinen in *Pinckney*, C-170/12, EU:C:2013:400, para 68.

[84] In this sense, see P Torremans, 'Jurisdiction in intellectual property cases' in P Torremans (ed), *Research Handbook on Cross-Border Enforcement of Intellectual Property* (Edward Elgar:2014), 386, and K Bercimuelle-Chamot, 'Accessibility is the relevant criterion to determine jurisdiction in online copyright infringement cases' (2015) 10(6) JIPLP 406, 407.

[85] In the same sense, see P Savola, 'The ultimate copyright shopping opportunity—jurisdiction and choice of law in website blocking injunctions' (2014) 45(3) IIC 287, 290–8. Cf, more critically, M Pryke, 'Online copyright infringement—is jurisdiction now simply a matter of accessibility' (2015) 26(4) Ent LR 152, 153–4.

[86] See also the interesting considerations of R Matulionyte, 'Enforcing copyright infringements online—In search of balanced private international law rules' (2015) 6(2) JIPITEC 132, 135.

[87] T Lutzi, 'Internet cases in EU private international law—developing a coherent approach' (2017) 66(3) ICLQ 687, 719; P Torremans, 'Copyright jurisdiction under EU private international law', in Torremans (ed), *Research Handbook on Copyright Law* 564–6.

PART III

THE LEGACY OF THE CJEU

Following a discussion of the role and action of the CJEU in the preceding two parts, this final part discusses the impact and, therefore, legacy of its case law in the area of copyright. It does so from two distinct perspectives: the first one is the effect that CJEU case law has had on national copyright laws; the second one is existing case law in the context of current policy discourse around EU copyright reform.

Chapter 7, 'Relevance of EU Copyright Law to (Future) non-EU Member States', is concerned with the first perspective. The choice has been to address in particular a current issue: the default consequences that the departure of a certain Member State from the EU would have. In this sense, the focus is primarily on the UK: the chapter seeks to explore to what extent this country's copyright law has been shaped, not just by EU legislation, but also by CJEU interpretation of the EU *acquis*. Further to an overview of what immediate changes the departure from the EU and the EEA would have on an EU Member State, an attempt to understand the extent to which CJEU case law has changed UK copyright law is made. The discussion therefore tackles issues such as: copyright subsistence, subject matter categorization, primary/accessory liability, the standard of infringement, exceptions and limitations, and enforcement (with particular regard to website blocking jurisprudence). Overall, this chapter shows that CJEU case law has had a profound impact on UK copyright, and that this legacy may be felt for a long time, even in a scenario of a 'hard' Brexit.

The final chapter, 'CJEU Case Law and the Interplay with Policy and Legislative Action in the DSM', tackles recent initiatives of the EU Commission to reform the EU copyright *acquis*. In particular, it focuses on a number of selected areas in the proposed DSM Directive, which need to be considered in light, not just of existing legislation, but also—and perhaps most importantly—of existing CJEU case law. These areas are: the 'value gap' ('transfer of value') proposal, the press publishers' right, fair compensation for private copying, and licensing of out-of-commerce works.

7

Relevance of EU Copyright Law to (Future) Non-EU Member States

Introduction

As discussed in Part II, the activity of the CJEU has often translated to a de facto activism of the Court, which has, on the one hand, pushed the boundaries of harmonization further than the text of directives has done per se and, on the other hand, created a principled framework for a set of legislative provisions that—considered in isolation—would not have the prescriptive force that, instead, the case law of the CJEU has been conferring upon them.

Exit from the EU—This being the state of EU copyright evolution, the question that arises is what legacy is left for those EU Member States that might decide to withdraw from the EU. The answer would be relatively straightforward for those countries that, while not part of the EU, are or remain part of the EEA, in that such countries would still be subject to EU law and, together with this, also CJEU case law and jurisdiction. The implications are more difficult to appreciate for those countries that, as well as withdrawing from the EU, would also leave the EEA. For the latter, in fact, EU law would cease to have the character of supremacy over national laws and the CJEU would cease to have jurisdiction.

Default effects of exit from the EU and the EEA—In such a scenario, for the sake of the present analysis, there would be three main consequences. First, that country would no longer be bound to transpose new EU directives into its own legal system or apply relevant EU regulations. Second, that country would no longer benefit from EU-wide rules and recognition principles found in certain EU legislation. Third, the CJEU would no longer have jurisdiction, including with regard to references for a preliminary ruling.

While the first consequence appears relatively straightforward (albeit whether there would be an obligation of the departing Member State to transpose into its own law EU directives that were adopted prior to the withdrawal date but for which the transposition term is still pending at the time of leaving the EU/EEA might prove contentious), the second and third consequences may be difficult to assess, due to their complexity. The second consequence relates to the implications that leaving the EU would have on the loss of EU citizenship for individual authors and rightholders or qualification as an EU business for corporate rightholders; the third consequence requires consideration of the legacy of CJEU case law, particularly in areas in which the Court has gone beyond the literal text of relevant EU provisions and carried out a de facto harmonization of certain copyright concepts. The analysis which follows will tackle both aspects in detail.

1. Loss of EU Citizenship or Qualification as an EU Business

Qualification as a third country—In a note sent to stakeholders in 2018, the EU Commission outlined some of the default legislative implications that the exit of a Member State from the EU/EEA would have on rightholders that are nationals of that country or are established there.[1] On the withdrawal date of a certain Member State that left both the EU and the EEA, relevant EU directives and regulations would cease to apply. Absent an ad hoc agreement, the relationships between the EU and the former EU Member State (which would qualify as a third country) would be governed by relevant international treaties to which both are parties. With particular regard to EU copyright instruments, the withdrawal of a Member State from the EU and the EEA would have consequences for both individuals and legal persons and businesses established therein, with reference to rights entitlement and mechanisms of mutual assistance/cooperation/recognition.

Consequences for individuals—With regard to individuals, withdrawal from the EU would have consequences in terms of access to and enjoyment of copyright content. Recently the EU adopted a directive to implement the obligations that the EU has to meet under the 2014 Marrakesh Treaty to Facilitate Access to Published Works for Persons Who Are Blind, Visually Impaired, or Otherwise Print Disabled (Marrakesh Treaty) in a harmonized fashion, with a view to ensuring that the corresponding measures are applied consistently throughout the internal market (Recital 6 of the Directive implementing the Marrakesh Treaty in the EU). In its Opinion 3/15 the CJEU held that the EU has exclusive competence to conclude that Treaty and it is settled case law that EU Member States may not enter, outside the framework of the EU institutions, into international commitments falling within an area that is already covered to a large extent by common EU rules, even if there is no possible contradiction between those commitments and the common EU rules.[2] The withdrawal from the EU would mean that blind/visually impaired/print-disabled persons based in a country that has left the EU would no longer be automatically entitled to obtain accessible format copies from authorized entities in the EU under Article 4 of that directive.

Also the right to 'port' one's own digital content subscriptions when travelling within the EU but outside the Member State of residence pursuant to the Portability Regulation would no longer be available to residents of such former EU Member State. The reason is that Article 3 of the Regulation only enables subscribers who are temporarily present in another EU Member State to access and use the online content service in the same manner as in the EU Member State of their own residence.

Broadcasters—Broadcasters established in a country that ceases to be an EU Member State would no longer benefit from the country of origin principle as enshrined in the Satellite and Cable Directive. This principle consists of a legal fiction according to which the act of communication to the public by satellite occurs solely in

---

[1] European Commission, *Notice to stakeholders: withdrawal of the United Kingdom and EU rules in the field of copyright*, 28 March 2018, available at <https://ec.europa.eu/digital-single-market/en/news/notice-stakeholders-withdrawal-united-kingdom-and-eu-rules-field-copyright> (last accessed 15 August 2018).

[2] Opinion 3/15 (*Avis rendu en vertu de l'article 218, paragraphe 11 TFUE (Traité de Marrakech sur l'accès aux œuvres publiées)*), of 14 February 2017, EU:C:2016:657, para 113 referring to: *Commission v Council*, C-114/12, EU:C:2014:2151, paras 70 and 71; and Opinion 1/13 (*Accession of third States to the Hague Convention*), of 14 October 2014, EU:C:2014:2303, para 86.

the EU Member State where, under the control and responsibility of the broadcasting organization, the programme-carrying signals are introduced into an uninterrupted chain of communication leading to the satellite and down towards the earth (Article 1(2)(b) of the Satellite and Cable Directive). Currently, an EU-based broadcasting organization is only required to clear rights in the EU Member State where the signal is introduced in order to transmit broadcasts containing copyright works or other protected subject matter.

Collective rights management—The end of the application of the Collective Rights Management Directive to a Member State that withdraws from the EU and the EEA would mean that the obligation of a collective management organization to represent another collective management organization for multi-territorial licensing (for the online rights in musical works) in certain cases (Article 30) would cease to be applicable. This means that the obligation of reciprocal representation would no longer subsist for collective rights management organizations based in the EU with regard to the collective rights management organizations established in the former EU Member State, and vice versa.

Sui generis **right in databases**—The availability of the *sui generis* right in databases would also be affected by a Member State's choice to withdraw from the EU. In this sense, nationals of the former Member State (unless they had their habitual residence in the EU) and companies/firms formed in accordance with the law of that country would no longer be entitled to maintain or obtain a *sui generis* right in respect of databases in the EU. Article 11 of the Database Directive, in fact, provides that the *sui generis* right within Article 7 only applies to databases whose makers or rightholders are nationals of a Member State or who have their habitual residence in the territory of the EU. The same applies to companies and firms formed in accordance with the law of a Member State and having their registered office, central administration, or principal place of business within the EU; however, where such a company or firm has only its registered office in the territory of the EU, its operations must be genuinely linked on an ongoing basis with the economy of a Member State. It is possible for the *sui generis* right to be available to databases made in third countries. However, any agreements extending the right within Article 7 to these kinds of databases must be concluded by the Council acting on a proposal from the EU Commission.

Orphan works—In addition, the rules on orphan works would also be affected by a country's withdrawal from the EU, in that the mechanism of mutual recognition of the 'orphan work' status provided for by the Orphan Works Directive would no longer apply between the former Member State and the EU. Article 4 of that directive provides, in fact, that a work or phonogram, which is considered orphan under Article 2 in a Member State, shall be considered orphan in all Member States. The result of such recognition is that the orphan work or phonogram may be used and accessed in accordance with the directive in all EU Member States. This would no longer be the case for orphans declared so in the former Member State, and vice versa.

2. Exhaustion of the Right of Distribution

Rationale of EU exhaustion—EU exhaustion rules are linked to the internal market-building project. In fact, in its proposal for a directive of the European Parliament and Council on the harmonization of certain aspects of copyright and related rights in the information society (that would eventually be adopted as the InfoSoc Directive), the EU Commission linked legislative action at the EU level to the need to align the laws of EU Member States and establish a system of regional (at that time, EC-wide) exhaustion that would replace national or international exhaustion regimes in place in certain Member States. Overall it was found that the smooth functioning of the internal market could not be guaranteed if EU Member States applied different regimes in respect of the exhaustion of copyright.[3] Indeed, in its proposal the EU Commission stressed the particular meaning of exhaustion in the EC/EU context, ie reconciling the principle of free movement of goods throughout the territory of the Union as per the provisions current in Articles 34–36 TFEU with the protection of the specific subject matter of intellectual property rights.[4]

The particular significance and rationale of EU exhaustion has been highlighted in relevant case law since the seminal decision of the then ECJ in *Metro v Commission*, C-26/76. In that case, which concerned whether an undertaking manufacturing sound recordings might rely on its exclusive right of distribution to prohibit the marketing in a certain Member State of sound recordings which it had itself supplied to an autonomous but fully subordinate subsidiary established in another Member State. The Court answered in the negative, holding that:

[12] If a right related to copyright is relied upon to prevent the marketing in a Member State of products distributed by the holder of the right or with his consent on the territory of another Member State on the sole ground that such distribution did not take place on the national territory, such a prohibition, which would legitimize the isolation of national markets, would be repugnant to the essential purpose of the Treaty, which is to unite national markets into a single market.

[13] That purpose could not be attained if, under the various legal systems of the Member States, nationals of those States were able to partition the market and bring about arbitrary discrimination of disguised restrictions on trade between Member States.[5]

This rationale of EU copyright exhaustion has been reiterated in subsequent case law. Referring to the decision in *Laserdisken*, C-479/04,[6] in *Art & Allposters International*, C-419/13, the CJEU confirmed that Article 4(2) of the InfoSoc Directive does not leave it open to the Member States to provide for an exhaustion rule other than the one set out in that provision. As follows from Recital 31 in the preamble to the same directive, differences in the national laws governing exhaustion of the right of distribution are likely to affect directly the smooth functioning of the internal market.[7]

Regional exhaustion—Similarly to other intellectual property rights, the EU legislative framework also envisages a system of regional (EU/EEA) exhaustion for copyright. Article 4(2) of the InfoSoc Directive states that:

[t]he distribution right shall not be exhausted within the Community in respect of the original or copies of the work, except where the first sale or other transfer of ownership in the Community of that object is made by the rightholder or with his consent.

---

[3] Commission of the European Communities, Proposal for a European Parliament and Council Directive on the harmonisation of certain aspects of copyright and related rights in the Information Society, /* COM/97/0628 final - COD 97/0359 */, OJ C 108, 7 April 1998, 6–13, 22.

[4] Ibid, 27. See also B Ubertazzi, 'The principle of free movement of goods: Community exhaustion and parallel imports', in I Stamatoudi and P Torremans (eds), *EU Copyright Law—A Commentary* (Edward Elgar:2014), §§3.04–3.05; P Mezei, *Copyright Exhaustion—Law and Policy in the United States and the European Union* (CUP:2018), 24–31.

[5] *Metro v Commission*, C-26/76, EU:C:1977:167, paras 12–13.

[6] *Laserdisken*, C-479/04, EU:C:2006:549, paras 24 and 56.

[7] *Art & Allposters International*, C-419/13, EU:C:2015:27, para 30.

This provision echoes the exhaustion rules contained in the Rental and Lending Rights Directive (Article 9(2)), Software Directive (Article 4(2)), and the Database Directive (Article 7(2)(b)). The phrase 'shall not be exhausted ... except where' is akin to 'shall be exhausted only where'. This means that the right of distribution shall be only exhausted when the relevant conditions are satisfied: first, there must be a first sale or other transfer of ownership that takes place in the EU/EEA; second, this must be made by the rightholder or be made with their consent.

No exhaustion in the EU/EEA if first sale occurs outside EU/EEA—Exhaustion within the EU/EEA may not take place if the first sale or other transfer of ownership occurs outside the EU/EEA.[8] This is confirmed by the wording of Recital 28 in the preamble to the InfoSoc Directive, which explicitly states that the right of distribution 'should not be exhausted in respect of the original or of copies thereof sold by the rightholder or with his consent outside the Community'.[9]

The decision to exit the EU, withdrawing from both the EU and EEA, would also lead—by default, and absent a unilateral decision by the departing Member State to *continue* recognizing and applying EU/EEA exhaustion to facilitate imports of goods coming from the EU/EEA into its own territory—to the inapplicability of the EU/ EEA exhaustion regime. The result would be that the first sale or other transfer of ownership in the former Member State alone would not exhaust the right of distribution as far as the EU/EEA is concerned, and vice versa. Hence, a copyright owner would be entitled to control subsequent transfers of ownership of a copyright work or a copy thereof from the former Member State to the EU/EEA or from the EU/EEA to the former Member State. This conclusion finds support in both the language of legislation and CJEU case law. The practical implications of all this would be that content circulation between a former Member State and the EU would be less smooth than is the case for protected subject matter first sold (or whose ownership is first transferred) within the EU/EEA.

3. Relevance of EU Copyright Case Law to (Future) Non-EU Member States

Inapplicability of EU law and case law—In addition to changes brought about by the supervening inapplicability of EU legislation to a country that decides to leave both the EU and the EEA, the other aspect to consider is the value and legacy of the case law of a court, the CJEU, which—at least in the area of copyright—has been having a decisive role in shaping the EU copyright framework. In this respect, three main points arise. The first one is the legal value of CJEU judgments issued after the exit of a Member State from the EU. The second one relates to the legal value of CJEU judgments issued before actual withdrawal from the EU. The final point concerns the room left for the copyright law of a certain country that is no longer part of the EU to develop in a different direction from the EU copyright *acquis*, as interpreted by the CJEU.

Value of EU judgments issued before and after exit from the EU—In relation to the first two points, the *substantial* value of judgments issued by the highest EU court

---

[8] See S von Lewinski, 'International exhaustion of the distribution right under EC copyright law?' (2005) 27(7) EIPR 233, 234. See also P Mezei, 'Digital first sale doctrine *ante portas*' (2015) 6(2) JIPITEC 23, 30.

[9] In this sense, see also *Laserdisken*, C-479/04, EU:C:2006:549, para 23.

concerning the interpretation of EU rules on which domestic rules are modelled—at least for the initial period following the withdrawal from the EU until (and whether) the copyright system of a former Member State departs substantially from the one in place at the EU level—is due to remain significant. With specific regard to the *formal* value of such judgments, this is a choice (also) left to the departing Member State and may be subject to negotiations with the EU.

The case of the UK—In the particular case of the UK, section 6 of the European Union (Withdrawal) Act 2018 provides a framework for the interpretation of retained EU law.[10] The provision states that, following the departure of the UK from the EU, a court or tribunal in that country would not be bound by any principles laid down, or any decisions made, on or after exit day by the CJEU, and would not be able to refer any matter to the CJEU on or after exit day. As regards CJEU decisions issued after exit day, a court or tribunal would need not to have regard to anything done on or after exit day by the CJEU, another EU entity, or the EU, but 'may do so if it considers it appropriate to do so'. In addition, any question concerning the validity, meaning, or effect of any retained EU law (this would also apply to copyright provisions adopted in light of EU obligations) would need to be decided—so far as that law is unmodified on or after exit day and so far as they are relevant to it—in accordance with any retained case law and any retained general principles of EU law, and having regard (among other things) to the limits, immediately before exit day, of EU competences. The UK Supreme Court would not be bound by any retained CJEU case law, nor would the High Court of Justiciary in certain scenarios or when no court or tribunal would be bound by any retained domestic case law that it would not otherwise have been bound by. In any case, in deciding whether to depart from any retained CJEU case law, the Supreme Court or the High Court of Justiciary would need to apply the same test as it would apply in deciding whether to depart from its own case law.

An actual and immediate freedom?—Whilst this arrangement might prima facie suggest a certain freedom to disentangle one's own domestic law (and case law) from the influence and effects of CJEU decisions, including those issued before the actual exit from the EU, things would actually be much more complex than this. The reason is twofold: first, the relatively high number and the content of CJEU judgments has contributed to also shaping the domestic interpretations of national statutes; second, national courts have been incorporating CJEU judgments into their own reasoning. For a country like the UK, also 'Brexiting' CJEU case law would require disentanglement from a wealth of national decisions that have the status of binding precedent.[11] In any case, CJEU decisions will continue to be relevant to the interpretation of EU-derived UK legislation. In addition, there will continue to be cases, for instance with regard to communication to the public, in which CJEU rulings will be refining earlier case law which will be 'retained' and hence binding below the Supreme Court. A number of examples, presented according to the order of the issues discussed in Chapters 4 to 6, are provided in what follows.

---

[10] European Union (Withdrawal) Act 2018.

[11] See further R Arnold, L Bently, E Derclaye, and G Dinwoodie, *The legal consequences of Brexit through the lens of IP law* (2017) University of Cambridge—Legal Studies Research Paper Series, No 21/2017, 6–8.

4. The Case of the UK: Impact and Legacy of CJEU Case Law on Economic Rights

The CJEU understanding and construction of economic rights has had a significant impact on corresponding UK rights, as well as on the subsistence of copyright protection, the notion of 'work', and the standard of infringement. Following the departure of the UK from the EU, and depending on the type of departure and new relationship (if any) with the EU, the complexity of UK copyright law would likely increase rather than decrease.[12] A change of legislative provisions would in any case be required to reflect the fact that this country would no longer be a Member State of the EU and, possibly, would also cease to be part of the EEA. However, without a major overhaul of its copyright statute, provisions that have been included to give effect to corresponding EU provisions would still need to be interpreted in light of EU law.

4.1 Impact on the originality requirement

Skill, labour, or effort—Traditionally, under UK law the requirement of originality has not represented a particularly meaningful threshold to copyright protection: the understanding of this requirement has in fact been that 'original' is akin to 'not copied', 'what is worth copying is worth protecting', and, ultimately, that originality is the result of employing 'sufficient skill, labour or effort'. After the introduction of an originality requirement into statutory copyright law in 1911, the authority often cited to define its meaning has been *University of London Press Ltd v University Tutorial Press Ltd*, in which Peterson J held that:

[t]he word 'original' does not in this connection mean that the work must be the expression of original or inventive thought. Copyright Acts are not concerned with the originality of ideas, but with the expression of thought ... The originality which is required relates to the expression of the thought. But the Act does not require that the expression must be in an original or novel form, but that the work must not be copied from another work—that it should originate from the author.[13]

Such understanding of originality has been challenged little since 1911, and the Copyright, Designs and Patents Act (CDPA), enacted in 1988, does not add clarity on this point. The CDPA only sets an express originality requirement for literary, dramatic, musical, or artistic works, and not also for sound recordings, films, broadcasts, and the typographical arrangement of published editions. The reason for this choice is that, while the former may be classified as contents (works that are protected regardless of the signals by which they are carried), the latter are signals (what is protected is the signal itself, as distinct from the content it carries).[14]

According to commentators, the reason why originality under UK law has been read in a limited sense is twofold: first of all, a loose understanding reduces the element of

---

[12] The need for a new UK copyright act was advocated well before the 2016 referendum: see R Arnold, 'The need for a new Copyright Act: a case study in law reform' (2015) 5(2) QMJIP 110.

[13] *University of London Press v University Tutorial* [1916] 2 Ch 601. On this case, see Centre for Intellectual Property and Information Law (University of Cambridge)—Virtual Museum, *University of London Press v University Tutorial* [1916] 2 Ch 601, available at <https://www.cipil.law.cam.ac.uk/virtual-museum/university-london-press-v-university-tutorial-1916-2-ch-601> (last accessed 15 August 2018).

[14] R Arnold, 'Content copyrights and signal copyrights: the case for a rational scheme of protection' (2011) 1(3) QMJIP 272, 276.

subjective judgement in deciding what qualifies for protection to a minimum; second, it allows protection of any investment of labour and capital which in some way produces a literary result.[15] The result has been that, to satisfy the traditional originality standard, two sole conditions need to be met: first, that the work has originated from the author, in the sense of not being slavishly copied from another work; second, that the creation of the work has required the expenditure of more than negligible or trivial effort or relevant skill.[16] However, for certain works (eg sculptures), courts have also (and rather oddly) required a demonstration of the intention of the author to create a work of art. So, for instance, among the reasons that led to the conclusion that copyright could not vest in the Stormtrooper Helmet from the *Star Wars* films there was the fact that its primary function was utilitarian:

> While it was intended to express something, that was for utilitarian purposes. While it has an interest as an object, and while it was intended to express an idea, it was not conceived, or created, with the intention that it should do so other than as part of character portrayal in the film.[17]

Infopaq International—In the immediate aftermath of the CJEU decision in *Infopaq International*, C-5/08 (see further Chapter 4, Section 1.1) its impact on the UK understanding of originality appeared limited, if any at all. In the first case decided after that CJEU ruling, the High Court of England and Wales reiterated that originality involves the application of skill or labour in the creation of the work,[18] and did not consider the CJEU decision as requiring a change in the approach to originality. At the same time, however, the court conceded that the full implications of that ruling had not yet been fully worked out.[19]

Subsequent CJEU decisions have clarified that the EU standard of 'author's own intellectual creation' requires more than simple 'skill, labour or effort': a work is protectable if it is the result of 'creative freedom'[20] and 'free and creative choices',[21] and ultimately carries the 'personal touch'[22] of the author. It is apparent, as AG Mengozzi noted in his Opinion in *Football Dataco and Others*, C-604/10 (with regard to the standard of originality for databases), that 'copyright protection is conditional upon the database being characterised by a "creative" aspect, and it is not sufficient that the creation of the database required labour and skill'.[23] The AG recalled that different standards of originality have traditionally been found across the various EU Member States.[24] However, the EU standard of originality for databases and—after

---

[15] W Cornish, D Llewelyn, and T Aplin, *Intellectual Property: Patents, Copyright, Trade Marks and Allied Rights* (Sweet & Maxwell:2013), 8th edn, 435–6.
[16] K Garnett, G Davies, and G Harbottle, *Copinger and Skone James on Copyright* (Sweet & Maxwell:2017), 17th edn, Vol I, §3.208.
[17] *Lucasfilm Ltd and Others v Ainsworth and Another* [2008] EWHC 1878 (Ch) (31 July 2008), para 121, cited with approval in *Lucasfilm Ltd and Others v Ainsworth and Another* [2011] UKSC 39 (27 July 2011) (Lord Walker and Lord Collins), para 40. See also the discussion in R Jacob, D Alexander, and M Fisher, *Guidebook to Intellectual Property* (Hart:2013), 6th edn, 148.
[18] *Newspaper Licensing Agency Ltd and Others v Meltwater Holding BV and Others* [2010] EWHC 3099 (Ch) (26 November 2010), para 30, referring to: *Interlego AG v Tyco Industries* [1989] 1 AC 217, paras 259–263; *Walter v Lane* [1900] AC 539; *Express Newspapers Plc v News (UK) Limited* [1990] 1 WLR 1320.
[19] *Newspaper Licensing Agency Ltd and Others v Meltwater Holding BV and Others* [2010] EWHC 3099 (Ch) (26 November 2010), para 81.
[20] *Football Association Premier League and Others*, C-403/08 and C-429/08, EU:C:2011:631, para 98.
[21] *Painer*, C-145/10, EU:C:2011:798, para 89.   [22] Ibid, para 92.
[23] Opinion of Advocate General Paolo Mengozzi in *Football Dataco and Others*, C-604/10, EU:C:2011:848, para 35.
[24] Ibid, para 36.

Infopaq International, C-5/08—also for works falling under the scope of the InfoSoc Directive—requires more than just skill, labour, or effort. The AG made this point clearly:

[T]here is no doubt that, as regards copyright protection, the [Database] Directive espouses a concept of originality which requires more than the mere 'mechanical' effort needed to collect the data and enter them in the database. To be protected by the copyright, a database must ... be the 'intellectual creation' of the person who has set it up. That expression leaves no room for doubt, and echoes a formula which is typical of the continental copyright tradition.[25]

Subsequent case law in the UK—The impact of CJEU case law, even after further rulings tackling the concept of originality, has not always been understood correctly by UK courts, with certain judgments suggesting that 'author's own intellectual creation' is an alternative phrase for 'sufficient skill, labour or effort'.[26] However, more recent judgments support the view that the bar to originality has also been raised under UK law: the string of CJEU decisions on this point has been incorporated into UK law. Hence, it is no longer correct to hold that satisfying originality merely requires exercising sufficient skill, labour, or effort (or judgement). This is so because, also under UK law, what is required to claim sufficient originality in a work 'is something on which the author has stamped his "personal touch" through the creative choices he has made'.[27] Hence, '[t]he requirement of originality under the [CDPA] is that the work must be an expression of the author's own intellectual creation'.[28] This does not mean that every constituent aspect of a work must be original: the work must be taken as a whole, and can include parts that are neither novel nor ingenious.[29]

4.2 Impact on the notion of 'work', subject matter categorization, and rights attached to categories

Notion of 'work' in Berne—The Berne Convention—which will continue to bind the UK following this country's departure from the EU (the UK is a member state of the Berne Union) adopts an open-ended definition of 'literary and artistic works' eligible for protection. Article 2(1) therein does not define the term 'work', although it clarifies that such expression 'shall include every production in the literary, scientific and artistic domain, whatever may be the mode or form of its expression'. According to the relevant WIPO Guide, the reason why Article 2(1) does not state explicitly that works are intellectual creations is that this element of the concept of 'work' was considered to be obvious (all this was stated explicitly at the 1948 Brussels revision conference).[30] In this sense, the expression 'literary and artistic works' is to be understood as including 'all intellectual creations irrespective of whether they may be regarded as belonging to

---

[25] Ibid, para 37.
[26] *Temple Island Collections Ltd v New English Teas Ltd and Another* [2012] EWPCC 1 (12 January 2012), para 27; *Taylor v Maguire* [2013] EWHC 3804 (IPEC) (3 December 2013), para 8.
[27] *SAS Institute Inc v World Programming Ltd* [2013] EWHC 69 (Ch) (25 January 2013), para 41. See also *Dramatico Entertainment Ltd and Others v British Sky Broadcasting Ltd and Others* [2012] EWHC 268 (Ch) (20 February 2012), paras 62–63.
[28] *Banner Universal Motion Pictures Ltd v Endemol Shine Group Ltd and Another* [2017] EWHC 2600 (Ch) (19 October 2017), para 26. In the same sense, also *Martin and Another v Kogan and Others* [2017] EWHC 2927 (IPEC) (22 November 2017), para 38.
[29] *Banner Universal Motion Pictures Ltd v Endemol Shine Group Ltd and Another* [2017] EWHC 2600 (Ch) (19 October 2017), para 26.
[30] World Intellectual Property Organization, *Guide to copyright and related rights treaties administered by WIPO and glossary of copyright and related rights terms* (2003), BC-2.4–BC-2.5.

the literary domain, to the artistic domain or to both at the same time'.[31] The list of protectable works within Article 2 of the Berne Convention is also a non-exhaustive one, and this is clearly indicated by the fact the provision uses the words 'such as'.[32]

Open-ended or closed lists of protectable subject matter—It is not entirely clear from the wording of EU directives like the InfoSoc Directive whether under EU law there is any obligation to intend the list of protectable works to be open-ended. If the latter was the case (see further Chapter 4, Section 1.2), then those Member States, like the UK, that envisage a closed categorization might be considered in breach of their own obligations under EU law. Section 1(1) CDPA provides that:

[c]opyright is a property right which subsists in accordance with this Part in the following descriptions of work—

(a) original literary, dramatic, musical or artistic works,
(b) sound recordings, films or broadcasts, and
(c) the typographical arrangement of published editions.

With particular regard to the UK, there are a few instances in which works have been denied copyright protection due to the impossibility of placing such works within one of the categories provided by the CDPA. Examples include the assembly of a scene[33] and the Stormtrooper Helmet from the *Star Wars* films.[34] Until recently, uncertainties have surrounded the protectability of TV formats by means of copyright, due also to the uncertain categorization thereof.[35]

CJEU case law—Yet, in light of CJEU case law, it is doubtful that EU Member States have the freedom to maintain closed systems of protectable subject matter (see further Chapter 4, Section 1.2). In fact, in its decisions in *Bezpečnostní softwarová asociace*, C-393/09, and *Football Association Premier League and Others*, C-403/08 and C-429/08, the CJEU held that under EU law copyright protection should arise any time a work is 'its author's own intellectual creation', ie a work is sufficiently original, without also considering whether the work at issue would be one of the 'right kind'.

In *Bezpečnostní softwarová asociace*, C-393/09, the CJEU considered whether a graphic user interface could be protected by copyright under the Software Directive. It ruled out that this would be the case, in that a graphic user interface is an interaction interface that enables the communication between a computer program and its user. Since it does not enable the reproduction of a computer program but merely constitutes an element of that program through which a user makes use of the features of a particular program, a graphic user interface does not constitute a form of expression of a computer program within Article 1(2) of the Software Directive. However, it may be eligible for copyright protection under the InfoSoc Directive: a graphic user interface 'can, as a work, be protected by copyright if it is its author's own intellectual creation'.[36] In *Football Association Premier League and Others*, C-403/08 and C-429/08, the CJEU had to consider—among other things—whether sporting events (English Premier League football matches) per se might be eligible for copyright protection. It responded in the negative, holding that they 'cannot be classified as works. To be so classified, the subject matter concerned would have to be original in the sense that it

[31] Ibid, BC-2.15.   [32] Ibid, BC-2.16.
[33] *Creation Records Ltd and Others v News Group Newspapers Ltd* [1997] EWHC Ch 370 (25 April 1997).
[34] *Lucasfilm Ltd and Others v Ainsworth and Another* [2011] UKSC 39 (27 July 2011).
[35] *Banner Universal Motion Pictures Ltd v Endemol Shine Group Ltd and Another* [2017] EWHC 2600 (Ch) (19 October 2017).
[36] *Bezpečnostní softwarová asociace*, C-393/09, EU:C:2010:816, para 46.

is its author's own intellectual creation.'[37] What the Court found in both *Bezpečnostní softwarová asociace*, C-393/09, and *Football Association Premier League and Others*, C-403/08 and C-429/08, is that it is sufficient for a certain subject matter to be original to be eligible for copyright protection under the InfoSoc Directive. The outcome of the pending CJEU referral in *Levola Hengelo*, C-310/17 (on which see further in Chapter 4, Section 1.2) has the potential to be decisive, in that the CJEU will likely tackle the conditions for copyright protection of 'works' under EU law.

Flos **and designs**—The CJEU has clarified that the scope of protection granted to 'works' under the InfoSoc Directive is not only broad (this is in line with one of the objectives the EU wished to pursue by adopting this piece of legislation), but also such as to complement—if not supersede—that of other directives. Besides the case of graphic user interfaces in *Bezpečnostní softwarová asociace*, C-393/09, the CJEU also applied this conclusion to designs and videogames. In *Flos*, C-168/09, the CJEU held that while unregistered designs in the public domain are outside the scope of Article 17 of the Design Directive, they might nonetheless qualify for copyright protection under the InfoSoc Directive 'if the conditions for that directive's application are met',[38] ie if they are their author's own intellectual creation.[39] The outcome of *Flos*, C-168/09, was admittedly ambiguous, yet it led the UK government to the decision to repeal section 52 CDPA, on the basis that a different scope of copyright protection for registered designs than was the case for other subject matter would be contrary to EU law.[40] The outcome of the current referral in *Cofemel*, C-683/17, might help determine more precisely the actual implications of *Flos*, C-168/09.[41]

---

[37] *Football Association Premier League and Others*, C-403/08 and C-429/08, EU:C:2011:631, paras 96–97.

[38] *Flos*, C-168/09, EU:C:2011:29, para 34.

[39] On the particular outcome of *Flos*, C-168/09, see (critically) L Bently, 'The return of industrial copyright?' (2012) 34(10) EIPR 654, 660–1.

[40] Section 52 CDPA so provided:

Effect of exploitation of design derived from artistic work.

(1) This section applies where an artistic work has been exploited, by or with the licence of the copyright owner, by—
   (a) making by an industrial process articles falling to be treated for the purposes of this Part as copies of the work, and
   (b) marketing such articles, in the United Kingdom or elsewhere.

(2) After the end of the period of 25 years from the end of the calendar year in which such articles are first marketed, the work may be copied by making articles of any description, or doing anything for the purpose of making articles of any description, and anything may be done in relation to articles so made, without infringing copyright in the work.

(3) Where only part of an artistic work is exploited as mentioned in subsection (1), subsection (2) applies only in relation to that part.

(4) The Secretary of State may by order make provision—
   (a) as to the circumstances in which an article, or any description of article, is to be regarded for the purposes of this section as made by an industrial process;
   (b) excluding from the operation of this section such articles of a primarily literary or artistic character as he thinks fit.

(5) An order shall be made by statutory instrument which shall be subject to annulment in pursuance of a resolution of either House of Parliament.

(6) In this section—
   (a) references to articles do not include films; and
   (b) references to the marketing of an article are to its being sold or let for hire or offered or exposed for sale or hire.

[41] See further: E Rosati, 'When does copyright protection arise in works of applied art and industrial models and designs? A new CJEU reference' (25 January 2018), The IPKat, available at <http://ipkitten.blogspot.com/2018/01/when-does-copyright-protection-arise-in.html> (last accessed 15

Nintendo and Others **and videogames**—Similarly, the CJEU excluded that videogames, being complex matter comprising not only a computer program but also graphic and sound elements, could be regarded as computer programs within the meaning of the Software Directive: insofar as the parts of a videogame are part of its originality, they are protected, together with the entire work, by copyright in the context of the system established by the InfoSoc Directive.[42]

UK approach to 'work' and subject matter categorization and impact of CJEU case law—Under UK law, a 'work' is 'a thing which satisfies the statutory description of a literary, dramatic, etc. work'.[43] Such 'thing' must be, first, a production in the Berne sense and, second, fall within one of the categories provided by the CDPA. Categorization has implications not just for determining whether a certain work may be actually protected by copyright under UK law, but also what rights attach to such work. So, for instance, section 21(1) of the UK Act excludes the right of adaptation for artistic works, while providing expressly for it in relation to literary, dramatic, and musical works. Similarly, section 17(3) includes conversion of a work into a three-dimensional form within the scope of the right of reproduction only for artistic works, not also literary works. In addition, differences between the various categories subsist also in relation to the topic of infringement. While copyright in a literary, dramatic, musical, or artistic work may be infringed without copying the medium on which the work was recorded by the author or published by the publisher, copyright in sound recordings, broadcasts, published editions, and films may only be infringed by reproducing the medium produced by the author.

The impact of CJEU case law is profound, although the full implications remain to be seen (see further Chapter 4, Section 1.2). In its decision in *SAS v WPL*, the High Court of England and Wales stated that:

[i]n the light of a number of recent judgments of the CJEU, it may be arguable that it is not a fatal objection to a claim that copyright subsists in a particular work that the work is not one of the kinds of work listed in section 1(1)(a) of the Copyright, Designs and Patents 1988 and defined elsewhere in that Act. Nevertheless, it remains clear that the putative copyright work must be a literary or artistic work within the meaning of Article 2(1) of the Berne Convention.[44]

Different rights for different works—With regard to maintaining different regimes for different categories of works, this may also be no longer justifiable in light of EU law beyond instances like the *sui generis* database right, for which EU law sets a reciprocal protection obligation across the EU. The 2012 *Abraham Moon* case concerned infringement of copyright in the design of woollen plaid fabric for use in upholstery and furnishing by a competitor's design. The defendants denied infringement, on the grounds that their design had been created independently from that of the claimant. Among other things, counsel for the latter pointed out that the definition of reproduction in section 17(2) CDPA is broad, also by reference to Article 2 of the InfoSoc Directive, as well as Recital 21 therein. Besides *Infopaq International*, C-5/08,[45] reference was made to the CJEU ruling in *Painer*, C-145/10,[46] in which it was stated that

---

August 2018); T Rendas, 'Copyright protection of designs in the EU: how many originality standards is too many?' (2018) 13(6) JIPLP 439.

[42] *Nintendo and Others*, C-355/12, EU:C:2014:25, para 23.

[43] K Garnett, G Davies, and G Harbottle, *Copinger and Skone James on Copyright* (Sweet & Maxwell:2011), 16th edn, Vol I, §3.06.

[44] *SAS Institute Inc v World Programming Ltd* [2010] EWHC 1829 (Ch) (23 July 2010), para 27.

[45] *Infopaq International*, C-5/08, EU:C:2009:465, para 43.

[46] *Painer*, C-145/10, EU:C:2011:798, para 96.

the scope of copyright protection should not depend on the possible differences in the degree of creative freedom in the production of various categories of works.

In other words, the InfoSoc Directive envisages the protection of all intellectual creations by the same reproduction right, and distinctions under the CDPA between literary and artistic works would no longer be justified. So, the limitation of three-dimensional copying in section 17(3) CDPA to artistic works would no longer be appropriate. Nonetheless, the Patents County Court (now Intellectual Property Enterprise Court) held that 'however tempting it may be', it would 'not propose to go down the road suggested by [the claimant's counsel] to the extent of denying the existence of differences between literary and artistic works'.[47]

4.3 Impact on the standard of infringement

Substantial taking—To establish prima facie infringement under UK law, a claimant needs to demonstrate—in accordance with section 16 CDPA—that the defendant has done any of the restricted acts in relation to the work as a whole or any substantial part of it. The notion of 'substantial taking' should not be intended in a quantitative sense. Lord Millett set out the test in the context of the landmark decision in *Designers Guild*, concerning alleged infringement of copyright in a fabric design (see Figure 7.1):

Once the judge has found that the defendants' design incorporates features taken from the copyright work, the question is whether what has been taken constitutes all or a substantial part of the copyright work. This is a matter of impression, for whether the part taken is substantial must be determined by its quality rather than its quantity. It depends upon its importance to the copyright work. It does not depend upon its importance to the defendants' work, as I have already pointed out. The pirated part is considered on its own.[48]

The House of Lords thus held that the test to be followed in assessing infringement cases is whether the alleged infringer has incorporated a substantial part of the independent skill, labour, and judgement contributed by the original author in creating the copyright work. Overall, the question whether the defendant has copied a substantial part depends much more on the quality, rather than the quantity, of what they have taken,[49] and is a question of degree.[50] To determine whether a substantial part has been taken, a court must have regard to all the facts of the case including: 'the nature and extent of the copying; the quality and importance of what has been taken; the degree of originality of what has been taken or whether it is commonplace; and whether a substantial part of the skill and labour contributed by the author in creating the original has been appropriated'.[51]

Substantial taking as taking of an original part—In light of the CJEU decision in *Infopaq International*, C-5/08 (which, before being a case about originality, is a case about infringement), it is apparent that, while the UK test for infringement might not have been affected substantially,[52] it needs to be qualified by the interpretation of the

---

[47] *Abraham Moon & Sons Ltd v Thornber and Others* [2012] EWPCC 37 (5 October 2012), para 99.
[48] *Designers Guild Limited v Russell Williams (Textiles) Limited (Trading As Washington Dc)* [2000] UKHL 58; [2001] 1 All ER 700; [2000] 1 WLR 2416 (23 November 2000) (Lord Millett).
[49] *Ladbroke v William Hill* [1964] 1 WLR 273, (Lord Reid), para 276.
[50] *Macmillan & Co Ltd v Cooper* (1923) 93 LJPC 113, (Atkinson J), para 121.
[51] *Allen v Bloomsbury Publishing Plc and Another* [2010] EWHC 2560 (Ch) (14 October 2010), para 85.
[52] Advancing a cautious reading of the implications of *Infopaq International*, C-5/0,8 for the UK standard of infringement, see M Vitoria and Others, *Laddie, Prescott and Vitoria—The Modern Law of Copyright and Designs* (LexisNexis:2011), 4th edn, Vol I, §3.136.

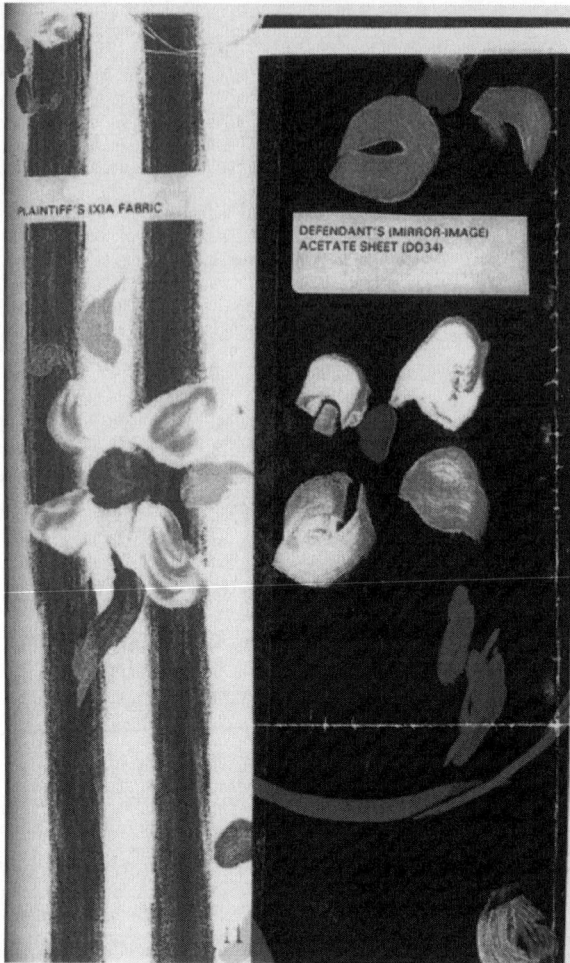

Figure 7.1 *Designers Guild* case: The claimant's work (L) and the infringing work (R) (source: Centre for Intellectual Property and Information Law (University of Cambridge)— Virtual Museum)

concept of 'reproduction in part' as provided by the CJEU. In this sense, there would be a substantial taking of a work when what is being reproduced is sufficiently original in the sense of being its author's own intellectual creation.

The UK test is thus now informed by EU law, despite the lack of any formal harmonization—whether at the international or EU levels—of the standard of infringement. The High Court of England and Wales correctly qualified prima facie infringement by referring to a passage that was strictly obiter in *NLA v Marks & Spencer*, ie that 'the quality relevant for the purposes of substantiality is the literary originality of that which has been copied'.[53] The court noted that this approach is the same as that adopted by the CJEU in *Infopaq International*, C-5/08:

---

[53] *Newspaper Licensing Agency Limited v Marks and Spencer Plc* [2001] UKHL 38 (12 July 2001), (Lord Hoffmann), para 19.

It follows from this that, when considering whether a substantial part has been reproduced, it is necessary to focus upon what has been reproduced and to consider whether it expresses the author's own intellectual creation. To that extent, some dissection is not merely permissible, but required. On the other hand, the Court of Justice also held in *Infopaq* at [49] that it is necessary to consider the cumulative effect of what has been reproduced.[54]

'Copyright Infringement Checklist'—For the benefit of readers who may not be familiar with UK law or students in the early stages of their adventures in UK copyright law, the document reproduced in Figure 7.2 is a 'Copyright Infringement Checklist'[55] meant to provide a visual aid of the main issues that need to be considered to establish infringement under the CDPA.

4.4 Potential impact on the distinction between primary and accessory liability

Primary and accessory liability—Another aspect in which CJEU activity might have had an impact on UK copyright law (though, at the time of writing, it is difficult to appreciate the full ramifications thereof) is the traditional distinction between primary and accessory (or secondary) liability for copyright infringement. While the former is an open-ended set of situations, which have been traditionally assessed from an objective standpoint, ie without considering the defendant's state of mind as determinative for the establishment of prima facie liability, the latter requires consideration of the defendant's state of mind. In the context of the present discussion, accessory liability by authorization deserves special mention. This type of liability is composed of a conduct element and a mental element, which must be intended as requiring demonstration of a sufficient degree of knowledge by the defendant of the circumstances and of the acts committed (or about to be committed) by the primary infringer.[56]

  Liability of Pirate Bay operators—From a formal standpoint, accessory liability is an area untouched by relevant EU directives, and in which EU Member States retain their own freedom. However, in its decision in *Stichting Brein*, C-610/15 (see further Chapter 4, Section 2.3) the CJEU considered the liability of the operators of a platform, The Pirate Bay, which is an engine for P2P file-sharing hosting no protected works. In a decision concerning the liability of the same platform operators, the High Court of England and Wales held the operators of The Pirate Bay liable as accessories for users' infringements.[57] Following the CJEU decision, this approach may be no longer correct. In that case, the EU Court held that the operators of an unlicensed online file-sharing platform may be primarily liable for copyright infringement, both when they have actual knowledge of the infringements committed by users of their services and when they could not be unaware that their platform provides access to protected subject matter published without the consent of the rightholders.

---

  [54] *SAS Institute Inc v World Programming Ltd* [2010] EWHC 1829 (Ch) (23 July 2010), para 43.

  [55] The 'checklist' was first published in E Rosati, 'Struggling to understand how to address a copyright infringement issue? Here's my checklist' (24 November 2014), available at <http://ipkitten. blogspot.com/2014/11/struggling-to-understand-how-to-address.html> (last accessed 15 August 2018). Other study aid materials that I have created for intellectual property students are available at <http://www.elawnora.com/#ip-materials> (last accessed 15 August 2018).

  [56] R Arnold and PS Davies, 'Accessory liability for intellectual property infringement: the case of authorisation' (2017) 133(Jul) LQR 442, 465.

  [57] *Dramatico Entertainment Ltd and Others v British Sky Broadcasting Ltd and Others* [2012] EWHC 268 (Ch) (20 February 2012).

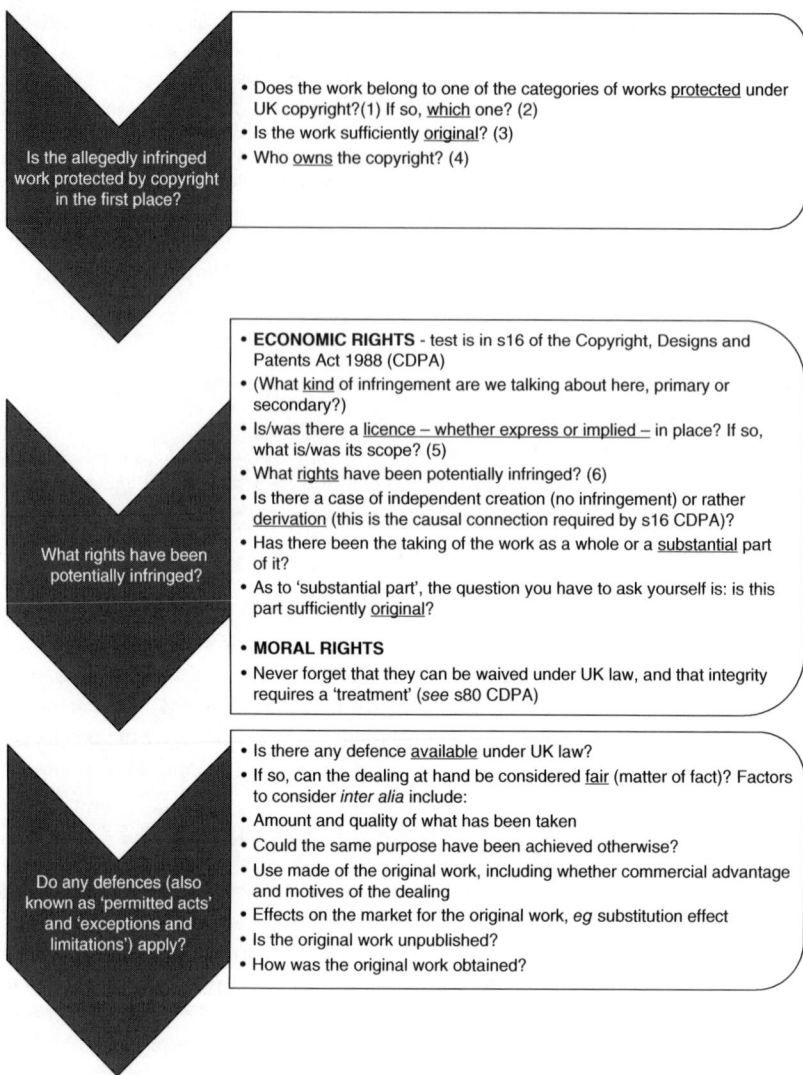

The flowchart contains three stages:

Is the allegedly infringed work protected by copyright in the first place?
- Does the work belong to one of the categories of works <u>protected</u> under UK copyright?(1) If so, <u>which</u> one? (2)
- Is the work sufficiently <u>original</u>? (3)
- Who <u>owns</u> the copyright? (4)

What rights have been potentially infringed?
- **ECONOMIC RIGHTS** - test is in s16 of the Copyright, Designs and Patents Act 1988 (CDPA)
- (What <u>kind</u> of infringement are we talking about here, primary or secondary?)
- Is/was there a <u>licence – whether express or implied –</u> in place? If so, what is/was its scope? (5)
- What <u>rights</u> have been potentially infringed? (6)
- Is there a case of independent creation (no infringement) or rather <u>derivation</u> (this is the causal connection required by s16 CDPA)?
- Has there been the taking of the work as a whole or a <u>substantial</u> part of it?
- As to 'substantial part', the question you have to ask yourself is: is this part sufficiently <u>original</u>?
- **MORAL RIGHTS**
- Never forget that they can be waived under UK law, and that integrity requires a 'treatment' (*see* s80 CDPA)

Do any defences (also known as 'permitted acts' and 'exceptions and limitations') apply?
- Is there any defence <u>available</u> under UK law?
- If so, can the dealing at hand be considered <u>fair</u> (matter of fact)? Factors to consider *inter alia* include:
- Amount and quality of what has been taken
- Could the same purpose have been achieved otherwise?
- Use made of the original work, including whether commercial advantage and motives of the dealing
- Effects on the market for the original work, *eg* substitution effect
- Is the original work unpublished?
- How was the original work obtained?

Figure 7.2 Copyright Infringement Checklist

(1) If not, *eg* it is an unconventional work, then you should recall potential implications of CJEU decisions in *Infopaq International*, C-5/08 and its progeny, notably *Bezpečnostní softwarová asociace*, C-393/09, as well as *Levola Hengelo*, C-310/17.

(2) This is key when the economic right that has been potentially infringed is one of those rights, eg adaptation, that are not available to each and every protected subject matter.

(3) This may prove tricky when dealing with works which might qualify for copyright protection under the traditional skill, labour, or effort approach, but might be considered sub-original if CJEU understanding of originality as author's own intellectual creation is to be intended as requiring something more than sufficient skill, labour, or effort.

(4) This requires consideration of issues such as authorship, joint authorship, works created in the course of employment, copyright assignment, etc.

(5) For instance, you might have granted a licence to reproduce a work, not also to communicate it to the public. If an act of communication to the public takes place, it may be an issue of infringement.

(6) See note (2) above.

(7) Do not forget that, except Article 5(1), all the exceptions in Article 5 of the InfoSoc Directive are optional for EU Member States to implement into their own national laws.

By introducing a knowledge requirement within the scope of primary liability, the CJEU has blurred the distinction between what has been traditionally regarded as a strict liability tort (primary infringement) and liability informed by the defendant's subjective state of actual or constructive knowledge (secondary infringement).[58] Liability should be determined, at least in relation to acts of communication to the public, by referring to the de facto EU standard, rather than national statutes and case law. All this is likely to result, for some time, in practical uncertainties for those jurisdictions, like the UK, which distinguish between primary and accessory liability. The practical effect is that, at least in instances like the present one, the liability by authorization regime might be regarded as absorbed within the system of primary liability.

5. The Case of the UK: Impact and Legacy of CJEU Case Law on Exceptions and Limitations

Autonomous concepts of EU law—The fact that several of the concepts found in EU copyright exceptions and limitations have been regarded by the CJEU as 'autonomous concepts' of EU law (see Chapter 2, Section 2.2) mandates a harmonized, common approach to corresponding national exceptions and limitations. In this sense, as discussed in Chapter 3, Section 4 and Chapter 5, it is necessary to reconsider both Member States' actual freedom in transposing into their own legal regimes provisions within Article 5 of the InfoSoc Directive and the need to adapt national interpretations and applications of copyright exceptions to relevant CJEU case law. This might be, for instance, the case of the UK defences of quotation (section 30(1ZA) CDPA) and parody (section 30A CDPA).[59] Introduced in the context of the 2014 reform further to the recommendations set forth in the Hargreaves Review,[60] both defences are framed within 'fair dealing'.

'Fair dealing'—A substantial number of UK copyright defences refer to the concept of 'fair dealing' with a third-party work. The Act does not contain a definition of it, nor does it stipulate what factors are to be considered when assessing whether a certain dealing with a work is to be considered fair. The notion has thus developed through case law from the perspective of a 'fair-minded and honest person',[61] and has been traditionally considered a matter of degree and impression.[62] Several factors inform the decision whether a certain use of a work is fair, although the relative importance of each of them will vary according to the case in hand and the dealing at issue.[63] In *Ashdown v Telegraph*, the Court of Appeal of England and Wales was not able to provide:

any hard-and-fast definition of what is fair dealing, for it is a matter of fact, degree and impression. However, by far the most important factor is whether the alleged fair dealing is in fact

---

[58] In this sense, see also P Savola, 'EU copyright liability for internet linking' (2017) 8(2) JIPITEC 139, 143.
[59] With regard to the treatment of parodies under UK law prior to the 2014 reform, see A Walsh, 'Parody of intellectual property: prospects for a fair use/dealing defence in the United Kingdom' (2010) 21(11) ICCLR 386, 386–8.
[60] I Hargreaves, *Digital Opportunity—A Review of Intellectual Property and Growth* (2011), available at <https://assets.publishing.service.gov.uk/government/uploads/system/uploads/attachment_data/file/32563/ipreview-finalreport.pdf> (last accessed 15 August 2018).
[61] *Hyde Park Residence Ltd v Yelland and Others* [2000] EWCA Civ 37 (10 February 2000), para 38.
[62] *Hubbard v Vosper* [1972] 2 QB 84.
[63] L Bently, B Sherman, D Gangjee, and P Johnson, *Intellectual Property Law* (OUP:2018), 5th edn, 229–32.

commercially competing with the proprietor's exploitation of the copyright work, a substitute for the probable purchase of authorised copies, and the like ... The second most important factor is whether the work has already been published or otherwise exposed to the public ... The third most important factor is the amount and importance of the work that has been taken. For, although it is permissible to take a substantial part of the work (if not, there could be no question of infringement in the first place), in some circumstances the taking of an excessive amount, or the taking of even a small amount if on a regular basis, would negative fair dealing.[64]

'UK Defences Checklist'—For the benefit of readers who may not be familiar with UK law or students in the early stages of their study of UK copyright law, the document reproduced in Figure 7.3 is a 'UK Defences Checklist'[65] meant to provide a visual aid of the issues that require consideration to establish the availability of a certain defence to copyright infringement under the CDPA.

As of today both the defences of quotation and parody remain unapplied at the judicial level. A correct interpretation and application of both provisions, however, could not disregard relevant CJEU case law concerning their corresponding exceptions in Article 5 of the InfoSoc Directive, from which both UK defences have been derived.

5.1 Lessons from the CJEU on the UK quotation defence

Section 30(1ZA)—The conditions for the availability of the UK quotation defence are that: the work has been made available to the public; the use of the quotation is a fair dealing with the work; the extent of the quotation is no more than is required by the specific purpose for which it is used, and the quotation is accompanied by a sufficient acknowledgement (unless this is impossible for reasons of practicality or otherwise). This defence has the potential to be interpreted fairly broadly due to the fact that, unlike other fair dealing defences, it does not require the quotation to be for any specified purpose. However, by referring to 'use of a quotation from that work', section 30(1ZA) may imply that the defence is only available to limited, partial reproductions of a work.[66]

Quotation in *Painer*—In any case, a UK court will need to take into account the understanding of 'quotation' as provided by the CJEU, notably in its decision in *Painer*, C-145/10 (see further Chapter 5, Section 2). Article 5(3)(d) of the InfoSoc Directive intends 'to preclude the exclusive right of reproduction conferred on authors from preventing the publication, by means of quotation accompanied by comments or criticism, of extracts from a work already available to the public'.[67] The CJEU also held, contrary to the Italian government's submission, that 'the part of the sentence "provided that they relate to a work or other subject matter which has already been lawfully made available to the public" in Article 5(3)(d) refers, unambiguously, to the work or other protected subject matter quoted and not to the subject matter in which the quotation is made'.[68] Whether the quotation is made as part of a work protected

---

[64] *Ashdown v Telegraph Group Ltd* [2001] EWCA Civ 1142 (18 July 2001), para 70.

[65] The 'checklist' was first published in E Rosati, 'Am I covered by that UK copyright exception? Here's my checklist' (11 April 2017), available at <http://ipkitten.blogspot.com/2017/04/am-i-covered-by-that-uk-copyright.html> (last accessed 15 August 2018). Other study aid materials that I have created for intellectual property students are available at <http://www.elawnora.com/#ip-materials> (last accessed 15 August 2018).

[66] A Cameron, 'Copyright exceptions for the digital age: new rights of private copying, parody and quotation' (2014) 9(12) 1002, 1007.

[67] *Painer*, C-145/10, EU:C:2011:798, para 120.   [68] Ibid, para 131.

```
(1) Is the defence limited to certain, specified beneficiaries?
```

```
(2) Is the defence limited to certain subject matter (types of works?)
```

```
(3) Are the conditions set by the relevant provision satisfied?
```

```
(4) Is the defence limited to certain, specified purpose?
```

```
(5) Must the use at issue be 'fair dealing' with the work in question?
```

```
(6) Other considerations (eg contractual override)?
```

Figure 7.3 UK Defences Checklist

Answering Questions (1) and (2) serves to rule out at the outset the availability to the particular case considered of defences (exceptions) whose beneficiaries are limited (eg, in the case of exceptions for libraries, archives, public administration, educational establishments, persons with disabilities) or only apply to certain types of works (eg, computer programs or databases). In a sense, these are preliminary questions to be considered and addressed. The core of the assessment regarding the availability of a defence in a certain case is answering Questions (3) to (5).

Question (3) requires consideration of whether a certain defence is subject to any conditions. For instance, quotation within section 30(1ZA) requires that: (i) the work has been made available to the public; (ii) the use of the quotation is fair dealing with the work (this would be relevant to Question (5)); (iii) the extent of the quotation is no more than is required by the specific purpose for which it is used, and (iv) the quotation is accompanied by a sufficient acknowledgement (unless this would be impossible for reasons of practicality or otherwise).

Question (4) requires one to determine whether the defence considered is only available to the use of a work for certain, specified purposes. While section 30(1ZA) does not require the quotation be made for any particular purposes, the same is not the case for other defences, eg, criticism or review (section 30(1)), news reporting (section 30(2)), caricature, parody, or pastiche (section 30A).

Question (5) is a crucial one for those defences that are framed within fair dealing. The CDPA does not contain a definition of 'fair dealing', nor does it stipulate what factors are to be considered when assessing whether a certain dealing with a work is to be considered fair. The notion of 'fair dealing' has been thus developed though case law from the perspective of a 'fair-minded and honest person', and has traditionally been considered a matter of degree and impression. A number of considerations may inform the decision whether a certain use of a work is fair, although the relative importance of each of them will vary according to the case in hand and the dealing at issue.

Finally, answering Question (6) requires one to consider other factors that might have an impact on the actual availability of a certain defence. So, for instance, while caricature, parody, or pastiche within section 30A cannot be overridden by contract (any such terms would be unenforceable), the defence is without prejudice to an author's moral rights.

by copyright or, instead, as part of a subject matter not protected by copyright, is irrelevant.[69] Thus, a quotation may be self-standing, ie not necessarily incorporated into another copyright work. However, it has to be accompanied by comments or criticism, though this does not appear a requirement stemming from the very wording of Article 5(3)(d) of the InfoSoc Directive. This conclusion might however be justified in light of Article 10(1) of the Berne Convention, which states that the quotation must be 'justified by the purpose', and also the three-step test in Article 5(5) of the InfoSoc Directive.

[69] Ibid, para 136.

5.2 Lessons from the CJEU on the UK parody defence

Section 30A—With particular regard to caricature, parody, and pastiche, the scope of the UK defence is unclear. Although using a 'minimalistic' wording[70] (eg without including references to the caricatured/parodied/'pastiched' work being published and receiving sufficient acknowledgement) when drafting section 30A of the CDPA, the UK government decided to include a reference to the need for a dealing with the original work to be fair, so as to minimize the potential harm to relevant copyright owners. Section 30A CDPA provides that '[f]air dealing with a work for the purposes of caricature, parody or pastiche does not infringe copyright in the work'.

The UK provision does not define the concept of 'parody': in *Deckmyn*, C-201/13, the CJEU clarified that this should, on the one hand, be intended as an autonomous concept of EU law (see further Chapter 2, Section 2.2) and, on the other hand, possess a (limited) number of characteristics (see further Chapter 5, Section 1). If and when the opportunity arises, UK courts will need to interpret the notion of 'parody' in line with the CJEU decision.[71] Relevant guidance on section 30A released by the UK Intellectual Property Office explains that, further to the introduction of this new defence, a comedian would be exempted from seeking a licence to use a few lines from a film or song for a parody sketch; a cartoonist might reference a well-known artwork or illustration for a caricature; and an artist would be able use small fragments from a range of films to compose a larger pastiche artwork.[72] Overall, fair dealing only allows one to make use of a limited, moderate amount of someone else's work. This means that any dealing that is not fair will still require a licence or permission from the copyright owner.[73] While this might be acceptable for, say, a literary work, one might wonder whether the same could be possible in relation to a parody of an artistic work that did not reproduce a substantial part—if not the whole—of it. A parody, in fact, depends upon recognition of the work being parodied.[74]

Parody and the moral right of integrity—Furthermore, the changes to the Act have had no impact on the law of libel or slander, and left unaffected the regulation of UK moral rights, including the right of integrity. Also this choice was meant as a safeguard for authors against the risk of lost sales due to the negative reputational effects of a parody of their work.[75] More often than not, a caricature, parody, or pastiche will involve a treatment of an earlier work. Such treatment might be prejudicial to the honour or reputation of the author of the original work and potentially amount to an

[70] J Griffiths, 'Fair dealing after *Deckmyn*: the United Kingdom's defence for caricature, parody and pastiche', in M Richardson M and S Ricketson (eds), *Research Handbook on Intellectual Property in Media and Entertainment* (Edward Elgar:2017), 64–101, 77.

[71] In this sense, see also S Jacques, 'Are the new 'fair dealing' provisions an improvement on the previous UK law, and why?' (2015) 10(9) JIPLP 699, 702.

[72] HM Government, *Technical Review of Draft Legislation on Copyright Exceptions: Government Response*, available at <https://assets.publishing.service.gov.uk/government/uploads/system/uploads/attachment_data/file/308732/response-copyright-techreview.pdf > (last accessed 15 August 2018). With regard to pastiche, E Hudson, 'The pastiche exception in copyright law: a case of mashed-up drafting?' (2017) 2017/4 IPQ 346, 352, has argued that its scope—albeit framed within fair dealing—might be broader than what anticipated by some commentators and the UK Intellectual Property Office in its guidance notes.

[73] HM Government, *Copyright Exception for Parody—Impact Assessment*, available at <http://webarchive.nationalarchives.gov.uk/20140603093549/http://www.ipo.gov.uk/ia-exception-parody.pdf> (last accessed 15 August 2018).

[74] Garnett, Davies, and Harbottle, *Copinger and Skone James on Copyright*, 17th edn, Vol I, §9.63.

[75] UK Intellectual Property Office, *Copyright Exception for Parody—Impact Assessment BIS 1057*, 13 December 2012, available at <http://webarchive.nationalarchives.gov.uk/20140603102738/http://www.ipo.gov.uk/consult-ia-bis1057.pdf> (last accessed 15 August 2018), 6.

infringement of the original author's right of integrity. Section 80 CDPA is drafted in such a way that there can be no defence based on freedom of expression against a claim brought on integrity grounds.[76]

It is however worth recalling that section 171(3) CDPA states that the enforcement of copyright may be prevented or restricted on grounds of public interest or otherwise. In *Hyde Park Residence v Yelland*, the Court of Appeal of England and Wales reviewed a number of authorities and concluded that such a provision could be used to prohibit the enforcement of copyright in the case of a work that is: '(i) immoral, scandalous or contrary to family life; (ii) injurious to public life, public health and safety or the administration of justice; (iii) incites or encourages others to act in a way referred to in (ii)'.[77] Having said so—even if the existence of a public interest defence were to be inferred from relevant statutory provisions and case law—its relevance would be residual, in the sense that it could only add to statutory exceptions in limited situations.

Deckmyn and Vrijheidsfonds—In any case, also in *Deckmyn and Vrijheidsfonds*, C-201/13, the CJEU did not envisage a 'limitless' right to parody. The CJEU held in fact that it follows from Recital 31 in the preamble to that directive that freedom of parody as an expression of one's own opinion is not guaranteed. A parody that conveys a message that is discriminatory/racist is not eligible for protection under Article 5(3)(k). To state otherwise would contradict the requirement that a fair balance between the rights and interests of the author of the parodied work and the rights of the parodist be set. Hence, a copyright holder (the CJEU did not refer to the 'author' in this part of the judgment) has a 'legitimate interest' not to be associated with parodies that convey discriminatory messages, contrary to the principles enshrined in Directive 2000/43 implementing the principle of equal treatment between persons irrespective of racial or ethnic origin[78] and Article 21(1) of the EU Charter.[79]

5.3 The (non-existent) UK three-step test

In the particular case of the UK an additional, potential, difficulty is the role of the InfoSoc three-step test within its copyright system. Unlike other Member States (see Chapter 5, Section 5.1), the UK has not transposed the language of the three-step test within Article 5(5) of the InfoSoc Directive into its own copyright law. The reason is that, at the time of implementing the InfoSoc Directive into its own legal system, the UK government took the view that relevant copyright exceptions already complied with Article 5(5). The lack of a specific provision outlining the three-step test in the CDPA, together with the idea that the three-step test would be akin to the UK concept of 'fair dealing',[80] is the principal reason why '[th]ere has been very little judicial consideration'[81] of the three-step test in UK case law.

---

[76] See also Jacques, 'Are the new 'fair dealing' provisions an improvement?' 705–6, and P Masiyakurima, 'Fair dealing defences', in PLC Torremans (ed), *Intellectual Property Law and Human Rights* (Wolters Kluwer:2015), 3rd edn, 285–6, both considering section 30A CDPA as having limited scope.

[77] *Hyde Park Residence Ltd v Yelland and Others* [2000] EWCA Civ 37 (10 February 2000), (Aldous LJ), para 66. According to Mance LJ, instead, it would not be possible to categorize the possible scenarios that would trigger section 171(3) (para 83).

[78] Council Directive 2000/43/EC of 29 June 2000 implementing the principle of equal treatment between persons irrespective of racial or ethnic origin, OJ L 180, 19 July 2000, 22–6.

[79] *Deckmyn and Vrijheidsfonds*, C-201/13, EU:C:2014:2132, para 30.

[80] *England And Wales Cricket Board Ltd & Another v Tixdaq Ltd & Another* [2016] EWHC 575 (Ch) (18 March 2016), para 89.

[81] Ibid, para 88.

6. The Case of the UK: Impact and Legacy of CJEU Case Law on Enforcement (Intermediary Injunctions)

The interpretation of the EU enforcement framework, notably in the context of injunctions against intermediaries, has contributed to shaping the corresponding UK framework. Among other things, reference to standards enshrined in relevant EU directives, as also interpreted by the CJEU, has assisted UK courts in formulating key rules, notably with regard to the allocation of costs of injunctions against intermediaries.

6.1 Copyright website blocking orders

Section 97A—With regard to copyright intermediary injunctions, the UK transposed Article 8(3) of the InfoSoc Directive into its own law by introducing section 97A CDPA. This domestic provision states that the High Court of England and Wales (in Scotland, the Court of Session) has the power to grant an injunction against a service provider (defined in accordance with the legislative instrument by which this country transposed the E-commerce Directive into its own law[82]), where that service provider has actual knowledge of another person using their service to infringe copyright. The second paragraph in section 97A further provides that, in determining whether a service provider has actual knowledge, a court must take into account all matters that are relevant in the particular circumstances and, among other things, have regard to whether a service provider has received a sufficiently detailed notice.

In 2011 the High Court of England and Wales utilized section 97A to grant the first injunction to block access to a website (*Newzbin 2*).[83] Since then, the High Court of England and Wales has ordered the blocking of access to hundreds of websites, with applications being filed by an increasingly diverse group of copyright owners (including film studios, the recording industry, the Football Association Premier League, UEFA, and publishers) and with the types of blocking orders sought evolving over time.

Live blocking orders—With regard to the latter, in 2017 the High Court of England and Wales granted the first live blocking order, ie a particular type of blocking limited in time to when the relevant content is being streamed unlawfully.[84] The decision originated from an application that the Football Association Premier League made to combat the growing problem of live Premier League footage being streamed online without authorization.

Since the blocking order granted in favour of the Football Association Premier League in 2013,[85] a number of changes have occurred. First, consumers have been increasingly turning to set-top boxes, media players, and mobile device apps to access infringing streams, rather than web browsers running on computers. The direct consequence of this is that traditional blocking orders (targeting websites) would not be able to prevent the growing number of infringements, because these devices do not rely upon access to

---

[82] Regulation 2 of the Electronic Commerce (EC Directive) Regulations 2002 clarifies that ' "service provider" means any person providing an information society service'.

[83] *Twentieth Century Fox Film Corp and Others v British Telecommunications Plc* [2011] EWHC 1981 (Ch) (28 July 2011).

[84] *The Football Association Premier League Ltd v British Telecommunications Plc and Others* [2017] EWHC 480 (Ch) (13 March 2017); *The Football Association Premier League Ltd v British Telecommunications Plc* [2017] EWHC 1877 (Ch) (25 July 2017).

[85] *The Football Association Premier League Ltd v British Sky Broadcasting Ltd and Others* [2013] EWHC 2058 (Ch) (16 July 2013).

a specific website in order to enable consumers to access infringing material. Instead, such devices can connect directly to streaming servers via their IP addresses. The court thus recognized that advances in technology mean new methods by which intellectual property rights may be infringed.[86] Second, access to and use of the devices mentioned above does not present many challenges. Third, there is a significant availability of high-quality infringing streams of footage of each match. Fourth, evidence suggests that a significantly higher proportion of UK consumers believes that it is lawful to access unauthorized streams using such devices and software than believes that it is lawful to access unlicensed content via file-sharing websites, Fifth, the streaming servers used to make available infringing streams to the public have increasingly been moved to offshore hosting providers that do not cooperate with rightholders' requests to take down infringing content either at all or in a timely manner.

All this prompted the applicant to seek a different type of order from those granted in the past by the High Court of England and Wales. First, it would be a 'live' blocking order which would only have effect at the times when live Premier League match footage would be broadcast. Second, the order would provide for the list of target servers to be 're-set' each match week during the Premier League season. Third, the order sought would be only for a short period. Fourth, in addition to the safeguards which have become standard in section 97A orders, the order would require a notice to be sent to each hosting provider each week when one of its IP addresses is subject to blocking. In 2018, the High Court extended the duration of the order granted in relation to the Premier League 2017/18 season[87] to the 2018/19 season, also noting the effectiveness of website live blocking as an enforcement measure and the lack of evidence of overblocking.[88]

6.2 Costs of injunctions against intermediaries

Costs allocation in copyright intermediary injunctions—Until recently the rule in the UK for intermediary injunctions in the field of intellectual property law (copyright and trade marks) has been that, when it comes to costs of injunctions, rightholders would bear the costs of application and the intermediaries to which the orders are addressed would need to pay the costs of implementation thereof. The justification for such a cost allocation is partly rooted within EU law. In the first case which resulted in the granting of a copyright blocking injunction (*Newzbin 2*), the High Court of England and Wales considered that the rather unusual nature of the remedy under Article 8(3) of the InfoSoc Directive[89] means that it is reasonable for an (innocent) intermediary to require a court order for its own protection, and to require the relevant copyright owners to adduce sufficient evidence to establish both that the court had jurisdiction to make the order and that it is appropriate in the exercise of the court's discretion to

---

[86] J Smith and L Deacon, 'Live blocking orders: the next step for the protection of copyright in the online world' (2017) 39(7) EIPR 438, 440.

[87] *The Football Association Premier League Ltd v British Telecommunications Plc* [2017] EWHC 1877 (Ch) (25 July 2017).

[88] *The Football Association Premier League Ltd v British Telecommunications Plc and Others* [2018] EWHC 1828 (Ch) (18 July 2018), para 5. A similar reasoning may also be discerned in relation to UEFA's application for a live blocking order and its subsequent extension: *Union des Associations Européennes de Football v British Telecommunications Plc and Others* [2017] EWHC 3414 (Ch) (21 December 2017); *Union des Associations Européennes de Football v British Telecommunications Plc and Others* [2018] EWHC 1900 (Ch) (24 July 2018).

[89] *Twentieth Century Fox Film Corp and Others v British Telecommunications Plc* [2011] EWHC 1981 (Ch) (28 July 2011), para 53.

do so. Hence, the costs of an application for a blocking order should be borne by the applicant.[90] However, the costs of implementing a blocking order should be borne by the addressee of the injunction. The reason is that an intermediary is a commercial enterprise that makes a profit from the provision of the services that the operators and users of target websites use to infringe the applicants' rights. Accordingly,

the costs of implementing the order can be regarded as a cost of carrying on that business. It seems … to be implicit in recital (59) of the Information Society Directive that the European legislature has chosen to impose that cost on the intermediary. Furthermore, that interpretation appears to be supported by the Court of Justice's statement in *L'Oréal v eBay* [C-324/09] at [139] that such measures 'must not be excessively costly'.[91]

This approach to cost allocation has been consistently followed in the area of copyright intermediary injunctions since 2011. However, developments occurring in the area of trade mark injunctions question whether the one described above remains the correct rule for allocating the costs of an injunction against an intermediary.

Trade mark intermediary injunctions—Unlike Article 8(3) of the InfoSoc Directive, the UK government did not take any specific steps to transpose the third sentence of Article 11 of the Enforcement Directive into this country's law.[92] In its 2009 decision in *L'Oréal v eBay* the High Court of England and Wales concluded that, despite lack of an express implementation, it had power under section 37(1) of the Senior Courts Act 1981 (SCA, formerly the Supreme Court Act 1981) to grant an injunction against an intermediary whose services had been used by third parties to infringe an intellectual property right (a registered trade mark), to the extent that this is what the third sentence in Article 11 of the Enforcement Directive requires.[93]

In the aftermath of this ruling it remained uncertain whether section 37(1) SCA could be used to obtain a particular type of injunction, ie an injunction against an intermediary to block access to a website where content that infringes intellectual property rights other than copyright can be found. Possibly unsurprisingly (considering the previous stance in *L'Oréal v eBay*), the High Court of England and Wales answered this question in the affirmative in its 2014 decision in *Cartier v BSkyB*.[94] A number of threshold conditions must however be satisfied: first, the ISPs against whom the order is sought must be intermediaries within the meaning of the third sentence of Article 11 of the Enforcement Directive; second, either the users or the operators of the website must be infringing the claimants' intellectual property rights; third, the users or the operators of the website must use the services of the intermediary; fourth, the provider must have actual knowledge of this. The first three conditions follow from the wording of Article 11 of the Enforcement Directive itself. The fourth follows from the E-commerce Directive: if ISPs could be required to block websites without having knowledge of the infringing activity, then this would effectively impose on them an obligation to monitor which would be contrary to Article 15 thereof.[95] Besides such

---

[90] Ibid, para 53.   [91] Ibid, para 32.

[92] For the different approaches to UK implementations of Article 8(3) of the InfoSoc Directive and the third sentence in Article 11 of the Enforcement Directive, see R Arnold, 'Website-blocking injunctions: the question of legislative basis' (2015) 37(10) EIPR 623, 624–5.

[93] *L'Oreal SA and Others v eBay International AG and Others* [2009] EWHC 1094 (Ch) (22 May 2009), paras 447–454.

[94] See further PS Davies, 'Costs of blocking injunctions' (2017) 2017/4 IPQ 330, 336–7; and J Cornwell, 'Injunctions and monetary remedies compared: the English judicial response to the IP Enforcement Directive' (2018) 40(8) EIPR 490, 497, both discussing the innovations in UK law brought about by this decision.

[95] *Cartier International AG and Others v British Sky Broadcasting Ltd and Others* [2014] EWHC 3354 (Ch) (17 October 2014), para 141. Some commentators have criticized the inclusion of a

threshold conditions, a number of principles must also be observed when considering whether to make a website blocking order, namely the relief must: (i) be necessary; (ii) be effective; (iii) be dissuasive; (iv) not be unnecessarily complicated or costly; (v) avoid barriers to legitimate trade; (vi) be fair and equitable and strike a 'fair balance' between the applicable fundamental rights; and (vii) be proportionate. These are also principles derived from the Enforcement Directive.[96]

Cartier v BSkyB—In line with the earlier judgment in *Newzbin 2*, in *Cartier v BSkyB* the High Court of England and Wales also took the view that the rightholders should pay the costs of an unopposed application and the ISPs should generally bear the costs of implementation as part of the costs of carrying on business in this sector. However the court did 'not rule out the possibility of ordering the rightholder to pay some or all of the implementation costs in an appropriate case'.[97]

The 'entirely correct'[98] decision at first instance was upheld on appeal. However, in his dissent Briggs LJ (as he then was) held the view that the rule on allocation of costs (as seemingly endorsed by the relevant EU framework) is not correct: the cost burden attributable to the implementation of a particular blocking order should fall upon the rightholder making the application for it. The reason would be a domestic one and consistent with general principles of equity.[99] It is true that both the Enforcement and the InfoSoc Directives state that rightholders should have the possibility of applying for an injunction against an intermediary who either carries a third party's infringement of a protected work in a network (in copyright cases) or whose services are being used by a third party to infringe the rightholder's industrial property right (in relation to trade marks). However, in both cases the conditions and modalities relating to such injunctions, or the conditions and procedures relating to such injunctions should be left to the national law of the Member States.[100] In the UK, courts have jurisdiction as per section 37(1) SCA, and this in substance reflects an originally unfettered jurisdiction exercised by the Court of Chancery on equitable principles. In the case of orders against innocent third parties, the law has evolved so as to ensure that a standard condition or 'modality' for the grant of an injunction is that the cost reasonably incurred by the innocent respondent should be reimbursed by the applicant.[101]

In 2018 the Supreme Court, to which the decision of the Court of Appeal of England and Wales had been appealed, delivered its judgment. It held that domestic law requires that innocent third parties as the ISPs are to bear no costs for the implementation of injunctions against them. According to the UK's highest judicature, neither EU directives nor CJEU judgments (notably those in *L'Oréal and Others*, C-324/09, and *UPC Telekabel Wien*, C-314/12) provide specific guidance in relation to the allocation of costs of intermediary injunctions.[102] Cost allocation is thus a matter for

---

'knowledge' requirement in the trade mark context: see A Marsoof 'The blocking injunction—a critical review of its implementation in the United Kingdom in the context of the European Union' (2015) 46(6) IIC 632, 638.

[96] *Cartier International AG and Others v British Sky Broadcasting Ltd and Others* [2014] EWHC 3354 (Ch) (17 October 2014), para 158.

[97] Ibid, para 240.

[98] *Cartier International AG and Others v British Sky Broadcasting Ltd and Others* [2016] EWCA Civ 658 (6 July 2016), para 35.

[99] Prior to the 2018 UK Supreme Court decision Davies, 'Costs of blocking injunctions' 342–4, held the dissenting judgment of Briggs LJ on this issue 'most persuasive, and should be adopted by the Supreme Court'.

[100] *Cartier International AG and Others v British Sky Broadcasting Ltd and Others* [2016] EWCA Civ 658, paras 198–199.

[101] Ibid, para 202.

[102] On whether any guidance is available at the EU level, see further E Rosati, 'Intermediary IP injunctions in the EU and UK experiences: when less (harmonization) is more?' (2017) 12(4) JIPLP 338, 347–8.

individual Member States to decide. However, while the incidence of compliance costs is a matter for UK law, this should be done 'within the broad limits set by the EU principles of effectiveness and equivalence, and the requirement that any remedy should be fair, proportionate and not unnecessarily costly'.[103]

Implications for copyright intermediary injunctions?—It is not entirely clear whether and to what extent the conclusion achieved in *Cartier v BSkyB* in relation to allocation of costs orders granted pursuant to section 37(1) SCA might also be applicable in the context of copyright intermediary injunctions, especially considering the different legal basis (section 97A of the CDPA) for those types of injunctions. However, the fact that EU law would not mandate the cost allocation as envisaged at the level of lower courts and as adopted in copyright website blocking orders, together with the consideration that—on the contrary—domestic law *prevents* the imposition of costs on innocent intermediaries targeted by an injunction, might result in a different approach to cost allocation *also* in copyright website blocking orders.

Conclusion

This chapter has focused on the potential, default impact that departure of a Member State from the EU would have on that country's copyright law. While the first part has highlighted some of the changes that might occur in legislation, the second part has attempted to show that, even in the case of a complete departure from both the EU and the EEA, the impact of CJEU case law would likely remain relevant. This would be so with regard to both future CJEU rulings interpreting relevant EU provisions from which national provisions are derived and consideration of how CJEU case law has contributed to defining domestic principles and concepts.

In this sense, the case of the UK is telling: the preceding sections have shown how courts in that country have relied upon CJEU case law and, in doing so, either changed their approaches to certain concepts (an example being the originality requirement) or construed domestic concepts in light of corresponding CJEU interpretations of EU standards and rules (eg with regard to economic rights, infringement, and enforcement). Overall, it is apparent how pervasive the work of the CJEU has been in the field of copyright: a clean break between a departing Member State and EU copyright law—subject to compliance with international law provisions—might be possible, but hardly feasible in a medium-term perspective.

---

[103] *Cartier International AG and Others v British Telecommunications Plc and Another* [2018] UKSC 28 (13 June 2018), para 31.

8

CJEU Case Law and the Interplay with Policy and Legislative Action in the DSM

Introduction

The Digital Single Market Strategy—In 2015 the EU Commission unveiled its Digital Single Market Strategy (DSMS). The Digital Single Market (DSM) is intended as an area 'in which the free movement of goods, persons, services and capital is ensured and where individuals and businesses can seamlessly access and exercise online activities under conditions of fair competition, and a high level of consumer and personal data protection, irrespective of their nationality or place of residence'.[1] Achieving it would allow the EU to maintain its leading position in the digital economy, and favour the growth of European companies on a global scale. To realize a DSM in Europe, a number of initiatives would need to be undertaken across a range of sectors. These include: implementing cross-border e-commerce rules that consumers and business can trust; making available affordable high-quality cross-border parcel delivery services; contrasting unjustified geo-blocking practices used for commercial reasons by online sellers that result in the denial of access to websites based in other Member States; reducing VAT-related burdens and obstacles when selling across borders; reforming telecom rules and the legislative framework for audiovisual media services; tackling the role and responsibilities of online platforms in combatting illegal content on the internet; reinforcing trust and security in digital services and in the handling of personal data; maximizing the growth potential by focusing on Big Data, cloud services and the Internet of Things, as well as interoperability and standardization, and investing in creating digital skills and expertise; and, finally, reforming the EU copyright framework.

With regard to the latter, the DSMS indicated that initiatives would be launched to reduce further the differences in the copyright regimes across EU Member States. Specific proposals would be tabled with regard to: content portability, cross-border access to content;[2] cross-border use of content for specific purposes (including research, education, text and data mining, etc) through harmonized exceptions. A clarification of the rules on the activities of intermediaries in relation to copyright content and a

---

[1] European Commission, Communication from the Commission to the European Parliament, the Council, the European Economic and Social Committee, and the Committee of the Regions, *A Digital Single Market Strategy for Europe*, {SWD(2015) 100 final} COM(2015) 192 final, §1.

[2] The EU Commission appeared prepared to tackle geo-blocking also in the copyright field (see European Commission, *Public consultation on the review of EU copyright rules*, 5 December 2013–5 March 2014, §II.A, available at <http://ec.europa.eu/internal_market/consultations/2013/copyright-rules/docs/consultation-document_en.pdf> (last accessed 15 August 2018); the report on the responses to the public consultation is available at <http://ec.europa.eu/internal_market/consultations/2013/copyright-rules/docs/contributions/consultation-report_en.pdf> (last accessed 15 August 2018). However, after the release of the DSMS it became apparent that geo-blocking would only be addressed at the e-commerce sector. For a critical discussion of overcoming geo-blocking in the copyright field, see G Mazziotti, 'Is geo-blocking a real cause for concern in Europe?' (2016) 38(6) EIPR 365.

modernization of the enforcement framework (with regard to both 'follow the money' approaches and cross-border scope) would also be required.[3]

Review of EU copyright rules—Following the release of the DSMS, a number of legislative proposals were tabled. For the sake of the present discourse, attention will be limited to the proposed DSM Directive and, more specifically, four areas in which the tackling of CJEU copyright case law—whether by means of a stated consolidation thereof or its rewriting *tout court*—is particularly apparent.[4] They are:

- The proposal on the 'value gap' (or 'transfer of value') within Article 13 of the draft DSM Directive and the interplay with CJEU case law on: the right of communication to the public within Article 3(1) of the InfoSoc Directive (discussed in Chapter 4, Section 2), filtering obligations and safe harbours for hosting providers within, respectively, Articles 15 and 14 of the E-commerce Directive (discussed in Chapter 6, Section 1);

- The press publishers' right within Article 11 of the proposed DSM Directive and the relationship with CJEU case law on originality under the InfoSoc Directive (discussed in Chapter 4, Section 1.1);

- Entitlement to a share of the fair compensation for private copying under Article 12 of the DSM Directive in relation to CJEU case law on fair compensation for private copying (discussed in Chapter 5, Section 3.2.4);

- The approach to out-of-commerce works with regard to the qualification of authors' economic rights as preventive in nature in the case law of the CJEU (discussed in Chapter 2, Section 2.10 and Chapter 3, Section 1).

1. The Value Gap (Transfer of Value) Proposal

Notion of 'value gap'—Article 13 of the DSM Directive as proposed by the EU Commission is intended to remedy what has come to be known in jargon as the 'value gap' or 'transfer of value'. This concept—the very existence of which remains controversial[5]—refers to an alleged mismatch between the value that some digital

---

[3] European Commission, Communication from the Commission to the European Parliament, the Council, the European Economic and Social Committee and the Committee of the Regions, *A Digital Single Market Strategy for Europe*, {SWD(2015) 100 final} COM(2015) 192 final, §2.4.

[4] Other areas have also attracted significant attention, including the proposal for a mandatory text and data mining (Article 3 of the draft DSM Directive). On the legal issues associated with text and data mining from an EU perspective see further: E Rosati, *The Exception for Text and Data Mining (TDM) in the Proposed Directive on Copyright in the Digital Single Market—Technical Aspects* (2018), Briefing requested by the JURI Committee of the European Parliament, available at <http://www.europarl.europa.eu/RegData/etudes/BRIE/2018/604942/IPOL_BRI(2018)604942_EN.pdf> (last accessed 15 August 2018), 5–6; C Geiger, G Frosio, and O Bulayenko, *The Exception for Text and Data Mining (TDM) in the Proposed Directive on Copyright in the Digital Single Market—Legal Aspects* (2018), Briefing requested by the JURI Committee of the European Parliament, available at <http://www.europarl.europa.eu/RegData/etudes/IDAN/2018/604941/IPOL_IDA(2018)604941_EN.pdf> (last accessed 15 August 2018), 7–12.

[5] Contesting the very foundation of the concept of 'value gap', see: WF Patry, 'The lack of value in the value gap' (2017) 30(4) Quarterly Copyright (Korea Copyright Commission) 189, available at <http://digital.kyobobook.co.kr/digital/article/articleDetail.ink?selectedLargeCategory=006&barcode=4010026168264> (last accessed 15 August 2018), §II.C; GF Frosio, 'From horizontal to vertical: an intermediary liability earthquake in Europe' (2017) 12(7) JIPLP 565, 568 (referring to it as 'a rhetorical device' for 'a discourse almost exclusively fabricated by the music and entertainment industry').

user-uploaded content (UUC) platforms are perceived as obtaining from protected content and the revenue returned to relevant rightholders. The argument for claiming that such a gap exists is the inconsistent application of the safe harbour for hosting providers under Article 14 of the E-commerce Directive. The allegedly resulting uncertainties 'have emboldened certain digital platforms to claim that they are not liable for the music they make available to the public'. The alleged result is that online platforms hosting large amounts of UUC would use all this 'as a shield to avoid licensing music like other digital services do, claiming they are not legally responsible for the music they distribute on their site'.[6] The consequence is said to be that, on the one hand, rightholders would not be appropriately compensated for the exploitation of content to which they own the rights and, on the other hand, competition in the market would be distorted.[7]

The structure of the original proposal—Read in combination with Recital 38 in the preamble to the proposed directive, the EU Commission's original proposal provides that, where a hosting provider stores and gives public access to large amounts of user-uploaded works (the concept of 'large amounts' is however undefined in the proposal), thereby performing an act of communication to the public within the meaning of Article 3(1) of the InfoSoc Directive, it is obliged to conclude a licensing agreement with the relevant rightholder(s), unless it is eligible for the safe harbour pursuant to Article 14 of the E-commerce Directive. Irrespective of whether the safe harbour in Article 14 of the E-commerce Directive applies, the provider that gives access to large amounts of works should take appropriate and proportionate measures to ensure protection of works or other subject matter, and also by implementing effective technologies.

By means of a simplification, the original formulation of the value gap proposal may be considered rooted within three core ideas. First, that the storing and making available of protected content uploaded by third parties would qualify as an act of communication to the public (the proposal does not, however, define this concept) by the hosting provider itself. Second, that despite the doing of restricted acts, the safe harbour protection within Article 14 of the E-commerce Directive would in principle remain available to the hosting provider. Recital 38 states however that, to determine the applicability of the safe harbour protection in Article 14 of the E-commerce Directive, 'it is necessary to verify whether the service provider plays an active role, including by optimizing the presentation of the uploaded works or subject matter or promoting them, irrespective of the nature of the means used therefor'. The third point is that hosting providers would be subjected to filtering obligations in order to prevent the making available of allegedly infringing content. Recital 39 suggests that this could be done in the context of a collaboration between hosting providers and rightholders, in that 'rightholders should provide the necessary data to allow the services to identify their content and the services should be transparent towards rightholders with regard to the deployed technologies, to allow the assessment of their appropriateness'.

The EU Commission's formulation of the value gap proposal has attracted significant discussion,[8] including criticisms concerning lack of

---

[6] International Federation of the Phonographic Industry, *Global Music Report 2018—Annual state of the industry* (2018), 26.

[7] Ibid, 27. Cf GF Frosio, 'The death of "no monitoring obligations"—A story of untameable monsters' (2017) 8(3) JIPITEC 199, 201, expressing reservations regarding the actual existence of such a 'value gap'.

[8] A helpful collection of academic commentary on Article 13 of the draft DSM Directive is available at <https://www.create.ac.uk/policy-responses/eu-copyright-reform/article-13-research/> (last accessed 15 August 2018). For an overall endorsement, see Association Littéraire et Artistique

clarity[9] and suggestions that it could be contrary to EU law, notably insofar as the filtering obligation is concerned.[10] A point that, however, has received less consideration is the assumption that hosting providers, by storing and making available copyright content uploaded by users, would be potentially liable—on a primary basis—for the doing of a restricted act but that, despite this, might be potentially still eligible for the protection offered by Article 14 of the E-commerce Directive.

1.1 The doing of acts of communication to the public

Essential/indispensable intervention—With consideration of the doing of an act of communication to the public online, CJEU case law has increasingly stressed the need to consider whether the user/defendant has made an *incontournable* intervention (see further Chapter 4, Section 2.1). Over time the CJEU has adopted an expansive approach to the interpretation of this concept. In this sense the decision in *GS Media*, C-160/15 (issued at nearly the same time as the proposed DSM Directive) is enlightening. In his Opinion in that case AG Wathelet attempted a rethinking of the earlier approach to linking, and excluded that the provision of a link to copyright content made available on a third-party site would be considered an act of communication to the public. He did so by suggesting that, to establish an act of communication, the intervention of the 'hyperlinker' must be vital or indispensable in order to benefit from or enjoy the relevant copyright work. Hyperlinks posted on a website that direct to copyright works freely accessible on another website could not be regarded as an 'act of communication': the intervention of the link provider would not be *incontournable* to the making available of the works in question to users.[11] The CJEU rejected this construction of the essentiality/indispensability of the user's role and, while confirming its broad understanding, attempted a modulation of potentially resulting liability by considering other criteria (notably the knowledge of the unlicensed character of the content linked to and the profit-making motives of the link providers).[12]

Incontournable **intervention as facilitation of access**—The subsequent decisions in *Stichting Brein*, C-527/15, and *Stichting Brein*, C-610/15, elaborated further on the notion of essential/indispensable intervention, and confirmed that essentiality/indispensability should be intended as akin to facilitation. In the former case, substantially

---

Internationale, *Resolution on the European proposals of 14 September 2016 to introduce fairer sharing of the value when works and other protected material are made available by electronic means* (18 February 2017), available at <http://www.alai.org/en/assets/files/resolutions/170218-value-gap-en.pdf> (last accessed 15 August 2018).

[9] Max Planck Institute for Innovation and Competition, *Position Statement of the Max Planck Institute for Innovation and Competition on the Proposed Modernisation of European Copyright Rules PART G Use of Protected Content on Online Platforms (Article 13 COM(2016) 593)* (2017), available at <https://www.ip.mpg.de/fileadmin/ipmpg/content/stellungnahmen/MPI_Position_Statement_PART_G_incl_Annex-2017_03_01.pdf > (last accessed 15 August 2018), 3–4.

[10] Concerns have been also expressed in relation to competition aspects (European Copyright Society, *General Opinion on the EU Copyright Reform Package* (24 January 2017), available at <https://europeancopyrightsocietydotorg.files.wordpress.com/2015/12/ecs-opinion-on-eu-copyright-reform-def.pdf> (last accessed 15 August 2018), 7) and the protection of cultural diversity (S Jacques, K Garstka, M Hviid, and J Street, 'Automated anti-piracy systems as copyright enforcement mechanism: a need to consider cultural diversity' (2018) 40(4) EIPR 218, 227–8).

[11] Opinion of Advocate General Melchior Wathelet in *GS Media*, C-160/15, EU:C:2016:221, paras 57 and 60. Also arguing in this sense, C Lim Saw, 'Linking on the internet and copyright liability: a clarion call for doctrinal clarity and legal certainty' (2018) 49(5) IIC 536, 541.

[12] *GS Media*, C-160/15, EU:C:2016:644, paras 43 and 48–55.

following the Opinion of AG Campos Sánchez-Bordona,[13] the CJEU rejected the notion that an essential/indispensable intervention could be limited to a 'merely direct' intervention. An intervention made 'with full knowledge of the consequences' of such conduct that facilitates access to unlicensed content that would otherwise be more difficult to locate is instead sufficient to lead to a finding of potential liability for the doing of unauthorized acts of communication to the public.[14]

In *Stichting Brein*, C-610/15, the CJEU confirmed this conclusion: by making their platform available and managing it, the operators of The Pirate Bay would provide their users with access to unlicensed content: '[t]hey can therefore be regarded as playing an essential role in making the works in question available.'[15]

In conclusion, the EU Commission's proposal was not necessarily problematic in respect of the idea that a hosting provider may, in certain conditions, be considered as doing an act of communication to the public together with users of its services. What, however, the proposal assumed, and in respect of which the case law of the CJEU (possibly with the exclusion of the decision in *Stichting Brein*, C-610/15) remains not entirely clear, is that a subject which does a restricted copyright act without a licence is nonetheless eligible, at least in principle, for the safe harbour protection.

1.2 The availability of the safe harbour within Article 14 of the E-commerce Directive

Eligibility for safe harbour protection—A central aspect of the value gap proposal is the interplay between this provision and the protection offered by, in particular, Article 14 of the E-commerce Directive. The Commission's version of the draft DSM Directive does not clarify what relationship there is between the provisions contained therein and those in the E-commerce Directive: Article 1(2) of the former does not include the latter among EU legislation that would not be affected by the proposed new EU provisions.

In addition, while Article 13 does not exclude the availability of the safe harbour protection to hosting providers that do acts of communication to the public, Recital 38 appears to provide a narrow scope for its actual application. The protection offered by Article 14 of the E-commerce Directive would be unavailable to providers that play an active role, including by optimizing the presentation of the uploaded works or subject matter or promoting them, irrespective of the nature of the means used therefor. This wording suggests that even the use of automatic optimization techniques, for example, algorithmic optimization, would be sufficient to remove the safe harbour protection within Article 14 of the E-commerce Directive. In this regard two points in particular are worth raising.

Notion of 'active role' in CJEU case law—The first one is whether a formulation of this kind would be consistent with existing CJEU case law regarding the availability of Article 14 protection, notably as interpreted in the decisions in *Google France and Google*, C-236/08 to C-238/08, and *L'Oréal and Others*, C-324/09. In those cases the CJEU held that the safe harbour protection under Article 14 of the E-commerce Directive is not available to a hosting provider that, 'instead of confining itself to providing that service neutrally by a merely technical and automatic processing of the data

---

[13] Opinion of Advocate General Manuel Campos Sánchez-Bordona in *Stichting Brein*, C-527/15, EU:C:2016:938, paras 52–53.
[14] *Stichting Brein*, C-527/15, EU:C:2017:300, para 41.
[15] *Stichting Brein*, C-610/15, EU:C:2017:456, para 37.

provided by its customers, plays an active role of such a kind as to give it knowledge of, or control over, those data'.[16]

In this sense, the original formulation of Recital 38 may not be regarded as an entirely loyal 'codification' of CJEU case law, in that an 'active role' alone is not enough to remove the availability of the safe harbour: a role of this kind must be such as to give the provider knowledge or control over third-party infringing activities. However, it is also worth highlighting that the situations at issue in *Google France and Google*, C-236/08 to C-238/08, and *L'Oréal and Others*, C-324/09, were different from the one envisaged in Article 13: while in those cases the type of liability at issue would be the one arising from third-party infringements, Article 13 posits that a provider itself would be directly liable—together with users of its service—for the unauthorized doing of restricted acts.

Safe harbour for hosts that communicate to the public?—This leads to the second point, which has become central to the subsequent development of the proposal, and that is whether the safe harbour protection may even be available in principle for own acts of the hosting provider. With the E-commerce Directive, the EU legislature attempted to clarify the conditions that need to be satisfied for a provider to be exempted from liability when transmitting and storing information at the request of third parties. In other words, the E-commerce Directive safe harbours would relate to situations in which a provider acts as a mere, passive intermediary.

Besides the general wording of Recital 42 in the preamble to the E-commerce Directive, for mere conduit and caching providers it is Recital 44 that explicitly excludes the applicability of the safe harbours in case of direct infringements in collaboration with the recipients of their services. For hosting providers the same regime applies.[17] The safe harbour relates to possible liability of a hosting provider for third-party infringements, not direct infringements by the provider (Recital 46 and Article 14(2)). This interpretation of the scope of application of Articles 12 to 14 of the E-commerce Directive is preferable in light of textual references, as well as the rationale of the safe harbour regime and case law developments (including the decision in *Stichting Brein*, C-610/15). Some commentators have however suggested a broader reading, in the sense that the safe harbour regime would not be available in relation to providers' own content (ie in cases in which they act as editors/publishers), but it would remain available for third-party content, irrespective of the form of liability.[18]

1.3 Filtering obligations

'Appropriate and proportionate measures'—In its original formulation, Recital 38 and Article 13 would impose on hosting providers that give public access to large amounts of UUC, in order to guarantee the functioning of any licensing agreement concluded with relevant rightholders, to 'take appropriate and proportionate measures to ensure protection of works or other subject matter, such as implementing effective technologies'. Recital 39 further provides that, to this end and to allow the providers to identify content, rightholders should provide 'necessary data' and the services should

---

[16] *Google France and Google*, C-236/08 to C-238/08, EU:C:2008:389, para 114; *L'Oréal and Others*, C-324/09, EU:C:2011:474, para 123. See also *SNB-REACT*, C-521/17, EU:C:2018:639, para 52.

[17] *SNB-REACT*, C-521/17, EU:C:2018:639, para 47.

[18] M Husovec, *Injunctions against Intermediaries in the European Union: Accountable but not Liable?* (CUP:2017), 56; C Angelopoulos, *European Intermediary Liability in Copyright: A Tort-based Analysis* (Wolters Kluwer:2017), 68; J Riordan, *The Liability of Internet Intermediaries* (OUP:2016), §§12.01 and 12.37.

be transparent towards rightholders with regard to the technologies employed, so to allow an assessment of their appropriateness. The services should in particular provide rightholders with information on the type of technologies used, the way they are operated, and their success rate for the recognition of rightholders' content. Those technologies should also allow rightholders to get information from providers on the use of the subject matter covered by the agreement.

Article 15 of the E-commerce Directive—The obligation, which would also apply when the providers are eligible for the liability exemption provided in Article 14 of the E-commerce Directive, has been deemed potentially incompatible with the prohibition of general monitoring obligations in Article 15 of the E-commerce Directive. As discussed further in Chapter 6, Section 1.1, the CJEU has addressed the compatibility of certain types of intermediary injunctions in a number of rulings. In *L'Oréal and Others*, C-324/ 09, and *Mc Fadden*, C-484/14, the Court was adamant that Article 15 of the E-commerce Directive only applies to general monitoring obligations.[19] General monitoring obligations would also be contrary to Article 3 of the Enforcement Directive, which states that the measures referred to by the directive must be fair and proportionate and must not be excessively costly.[20] That said, the EU allows both the imposition on hosting providers of specific duties of care, and for injunctions to be issued against intermediaries to put an end to existing infringements and prevent further ones from occurring.[21]

CJEU case law on filtering—In *UPC Telekabel*, C-314/12, the CJEU considered website blocking compatible with EU law. In relation to this, the Court envisaged blocking as an enforcement goal, and stated that intermediaries should define how such a goal is to be achieved. Blocking may also include filtering measures.[22]

In *Scarlet Extended*, C-70/10, and *Netlog*, C-360/10 the CJEU addressed the availability of injunctions that would impose on a provider an obligation to filter to prevent the making available of infringing content. These rulings are narrow in scope and specific in content. In fact, what the CJEU found incompatible with EU law in those cases (see also the operative part of the decision) would be *only* a filtering system imposed on a provider that would: (1) filter information which is stored on its servers by its service users; (2) which applies indiscriminately to all of those users; (3) as a preventative measure; (4) exclusively at its expense; *and* (5) for an unlimited period, which is capable of identifying electronic files containing copyright material, with a view to preventing those works from being made available to the public without a licence.[23]

In *Stichting Brein*, C-610/15, the CJEU held that liability for unauthorized acts of communication to the public arises in case of actual and constructive knowledge and—potentially—also in cases in which knowledge is presumed. In this sense, operators of platforms with a profit-making intention would have an *ex ante* reasonable duty of care and be subject to an *ex post* notice-and-takedown system, which would also include an obligation to prevent infringements of the same kind, for example, by means of re-uploads of the same content. This appears in line with *L'Oréal and Others*, C-324/09, in which the CJEU clarified the obligations of a 'diligent economic operator'[24] and also held that an injunction against an intermediary may be aimed not just

---

[19] *L'Oréal and Others*, C-324/09, EU:C:2011:474, para 139; *Mc Fadden*, C-484/14, EU:C:2016:689, para 87.

[20] Ibid.   [21] See further GF Frosio, 'The death of "no monitoring obligations"' 203–4.

[22] M Husovec, *Injunctions against* 119–20.

[23] Also submitting that the CJEU 'prohibited generic filtering but allowed individualized blocking', see A Savin, *EU Internet Law* (Edward Elgar:2017), 2nd edn, 166. Cf, critically, C Angelopoulos, *European Intermediary Liability in Copyright* 103–4.

[24] *L'Oréal and Others*, C-324/09, EU:C:2011:474, paras 120–124.1

at repressing existing infringements but also preventing new ones from occurring. Also, national courts have reached similar conclusions regarding preventing re-uploads of infringing content.[25]

2. The Press Publishers' Right

Article 11—Another provision in the proposed DSM Directive, which requires to be assessed against the body of CJEU case law, is the one contained in Article 11. The EU Commission proposed the introduction of a new related right in favour of press publishers for the digital use of their press publications. In its original formulation, the press publishers' right would mandate Member States to provide publishers of press publications with the rights of reproduction and making available to the public, as envisaged by the InfoSoc Directive, for the digital use of their press publications. Such a right would leave intact and in no way affect—including by means of deprivation—any rights of authors and other rightholders, in respect of the works and other subject matter incorporated in a press publication. The duration would be twenty years following the publication of the subject matter at issue.

Rationale—The proposal is meant to help press publishers 'increase their legal certainty, strengthen their bargaining position and have a positive impact on their ability to license content and enforce the rights on their press publications'.[26] The stated rationale stems from awareness of the difficulties facing press publishers when seeking to license their publications and prevent unauthorized uses by online services.[27]

Achievement of underlying objectives—Besides considerations concerning whether the introduction of a new right is supported by an internal market rationale, would achieve its underlying objective (notably by improving press publishers' bargaining position), and would appropriately support the evolution of business models in the press sector,[28] in the context of the present contribution a question is whether the introduction of a press publishers' right would actually grant press publishers broader and more certain protection than the one already enjoyed under the *acquis*.[29] The answer

---

[25] In relation to Germany see eg JB Nordemann, 'Recent CJEU case law on communication to the public and its application in Germany: a new EU concept of liability' (2018) 13(9) JIPLP 744, 748–51. See also JB Nordemann, *Liability of Online Service Providers for Copyrighted Content—Regulatory Action Needed?* (2018) Directorate General for Internal Policies—Policy Department A: Economic and Scientific Policy, IP/A/IMCO/2017-08 - PE 614.207, 16–17.

[26] European Commission, *Commission staff working document—Executive summary of the Impact Assessment on the modernisation of EU copyright rules accompanying the document Proposal for a Directive of the European Parliament and of the Council on copyright in the Digital Single Market*, SWD(2016) 302 final, 3.

[27] European Commission, *Commission staff working document—Impact Assessment on the modernisation of EU copyright rules accompanying the document Proposal for a Directive of the European Parliament and of the Council on copyright in the Digital Single Market and Proposal for a Regulation of the European Parliament and of the Council laying down rules on the exercise of copyright and related rights applicable to certain online transmissions of broadcasting organisations and retransmissions of television and radio programmes*, SWD(2016) 301 final, 155.

[28] In relation to this last point, see, critically, European Copyright Society, *General Opinion on the EU Copyright Reform Package* (24 January 2017), available at <https://europeancopyrightsocietydotorg.files.wordpress.com/2015/12/ecs-opinion-on-eu-copyright-reform-def.pdf> (last accessed 15 August 2018), 6; M Senftleben, M Kerk, M Buiten, and K Heine, 'New rights or new business models? An inquiry into the future of publishing in the digital era' (2017) 48(5) IIC 538, 551–5.

[29] A collection of academic commentary on Article 11 of the draft DSM Directive is available at <https://www.create.ac.uk/policy-responses/eu-copyright-reform/article-11-research/> (last accessed 15 August 2018).

in relation to the Commission's original proposal appears to be in the negative.[30] The scope of the proposed press publishers' right as proposed by the Commission would not in fact be broader than the protection already available under existing legislation. Not only would the rights of reproduction and making available to the public be akin to those already envisaged under the InfoSoc Directive and relevant CJEU case law, but the new right would be also subject to relevant copyright exceptions and limitations under national copyright regimes (Recital 34 of the proposed DSM Directive). In this sense, the press publishers' right, in the EU Commission's version, would not offer broader scope of protection, especially to those publishers who have been transferred the copyright in relevant press publications. As will be however explained further in what follows, protection broader than what EU law (as interpreted by the CJEU) already envisaged prior to the proposal would be provided should the right be applicable also in relation to press content that failed to reach the required level of originality necessary to attract copyright protection.

3. Fair Compensation for Private Copying

The proposed DSM Directive also contains a provision, Article 12, which—compared to other provisions in the draft DSM Directive—has not been subject to particularly extensive commentary.[31] Yet this is a provision by which the EU Commission sought to depart from CJEU case law—discussed in Chapter 5, Section 3.2.4—concerning the beneficiaries of the fair compensation for private copying.

CJEU case law—In both its judgments in *Luksan*, C-277/10, and *Hewlett-Packard Belgium*, C-572/13, the Court found that the system of the InfoSoc Directive envisages that only authors are entitled to receive fair compensation for private copying. The rationale of such a requirement is in fact to compensate for the harm caused by the unauthorized making of reproductions for private use. In *Hewlett-Packard Belgium*, C-572/13, this led the Court to conclude that a national law, which provides that part of the fair compensation for private copying is to be allocated *ab initio* to publishers, would be incompatible with EU law. Not only are publishers not exclusive reproduction rightholders under Article 2 of the InfoSoc Directive, but they are not subject to any harm for the purpose of the limitations for reprography and private copying either. As such, they could not be the beneficiaries of any fair compensation.

Article 12 and its rationale—If adopted in the form proposed by the EU Commission, Article 12 would substantially overcome rulings like those in *Luksan*, C-277/10, and *Hewlett-Packard Belgium*, C-572/13. The provision states in fact that:

Member States may provide that where an author has transferred or licensed a right to a publisher, such a transfer or a licence constitutes a sufficient legal basis for the publisher to claim a share of the compensation for the uses of the work made under an exception or limitation to the transferred or licensed right.

---

[30] Cf, however, T Höppner 'EU copyright reform: the case for a publisher's right' (2018) 2018/1 IPQ 1, in particular 13–15, outlining the benefits that the introduction of a right in favour of press publishers would produce. See also U Furgal, 'Ancillary right for press publishers: an alternative answer to the linking conundrum? (2018) 13(9) JIPLP 700, 705–6, suggesting that this new right would result in a different treatment of acts of linking.

[31] A notable exception is the critical assessment of the European Copyright Society, *General Opinion on the EU Copyright Reform Package* (24 January 2017), available at <https:// europeancopyrightsocietydotorg.files.wordpress.com/2015/12/ecs-opinion-on-eu-copyright-reform-def.pdf> (last accessed 15 August 2018), 6–7.

The rationale of this provision is explained in Recital 36 in the preamble to the draft directive:

Publishers, including those of press publications, books or scientific publications, often operate on the basis of the transfer of authors' rights by means of contractual agreements or statutory provisions. In this context, publishers make an investment with a view to the exploitation of the works contained in their publications and may in some instances be deprived of revenues where such works are used under exceptions or limitations such as the ones for private copying and rep-rography. In a number of Member States compensation for uses under those exceptions is shared between authors and publishers. In order to take account of this situation and improve legal certainty for all concerned parties, Member States should be allowed to determine that, when an author has transferred or licensed his rights to a publisher or otherwise contributes with his works to a publication and there are systems in place to compensate for the harm caused by an exception or limitation, publishers are entitled to claim a share of such compensation, whereas the burden on the publisher to substantiate his claim should not exceed what is required under the system in place.

One may wonder whether a proposal of this kind, which is meant to safeguard existing business practices and contrast (correct) interpretations of the EU framework, may be regarded as compatible with one of the key objectives of the InfoSoc Directive, that is, ensuring a high level of protection of rightholders, intended as those who are actually recognized as holders of exclusive rights like the right of reproduction under the InfoSoc Directive.

4. Out-of-Commerce Works

Article 7—Also for out-of-commerce works the EU Commission's proposal envisages a mechanism of 'erasure' (or limitation) of CJEU case law similar to the one designed for beneficiaries of fair compensation for private copying. Article 7 of the proposed directive provides in fact that, when a collective management organization—on be-half of its members—concludes a non-exclusive licence for non-commercial purposes with a cultural heritage institution for the digitization, distribution, communication to the public, or making available of out-of-commerce works or other subject matter permanently in the collection of the institution, such a non-exclusive licence might be extended or presumed to apply to rightholders of the same category as those covered by the licence who are not represented by the collective management organization. Although a number of conditions need be satisfied for the extension of the effects of the licensing agreement concluded, this is a mechanism that would not have been pos-sible under the InfoSoc Directive alone, despite that directive being without prejudice to the arrangements in the Member States concerning the management of rights, such as extended collective licences (Recital 18 in the preamble to the InfoSoc Directive).

Soulier and Doke—Support for this conclusion comes from the CJEU decision in *Soulier and Doke*, C-301/15 (discussed in Chapter 3, Section 1). In that ruling the Court stressed how the exclusive rights within that directive are to be given a broad interpretation and considered preventive in nature.[32] The scope of protection is such as to include not only the ownership of those rights, but also their *exercise*. In this sense the decision in *Soulier and Doke*, C-301/15, implicitly qualifies the actual room left by Recital 18 in the preamble to the InfoSoc Directive as regards the creation by Member

---

[32] The preventive character of economic rights has also been recently reiterated in *Renckhoff*, C-161/17, EU:C:2018:634, para 29.

States of licensing mechanisms, which would prevent authors from exercising their rights and express their consent to third-party exploitations of their works and other subject matter.

5. Towards the Adoption of the DSM Directive: The Council's Mid-2018 Agreed Text

Following a number of compromise proposals drafted by the Estonian and Bulgarian presidencies of the Council, in May 2018 the Council's permanent representatives committee (Coreper) agreed a common position on the text of the draft DSM Directive, which would serve as a basis for negotiation with the European Parliament and the Commission.[33] For the sake of the present discussion the most notable features of the text in relation to the issues discussed earlier in the chapter appear to be the following.

5.1 Value gap proposal

Relationship with E-commerce Directive—With regard to Article 13, unlike the initial Commission's text, the Coreper version explicitly refers to the E-commerce Directive, clarifying that the DSM Directive is based upon and complements the rules contained therein.

Online content sharing service providers—Contrary to the Commission's original proposal, which used the language of the E-commerce Directive in that it was addressed to information society service providers, the Coreper's version refers to online content sharing service providers (OCSSPs), this being a notion that encompasses providers whose 'main or one of the main purposes … is to provide access to a large amount of copyright-protected content uploaded by their users with the purpose of obtaining profit therefrom, either directly or indirectly, by organising it and promoting it in order to attract more audiences'.

While this notion is potentially broad, the text states that the resulting obligations would not apply to OCSSPs whose main purpose is not to provide access to protected content to profit from this activity, for example, internet access providers, cloud providers, or online marketplaces. In addition, the draft text clarifies that, on the one hand, organizing and promoting content involves, among other things, indexing the content, presenting it in a certain manner, and categorizing it, as well as using targeted promotion on it; on the other hand, whether an OCSSP stores and gives access to a large amount of protected content needs to be decided on a case-by-case basis.

The most significant points of departure from the Commission's original version concern, first, the attempted definition of what constitutes an act of communication to the public by the addressees of Article 13 and, second, the unavailability of the safe harbour protection for OCSSPs that are deemed to do acts of communication to the public.

Communication to the public—With regard to the former, pursuant to Article 13(1) 'an online content sharing service provider performs an act of communication to the public or an act of making available to the public when it gives the public

---

[33] Council of the European Union, Proposal for a Directive of the European Parliament and of the Council on copyright in the Digital Single Market—Agreed negotiating mandate (25 May 2018), Interinstitutional File: 2016/0280 (COD), 9134/18, available at <http://www.consilium.europa.eu/media/35373/st09134-en18.pdf> (last accessed 15 August 2018).

access to copyright protected works or other protected subject matter uploaded by its users.' This appears a rather simplified reading of relevant CJEU case law on the right of communication to the public, and might lead interpreters to believe that the mere displaying of copyright content uploaded by third parties qualifies as an act of communication to the public. In its case law, the CJEU has found that this would not be sufficient, in that it is necessary to consider a number of additional factors, including—amongst others—whether the intervention of the subject in question may be considered essential/indispensable (see further Chapter 4, Section 2.1).

Unavailability of safe harbour—Turning to the second point, the Coreper text considers that, if an OCSSP is deemed to engage in acts of communication to the public/making available to the public, then it should not enjoy the safe harbour protection within Article 14 of the E-commerce Directive in relation to the doing of restricted acts (Recital 38b and Article 13(3)). However, this subject might be exempted from any resulting liability in a number of situations as per Article 13(4). OCSSPs are in fact subject to a 'diligent operator' obligation (Recital 38c). This means that 'they should not be liable if some unauthorised content is available on their services despite their best efforts to prevent its availability by applying effective and proportionate measures based on the information provided by rightholders'. In addition, the text refers to the duty of OCSSPs to act expeditiously to remove or disable access to content upon being notified by rightholders, and also a subsequent obligation to 'make their best efforts to prevent their future availability' (how this is to be done depends on the type of content: see Recital 38e). Furthermore, a licence granted to OCSSPs should also cover the doing of restricted acts in respect of uploads by users but only in cases where these act in their private capacity and for non-commercial purposes (Recital 38d), and applicable exceptions and limitations shall remain unaffected. Finally, Recital 45 mandates an interpretation and application of the directive in accordance with the rights and principles found in the EU Charter.

5.2 Press publishers' right

Limitation to publishers established in the EU—In relation to the press publishers' right, besides limiting its availability to publishers established in the EU and the duration to one year from the publication of the press publication in question (without the possibility of a retroactive application of the right), the Coreper text states that the use of *insubstantial parts* of press publications should not fall within the scope of the right.

Notion of 'insubstantial part'—It would be left to Member States to determine the 'insubstantial' character of parts of press publications (Recital 34a and Art 11(1)): to this end they might take into account whether these parts are the expression of the intellectual creation of their authors, and, hence, are sufficiently original to qualify for copyright protection (in accordance with *Infopaq International*, C-5/08, on which see further Chapter 4, Sections 1 and 1.1), or whether these parts are limited to individual words or very short excerpts, without independent economic significance, or both criteria. This attempted clarification of the scope of application of the press publishers' right appears to conflate concepts that belong to copyright with concepts that are found in respect of, for example, the protection of the investment in the *sui generis* database right. It also begs the question whether an actual harmonization would be achieved if EU Member States were free to determine the limits of the right.

5.3 Fair compensation for private copying

The formulation of Article 12 in the Coreper version is substantially identical to the original proposal of the EU Commission, the only significant difference being that Coreper's version, besides being referred to fair compensation for private copying and reprography, also envisages the possibility of extending publishers' entitlement to a share of the remuneration for public lending within Article 6(1) of the Rental and Lending Rights Directive.

5.4 Out-of-commerce works

Sufficient representativeness—Also with regard to out-of-commerce works, the Coreper version of Article 7 is not substantially different from the Commission's original proposal, but the requirements set in Coreper's text appear more relaxed. In fact, among other things, unlike the Commission's original proposal, the Coreper's version does not require the collective management organization, entrusted with the power to conclude licensing agreements with cultural heritage institutions, to be broadly representative of rightholders in the category of works or other subject matter and of the rights which are the subject of the licence, but merely 'sufficiently' representative.

Notion of 'out-of-commerce'—In addition, the definition of when a work or other subject matter is to be regarded as out-of-commerce is less stringent than in the original proposal: this would be the case 'when it can be presumed in good faith that the whole work or other subject matter is not available to the public through customary channels of commerce after a reasonable effort is made to determine such availability'. The original proposal held that a work or other subject matter would be deemed out-of-commerce when 'the whole work or other subject matter, in all its translations, versions and manifestations, is not available to the public through customary channels of commerce and cannot be reasonably expected to become so'.

6. Towards the Adoption of the DSM Directive: The JURI Committee's Text

Following a number of delays, in June 2018 the JURI Committee (Committee on Legal Affairs) of the European Parliament adopted the text of the Report on the proposed DSM Directive as drafted by its Rapporteur, MEP Voss.[34] This text would serve as a basis for the European Parliament to begin trilogue negotiations and eventually adopt formally the text of the DSM Directive as EU legislation. In early July 2018 the European Parliament (plenary) voted against the JURI text, postponing to September 2018 a decision on whether the trilogue negotiations—on the basis of the JURI text or an amended version thereof—would begin. With regard to the issues discussed in this chapter, the following may be noted in the version of the directive as proposed by the JURI Committee.

---

[34] European Parliament—Committee on Legal Affairs, *Report on the proposal for a directive of the European Parliament and of the Council on copyright in the Digital Single Market* (Rapporteur: Axel Voss), COM(2016)0593 – C8-0383/2016 – 2016/0280(COD).

6.1 Value gap proposal

Notion of 'online content sharing service providers'—OCSSPs that would be subject to Article 13 obligations are defined (Recital 37a and Article 2) as 'information society service providers one of the main purposes of which is to store and give access to the public or to stream copyright protected content uploaded/made available by its users and that optimise content, including amongst others promoting displaying, tagging, curating, sequencing the uploaded works or other subject matter, irrespective of the means used therefor, and therefore act in an active way'. The following are excluded from the definition of OCSSPs and, therefore, Article 13 of the DSM Directive: non-commercial service providers (eg online encyclopaedias), providers which allow content be uploaded with the authorization of all rightholders concerned, providers of private, open source software developing platforms, and online marketplaces whose main activity is online retail of physical goods.

Resulting obligations—The JURI Committee Report (Article 13 and Recitals 37–39c) states that providers included in the definition above:

- are deemed to perform acts of communication to the public and are therefore responsible (and potentially liable) for UUC made available through their services;
- if they perform acts of communication to the public, are not eligible for the safe harbour within Article 14 of the E-commerce Directive (which the directive would be based upon and complement: Recital 4). In any case, the safe harbour would not apply when a service provider plays an active role, including by optimizing the presentation of the uploaded works or subject matter or promoting them, irrespective of the nature of the means used therefor;
- are under an obligation to conclude 'fair and appropriate' licensing agreements with relevant rightholders (the latter are, however, under no obligation to issue licences). Said obligation also applies to information society service providers that automatically reproduce or refer to significant amounts to copyright works and make them available to the public for the purpose of indexing and referencing (Article 13b);
- would be subjected to licences that also cover any liability of users of the service for non-commercial UUC in line with the terms of the relevant licence (users, but not OCSSPs, would also benefit from the introduction of a new exception or limitation permitting the legitimate uses of extracts of pre-existing protected works or other subject matter in content that is uploaded or made available by users: Recitals 21b and 21c);
- shall, in cooperation with rightholders, take 'appropriate and proportionate' measures to ensure the functioning of the licensing agreements concluded for use of relevant works on their services;
- are under an obligation to prevent the availability of infringing content by adopting proportionate and effective measures—based on information provided by rightholders—while not preventing the availability of lawful UUC (this obligation subsists also when the safe harbour protection applies and in the absence of licensing agreements);
- are under an obligation of transparency towards rightholders and users alike regarding the use and implementation of relevant measures.

Obligations for EU Member States—The JURI version also sets out a number of obligations for EU Member States. They, in fact:

- are under an obligation to ensure that the implementation of the measures referred to in Article 13 is: (i) proportionate; (ii) strikes an appropriate balance between different fundamental rights protected by the EU Charter; and (iii) is in accordance with the prohibition of general monitoring within Article 15 of the E-commerce Directive;
- must ensure that: (i) providers put in place effective and expeditious complaints and redress mechanisms to prevent misuses or limitations to the exercise of relevant exceptions and limitations (any complaint filed under such mechanisms is to be processed without undue delay); (ii) the measures adopted by online content sharing service providers to prevent the availability of infringing content comply with Regulation 2016/679[35] (General Data Protection Regulation—GDPR) and Directive 2002/58[36] (Directive on privacy and electronic communications) and require no identification of individual users and the processing of their personal data; (iii) users have access to judicial remedies to assert reliance on an exception or limitation; (iv) authors and performers, who do not opt for a non-exclusive usage right for all users free of charge, receive fair and proportionate remuneration for the exploitation of their works, including online.

Compared to the original proposal of the EU Commission, the text and content of the value gap proposal has become increasingly complex and envisages a greater number of safeguards, arguably as a result of close scrutiny and criticisms of the original proposal.

6.2 Press publishers' right

Rationale—In relation to the press publishers' right, the text of the JURI Committee version would be the same as the original EU Commission's proposal. However, there are two points worth highlighting. The first is that in the JURI text the rationale for such an initiative would not be just favouring the sustainability of the publishing industry, but also contrasting 'fake news' (Recital 32):

The organisational and financial contribution of publishers in producing press publications needs to be recognised and further encouraged to ensure the sustainability of the publishing industry *and thereby to guarantee the availability of reliable information.* (emphasis added)

Royalty sharing—The second point is that the royalties deriving from the authorized exploitation of press content would need to be shared between publishers and authors of the relevant press content. Recital 35 states in fact that:

[n]otwithstanding the fact that authors of the works incorporated in a press publication receive an appropriate reward for the use of their works on the basis of the terms for licensing of their work to the press publisher, authors whose work is incorporated in a press publication should

---

[35] Regulation (EU) 2016/679 of the European Parliament and of the Council of 27 April 2016 on the protection of natural persons with regard to the processing of personal data and on the free movement of such data, and repealing Directive 95/46/EC (General Data Protection Regulation), OJ L 119, 4 May 2016, 1–88.

[36] Directive 2002/58/EC of the European Parliament and of the Council of 12 July 2002 concerning the processing of personal data and the protection of privacy in the electronic communications sector (Directive on privacy and electronic communications), OJ L 201, 31 July 2002, 37–47.

be entitled to an appropriate share of the new additional revenues press publishers receive for certain types of secondary use of their press publications by information society service providers in respect of the rights provided for in Article 11(1) of this Directive. The amount of the compensation attributed to the authors should take into account the specific industry licensing standards regarding works incorporated in a press publication which are accepted as appropriate in the respective Member State; and the compensation attributed to authors should not affect the licensing terms agreed between the author and the press publisher for the use of the author's article by the press publisher.

6.3 Fair compensation for private copying

The JURI text does not propose any substantial amendments to the original proposal.

6.4 Out-of-commerce works

Adequate protection—With regard to out-of-commerce works, the most notable elements are that, one the one hand, the JURI version stresses the importance of adequately protecting rightholders. So, Recital 28a provides that, in order to ensure that the licensing mechanisms established for out-of-commerce works are relevant and function properly, also ensuring rightholders adequate protection, licences are properly publicized and that legal clarity is ensured with regard to the representativeness of collective management organizations and the categorization of works.

Exception for cultural heritage institutions—The JURI Committee version also proposes the introduction of an exception in favour of cultural heritage institutions: considering the variety of works and other subject matter in the collections of cultural heritage institutions and the variance between collective management practices across Member States and sectors of cultural production, a licensing mechanism might in fact be inapplicable in cases where, for example, there is no practice of collective management. In situations of this kind, therefore, cultural heritage institutions should be entitled to make out-of-commerce works held in their permanent collection available online under an exception to copyright and related rights. Any uses under this exception should be subject to the same opt-out and publicity requirements as uses authorized by a licensing mechanism (Recital 22a).

7. Next Steps

At the time of writing the adoption of the DSM Directive remains pending. In September 2018 the European Parliament adopted its own (amended) version of the draft DSM Directive.[37] This would serve as the basis for a negotiating mandate in the context of trilogue negotiations, ie one of the final phases in the legislative process, which would eventually lead to the adoption, by the Council and the European Parliament, of the DSM Directive as a new piece of EU legislation. The DSM Directive, once adopted, would then require transposition by the individual EU Member States into their own legal systems.

---

[37] European Parliament, *Copyright in the Digital Single Market ***I Amendments adopted by the European Parliament on 12 September 2018 on the Proposal for a Directive of the European Parliament and of the Council on Copyright in the Digital Single Market*, (COM(2016)0593 – C8-0383/2016 – 2016/0280(COD)), P8_TA-PROV(2018)0337.

Conclusion

Reform of the EU copyright framework has been indicated as a priority, yet the proposals tabled by the EU Commission have faced significant resistance. Overall, discourse around EU copyright reform has proved to be highly polarized, up to the point that EU Commission Vice-President Ansip stated:

I said copyright reform was controversial. That is an understatement.

The scale of lobbying, from all sides, has been astonishing.

Everyone claims that their rivals will kill creativity, or kill innovation, or kill the internet—or kill all of it at the same time. This all has to stop. It is getting us nowhere.

It is good to have a lively debate about copyright—but not one which has descended into slogans and exaggeration.[38]

One of the criticisms advanced is that, in respect of certain draft provisions in the proposed DSM Directive, the EU Commission's proposal would go against the existing legislative framework and, above all, the interpretation that the CJEU has given of it. Overall, it appears that the reform discourse also needs to develop in such a way that CJEU case law and its implications are taken in due account, on consideration that, if in some instances the Court has clarified the meaning of legislative provisions, in other instances it has acted as de facto legislator. As such, reform of the EU *acquis* may not be just about reforming the legislative framework, but also tackling existing case law.

---

[38] A Ansip, 'Crunch time for copyright: Europe needs to find the best way forward' (23 July 2018), available at <https://ec.europa.eu/commission/commissioners/2014-2019/ansip/blog/crunch-time-copyright-europe-needs-find-best-way-forward_en> (last accessed 15 August 2018).

Summary and Conclusion—Copyright and the CJEU: Role, Action, Legacy

1. EU Copyright after Twenty Years of Case Law

The role of the CJEU in shaping the EU copyright framework has been of paramount importance. Further to a fragmentary approach to copyright harmonization and a resulting legislative framework whose provisions have proved to be rather inscrutable or altogether challenging to interpret, also in light of the issues arising out of technological advancement and new modalities of exploitation and infringement of copyright works and other protected subject matter, national courts have increasingly relied on the instrument of references for a preliminary ruling. As of today, in the context of the relatively brief history of EU copyright and within a timeframe of less than twenty years, the CJEU has issued several key preliminary rulings.

Factors that have contributed to the construction of EU copyright—Despite the lack of formal specialization within the Court, as a matter of fact a subject matter specialization has occurred through the selection of relevant Judges-Rapporteur and AGs from rather a narrow pool. This has been one factor that has contributed to developing a rich body of case law. The other key factor has been the employment, by the CJEU, of a set of standards that have served to address copyright issues from a certain perspective, and—admittedly—to achieve certain results. At times, reliance on certain standards, including the need to guarantee a high level of protection, has been more formal than substantial, in that the Court has referred to this objective to justify certain outcomes. Nonetheless, the guarantee of a high level of protection has indeed played a key role, and has allowed the Court to develop an expansive approach to the scope of copyright protection with regard to the construction of economic rights, while interpreting narrowly exceptions and limitations. However, it would not be correct to sum up the work of the CJEU as mostly or even solely concerned with this objective. Another key standard has been that of referring to certain notions in relevant legislation as autonomous concepts of EU law: this has resulted in a greater harmonization of EU Member States' laws, at a level that legislation alone—due to both the fragmentary character of its provisions and the approach of various EU Member States to the process of transposition of relevant directives into national law—would have not achieved. In addition, the Court has relied on other key standards—including proportionality and effectiveness—in its approach to the construction of the copyright framework. The need to ensure that a fair balance be achieved for contrasting rights and interests has also guided its interpretative efforts, with the EU Charter playing an increasingly relevant role.

Building an internal market—As a result of the application of this complex set of standards, the Court has given a certain shape to EU copyright law and, in significant instances, pushed the boundaries of EU harmonization beyond the text of EU legislation. In this sense, the Court's action has been informed by an overarching internal market goal. Speaking of a harmonizing 'agenda' should not lead one to believe that harmonization has been a goal per se. What the CJEU has done has been to extract and apply the primary rationale of EU harmonization: removing those differences that amount to barriers to the free movement of copyright works and protected subject matter across the EU. This has been the case, as illustrated, with regard to the construction of economic rights, exceptions and limitations, and enforcement tools alike.

An EU (CJEU) approach to copyright—The result has been a profound impact of CJEU case law on individual EU Member States, to the point that it is possible to speak of an EU (or, rather, a CJEU) approach to copyright that has rendered the traditional dichotomy between continental Europe *droit d'auteur*/common law copyright less acute than was the case before the EC/EU harmonization process began. In this sense, as the case of the UK demonstrates, CJEU case law—rather than the transposition of EU copyright directives alone—has contributed to re-shaping key copyright concepts and approaches to copyright protection.

The legacy of CJEU case law is also apparent in the context of the EU copyright reform debate: any review of EU copyright rules would not just need to consider the (formally rich but substantially thin) legislative framework, but also—and possibly above all—the CJEU interpretation of existing sets of rules. In this sense, the discussion around certain provisions in the proposed DSM Directive shows how the core of the analysis is the relationship with existing CJEU case law and whether and to what extent the EU legislature wishes to retain the legacy of CJEU rulings.

2. The Next Twenty Years?

Further harmonization and the role of the Court—It is difficult, if even at all possible, to think what EU copyright law will look like at the end of the next two decades. On the one hand, the process of legislative harmonization might lose the input of EU Member States, like the UK, that have played a central role so far, contributing from a particular perspective (that of common law copyright) to this process. This might have the effect of creating the conditions for a closer approximation between the continental European understanding of the role of copyright protection and the progression of EU harmonization. On the other hand, it is anticipated that the role of the Court will remain central: this may be due to a number of factors. First, as the draft DSM Directive suggests, law-making and resulting legislative provisions might become increasingly complex: in this sense, it would be a mistake to think that the formal complexity and density of new EU law provisions would necessarily be a way to enhance the clarity thereof. Second, progressive enlargements of the EU, for example, granting EU membership to Western Balkan countries, would require incorporation of the EU copyright *acquis* into those countries' copyright laws and, as a result of such an operation, interpretative uncertainties might arise that would require the involvement of the CJEU. Third, over the past few years a substantial number of referrals have been made in relation to technologically enabled uses of copyright works and other protected subject matter: this trend is likely to stay.

A reform of the Court?—An issue that is often raised concerns how the Court works, notably its alleged lack of specialization in copyright matters. According to a criticism often made, the CJEU should envisage specialist chambers and a system of dissenting judgments, on the model of common law countries. Is this something that is needed? Probably not, and this may be so essentially for two reasons. The first relates to the role of the Court in preliminary rulings, which is to provide guidance to national courts on how certain EU law provisions are to be interpreted: would dissenting judgments improve the clarity of CJEU rulings? The second reason relates to something that has been already discussed, and is that a de facto specialization has occurred within the CJEU. In the particular context of preliminary rulings, the role of the Court remains that of interpreting EU law provisions, also in light of the rationale for which a process of EU integration began in the first place. In this sense, EU copyright is not and should probably not become just something for copyright lawyers.

The power of the Court—I would like to conclude with a thought about the role of the CJEU over the past few years, by using an analogy, though one *a contrario*. Readers will be familiar with *The Wizard of Oz*, whether the original novel by Frank L Baum or the various film versions, including the best-known one starring Judy Garland, or both. They will also remember that the reason why Dorothy, the Cowardly Lion, the Scarecrow, and the Tin Woodman wish to reach the Emerald City is to ask the Wonderful Wizard of Oz to help them go back to Kansas, become brave, have a brain, and have a heart, respectively. After a series of adventures and incidents, they finally reach the Emerald City. However, something *very* bad happens there: Dorothy and her friends discover that the great and powerful wizard is nothing but a crook, with no power whatsoever to grant their wishes. Nonetheless, the wizard is also a wise guy: he tells Dorothy and the others that they actually do not need him: Dorothy would be able to go back to Kansas, just by using her magical red slippers; the Cowardly Lion has already proved to have courage; the Scarecrow has demonstrated his intelligence; and the Tin Man has proved to be sensitive. So, what Dorothy and the others need is already with them. They just have to realize that.

The CJEU is *not* like the Wizard of Oz. The Court has actually had and exercised a great *power* in building EU copyright, achieving a degree of harmonization that legislation alone—by this meaning both at the EU and national levels—has so far failed to realize. Harmonization as an end in itself is not however what has guided the Court's action: in its case law the CJEU has developed a principled approach to copyright protection, that is likely to continue developing over the next few years. Whether, in all this, the Court will be also able to *solve* all the issues facing EU copyright today (with some of them—admittedly—being due to the Court itself and all its activism), well … that is a story for another time.

Appendix 1

Directive 2001/29/EC of the European Parliament and of the Council of 22 May 2001 on the Harmonisation of Certain Aspects of Copyright and Related Rights in the Information Society

THE EUROPEAN PARLIAMENT AND THE COUNCIL OF THE EUROPEAN UNION,

Having regard to the Treaty establishing the European Community, and in particular Articles 47(2), 55 and 95 thereof,

Having regard to the proposal from the Commission ([1]),

Having regard to the opinion of the Economic and Social Committee ([2]),

Acting in accordance with the procedure laid down in Article 251 of the Treaty ([3]),

Whereas:

(1) The Treaty provides for the establishment of an internal market and the institution of a system ensuring that competition in the internal market is not distorted. Harmonisation of the laws of the Member States on copyright and related rights contributes to the achievement of these objectives.

(2) The European Council, meeting at Corfu on 24 and 25 June 1994, stressed the need to create a general and flexible legal framework at Community level in order to foster the development of the information society in Europe. This requires, *inter alia*, the existence of an internal market for new products and services. Important Community legislation to ensure such a regulatory framework is already in place or its adoption is well under way. Copyright and related rights play an important role in this context as they protect and stimulate the development and marketing of new products and services and the creation and exploitation of their creative content.

(3) The proposed harmonisation will help to implement the four freedoms of the internal market and relates to compliance with the fundamental principles of law and especially of property, including intellectual property, and freedom of expression and the public interest.

(4) A harmonised legal framework on copyright and related rights, through increased legal certainty and while providing for a high level of protection of intellectual property, will foster substantial investment in creativity and innovation, including network infrastructure, and lead in turn to growth and increased competitiveness of European industry, both in the area of content provision and information technology and more generally across a wide range of industrial and cultural sectors. This will safeguard employment and encourage new job creation.

---

[1] OJ C 108, 7.4.1998, p. 6 and OJ C 180, 25.6.1999, p. 6.
[2] OJ C 407, 28.12.1998, p. 30.
[3] Opinion of the European Parliament of 10 February 1999 (OJ C 150, 28.5.1999, p. 171), Council Common Position of 28 September 2000 (OJ C 344, 1.12.2000, p. 1) and Decision of the European Parliament of 14 February 2001 (not yet published in the Official Journal). Council Decision of 9 April 2001.

(5) Technological development has multiplied and diversified the vectors for creation, production and exploitation. While no new concepts for the protection of intellectual property are needed, the current law on copyright and related rights should be adapted and supplemented to respond adequately to economic realities such as new forms of exploitation.

(6) Without harmonisation at Community level, legislative activities at national level which have already been initiated in a number of Member States in order to respond to the technological challenges might result in significant differences in protection and thereby in restrictions on the free movement of services and products incorporating, or based on, intellectual property, leading to a refragmentation of the internal market and legislative inconsistency. The impact of such legislative differences and uncertainties will become more significant with the further development of the information society, which has already greatly increased transborder exploitation of intellectual property. This development will and should further increase. Significant legal differences and uncertainties in protection may hinder economies of scale for new products and services containing copyright and related rights.

(7) The Community legal framework for the protection of copyright and related rights must, therefore, also be adapted and supplemented as far as is necessary for the smooth functioning of the internal market. To that end, those national provisions on copyright and related rights which vary considerably from one Member State to another or which cause legal uncertainties hindering the smooth functioning of the internal market and the proper development of the information society in Europe should be adjusted, and inconsistent national responses to the technological developments should be avoided, whilst differences not adversely affecting the functioning of the internal market need not be removed or prevented.

(8) The various social, societal and cultural implications of the information society require that account be taken of the specific features of the content of products and services.

(9) Any harmonisation of copyright and related rights must take as a basis a high level of protection, since such rights are crucial to intellectual creation. Their protection helps to ensure the maintenance and development of creativity in the interests of authors, performers, producers, consumers, culture, industry and the public at large. Intellectual property has therefore been recognised as an integral part of property.

(10) If authors or performers are to continue their creative and artistic work, they have to receive an appropriate reward for the use of their work, as must producers in order to be able to finance this work. The investment required to produce products such as phonograms, films or multimedia products, and services such as 'on-demand' services, is considerable. Adequate legal protection of intellectual property rights is necessary in order to guarantee the availability of such a reward and provide the opportunity for satisfactory returns on this investment.

(11) A rigorous, effective system for the protection of copyright and related rights is one of the main ways of ensuring that European cultural creativity and production receive the necessary resources and of safeguarding the independence and dignity of artistic creators and performers.

(12) Adequate protection of copyright works and subject-matter of related rights is also of great importance from a cultural standpoint. Article 151 of the Treaty requires the Community to take cultural aspects into account in its action.

(13) A common search for, and consistent application at European level of, technical measures to protect works and other subject-matter and to provide the necessary information on rights are essential insofar as the ultimate aim of these measures is to give effect to the principles and guarantees laid down in law.

(14) This Directive should seek to promote learning and culture by protecting works and other subject-matter while permitting exceptions or limitations in the public interest for the purpose of education and teaching.

(15) The Diplomatic Conference held under the auspices of the World Intellectual Property Organisation (WIPO) in December 1996 led to the adoption of two new Treaties, the 'WIPO Copyright Treaty' and the 'WIPO Performances and Phonograms Treaty', dealing respectively with the protection of authors and the protection of performers and phonogram producers. Those Treaties update the international protection for copyright and related rights significantly, not least with regard to the so-called 'digital agenda', and improve the means to fight piracy world-wide. The Community and a majority of Member States have already signed the Treaties and the process of making arrangements for the ratification of the Treaties by the Community and the Member States is under way. This Directive also serves to implement a number of the new international obligations.

(16) Liability for activities in the network environment concerns not only copyright and related rights but also other areas, such as defamation, misleading advertising, or infringement of trademarks, and is addressed horizontally in Directive 2000/31/EC of the European Parliament and of the Council of 8 June 2000 on certain legal aspects of information society services, in particular electronic commerce, in the internal market ('Directive on electronic commerce') ([1]), which clarifies and harmonises various legal issues relating to information society services including electronic commerce. This Directive should be implemented within a timescale similar to that for the implementation of the Directive on electronic commerce, since that Directive provides a harmonised framework of principles and provisions relevant *inter alia* to important parts of this Directive. This Directive is without prejudice to provisions relating to liability in that Directive.

(17) It is necessary, especially in the light of the requirements arising out of the digital environment, to ensure that collecting societies achieve a higher level of rationalisation and transparency with regard to compliance with competition rules.

(18) This Directive is without prejudice to the arrangements in the Member States concerning the management of rights such as extended collective licences.

(19) The moral rights of rightholders should be exercised according to the legislation of the Member States and the provisions of the Berne Convention for the Protection of Literary and Artistic Works, of the WIPO Copyright Treaty and of the WIPO Performances and Phono-grams Treaty. Such moral rights remain outside the scope of this Directive.

(20) This Directive is based on principles and rules already laid down in the Directives currently in force in this area, in particular Directives 91/250/EEC ([2]), 92/ 100/EEC ([3]), 93/83/EEC ([4]), 93/98/EEC ([5]) and 96/9/ EC ([6]), and it develops those principles and rules and places them in the context of the information society. The provisions of this Directive should be without prejudice to the provisions of those Directives, unless otherwise provided in this Directive.

---

[1] OJ L 178, 17.7.2000, p. 1.
[2] Council Directive 91/250/EEC of 14 May 1991 on the legal protection of computer programs (OJ L 122, 17.5.1991, p. 42). Directive as amended by Directive 93/98/EEC.
[3] Council Directive 92/100/EEC of 19 November 1992 on rental right and lending right and on certain rights related to copyright in the field of intellectual property (OJ L 346, 27.11.1992, p. 61). Directive as amended by Directive 93/98/EEC.
[4] Council Directive 93/83/EEC of 27 September 1993 on the coordination of certain rules concerning copyright and rights related to copyright applicable to satellite broadcasting and cable retransmission (OJ L 248, 6.10.1993, p. 15).
[5] Council Directive 93/98/EEC of 29 October 1993 harmonising the term of protection of copyright and certain related rights (OJ L 290, 24.11.1993, p. 9).
[6] Directive 96/9/EC of the European Parliament and of the Council of 11 March 1996 on the legal protection of databases (OJ L 77, 27.3.1996, p. 20).

Appendix 1

(21) This Directive should define the scope of the acts covered by the reproduction right with regard to the different beneficiaries. This should be done in conformity with the acquis communautaire. A broad definition of these acts is needed to ensure legal certainty within the internal market.

(22) The objective of proper support for the dissemination of culture must not be achieved by sacrificing strict protection of rights or by tolerating illegal forms of distribution of counterfeited or pirated works.

(23) This Directive should harmonise further the author's right of communication to the public. This right should be understood in a broad sense covering all communication to the public not present at the place where the communication originates. This right should cover any such transmission or retransmission of a work to the public by wire or wireless means, including broadcasting. This right should not cover any other acts.

(24) The right to make available to the public subject-matter referred to in Article 3(2) should be understood as covering all acts of making available such subject-matter to members of the public not present at the place where the act of making available originates, and as not covering any other acts.

(25) The legal uncertainty regarding the nature and the level of protection of acts of on-demand transmission of copyright works and subject-matter protected by related rights over networks should be overcome by providing for harmonised protection at Community level. It should be made clear that all rightholders recognised by this Directive should have an exclusive right to make available to the public copyright works or any other subject-matter by way of interactive on-demand transmissions. Such interactive on-demand transmissions are characterised by the fact that members of the public may access them from a place and at a time individually chosen by them.

(26) With regard to the making available in on-demand services by broadcasters of their radio or television productions incorporating music from commercial phonograms as an integral part thereof, collective licensing arrangements are to be encouraged in order to facilitate the clearance of the rights concerned.

(27) The mere provision of physical facilities for enabling or making a communication does not in itself amount to communication within the meaning of this Directive.

(28) Copyright protection under this Directive includes the exclusive right to control distribution of the work incorporated in a tangible article. The first sale in the Community of the original of a work or copies thereof by the rightholder or with his consent exhausts the right to control resale of that object in the Community. This right should not be exhausted in respect of the original or of copies thereof sold by the rightholder or with his consent outside the Community. Rental and lending rights for authors have been established in Directive 92/100/EEC. The distribution right provided for in this Directive is without prejudice to the provisions relating to the rental and lending rights contained in Chapter I of that Directive.

(29) The question of exhaustion does not arise in the case of services and on-line services in particular. This also applies with regard to a material copy of a work or other subject-matter made by a user of such a service with the consent of the rightholder. Therefore, the same applies to rental and lending of the original and copies of works or other subject-matter which are services by nature. Unlike CD-ROM or CD-I, where the intellectual property is incorporated in a material medium, namely an item of goods, every on-line service is in fact an act which should be subject to authorisation where the copyright or related right so provides.

(30) The rights referred to in this Directive may be transferred, assigned or subject to the granting of contractual licences, without prejudice to the relevant national legislation on copyright and related rights.

(31) A fair balance of rights and interests between the different categories of rightholders, as well as between the different categories of rightholders and users of protected

subject-matter must be safeguarded. The existing exceptions and limitations to the rights as set out by the Member States have to be reassessed in the light of the new electronic environment. Existing differences in the exceptions and limitations to certain restricted acts have direct negative effects on the functioning of the internal market of copyright and related rights. Such differences could well become more pronounced in view of the further development of transborder exploitation of works and cross-border activities. In order to ensure the proper functioning of the internal market, such exceptions and limitations should be defined more harmoniously. The degree of their harmonisation should be based on their impact on the smooth functioning of the internal market.

(32) This Directive provides for an exhaustive enumeration of exceptions and limitations to the reproduction right and the right of communication to the public. Some exceptions or limitations only apply to the reproduction right, where appropriate. This list takes due account of the different legal traditions in Member States, while, at the same time, aiming to ensure a functioning internal market. Member States should arrive at a coherent application of these exceptions and limitations, which will be assessed when reviewing implementing legislation in the future.

(33) The exclusive right of reproduction should be subject to an exception to allow certain acts of temporary reproduction, which are transient or incidental reproductions, forming an integral and essential part of a technological process and carried out for the sole purpose of enabling either efficient transmission in a network between third parties by an intermediary, or a lawful use of a work or other subject-matter to be made. The acts of reproduction concerned should have no separate economic value on their own. To the extent that they meet these conditions, this exception should include acts which enable browsing as well as acts of caching to take place, including those which enable transmission systems to function efficiently, provided that the intermediary does not modify the information and does not interfere with the lawful use of technology, widely recognised and used by industry, to obtain data on the use of the information. A use should be considered lawful where it is authorised by the rightholder or not restricted by law.

(34) Member States should be given the option of providing for certain exceptions or limitations for cases such as educational and scientific purposes, for the benefit of public institutions such as libraries and archives, for purposes of news reporting, for quotations, for use by people with disabilities, for public security uses and for uses in administrative and judicial proceedings.

(35) In certain cases of exceptions or limitations, rightholders should receive fair compensation to compensate them adequately for the use made of their protected works or other subject-matter. When determining the form, detailed arrangements and possible level of such fair compensation, account should be taken of the particular circumstances of each case. When evaluating these circumstances, a valuable criterion would be the possible harm to the rightholders resulting from the act in question. In cases where rightholders have already received payment in some other form, for instance as part of a licence fee, no specific or separate payment may be due. The level of fair compensation should take full account of the degree of use of technological protection measures referred to in this Directive. In certain situations where the prejudice to the rightholder would be minimal, no obligation for payment may arise.

(36) The Member States may provide for fair compensation for rightholders also when applying the optional provisions on exceptions or limitations which do not require such compensation.

(37) Existing national schemes on reprography, where they exist, do not create major barriers to the internal market. Member States should be allowed to provide for an exception or limitation in respect of reprography.

(38) Member States should be allowed to provide for an exception or limitation to the reproduction right for certain types of reproduction of audio, visual and audiovisual material for private use, accompanied by fair compensation. This may include the introduction or continuation of remuneration schemes to compensate for the prejudice to rightholders. Although differences between those remuneration schemes affect the functioning of the internal market, those differences, with respect to analogue private reproduction, should not have a significant impact on the development of the information society. Digital private copying is likely to be more widespread and have a greater economic impact. Due account should therefore be taken of the differences between digital and analogue private copying and a distinction should be made in certain respects between them.

(39) When applying the exception or limitation on private copying, Member States should take due account of technological and economic developments, in particular with respect to digital private copying and remuneration schemes, when effective technological protection measures are available. Such exceptions or limitations should not inhibit the use of technological measures or their enforcement against circumvention.

(40) Member States may provide for an exception or limitation for the benefit of certain non-profit making establishments, such as publicly accessible libraries and equivalent institutions, as well as archives. However, this should be limited to certain special cases covered by the reproduction right. Such an exception or limitation should not cover uses made in the context of on-line delivery of protected works or other subject-matter. This Directive should be without prejudice to the Member States' option to derogate from the exclusive public lending right in accordance with Article 5 of Directive 92/100/EEC. Therefore, specific contracts or licences should be promoted which, without creating imbalances, favour such establishments and the disseminative purposes they serve.

(41) When applying the exception or limitation in respect of ephemeral recordings made by broadcasting organisations it is understood that a broadcaster's own facilities include those of a person acting on behalf of and under the responsibility of the broadcasting organisation.

(42) When applying the exception or limitation for noncommercial educational and scientific research purposes, including distance learning, the non-commercial nature of the activity in question should be determined by that activity as such. The organisational structure and the means of funding of the establishment concerned are not the decisive factors in this respect.

(43) It is in any case important for the Member States to adopt all necessary measures to facilitate access to works by persons suffering from a disability which constitutes an obstacle to the use of the works themselves, and to pay particular attention to accessible formats.

(44) When applying the exceptions and limitations provided for in this Directive, they should be exercised in accordance with international obligations. Such exceptions and limitations may not be applied in a way which prejudices the legitimate interests of the rightholder or which conflicts with the normal exploitation of his work or other subject-matter. The provision of such exceptions or limitations by Member States should, in particular, duly reflect the increased economic impact that such exceptions or limitations may have in the context of the new electronic environment. Therefore, the scope of certain exceptions or limitations may have to be even more limited when it comes to certain new uses of copyright works and other subject-matter.

(45) The exceptions and limitations referred to in Article 5(2), (3) and (4) should not, however, prevent the definition of contractual relations designed to ensure fair compensation for the rightholders insofar as permitted by national law.

(46) Recourse to mediation could help users and rightholders to settle disputes. The Commission, in cooperation with the Member States within the Contact Committee,

should undertake a study to consider new legal ways of settling disputes concerning copyright and related rights.

(47) Technological development will allow rightholders to make use of technological measures designed to prevent or restrict acts not authorised by the rightholders of any copyright, rights related to copyright or the *sui generis* right in databases. The danger, however, exists that illegal activities might be carried out in order to enable or facilitate the circumvention of the technical protection provided by these measures. In order to avoid fragmented legal approaches that could potentially hinder the functioning of the internal market, there is a need to provide for harmonised legal protection against circumvention of effective technological measures and against provision of devices and products or services to this effect.

(48) Such legal protection should be provided in respect of technological measures that effectively restrict acts not authorised by the rightholders of any copyright, rights related to copyright or the *sui generis* right in databases without, however, preventing the normal operation of electronic equipment and its technological development. Such legal protection implies no obligation to design devices, products, components or services to correspond to technological measures, so long as such device, product, component or service does not otherwise fall under the prohibition of Article 6. Such legal protection should respect proportionality and should not prohibit those devices or activities which have a commercially significant purpose or use other than to circumvent the technical protection. In particular, this protection should not hinder research into cryptography.

(49) The legal protection of technological measures is without prejudice to the application of any national provisions which may prohibit the private possession of devices, products or components for the circumvention of technological measures.

(50) Such a harmonised legal protection does not affect the specific provisions on protection provided for by Directive 91/250/EEC. In particular, it should not apply to the protection of technological measures used in connection with computer programs, which is exclusively addressed in that Directive. It should neither inhibit nor prevent the development or use of any means of circumventing a technological measure that is necessary to enable acts to be undertaken in accordance with the terms of Article 5(3) or Article 6 of Directive 91/250/EEC. Articles 5 and 6 of that Directive exclusively determine exceptions to the exclusive rights applicable to computer programs.

(51) The legal protection of technological measures applies without prejudice to public policy, as reflected in Article 5, or public security. Member States should promote voluntary measures taken by rightholders, including the conclusion and implementation of agreements between rightholders and other parties concerned, to accommodate achieving the objectives of certain exceptions or limitations provided for in national law in accordance with this Directive. In the absence of such voluntary measures or agreements within a reasonable period of time, Member States should take appropriate measures to ensure that rightholders provide beneficiaries of such exceptions or limitations with appropriate means of benefiting from them, by modifying an implemented technological measure or by other means. However, in order to prevent abuse of such measures taken by right-holders, including within the framework of agreements, or taken by a Member State, any technological measures applied in implementation of such measures should enjoy legal protection.

(52) When implementing an exception or limitation for private copying in accordance with Article 5(2)(b), Member States should likewise promote the use of voluntary measures to accommodate achieving the objectives of such exception or limitation. If, within a reasonable period of time, no such voluntary measures to make reproduction for private use possible have been taken, Member States may take measures to enable beneficiaries of the exception or limitation concerned to benefit from it. Voluntary measures taken by right-holders, including agreements between rightholders and other parties concerned,

as well as measures taken by Member States, do not prevent rightholders from using technological measures which are consistent with the exceptions or limitations on private copying in national law in accordance with Article 5(2)(b), taking account of the condition of fair compensation under that provision and the possible differentiation between various conditions of use in accordance with Article 5(5), such as controlling the number of reproductions. In order to prevent abuse of such measures, any technological measures applied in their implementation should enjoy legal protection.

(53) The protection of technological measures should ensure a secure environment for the provision of interactive on-demand services, in such a way that members of the public may access works or other subject-matter from a place and at a time individually chosen by them. Where such services are governed by contractual arrangements, the first and second subparagraphs of Article 6(4) should not apply. Non-interactive forms of online use should remain subject to those provisions.

(54) Important progress has been made in the international standardisation of technical systems of identification of works and protected subject-matter in digital format. In an increasingly networked environment, differences between technological measures could lead to an incompatibility of systems within the Community. Compatibility and interoperability of the different systems should be encouraged. It would be highly desirable to encourage the development of global systems.

(55) Technological development will facilitate the distribution of works, notably on networks, and this will entail the need for rightholders to identify better the work or other subject-matter, the author or any other rightholder, and to provide information about the terms and conditions of use of the work or other subject-matter in order to render easier the management of rights attached to them. Rightholders should be encouraged to use markings indicating, in addition to the information referred to above, *inter alia* their authorisation when putting works or other subject-matter on networks.

(56) There is, however, the danger that illegal activities might be carried out in order to remove or alter the electronic copyright-management information attached to it, or otherwise to distribute, import for distribution, broadcast, communicate to the public or make available to the public works or other protected subject-matter from which such information has been removed without authority. In order to avoid fragmented legal approaches that could potentially hinder the functioning of the internal market, there is a need to provide for harmonised legal protection against any of these activities.

(57) Any such rights-management information systems referred to above may, depending on their design, at the same time process personal data about the consumption patterns of protected subject-matter by individuals and allow for tracing of on-line behaviour. These technical means, in their technical functions, should incorporate privacy safeguards in accordance with Directive 95/ 46/EC of the European Parliament and of the Council of 24 October 1995 on the protection of individuals with regard to the processing of personal data and the free movement of such data ([1]).

(58) Member States should provide for effective sanctions and remedies for infringements of rights and obligations as set out in this Directive. They should take all the measures necessary to ensure that those sanctions and remedies are applied. The sanctions thus provided for should be effective, proportionate and dissuasive and should include the possibility of seeking damages and/or injunctive relief and, where appropriate, of applying for seizure of infringing material.

(59) In the digital environment, in particular, the services of intermediaries may increasingly be used by third parties for infringing activities. In many cases such intermediaries are best placed to bring such infringing activities to an end. Therefore, without prejudice to

---

[1] OJ L 281, 23.11.1995, p. 31.

any other sanctions and remedies available, rightholders should have the possibility of applying for an injunction against an intermediary who carries a third party's infringement of a protected work or other subject-matter in a network. This possibility should be available even where the acts carried out by the intermediary are exempted under Article 5. The conditions and modalities relating to such injunctions should be left to the national law of the Member States.

(60) The protection provided under this Directive should be without prejudice to national or Community legal provisions in other areas, such as industrial property, data protection, conditional access, access to public documents, and the rule of media exploitation chronology, which may affect the protection of copyright or related rights.

(61) In order to comply with the WIPO Performances and Phonograms Treaty, Directives 92/100/EEC and 93/98/EEC should be amended,

HAVE ADOPTED THIS DIRECTIVE:

CHAPTER I

OBJECTIVE AND SCOPE

Article 1
Scope

1. This Directive concerns the legal protection of copyright and related rights in the framework of the internal market, with particular emphasis on the information society.
2. Except in the cases referred to in Article 11, this Directive shall leave intact and shall in no way affect existing Community provisions relating to:
   (a) the legal protection of computer programs;
   (b) rental right, lending right and certain rights related to copyright in the field of intellectual property;
   (c) copyright and related rights applicable to broadcasting of programmes by satellite and cable retransmission;
   (d) the term of protection of copyright and certain related rights;
   (e) the legal protection of databases.

CHAPTER II

RIGHTS AND EXCEPTIONS

Article 2
Reproduction right

Member States shall provide for the exclusive right to authorise or prohibit direct or indirect, temporary or permanent reproduction by any means and in any form, in whole or in part:

(a) for authors, of their works;
(b) for performers, of fixations of their performances;
(c) for phonogram producers, of their phonograms;
(d) for the producers of the first fixations of films, in respect of the original and copies of their films;
(e) for broadcasting organisations, of fixations of their broadcasts, whether those broadcasts are transmitted by wire or over the air, including by cable or satellite.

Article 3

Right of communication to the public of works and right of making available to the public other subject-matter

1. Member States shall provide authors with the exclusive right to authorise or prohibit any communication to the public of their works, by wire or wireless means, including the making available to the public of their works in such a way that members of the public may access them from a place and at a time individually chosen by them.
2. Member States shall provide for the exclusive right to authorise or prohibit the making available to the public, by wire or wireless means, in such a way that members of the public may access them from a place and at a time individually chosen by them:
   (a) for performers, of fixations of their performances;
   (b) for phonogram producers, of their phonograms;
   (c) for the producers of the first fixations of films, of the original and copies of their films;
   (d) for broadcasting organisations, of fixations of their broadcasts, whether these broadcasts are transmitted by wire or over the air, including by cable or satellite.
3. The rights referred to in paragraphs 1 and 2 shall not be exhausted by any act of communication to the public or making available to the public as set out in this Article.

Article 4

Distribution right

1. Member States shall provide for authors, in respect of the original of their works or of copies thereof, the exclusive right to authorise or prohibit any form of distribution to the public by sale or otherwise.
2. The distribution right shall not be exhausted within the Community in respect of the original or copies of the work, except where the first sale or other transfer of ownership in the Community of that object is made by the rightholder or with his consent.

Article 5

Exceptions and limitations

1. Temporary acts of reproduction referred to in Article 2, which are transient or incidental [and] an integral and essential part of a technological process and whose sole purpose is to enable:
   (a) a transmission in a network between third parties by an intermediary, or
   (b) a lawful use

of a work or other subject-matter to be made, and which have no independent economic significance, shall be exempted from the reproduction right provided for in Article 2.

2. Member States may provide for exceptions or limitations to the reproduction right provided for in Article 2 in the following cases:
   (a) in respect of reproductions on paper or any similar medium, effected by the use of any kind of photographic technique or by some other process having similar effects, with the exception of sheet music, provided that the right-holders receive fair compensation;
   (b) in respect of reproductions on any medium made by a natural person for private use and for ends that are neither directly nor indirectly commercial, on condition that the rightholders receive fair compensation which takes account of the application or non-application of technological measures referred to in Article 6 to the work or subject-matter concerned;
   (c) in respect of specific acts of reproduction made by publicly accessible libraries, educational establishments or museums, or by archives, which are not for direct or indirect economic or commercial advantage;

(d) in respect of ephemeral recordings of works made by broadcasting organisations by means of their own facilities and for their own broadcasts; the preservation of these recordings in official archives may, on the grounds of their exceptional documentary character, be permitted;

(e) in respect of reproductions of broadcasts made by social institutions pursuing non-commercial purposes, such as hospitals or prisons, on condition that the rightholders receive fair compensation.

3. Member States may provide for exceptions or limitations to the rights provided for in Articles 2 and 3 in the following cases:

(a) use for the sole purpose of illustration for teaching or scientific research, as long as the source, including the author's name, is indicated, unless this turns out to be impossible and to the extent justified by the non-commercial purpose to be achieved;

(b) uses, for the benefit of people with a disability, which are directly related to the disability and of a non-commercial nature, to the extent required by the specific disability;

(c) reproduction by the press, communication to the public or making available of published articles on current economic, political or religious topics or of broadcast works or other subject-matter of the same character, in cases where such use is not expressly reserved, and as long as the source, including the author's name, is indicated, or use of works or other subject-matter in connection with the reporting of current events, to the extent justified by the informatory purpose and as long as the source, including the author's name, is indicated, unless this turns out to be impossible;

(d) quotations for purposes such as criticism or review, provided that they relate to a work or other subject-matter which has already been lawfully made available to the public, that, unless this turns out to be impossible, the source, including the author's name, is indicated, and that their use is in accordance with fair practice, and to the extent required by the specific purpose;

(e) use for the purposes of public security or to ensure the proper performance or reporting of administrative, parliamentary or judicial proceedings;

(f) use of political speeches as well as extracts of public lectures or similar works or subject-matter to the extent justified by the informatory purpose and provided that the source, including the author's name, is indicated, except where this turns out to be impossible;

(g) use during religious celebrations or official celebrations organised by a public authority;

(h) use of works, such as works of architecture or sculpture, made to be located permanently in public places;

(i) incidental inclusion of a work or other subject-matter in other material;

(j) use for the purpose of advertising the public exhibition or sale of artistic works, to the extent necessary to promote the event, excluding any other commercial use;

(k) use for the purpose of caricature, parody or pastiche;

(l) use in connection with the demonstration or repair of equipment;

(m) use of an artistic work in the form of a building or a drawing or plan of a building for the purposes of reconstructing the building;

(n) use by communication or making available, for the purpose of research or private study, to individual members of the public by dedicated terminals on the premises of establishments referred to in paragraph 2(c) of works and other subject-matter not subject to purchase or licensing terms which are contained in their collections;

(o) use in certain other cases of minor importance where exceptions or limitations already exist under national law, provided that they only concern analogue uses and do not affect the free circulation of goods and services within the Community, without prejudice to the other exceptions and limitations contained in this Article.

4. Where the Member States may provide for an exception or limitation to the right of reproduction pursuant to paragraphs 2 and 3, they may provide similarly for an exception or limitation to the right of distribution as referred to in Article 4 to the extent justified by the purpose of the authorised act of reproduction.

5. The exceptions and limitations provided for in paragraphs 1, 2, 3 and 4 shall only be applied in certain special cases which do not conflict with a normal exploitation of the work or other subject-matter and do not unreasonably prejudice the legitimate interests of the rightholder.

CHAPTER III

PROTECTION OF TECHNOLOGICAL MEASURES AND RIGHTS-MANAGEMENT INFORMATION

Article 6
Obligations as to technological measures

1. Member States shall provide adequate legal protection against the circumvention of any effective technological measures, which the person concerned carries out in the knowledge, or with reasonable grounds to know, that he or she is pursuing that objective.

2. Member States shall provide adequate legal protection against the manufacture, import, distribution, sale, rental, advertisement for sale or rental, or possession for commercial purposes of devices, products or components or the provision of services which:
   (a) are promoted, advertised or marketed for the purpose of circumvention of, or
   (b) have only a limited commercially significant purpose or use other than to circumvent, or
   (c) are primarily designed, produced, adapted or performed for the purpose of enabling or facilitating the circumvention of, any effective technological measures.

3. For the purposes of this Directive, the expression 'technological measures' means any technology, device or component that, in the normal course of its operation, is designed to prevent or restrict acts, in respect of works or other subject-matter, which are not authorised by the rightholder of any copyright or any right related to copyright as provided for by law or the *sui generis* right provided for in Chapter III of Directive 96/9/EC. Technological measures shall be deemed 'effective' where the use of a protected work or other subject-matter is controlled by the rightholders through application of an access control or protection process, such as encryption, scrambling or other transformation of the work or other subject-matter or a copy control mechanism, which achieves the protection objective.

4. Notwithstanding the legal protection provided for in paragraph 1, in the absence of voluntary measures taken by rightholders, including agreements between rightholders and other parties concerned, Member States shall take appropriate measures to ensure that rightholders make available to the beneficiary of an exception or limitation provided for in national law in accordance with Article 5(2)(a), (2)(c), (2)(d), (2)(e), (3)(a), (3)(b) or (3)(e) the means of benefiting from that exception or limitation, to the extent necessary to benefit from that exception or limitation and where that beneficiary has legal access to the protected work or subject-matter concerned.

   A Member State may also take such measures in respect of a beneficiary of an exception or limitation provided for in accordance with Article 5(2)(b), unless reproduction for private use has already been made possible by rightholders to the extent necessary to benefit from the exception or limitation concerned and in accordance with the provisions of Article 5(2)(b) and (5), without preventing rightholders from adopting adequate measures regarding the number of reproductions in accordance with these provisions.

The technological measures applied voluntarily by rightholders, including those applied in implementation of voluntary agreements, and technological measures applied in implementation of the measures taken by Member States, shall enjoy the legal protection provided for in paragraph 1.

The provisions of the first and second subparagraphs shall not apply to works or other subject-matter made available to the public on agreed contractual terms in such a way that members of the public may access them from a place and at a time individually chosen by them.

When this Article is applied in the context of Directives 92/ 100/EEC and 96/9/EC, this paragraph shall apply *mutatis mutandis.*

Article 7
Obligations concerning rights-management information

1. Member States shall provide for adequate legal protection against any person knowingly performing without authority any of the following acts:
   (a) the removal or alteration of any electronic rights-management information;
   (b) the distribution, importation for distribution, broadcasting, communication or making available to the public of works or other subject-matter protected under this Directive or under Chapter III of Directive 96/9/EC from which electronic rights-management information has been removed or altered without authority, if such person knows, or has reasonable grounds to know, that by so doing he is inducing, enabling, facilitating or concealing an infringement of any copyright or any rights related to copyright as provided by law, or of the *sui generis* right provided for in Chapter III of Directive 96/9/EC.

2. For the purposes of this Directive, the expression 'rights-management information' means any information provided by rightholders which identifies the work or other subject-matter referred to in this Directive or covered by the *sui generis* right provided for in Chapter III of Directive 96/9/EC, the author or any other rightholder, or information about the terms and conditions of use of the work or other subject-matter, and any numbers or codes that represent such information.

   The first subparagraph shall apply when any of these items of information is associated with a copy of, or appears in connection with the communication to the public of, a work or other subject-matter referred to in this Directive or covered by the *sui generis* right provided for in Chapter III of Directive 96/9/EC.

CHAPTER IV

COMMON PROVISIONS

Article 8
Sanctions and remedies

1. Member States shall provide appropriate sanctions and remedies in respect of infringements of the rights and obligations set out in this Directive and shall take all the measures necessary to ensure that those sanctions and remedies are applied. The sanctions thus provided for shall be effective, proportionate and dissuasive.

2. Each Member State shall take the measures necessary to ensure that rightholders whose interests are affected by an infringing activity carried out on its territory can bring an action for damages and/or apply for an injunction and, where appropriate, for the seizure of infringing material as well as of devices, products or components referred to in Article 6(2).

3. Member States shall ensure that rightholders are in a position to apply for an injunction against intermediaries whose services are used by a third party to infringe a copyright or related right.

Article 9
Continued application of other legal provisions

This Directive shall be without prejudice to provisions concerning in particular patent rights, trade marks, design rights, utility models, topographies of semi-conductor products, type faces, conditional access, access to cable of broadcasting services, protection of national treasures, legal deposit requirements, laws on restrictive practices and unfair competition, trade secrets, security, confidentiality, data protection and privacy, access to public documents, the law of contract.

Article 10
Application over time

1. The provisions of this Directive shall apply in respect of all works and other subject-matter referred to in this Directive which are, on 22 December 2002, protected by the Member States' legislation in the field of copyright and related rights, or which meet the criteria for protection under the provisions of this Directive or the provisions referred to in Article 1(2).
2. This Directive shall apply without prejudice to any acts concluded and rights acquired before 22 December 2002.

Article 11
Technical adaptations

1. Directive 92/100/EEC is hereby amended as follows:
   (a) Article 7 shall be deleted;
   (b) Article 10(3) shall be replaced by the following:

   '3. The limitations shall only be applied in certain special cases which do not conflict with a normal exploitation of the subject-matter and do not unreasonably prejudice the legitimate interests of the rightholder.'

2. Article 3(2) of Directive 93/98/EEC shall be replaced by the following:

   '2. The rights of producers of phonograms shall expire 50 years after the fixation is made. However, if the phonogram has been lawfully published within this period, the said rights shall expire 50 years from the date of the first lawful publication. If no lawful publication has taken place within the period mentioned in the first sentence, and if the phonogram has been lawfully communicated to the public within this period, the said rights shall expire 50 years from the date of the first lawful communication to the public.

   However, where through the expiry of the term of protection granted pursuant to this paragraph in its version before amendment by Directive 2001/29/EC of the European Parliament and of the Council of 22 May 2001 on the harmonisation of certain aspects of copyright and related rights in the information society (⁽*⁾*) the rights of producers of phonograms are no longer protected on 22 December 2002, this paragraph shall not have the effect of protecting those rights anew.

Article 12
Final provisions

1. Not later than 22 December 2004 and every three years thereafter, the Commission shall submit to the European Parliament, the Council and the Economic and Social Committee a report on the application of this Directive, in which, *inter alia*, on the basis of specific

---

⁽*⁾ OJ L 167, 22.6.2001, p. 10.'

information supplied by the Member States, it shall examine in particular the application of Articles 5, 6 and 8 in the light of the development of the digital market. In the case of Article 6, it shall examine in particular whether that Article confers a sufficient level of protection and whether acts which are permitted by law are being adversely affected by the use of effective technological measures. Where necessary, in particular to ensure the functioning of the internal market pursuant to Article 14 of the Treaty, it shall submit proposals for amendments to this Directive.

2. Protection of rights related to copyright under this Directive shall leave intact and shall in no way affect the protection of copyright.

3. A contact committee is hereby established. It shall be composed of representatives of the competent authorities of the Member States. It shall be chaired by a representative of the Commission and shall meet either on the initiative of the chairman or at the request of the delegation of a Member State.

4. The tasks of the committee shall be as follows:
   (a) to examine the impact of this Directive on the functioning of the internal market, and to highlight any difficulties;
   (b) to organise consultations on all questions deriving from the application of this Directive;
   (c) to facilitate the exchange of information on relevant developments in legislation and case-law, as well as relevant economic, social, cultural and technological developments;
   (d) to act as a forum for the assessment of the digital market in works and other items, including private copying and the use of technological measures.

Article 13
Implementation

1. Member States shall bring into force the laws, regulations and administrative provisions necessary to comply with this Directive before 22 December 2002. They shall forthwith inform the Commission thereof.

When Member States adopt these measures, they shall contain a reference to this Directive or shall be accompanied by such reference on the occasion of their official publication. The methods of making such reference shall be laid down by Member States.

2. Member States shall communicate to the Commission the text of the provisions of domestic law which they adopt in the field governed by this Directive.

Article 14
Entry into force

This Directive shall enter into force on the day of its publication in the *Official Journal of the European Communities*.

Article 15
Addressees

This Directive is addressed to the Member States.
Done at Brussels, 22 May 2001.

For the European Parliament	*For the Council*
The President	*The President*
N. FONTAINE	M. WINBERG

Appendix 2

Corrigendum to Directive 2004/48/EC of the European Parliament and of the Council of 29 April 2004 on the Enforcement of Intellectual Property Rights

(Official Journal of the European Union L 157 of 30 April 2004)

Directive 2004/48/EC should read as follows:

DIRECTIVE 2004/48/EC OF THE EUROPEAN PARLIAMENT AND OF THE COUNCIL

of 29 April 2004

on the enforcement of intellectual property rights

(Text with EEA relevance)

THE EUROPEAN PARLIAMENT AND THE COUNCIL OF THE EUROPEAN UNION,

Having regard to the Treaty establishing the European Community, and in particular Article 95 thereof,

Having regard to the proposal from the Commission,

Having regard to the opinion of the European Economic and Social Committee [(1)],

After consulting the Committee of the Regions,

Acting in accordance with the procedure laid down in Article 251 of the Treaty [(2)],

Whereas:

(1) The achievement of the internal market entails eliminating restrictions on freedom of movement and distortions of competition, while creating an environment conducive to innovation and investment. In this context, the protection of intellectual property is an essential element for the success of the internal market. The protection of intellectual property is important not only for promoting innovation and creativity, but also for developing employment and improving competitiveness.

(2) The protection of intellectual property should allow the inventor or creator to derive a legitimate profit from his/her invention or creation. It should also allow the widest possible dissemination of works, ideas and new know-how. At the same time, it should not hamper freedom of expression, the free movement of information, or the protection of personal data, including on the Internet.

(3) However, without effective means of enforcing intellectual property rights, innovation and creativity are discouraged and investment diminished. It is therefore necessary to ensure that the substantive law on intellectual property, which is nowadays largely part of the *acquis communautaire*, is applied effectively in the Community. In this respect,

---

[(1)] OJ C 32, 5.2.2004, p. 15.
[(2)] Opinion of the European Parliament of 9 March 2004 (not yet published in the Official Journal) and Council Decision of 26 April 2004.

the means of enforcing intellectual property rights are of paramount importance for the success of the internal market.

(4) At international level, all Member States, as well as the Community itself as regards matters within its competence, are bound by the Agreement on trade-related aspects of intellectual property (the TRIPS Agreement), approved, as part of the multilateral negotiations of the Uruguay Round, by Council Decision 94/800/EC ([3]) and concluded in the framework of the World Trade Organisation.

(5) The TRIPS Agreement contains, in particular, provisions on the means of enforcing intellectual property rights, which are common standards applicable at international level and implemented in all Member States. This Directive should not affect Member States' international obligations, including those under the TRIPS Agreement.

(6) There are also international conventions to which all Member States are parties and which also contain provisions on the means of enforcing intellectual property rights. These include, in particular, the Paris Convention for the Protection of Industrial Property, the Berne Convention for the Protection of Literary and Artistic Works, and the Rome Convention for the Protection of Performers, Producers of Phonograms and Broadcasting Organisations.

(7) It emerges from the consultations held by the Commission on this question that, in the Member States, and despite the TRIPS Agreement, there are still major disparities as regards the means of enforcing intellectual property rights. For instance, the arrangements for applying provisional measures, which are used in particular to preserve evidence, the calculation of damages, or the arrangements for applying injunctions, vary widely from one Member State to another. In some Member States, there are no measures, procedures and remedies such as the right of information and the recall, at the infringer's expense, of the infringing goods placed on the market.

(8) The disparities between the systems of the Member States as regards the means of enforcing intellectual property rights are prejudicial to the proper functioning of the Internal Market and make it impossible to ensure that intellectual property rights enjoy an equivalent level of protection throughout the Community. This situation does not promote free movement within the internal market or create an environment conducive to healthy competition.

(9) The current disparities also lead to a weakening of the substantive law on intellectual property and to a fragmentation of the internal market in this field. This causes a loss of confidence in the internal market in business circles, with a consequent reduction in investment in innovation and creation. Infringements of intellectual property rights appear to be increasingly linked to organised crime. Increasing use of the Internet enables pirated products to be distributed instantly around the globe. Effective enforcement of the substantive law on intellectual property should be ensured by specific action at Community level. Approximation of the legislation of the Member States in this field is therefore an essential prerequisite for the proper functioning of the internal market.

(10) The objective of this Directive is to approximate legislative systems so as to ensure a high, equivalent and homogeneous level of protection in the internal market.

(11) This Directive does not aim to establish harmonised rules for judicial cooperation, jurisdiction, the recognition and enforcement of decisions in civil and commercial matters, or deal with applicable law. There are Community instruments which govern such matters in general terms and are, in principle, equally applicable to intellectual property.

(12) This Directive should not affect the application of the rules of competition, and in particular Articles 81 and 82 of the Treaty. The measures provided for in this Directive should not be used to restrict competition unduly in a manner contrary to the Treaty.

---

[3] OJ L 336, 23.12.1994, p. 1.

(13) It is necessary to define the scope of this Directive as widely as possible in order to encompass all the intellectual property rights covered by Community provisions in this field and/or by the national law of the Member State concerned. Nevertheless, that requirement does not affect the possibility, on the part of those Member States which so wish, to extend, for internal purposes, the provisions of this Directive to include acts involving unfair competition, including parasitic copies, or similar activities.

(14) The measures provided for in Articles 6(2), 8(1) and 9(2) need to be applied only in respect of acts carried out on a commercial scale. This is without prejudice to the possibility for Member States to apply those measures also in respect of other acts. Acts carried out on a commercial scale are those carried out for direct or indirect economic or commercial advantage; this would normally exclude acts carried out by end consumers acting in good faith.

(15) This Directive should not affect substantive law on intellectual property, Directive 95/46/EC of 24 October 1995 of the European Parliament and of the Council on the protection of individuals with regard to the processing of personal data and on the free movement of such data ([1]), Directive 1999/93/EC of the European Parliament and of the Council of 13 December 1999 on a Community framework for electronic signatures ([2]) and Directive 2000/31/EC of the European Parliament and of the Council of 8 June 2000 on certain legal aspects of information society services, in particular electronic commerce, in the internal market ([3]).

(16) The provisions of this Directive should be without prejudice to the particular provisions for the enforcement of rights and on exceptions in the domain of copyright and related rights set out in Community instruments and notably those found in Council Directive 91/250/EEC of 14 May 1991 on the legal protection of computer programs ([4]) or in Directive 2001/29/EC of the European Parliament and of the Council of 22 May 2001 on the harmonisation of certain aspects of copyright and related rights in the information society ([5]).

(17) The measures, procedures and remedies provided for in this Directive should be determined in each case in such a manner as to take due account of the specific characteristics of that case, including the specific features of each intellectual property right and, where appropriate, the intentional or unintentional character of the infringement.

(18) The persons entitled to request application of those measures, procedures and remedies should be not only the rightholders but also persons who have a direct interest and legal standing in so far as permitted by and in accordance with the applicable law, which may include professional organisations in charge of the management of those rights or for the defence of the collective and individual interests for which they are responsible.

(19) Since copyright exists from the creation of a work and does not require formal registration, it is appropriate to adopt the rule laid down in Article 15 of the Berne Convention, which establishes the presumption whereby the author of a literary or artistic work is regarded as such if his/her name appears on the work. A similar presumption should be applied to the owners of related rights since it is often the holder of a related right, such as a phonogram producer, who will seek to defend rights and engage in fighting acts of piracy.

(20) Given that evidence is an element of paramount importance for establishing the infringement of intellectual property rights, it is appropriate to ensure that effective means of presenting, obtaining and preserving evidence are available. The procedures should have regard to the rights of the defence and provide the necessary guarantees, including

---

[1] OJ L 281, 23.11.1995, p. 31. Directive as amended by Regulation (EC) No 1882/2003 (OJ L 284, 31.10.2003, p. 1).
[2] OJ L 13, 19.1.2000, p. 12.   [3] OJ L 178, 17.7.2000, p. 1.
[4] OJ L 122, 17.5.1991, p. 42. Directive as amended by Directive 93/98/EEC (OJ L 290, 24.11.1993, p. 9).
[5] OJ L 167, 22.6.2001, p. 10.

the protection of confidential information. For infringements committed on a commercial scale it is also important that the courts may order access, where appropriate, to banking, financial or commercial documents under the control of the alleged infringer.

(21) Other measures designed to ensure a high level of protection exist in certain Member States and should be made available in all the Member States. This is the case with the right of information, which allows precise information to be obtained on the origin of the infringing goods or services, the distribution channels and the identity of any third parties involved in the infringement.

(22) It is also essential to provide for provisional measures for the immediate termination of infringements, without awaiting a decision on the substance of the case, while observing the rights of the defence, ensuring the proportionality of the provisional measures as appropriate to the characteristics of the case in question and providing the guarantees needed to cover the costs and the injury caused to the defendant by an unjustified request. Such measures are particularly justified where any delay would cause irreparable harm to the holder of an intellectual property right.

(23) Without prejudice to any other measures, procedures and remedies available, rightholders should have the possibility of applying for an injunction against an intermediary whose services are being used by a third party to infringe the rightholder's industrial property right. The conditions and procedures relating to such injunctions should be left to the national law of the Member States. As far as infringements of copyright and related rights are concerned, a comprehensive level of harmonisation is already provided for in Directive 2001/29/EC. Article 8(3) of Directive 2001/29/EC should therefore not be affected by this Directive.

(24) Depending on the particular case, and if justified by the circumstances, the measures, procedures and remedies to be provided for should include prohibitory measures aimed at preventing further infringements of intellectual property rights. Moreover there should be corrective measures, where appropriate at the expense of the infringer, such as the recall and definitive removal from the channels of commerce, or destruction, of the infringing goods and, in appropriate cases, of the materials and implements principally used in the creation or manufacture of these goods. These corrective measures should take account of the interests of third parties including, in particular, consumers and private parties acting in good faith.

(25) Where an infringement is committed unintentionally and without negligence and where the corrective measures or injunctions provided for by this Directive would be disproportionate, Member States should have the option of providing for the possibility, in appropriate cases, of pecuniary compensation being awarded to the injured party as an alternative measure. However, where the commercial use of counterfeit goods or the supply of services would constitute an infringement of law other than intellectual property law or would be likely to harm consumers, such use or supply should remain prohibited.

(26) With a view to compensating for the prejudice suffered as a result of an infringement committed by an infringer who engaged in an activity in the knowledge, or with reasonable grounds for knowing, that it would give rise to such an infringement, the amount of damages awarded to the rightholder should take account of all appropriate aspects, such as loss of earnings incurred by the rightholder, or unfair profits made by the infringer and, where appropriate, any moral prejudice caused to the rightholder. As an alternative, for example where it would be difficult to determine the amount of the actual prejudice suffered, the amount of the damages might be derived from elements such as the royalties or fees which would have been due if the infringer had requested authorisation to use the intellectual property right in question. The aim is not to introduce an obligation to provide for punitive damages but to allow for compensation based on an objective criterion while taking account of the expenses incurred by the rightholder, such as the costs of identification and research.

(27) To act as a supplementary deterrent to future infringers and to contribute to the awareness of the public at large, it is useful to publicise decisions in intellectual property infringement cases.

(28) In addition to the civil and administrative measures, procedures and remedies provided for under this Directive, criminal sanctions also constitute, in appropriate cases, a means of ensuring the enforcement of intellectual property rights.

(29) Industry should take an active part in the fight against piracy and counterfeiting. The development of codes of conduct in the circles directly affected is a supplementary means of bolstering the regulatory framework. The Member States, in collaboration with the Commission, should encourage the development of codes of conduct in general. Monitoring of the manufacture of optical discs, particularly by means of an identification code embedded in discs produced in the Community, helps to limit infringements of intellectual property rights in this sector, which suffers from piracy on a large scale. However, these technical protection measures should not be misused to protect markets and prevent parallel imports.

(30) In order to facilitate the uniform application of this Directive, it is appropriate to provide for systems of cooperation and the exchange of information between Member States, on the one hand, and between the Member States and the Commission on the other, in particular by creating a network of correspondents designated by the Member States and by providing regular reports assessing the application of this Directive and the effectiveness of the measures taken by the various national bodies.

(31) Since, for the reasons already described, the objective of this Directive can best be achieved at Community level, the Community may adopt measures, in accordance with the principle of subsidiarity as set out in Article 5 of the Treaty. In accordance with the principle of proportionality as set out in that Article, this Directive does not go beyond what is necessary in order to achieve that objective.

(32) This Directive respects the fundamental rights and observes the principles recognised in particular by the Charter of Fundamental Rights of the European Union. In particular, this Directive seeks to ensure full respect for intellectual property, in accordance with Article 17(2) of that Charter,

HAVE ADOPTED THIS DIRECTIVE:

CHAPTER I

OBJECTIVE AND SCOPE

Article 1
Subject matter

This Directive concerns the measures, procedures and remedies necessary to ensure the enforcement of intellectual property rights. For the purposes of this Directive, the term 'intellectual property rights' includes industrial property rights.

Article 2
Scope

1. Without prejudice to the means which are or may be provided for in Community or national legislation, in so far as those means may be more favourable for rightholders, the measures, procedures and remedies provided for by this Directive shall apply, in accordance with Article 3, to any infringement of intellectual property rights as provided for by Community law and/or by the national law of the Member State concerned.

2. This Directive shall be without prejudice to the specific provisions on the enforcement of rights and on exceptions contained in Community legislation concerning copyright and rights related to copyright, notably those found in Directive 91/250/EEC and, in particular, Article 7 thereof or in Directive 2001/29/EC and, in particular, Articles 2 to 6 and Article 8 thereof.
3. This Directive shall not affect:
    (a) the Community provisions governing the substantive law on intellectual property, Directive 95/46/EC, Directive 1999/93/EC or Directive 2000/31/EC, in general, and Articles 12 to 15 of Directive 2000/31/EC in particular;
    (b) Member States' international obligations and notably the TRIPS Agreement, including those relating to criminal procedures and penalties;
    (c) any national provisions in Member States relating to criminal procedures or penalties in respect of infringement of intellectual property rights.

CHAPTER II

MEASURES, PROCEDURES AND REMEDIES

Section 1
General provisions
Article 3
General obligation

1. Member States shall provide for the measures, procedures and remedies necessary to ensure the enforcement of the intellectual property rights covered by this Directive. Those measures, procedures and remedies shall be fair and equitable and shall not be unnecessarily complicated or costly, or entail unreasonable time-limits or unwarranted delays.
2. Those measures, procedures and remedies shall also be effective, proportionate and dissuasive and shall be applied in such a manner as to avoid the creation of barriers to legitimate trade and to provide for safeguards against their abuse.

Article 4

Persons entitled to apply for the application of the measures, procedures and remedies

Member States shall recognise as persons entitled to seek application of the measures, procedures and remedies referred to in this chapter:

(a) the holders of intellectual property rights, in accordance with the provisions of the applicable law;
(b) all other persons authorised to use those rights, in particular licensees, in so far as permitted by and in accordance with the provisions of the applicable law;
(c) intellectual property collective rights-management bodies which are regularly recognised as having a right to represent holders of intellectual property rights, in so far as permitted by and in accordance with the provisions of the applicable law;
(d) professional defence bodies which are regularly recognised as having a right to represent holders of intellectual property rights, in so far as permitted by and in accordance with the provisions of the applicable law.

Article 5
Presumption of authorship or ownership

For the purposes of applying the measures, procedures and remedies provided for in this Directive,

(a) for the author of a literary or artistic work, in the absence of proof to the contrary, to be regarded as such, and consequently to be entitled to institute infringement proceedings, it shall be sufficient for his/her name to appear on the work in the usual manner;

(b) the provision under (a) shall apply *mutatis mutandis* to the holders of rights related to copyright with regard to their protected subject matter.

Section 2
Evidence
Article 6
Evidence

1. Member States shall ensure that, on application by a party which has presented reasonably available evidence sufficient to support its claims, and has, in substantiating those claims, specified evidence which lies in the control of the opposing party, the competent judicial authorities may order that such evidence be presented by the opposing party, subject to the protection of confidential information. For the purposes of this paragraph, Member States may provide that a reasonable sample of a substantial number of copies of a work or any other protected object be considered by the competent judicial authorities to constitute reasonable evidence.

2. Under the same conditions, in the case of an infringement committed on a commercial scale Member States shall take such measures as are necessary to enable the competent judicial authorities to order, where appropriate, on application by a party, the communication of banking, financial or commercial documents under the control of the opposing party, subject to the protection of confidential information.

Article 7
Measures for preserving evidence

1. Member States shall ensure that, even before the commencement of proceedings on the merits of the case, the competent judicial authorities may, on application by a party who has presented reasonably available evidence to support his/her claims that his/her intellectual property right has been infringed or is about to be infringed, order prompt and effective provisional measures to preserve relevant evidence in respect of the alleged infringement, subject to the protection of confidential information. Such measures may include the detailed description, with or without the taking of samples, or the physical seizure of the infringing goods, and, in appropriate cases, the materials and implements used in the production and/or distribution of these goods and the documents relating thereto. Those measures shall be taken, if necessary without the other party having been heard, in particular where any delay is likely to cause irreparable harm to the rightholder or where there is a demonstrable risk of evidence being destroyed.

   Where measures to preserve evidence are adopted without the other party having been heard, the parties affected shall be given notice, without delay after the execution of the measures at the latest. A review, including a right to be heard, shall take place upon request of the parties affected with a view to deciding, within a reasonable period after the notification of the measures, whether the measures shall be modified, revoked or confirmed.

2. Member States shall ensure that the measures to preserve evidence may be subject to the lodging by the applicant of adequate security or an equivalent assurance intended to ensure compensation for any prejudice suffered by the defendant as provided for in paragraph 4.

3. Member States shall ensure that the measures to preserve evidence are revoked or otherwise cease to have effect, upon request of the defendant, without prejudice to the damages which may be claimed, if the applicant does not institute, within a reasonable period, proceedings leading to a decision on the merits of the case before the competent judicial authority, the period to be determined by the judicial authority ordering the measures where

the law of a Member State so permits or, in the absence of such determination, within a period not exceeding 20 working days or 31 calendar days, whichever is the longer.

4. Where the measures to preserve evidence are revoked, or where they lapse due to any act or omission by the applicant, or where it is subsequently found that there has been no infringement or threat of infringement of an intellectual property right, the judicial authorities shall have the authority to order the applicant, upon request of the defendant, to provide the defendant appropriate compensation for any injury caused by those measures.

5. Member States may take measures to protect witnesses' identity.

Section 3
Right of information
Article 8
Right of information

1. Member States shall ensure that, in the context of proceedings concerning an infringement of an intellectual property right and in response to a justified and proportionate request of the claimant, the competent judicial authorities may order that information on the origin and distribution networks of the goods or services which infringe an intellectual property right be provided by the infringer and/or any other person who:
   (a) was found in possession of the infringing goods on a commercial scale;
   (b) was found to be using the infringing services on a commercial scale;
   (c) was found to be providing on a commercial scale services used in infringing activities; or
   (d) was indicated by the person referred to in point (a), (b) or (c) as being involved in the production, manufacture or distribution of the goods or the provision of the services.

2. The information referred to in paragraph 1 shall, as appropriate, comprise:
   (a) the names and addresses of the producers, manufacturers, distributors, suppliers and other previous holders of the goods or services, as well as the intended wholesalers and retailers;
   (b) information on the quantities produced, manufactured, delivered, received or ordered, as well as the price obtained for the goods or services in question.

3. Paragraphs 1 and 2 shall apply without prejudice to other statutory provisions which:
   (a) grant the rightholder rights to receive fuller information;
   (b) govern the use in civil or criminal proceedings of the information communicated pursuant to this Article;
   (c) govern responsibility for misuse of the right of information; or
   (d) afford an opportunity for refusing to provide information which would force the person referred to in paragraph 1 to admit to his/her own participation or that of his/her close relatives in an infringement of an intellectual property right; or
   (e) govern the protection of confidentiality of information sources or the processing of personal data.

Section 4
Provisional and precautionary measures
Article 9
Provisional and precautionary measures

1. Member States shall ensure that the judicial authorities may, at the request of the applicant:
   (a) issue against the alleged infringer an interlocutory injunction intended to prevent any imminent infringement of an intellectual property right, or to forbid, on a provisional basis and subject, where appropriate, to a recurring penalty payment where provided

for by national law, the continuation of the alleged infringements of that right, or to make such continuation subject to the lodging of guarantees intended to ensure the compensation of the rightholder; an interlocutory injunction may also be issued, under the same conditions, against an intermediary whose services are being used by a third party to infringe an intellectual property right; injunctions against intermediaries whose services are used by a third party to infringe a copyright or a related right are covered by Directive 2001/29/EC;

(b) order the seizure or delivery up of the goods suspected of infringing an intellectual property right so as to prevent their entry into or movement within the channels of commerce.

2. In the case of an infringement committed on a commercial scale, the Member States shall ensure that, if the injured party demonstrates circumstances likely to endanger the recovery of damages, the judicial authorities may order the precautionary seizure of the movable and immovable property of the alleged infringer, including the blocking of his/her bank accounts and other assets. To that end, the competent authorities may order the communication of bank, financial or commercial documents, or appropriate access to the relevant information.

3. The judicial authorities shall, in respect of the measures referred to in paragraphs 1 and 2, have the authority to require the applicant to provide any reasonably available evidence in order to satisfy themselves with a sufficient degree of certainty that the applicant is the rightholder and that the applicant's right is being infringed, or that such infringement is imminent.

4. Member States shall ensure that the provisional measures referred to in paragraphs 1 and 2 may, in appropriate cases, be taken without the defendant having been heard, in particular where any delay would cause irreparable harm to the rightholder. In that event, the parties shall be so informed without delay after the execution of the measures at the latest.

A review, including a right to be heard, shall take place upon request of the defendant with a view to deciding, within a reasonable time after notification of the measures, whether those measures shall be modified, revoked or confirmed.

5. Member States shall ensure that the provisional measures referred to in paragraphs 1 and 2 are revoked or otherwise cease to have effect, upon request of the defendant, if the applicant does not institute, within a reasonable period, proceedings leading to a decision on the merits of the case before the competent judicial authority, the period to be determined by the judicial authority ordering the measures where the law of a Member State so permits or, in the absence of such determination, within a period not exceeding 20 working days or 31 calendar days, whichever is the longer.

6. The competent judicial authorities may make the provisional measures referred to in paragraphs 1 and 2 subject to the lodging by the applicant of adequate security or an equivalent assurance intended to ensure compensation for any prejudice suffered by the defendant as provided for in paragraph 7.

7. Where the provisional measures are revoked or where they lapse due to any act or omission by the applicant, or where it is subsequently found that there has been no infringement or threat of infringement of an intellectual property right, the judicial authorities shall have the authority to order the applicant, upon request of the defendant, to provide the defendant appropriate compensation for any injury caused by those measures.

Section 5
Measures resulting from a decision on the merits of the case
Article 10
Corrective measures

1. Without prejudice to any damages due to the rightholder by reason of the infringement, and without compensation of any sort, Member States shall ensure that the competent judicial authorities may order, at the request of the applicant, that appropriate measures be

taken with regard to goods that they have found to be infringing an intellectual property right and, in appropriate cases, with regard to materials and implements principally used in the creation or manufacture of those goods. Such measures shall include:

(a) recall from the channels of commerce;

(b) definitive removal from the channels of commerce;

or

(c) destruction.

2. The judicial authorities shall order that those measures be carried out at the expense of the infringer, unless particular reasons are invoked for not doing so.

3. In considering a request for corrective measures, the need for proportionality between the seriousness of the infringement and the remedies ordered as well as the interests of third parties shall be taken into account.

Article 11
Injunctions

Member States shall ensure that, where a judicial decision is taken finding an infringement of an intellectual property right, the judicial authorities may issue against the infringer an injunction aimed at prohibiting the continuation of the infringement. Where provided for by national law, non-compliance with an injunction shall, where appropriate, be subject to a recurring penalty payment, with a view to ensuring compliance. Member States shall also ensure that rightholders are in a position to apply for an injunction against intermediaries whose services are used by a third party to infringe an intellectual property right, without prejudice to Article 8(3) of Directive 2001/29/EC.

Article 12
Alternative measures

Member States may provide that, in appropriate cases and at the request of the person liable to be subject to the measures provided for in this section, the competent judicial authorities may order pecuniary compensation to be paid to the injured party instead of applying the measures provided for in this section if that person acted unintentionally and without negligence, if execution of the measures in question would cause him/her disproportionate harm and if pecuniary compensation to the injured party appears reasonably satisfactory.

Section 6
Damages and legal costs
Article 13
Damages

1. Member States shall ensure that the competent judicial authorities, on application of the injured party, order the infringer who knowingly, or with reasonable grounds to know, engaged in an infringing activity, to pay the rightholder damages appropriate to the actual prejudice suffered by him/her as a result of the infringement.

   When the judicial authorities set the damages:

   (a) they shall take into account all appropriate aspects, such as the negative economic consequences, including lost profits, which the injured party has suffered, any unfair profits made by the infringer and, in appropriate cases, elements other than economic factors, such as the moral prejudice caused to the rightholder by the infringement;

   or

   (b) as an alternative to (a), they may, in appropriate cases, set the damages as a lump sum on the basis of elements such as at least the amount of royalties or fees which would have been due if the infringer had requested authorisation to use the intellectual property right in question.

2. Where the infringer did not knowingly, or with reasonable grounds know, engage in infringing activity, Member States may lay down that the judicial authorities may order the recovery of profits or the payment of damages, which may be pre-established.

Article 14
Legal costs

Member States shall ensure that reasonable and proportionate legal costs and other expenses incurred by the successful party shall, as a general rule, be borne by the unsuccessful party, unless equity does not allow this.

Section 7
Publicity measures
Article 15
Publication of judicial decisions

Member States shall ensure that, in legal proceedings instituted for infringement of an intellectual property right, the judicial authorities may order, at the request of the applicant and at the expense of the infringer, appropriate measures for the dissemination of the information concerning the decision, including displaying the decision and publishing it in full or in part. Member States may provide for other additional publicity measures which are appropriate to the particular circumstances, including prominent advertising.

CHAPTER III

SANCTIONS BY MEMBER STATES

Article 16
Sanctions by Member States

Without prejudice to the civil and administrative measures, procedures and remedies laid down by this Directive, Member States may apply other appropriate sanctions in cases where intellectual property rights have been infringed.

CHAPTER IV

CODES OF CONDUCT AND ADMINISTRATIVE COOPERATION

Article 17
Codes of conduct

Member States shall encourage:

(a) the development by trade or professional associations or organisations of codes of conduct at Community level aimed at contributing towards the enforcement of the intellectual property rights, particularly by recommending the use on optical discs of a code enabling the identification of the origin of their manufacture;

(b) the submission to the Commission of draft codes of conduct at national and Community level and of any evaluations of the application of these codes of conduct.

Article 18
Assessment

1. Three years after the date laid down in Article 20(1), each Member State shall submit to the Commission a report on the implementation of this Directive.

On the basis of those reports, the Commission shall draw up a report on the application of this Directive, including an assessment of the effectiveness of the measures taken, as well as an evaluation of its impact on innovation and the development of the information society. That report shall then be transmitted to the European Parliament, the Council and the European Economic and Social Committee. It shall be accompanied, if necessary and in the light of developments in the Community legal order, by proposals for amendments to this Directive.

2. Member States shall provide the Commission with all the aid and assistance it may need when drawing up the report referred to in the second subparagraph of paragraph 1.

Article 19
Exchange of information and correspondents

For the purpose of promoting cooperation, including the exchange of information, among Member States and between Member States and the Commission, each Member State shall designate one or more national correspondents for any question relating to the implementation of the measures provided for by this Directive. It shall communicate the details of the national correspondent(s) to the other Member States and to the Commission.

CHAPTER V

FINAL PROVISIONS

Article 20
Implementation

1. Member States shall bring into force the laws, regulations and administrative provisions necessary to comply with this Directive by 29 April 2006. They shall forthwith inform the Commission thereof.

   When Member States adopt these measures, they shall contain a reference to this Directive or shall be accompanied by such reference on the occasion of their official publication. The methods of making such reference shall be laid down by Member States.
2. Member States shall communicate to the Commission the texts of the provisions of national law which they adopt in the field governed by this Directive.

Article 21
Entry into force

This Directive shall enter into force on the 20th day following that of its publication in the *Official Journal of the European Union*.

Article 22
Addressees

This Directive is addressed to the Member States.
Done at Strasbourg, 29 April 2004.

For the European Parliament	*For the Council*
The President	*The President*
P. COX	M. McDOWELL

References

Memorandum of Understanding Key Principles on the Digitisation and Making Available of Out-of-Commerce Works (2011), available at <http://ec.europa.eu/internal_market/copyright/docs/copyright-infso/20110920-mou_en.pdf> (last accessed 15 August 2018).

Abrar, S, 'GS Media finds its first application in Germany' (12 December 2016), The IPKat, available at <http://ipkitten.blogspot.com/2016/12/gs-media-finds-its-first-application-in.html> (last accessed 15 August 2018).

Adeney, E, 'How much is too much? The gradual coalescence of the law on sampling' (2018) 2018(2) IPQ 91.

Angelopoulos, C, 'Freedom of expression and copyright: the double balancing act' (2008) 2008(3) IPQ 328.

Angelopoulos, C, 'Are blocking injunctions against ISPs allowed in Europe? Copyright enforcement in the post-*Telekabel* EU legal landscape' (2014) 9(10) JIPLP 812.

Angelopoulos, C, 'CJEU decision on *Ziggo*: The Pirate Bay communicates works to the public' (30 June 2017), Kluwer Copyright Blog, available at <http://copyrightblog.kluweriplaw.com/2017/06/30/cjeu-decision-ziggo-pirate-bay-communicates-works-public/> (last accessed 15 August 2018).

Angelopoulos, C, 'Communication to the public and accessory copyright infringement' (2017) 76(3) CLJ 496.

Angelopoulos, C, European Intermediary Liability in Copyright: A Tort-based Analysis (Wolters Kluwer:2017).

Angelopoulos, C and Smet, S, 'Notice-and-fair-balance: how to reach a compromise between fundamental rights in European intermediary liability' (2016) 8(2) JML 266.

Ansip, A, 'Crunch time for copyright: Europe needs to find the best way forward' (23 July 2018), available at <https://ec.europa.eu/commission/commissioners/2014-2019/ansip/blog/crunch-time-copyright-europe-needs-find-best-way-forward_en> (last accessed 15 August 2018).

Aplin, T and Bently, L, Displacing the Dominance of the Three-Step Test: The Role of Global, Mandatory Fair Use (2018), University of Cambridge Faculty of Law Research Paper No 33/2018 (forthcoming in WL Ng, H Sun, and S Balganesh (eds), Comparative Aspects of Limitations and Exceptions in Copyright Law (CUP:2018)).

Arezzo, E, 'Hyperlinks and making available right in the European Union—what future for the Internet after *Svensson*?' (2014) 45(5) IIC 524.

Arnold, R, 'Content copyrights and signal copyrights: the case for a rational scheme of protection' (2011) 1(3) QMJIP 272.

Arnold, R, 'The need for a new Copyright Act: a case study in law reform' (2015) 5(2) QMJIP 110.

Arnold, R, 'Website-blocking injunctions: the question of legislative basis' (2015) 37(10) EIPR 623.

Arnold, R and Davies, PS, 'Accessory liability for intellectual property infringement: the case of authorisation' (2017) 133(Jul) LQR 442.

Arnold, R and Rosati, E, 'Are national courts the addressees of the InfoSoc three-step test? (2015) 10(10) JIPLP 741.

Arnold, R, Bently, L, Derclaye, E, and Dinwoodie, G, The Legal Consequences of Brexit through the Lens of IP Law (2017) University of Cambridge—Legal Studies Research Paper Series, No 21/2017.

Arnull, A, The European Union and its Court of Justice (OUP:1999).

Association Littéraire et Artistique Internationale, Report and Opinion on the making available and communication to the public in the internet environment—focus on linking techniques on *the Internet* (16 September 2013), available at <http://www.alai.org/en/assets/files/resolutions/making-available-right-report-opinion.pdf> (last accessed 15 August 2018).

Association Littéraire et Artistique Internationale, *Opinion proposed to the Executive Committee and adopted at its meeting, 17 September 2014 on the criterion "New Public", developed by the Court of Justice of the European Union (CJEU), put in the context of making available and communication to the public* (17 September 2014), available at <http://www.alai.org/en/assets/files/resolutions/2014-opinion-new-public.pdf> (last accessed 15 August 2018).

Association Littéraire et Artistique Internationale, *Resolution on the European proposals of 14 September 2016 to introduce fairer sharing of the value when works and other protected material are made available by electronic means* (18 February 2017), available at <http://www.alai.org/en/assets/files/resolutions/170218-value-gap-en.pdf> (last accessed 15 August 2018).

Axhamn, J, 'Internet linking and the notion of "new public" ' (2014) 2014(2) NIR 110.

Barnard, C and Peers, S (eds), *European Union Law* (OUP:2018), 2nd edn.

Bellan, A, *Linking e comunicazione al pubblico nel sistema della Corte di Giustizia dell'Unione Europea* (2016), Tesi di dottorato—Scuola di Dottorato in Scienze Giuridiche, Dipartimento di Diritto Privato e Storia del Diritto (Università degli Studi di Milano—Facoltà di Giurisprudenza), Curriculum di Diritto Industriale:Ciclo XXVIII.

Benabou, V, 'Retour sur dix ans de jurisprudence de la Cour de Justice de l'Union Européenne en matière de propriété littéraire et artistique' (2012) 43 Propriétés Intellectuelles 140.

Benabou, V, 'Digital exhaustion of copyright in the EU or shall we cease being so schizophrenic?', in IA Stamatoudi (ed), *New Developments in EU and International Copyright Law* (Wolters Kluwer:2016).

Bently, L, *Harmonization by Stealth: Copyright and the ECJ*, Fordham IP Conference 2010, available at <http://fordhamipconference.com/wp-content/uploads/2010/08/Bently_Harmonization.pdf> (last accessed 15 August 2018).

Bently, L, 'The return of industrial copyright?' (2012) 34(10) EIPR 654.

Bently, L and Aplin, T, *Whatever Became of Global Mandatory Fair Use? A Case Study in Dysfunctional Pluralism* (2018) University of Cambridge Faculty of Law Research Paper No 34/2018 (forthcoming in S Frankel (ed), *Is Intellectual Property Pluralism Functional?* (Edward Elgar:2018).

Bently, L and Others, *Draft Statutory Instruments on Exceptions to Copyright* (6 June 2014), available at <http://www.create.ac.uk/wpcontent/uploads/2014/03/Scrutiny-Committee-Profs-letter-June2014.pdf> (last accessed 15 August 2018).

Bently, L and Radauer, A, 'European intellectual property law: what lies ahead', in Directorate General for Internal Policies—Policy Department C: Citizens' Rights and Constitutional Affairs, *Upcoming Issues of EU law—Compilation of In-depth Analyses* (2014), available at <http://www.europarl.europa.eu/RegData/etudes/IDAN/2014/509987/IPOL_IDA(2014)509987_EN.pdf?utm_content=buffer3f39b&utm_medium=social&utm_source=twitter.com&utm_campaign=buffer> (last accessed 15 August 2018).

Bently, L, Sherman, B, Gangjee, D, and Johnson, P, *Intellectual Property Law* (OUP:2018), 5th edn.

Bercimuelle-Chamot, K, 'Accessibility is the relevant criterion to determine jurisdiction in online copyright infringement cases' (2015) 10(6) JIPLP 406.

Bonadio, E, 'Trade marks in online marketplaces: the CJEU's stance in *L'Oreal v eBay*' (2012) 18(2) CTLR 37.

Brison, F and Depreeuw, S, 'The right of "communication to the public" in the European Union', in P Torremans (ed), *Research Handbook on Copyright Law* (Edward Elgar:2017), 2nd edn.

Brüß, M, 'CJEU *GS Media* decision finds its first application in Germany' (9 December 2016), The 1709 Blog, available at <http://the1709blog.blogspot.com/2016/12/cjeu-gs-media-decision-finds-its-first.html> (last accessed 15 August 2018).

Bulayenko, O, 'Permissibility of non-voluntary collective management of copyright under EU law—The case of the French law on out-of-commerce books' (2016) 7(1) JIPITEC 51.

Butriy, O, 'Letters on copyright law: Hyperlinking and content embedding as "communication to the public" in the digital space' (28 January 2017), available at <https://www.linkedin.com/pulse/letters-copyright-law-hyperlinking-content-embedding-public-butriy/?trk=hp-feed-article-title-publish> (last accessed 15 August 2018).

Cameron, A, 'Copyright exceptions for the digital age: new rights of private copying, parody and quotation (2014) 9(12) JIPLP 1002.

Centre for Intellectual Property and Information Law (University of Cambridge)—Virtual Museum, *University of London Press v University Tutorial* [1916] 2 Ch 601, available at <https://www.cipil.law.cam.ac.uk/virtual-museum/university-london-press-v-university-tutorial-1916-2-ch-601> (last accessed 15 August 2018).

Chalmers, D, Davies, G, and Monti, G, *European Union Law*, (CUP:2014), 3rd edn.

Chiou, T, 'Lifting the (dogmatic) barriers in intellectual property law: fragmentation v integration and the practicability of a European Copyright Code' (2015) 37(3) EIPR 138.

Chiou, T, 'Athens Court of Appeal applies CJEU *GS Media* linking decision and interprets "profit-making intention" restrictively' (20 November 2017), The IPKat, available at <http://ipkitten.blogspot.com/2017/11/athens-court-of-appeal-applies-cjeu-gs.html> (last accessed 15 August 2018).

Christoffersen, J, 'Human rights and balancing: The principle of proportionality', in C Geiger (ed), *Research Handbook on Human Rights and Intellectual Property* (Edward Elgar:2015).

Clark, B and Dickinson, J, 'Theseus and the labyrinth? An overview of "communication to the public" under EU copyright law: after *Reha Training* and *GS Media* where are we now and where do we go from here?' (2017) 39(5) EIPR 265.

Clark, B and Tozzi, S, ' "Communication to the public" under EU copyright law: an increasingly Delphic concept or intentional fragmentation?' (2016) 38(12) EIPR 715.

Cohen Jeroham, H, 'European copyright law—ever more horizontal' (2001) 32(5) IIC 532.

Cohen Jeroham, H, 'Restrictions on copyright and their abuse' (2005) 27(10) EIPR 359.

Cohen Jeroham, H, 'Is there a hidden agenda behind the general non-implementation of the EU three-step test?' (2009) 31(8) EIPR 408.

Commission of the European Communities, *Green Paper on copyright and the challenge of technology—Copyright issues requiring immediate action*, COM(88) 172 final.

Commission of the European Communities, Proposal for a European Parliament and Council Directive on the harmonisation of certain aspects of copyright and related rights in the Information Society, /* COM/97/0628 final - COD 97/0359 */, OJ C 108, 7 April 1998, 6–13.

Commission of the European Communities, *DG Internal Market and Services Working Paper—First evaluation of Directive 96/9/EC on the legal protection of databases*, 12 December 2005.

Commission of the European Communities, *Green Paper on copyright in the knowledge economy*, COM(2008) 466/3.

Commission of the European Communities, Communication from the Commission—*Copyright in the knowledge economy*, COM(2009) 532 final.

Cook, T, 'Exhaustion—a casualty of the borderless digital era', in L Bently, U Suthersanen, and E Torremans (eds), *Global Copyright—Three Hundred Years since the Statute of Anne, from 1709 to Cyberspace* (Edward Elgar:2010).

Cook, T and Derclaye, E, 'An EU Copyright Code: what and how, if ever?' (2011) 2011(3) IPQ 259.

Cordell, N and Potts, B, 'Communication to the public or accessory liability? Is the CJEU using communication to the public to harmonise accessory liability across the EU?' (2018) 40(5) EIPR 289.

Cornwell, J, 'Injunctions and monetary remedies compared: the English judicial response to the IP Enforcement Directive' (2018) 40(8) EIPR 490.

Cornish, W, Llewelyn, D, and Aplin, T, *Intellectual Property: Patents, Copyright, Trade Marks and Allied Rights* (Sweet & Maxwell:2013), 8th edn.

Council of the European Union, Proposal for a Directive of the European Parliament and of the Council on copyright in the Digital Single Market—agreed negotiating mandate (25 May 2018), Interinstitutional File: 2016/0280 (COD), 9134/18, available at <http://www.consilium.europa.eu/media/35373/st09134-en18.pdf> (last accessed 15 August 2018).

Craig, P and de Búrca, G, *EU Law. Text, Cases and Materials* (OUP:2015), 6th edn.

Danaher, B, Smith, MD, and Telang, R, 'Copyright enforcement in the digital age: empirical evidence and policy implications' (2017) 60(2) Communications of the ACM 68.

Davies, G, 'The convergence of copyright and authors' rights—reality or chimera?' (1995) 26(6) IIC 964.

Davies, G, Caddick, N, and Harbottle, G, *Copinger and Skone James on Copyright* (Sweet & Maxwell:2016), 17th edn.

Davies, PS, 'Costs of blocking injunctions' (2017) 2017(4) IPQ 330.

Depreeuw, S, *The Variable Scope of the Exclusive Economic Rights in Copyright* (Wolters Kluwer:2014).

Derclaye, E, 'The Court of Justice copyright case law: quo vadis?' (2014) 36(11) EIPR 716.

Dias Pereira, AL, 'Levies in EU copyright law: an overview of the CJEU's judgments on the fair compensation of private copying and reprography' (2017) 12(7) JIPLP 591.

Dietz, A, *Copyright Law in the European Community* (Sijthoff & Noordhoff:1978).

Dietz, A, 'The protection of intellectual property in the information age—the draft E.U. Copyright Directive of November 1997' (1998) 1998(4) IPQ 335.

Dinwoodie, GB, 'A comparative analysis of the secondary liability of online service providers', in GB Dinwoodie, (ed), *Secondary Liability of Internet Service Providers* (Springer:2017).

Dreier, T and Hugenholtz, PB (eds), *Concise European Copyright Law* (Wolters Kluwer:2016), 2nd edn.

Dworkin, RM, 'The model of rules' (1967) 35(1) U Chi L Rev 14.

Elkin-Koren, N, 'After twenty years: revisiting copyright liability of online intermediaries', in S Frankel and D Gervais (eds), *The Evolution and Equilibrium of Copyright in the Digital Age* (CUP:2014).

European Commission, *Commission Staff Working Document—Evaluation of Directive 96/9 on the legal protection of databases*, SWD(2018) 146 final.

European Commission, *Commission Staff Working Document—Executive summary of the Impact Assessment on the modernisation of EU copyright rules accompanying the document Proposal for a Directive of the European Parliament and of the Council on copyright in the Digital Single Market*, SWD(2016) 302 final.

European Commission, *Commission Staff Working Paper Impact Assessment on the cross-border online access to orphan works accompanying the document 'Proposal for a directive of the European Parliament and of the Council on certain permitted uses of orphan works'* (24 May 2011), SEC(2011) 615 final.

European Commission, *Commission Staff Working Document—Impact Assessment on the modernisation of EU copyright rules accompanying the document Proposal for a Directive of the European Parliament and of the Council on copyright in the Digital Single Market and Proposal for a Regulation of the European Parliament and of the Council laying down rules on the exercise of copyright and related rights applicable to certain online transmissions of broadcasting organisations and retransmissions of television and radio programmes*, SWD(2016) 301 final.

European Commission, *Commission Staff Working Paper on the review of the EC legal framework in the field of copyright and related rights* (2004) 995.

European Commission, Communication from the Commission, *Follow-up to the Green Paper on copyright and related rights in the information society*, COM(1996) 568 final.

European Commission, Communication from the Commission *On content in the Digital Single Market*, /* COM/2012/0789 final */.

European Commission, Communication from the Commission to the European Parliament, the Council, the European Economic and Social Committee and the Committee of the Regions, *A Digital Single Market Strategy for Europe*, /* COM/2015/0192 final */.

European Commission, Communication from the Commission to the European Parliament, the Council, the European Economic and Social Committee and the Committee of the Regions, *A Single Market for Intellectual Property Rights boosting creativity and innovation to provide economic growth, high quality jobs and first class products and services in Europe*, COM(2011) 287 final.

European Commission, Communication from the Commission to the European Parliament, the Council, the Economic and Social Committee and the Committee of the Regions, Single Market Act—*Twelve levers to boost growth and strengthen confidence*—'*Working together to create new growth*', COM(2011) 206 final.

European Commission, Communication from the Commission to the Council, the European Parliament and the European Economic and Social Committee, *The management of copyright and related rights in the internal market*, COM(2004) 261 final.

European Commission, Communication from the Commission to the European Parliament, the Council, the European Economic and Social Committee and the Committee of the Regions, *Towards a modern, more European copyright framework*, COM(2015) 626 final.

European Commission, Communication from the Commission to the European Parliament, the Council, the Economic and Social Committee and the Committee of the Regions, *Towards a Single Market Act for a highly competitive social market economy—50 proposals for improving our work, business and exchanges with one another*, COM(2010) 608 final.

European Commission, *Green Paper of 27 July 1995 on Copyright and Related Rights in the Information Society*, COM(95) 382 final.

European Commission, *Growth, competitiveness and employment. White Paper follow-up, Europe and the global information society. Recommendations of the high-level group on the information society to the Corfu European Council* (Bangemann Group), Bulletin of the European Union, Supplement 2/94.

European Commission, *Letter to the attention of the competent national authorities on the application of Regulation (EU) 2017/1128*, 1 June 2018, available at <https://ec.europa.eu/digital-single-market/en/news/portability-regulation-letter-sent-competent-national-authorities> (last accessed 15 August 2018).

European Commission, *Notice to stakeholders: withdrawal of the United Kingdom and EU rules in the field of copyright*, 28 March 2018, available at <https://ec.europa.eu/digital-single-market/en/news/notice-stakeholders-withdrawal-united-kingdom-and-eu-rules-field-copyright> (last accessed 15 August 2018).

European Commission, *Public consultation on the review of EU copyright rules*, 5 December 2013–5 March 2014, available at <http://ec.europa.eu/internal_market/consultations/2013/copyright-rules/docs/consultation-document_en.pdf> (last accessed 15 August 2018).

European Commission, *Reflection Document of DG INFSO and DG MARKT on Creative Content in a European digital single market: challenges for the future*, 22 October 2009.

European Commission, *White Paper on growth, competitiveness, employment. The challenges and ways forward into the 21st century*, COM(93) 700, Bulletin of the European Communities, Supplement 6/93.

European Copyright Society, *Opinion on the reference to the CJEU in Case C466/12* Svensson (15 February 2013), available at <https://europeancopyrightsocietydotorg.files.wordpress.com/2015/12/european-copyright-society-opinion-on-svensson-first-signatoriespaginatedv31.pdf> (last accessed 15 August 2018).

European Copyright Society, *Limitations and exceptions as key elements of the legal framework for copyright in the European Union—Opinion on the Judgment of the CJEU in Case C201/13* Deckmyn (20 October 2014), available at <https://europeancopyrightsocietydotorg.files.wordpress.com/2015/12/deckmyn-opinion-final-with-signatures.pdf> (last accessed 15 August 2018).

European Copyright Society, *Opinion on the reference to the CJEU in Case C-572/13* Hewlett-Packard Belgium SPRL v Reprobel SCRL (5 September 2015), available at <https://europeancopyrightsociety.org/opinion-on-reprobel/> (last accessed 15 August 2018).

European Copyright Society, *General Opinion on the EU Copyright Reform Package* (24 January 2017), available at <https://europeancopyrightsocietydotorg.files.wordpress.com/2015/12/ecs-opinion-on-eu-copyright-reform-def.pdf> (last accessed 15 August 2018).

European Copyright Society, *Opinion on the pending reference before the CJEU in Case 310/17 (copyright protection of tastes)* (19 February 2018), available at <https://europeancopyrightsocietydotorg.files.wordpress.com/2018/03/ecs-opinion-on-protection-for-tastes-final1.pdf > (last accessed 15 August 2018).

European Copyright Society, *Opinion of the European Copyright Society in relation to the pending reference before the CJEU in Case C-476/17,* Hutter v Pelham (2018), available at <https://europeancopyrightsocietydotorg.files.wordpress.com/2018/03/opinion-metall-auf-metall-fin4.pdf> (last accessed 15 August 2018).

European Max Planck Group on Conflict of Laws in Intellectual Property (CLIP), *Principles on Conflict of Laws in Intellectual Property* (2011).

European Parliament, *Copyright in the Digital Single Market ***I Amendments Adopted by the European Parliament on 12 September 2018 on the Proposal for a Directive of the European Parliament and of the Council on Copyright in the Digital Single Market,* (COM(2016)0593 – C8-0383/2016 – 2016/0280(COD)), P8_TA-PROV(2018)0337.

European Parliament—Committee on Legal Affairs, *Report on the Proposal for a Directive of the European Parliament and of the Council on Copyright in the Digital Single Market* (Rapporteur: Axel Voss), COM(2016)0593 – C8-0383/2016 – 2016/0280(COD).

Favale, M, 'Fine-tuning European copyright law to strike a balance between the rights of owners and users' (2008) 33(5) EL Rev 687.

Favale, M, Kretschmer, M, and Torremans, P, 'Is there a EU copyright jurisprudence? An empirical analysis of the workings of the European Court of Justice' (2016) 79(1) MLR 31.

Fawcett, JJ and Torremans, P, *Intellectual Property and Private International Law* (OUP:2011), 2nd edn.

Ficsor, M, *The Law of Copyright and the Internet: The 1996 WIPO Treaties, their Interpretation and Implementation* (OUP:2002).

Fischman Afori, O, 'Proportionality: a new mega standard in European copyright law' (2014) 45(8) IIC 889.

Frolova, K, 'Auteurswhat? Dutch copyright law not tolerated by the CJEU: *ACI Adam BV and Others v Stichting de Thuiskopie and Stichting Onderhandelingen Thuiskopie vergoeding* (C-435/12)' (2014) 36(1) EIPR 738.

Frolova, K, 'The UK public is a titillating target: a case comment on *Omnibill v Egpsxx*' (2015) 37(6) EIPR 383.

Frosio, GF, 'From horizontal to vertical: an intermediary liability earthquake in Europe' (2017) 12(7) JIPLP 565.

Frosio, GF, 'The death of "no monitoring obligations"—A story of untameable monsters' (2017) 8(3) JIPITEC 199.

Frosio, GF, 'To filter or not to filter? That is the question in EU copyright reform' (2018) 36(2) AELJ 101.

Furgal, U, 'Ancillary right for press publishers: an alternative answer to the linking conundrum? (2018) 13(9) JIPLP 700.

Garnett, K, Davies, G, and Harbottle, G, *Copinger and Skone James on Copyright* (Sweet & Maxwell:2011), 16th edn.

Geiger, C, ' "Constitutionalising" intellectual property law? The influence of fundamental rights on intellectual property in the European Union' (2006) 37(4) IIC 371.

Geiger, C, 'The three-step test, a threat to a balanced copyright law?' (2006) 37(6) IIC 683.

Geiger, C, 'From Berne to national law, via the Copyright Directive: the dangerous mutations of the three-step test' (2007) 29(12) EIPR 486.

Geiger, C, 'Intellectual property shall be protected!? Article 17(2) of the Charter of Fundamental Rights of the European Union: a mysterious provision with an unclear scope' (2009) 31(3) EIPR 113.

Geiger, C, 'Intellectual "property" after the Treaty of Lisbon: towards a different approach in the new European legal order?' (2010) 32(6) EIPR 255.

Geiger, C and Schönherr, F, 'Limitations to copyright in the digital age', in A Savin and J Trzaskowski (eds), *Research Handbook on EU Internet Law* (Edward Elgar:2014).

Geiger, C, Frosio, G, and Bulayenko, O, *The Exception for Text and Data Mining (TDM) in the Proposed Directive on Copyright in the Digital Single Market—Legal Aspects*, (2018), Briefing requested by the JURI Committee of the European Parliament, available at <http://www.europarl.europa.eu/RegData/etudes/IDAN/2018/604941/IPOL_IDA(2018)604941_EN.pdf> (last accessed 15 August 2018).

Geiger, C, Gervais, DJ, and Senftleben, M, 'Understanding the "three-step test"', in DJ Gervais, (ed), *International Intellectual Property—A Handbook of Contemporary Research* (Edward Elgar:2015).

Geiger, C, Hilty, RM, Griffiths, J, and Suthersanen, U, 'Declaration—A balanced interpretation of the "three-step test" in copyright law' (2010) 1(2) JIPITEC 119.

Georgopoulos, T, 'The legal foundation of European copyright law', in TE Synodinou (ed), *Codification of European Copyright Law. Challenges and Perspectives* (Kluwer Law International:2012), 31.

Gera, M, 'A tectonic shift in the European system of collective management of copyright? Possible effects of the *Soulier & Doke* decision' (2017) 39(5) EIPR 261.

Ginsburg, JC, 'Hyperlinking and infringement: The CJEU decides (sort of)' (17 May 2014), available at <https://www.mediainstitute.org/2014/03/17/hyperlinking-and-infringement-the-cjeu-decides-sort-of/> (last accessed 15 August 2018).

Ginsburg, JC and Budiardjo, LA, 'Liability for providing hyperlinks to copyright-infringing content: international and comparative law perspectives' (2018) 41 Colum JL & Arts 153.

Goldstein, P and Hugenholtz, B, *International Copyright. Principles, Law, and Practice*, 3rd edn (OUP:2013).

Gotzen, F, 'The European legislator's strategy in the field of copyright', in TE Synodinou (ed), *Codification of European Copyright Law—Challenges and Perspectives* (Wolters Kluwer:2012).

Griffiths, J, 'The "three-step test" in European copyright law—problems and solutions' (2009) 2009(4) IPQ 428.

Griffiths, J, 'Constitutionalising or harmonising? The Court of Justice, the right to property and European copyright law' (2013) 38(1) EL Rev 65.

Griffiths, J, 'The role of the Court of Justice in the development of European Union copyright law', in I Stamatoudi and Torremans (eds), *EU Copyright Law—A Commentary* (Edward Elgar:2014).

Griffiths, J, 'Fair dealing after *Deckmyn*: the United Kingdom's defence for caricature, parody and pastiche', in M Richardson and S Ricketson (eds), *Research Handbook on Intellectual Property in Media and Entertainment* (Edward Elgar:2017).

Grisse, K and Koroch, S, 'The British private copying exception and its compatibility with the Information Society Directive' (2015) 10(7) JIPLP 562.

Guadamuz, A, 'Do androids dream of electric copyright? Comparative analysis of originality in artificial intelligence generated works' (2017) 2017(2) IPQ 169.

Guibault, L, Westkamp, G, and RieberMohn, T, *Study on the Implementation and Effect in Member States' laws of Directive 2001/29/EC on the Harmonisation of Certain Aspects of Copyright and Related Rights in the Information Society* (2012), Amsterdam Law School Research Paper No 2012-28.

Günther, P, 'The principle of exhaustion and the resale of digital music in Europe: a comparative analysis of the *UsedSoft GmbH v. Oracle International Corp.* and *Capitol Records, LLC v. ReDigi, Inc.* cases' (2014) 2014(3) NIR 205.

Handig, C, 'The copyright term "work"—European harmonisation at an unknown level' (2009) 40(6) IIC 665.

Handig, C, 'The "sweat of the brow" is not enough!—more than a blueprint of the European copyright term "work"' (2013) 35(6) EIPR 334.

Hargreaves, I, *Digital Opportunity—A Review of Intellectual Property and Growth* (2011), available at <https://assets.publishing.service.gov.uk/government/uploads/system/uploads/attachment_data/file/32563/ipreview-finalreport.pdf> (last accessed 15 August 2018).

Hart, M, 'The proposed directive for copyright in the information society: nice rights, shame about the exceptions' (1998) 20(5) EIPR 169.

Hazucha, B, 'Private copying and harm to authors—compensation versus remuneration' (2017) 133(Apr) LQR 269.

Headdon, T, 'Beyond liability: on the availability and scope of injunctions against online intermediaries after *L'Oreal v Ebay*' (2012) 34(3) EIPR 137.

Headdon, T, 'The *Allposters* problem: reproduction, alteration and the misappropriation of value' (2018) 40(8) EIPR 501.

Heide, T, 'The Berne three-step test and the proposed Copyright Directive' (1999) 21(3) EIPR 105.

Heide, T, 'The approach to innovation under the proposed Copyright Directive: time for mandatory exceptions?' (2000) 2000/3 IPQ 215.

Hilty, RM, Köklü, K, and Hafenbrädl, F, 'Software agreements: stocktaking and outlook—lessons from the *UsedSoft v. Oracle* case from a comparative law perspective' (2013) 44(3) IIC 263.

HM Government, *Copyright Exception for Parody—Impact Assessment*, available at <http://webarchive.nationalarchives.gov.uk/20140603093549/http://www.ipo.gov.uk/ia-exception-parody.pdf> (last accessed 15 August 2018).

HM Government, *Technical Review of Draft Legislation on Copyright Exceptions: Government Response*, available at <http://webarchive.nationalarchives.gov.uk/20140603093549/http://www.ipo.gov.uk/response-copyrighttechreview.pdf> (last accessed 15 August 2018).

Höppner, T, 'EU copyright reform: the case for a publisher's right' (2018) 2018(1) IPQ 1.

Hudson, E, 'The pastiche exception in copyright law: a case of mashed-up drafting?' (2017) 2017(4) IPQ 346.

Hugenholtz, PB, 'Is harmonization a good thing? The case of the copyright acquis', in A Ohly and J Pila (eds), *The Europeanization of Intellectual Property Law—Towards a European Legal Methodology* (OUP:2013).

Hugenholtz, PB, 'Why the Copyright Directive is unimportant, and possibly invalid' (2000) 22(11) EIPR 499.

Hugenholtz, B and Sentleben, MRF, *Fair Use in Europe. In Search of Flexibilities* (2012), Amsterdam Law School Research Paper No 2012-39; Institute for Information Law Research Paper No 2012-33, available at <https://papers.ssrn.com/sol3/papers.cfm?abstract_id=2013239> (last accessed 15 August 2018).

Hugenholtz, PB and Van Velze, SC, 'Communication to a new public? Three reasons why EU copyright law can do without a "new public"' (2016) 47(7) IIC 797.

Husovec, M, 'European Union: comment on *Pinckney*' (2014) 45(3) IIC 370.

Husovec, M, 'Holey cap! CJEU drills (yet) another hole in the e-Commerce Directive's safe harbours' (2017) 12(2) JIPLP 115.

Husovec, M, *Injunctions Against Intermediaries in the European Union: Accountable but not Liable?* (CUP:2017).

Husovec, M and Peguera, M, 'Much ado about little—privately litigated internet disconnection injunctions' (2015) 46(1) IIC 10.

International Federation of the Phonographic Industry, *Global Music Report 2018—Annual State of the Industry* (2018).

Jääskinen, N, 'Europeanisation of national law: a legal-theoretical analysis' (2015) 40(5) EL Rev 667.

Jacob, R, 'The relationship between European and national courts in intellectual property law', A Ohly and J Pila (eds), *The Europeanization of Intellectual Property Law—Towards a European Legal Methodology* (OUP:2013).

Jacob, R, Alexander, D, and Fisher, M, *Guidebook to Intellectual Property* (Hart:2013), 6th edn.

Jacques, S, 'Are the new "fair dealing" provisions an improvement on the previous UK law, and why?' (2015) 10(9) JIPLP 699.

Jacques, S, *The Parody Exception in Copyright Law* (OUP: forthcoming).

Jacques, S, Garstka, K, Hviid, M, and Street, J, 'Automated anti-piracy systems as copyright enforcement mechanism: a need to consider cultural diversity' (2018) 40(4) EIPR 218.

Janssens, MC, 'Invitation for a 'Europeanification' of moral rights', in P Torremans (ed), *Research Handbook on Copyright Law* (Edward Elgar:2017), 2nd edn.

Janssens, MC, 'The issue of exceptions: reshaping the keys to the gates in the territory of literary, musical and artistic creation', in E Derclaye (ed), *Research Handbook on the Future of EU Copyright* (Edward Elgar:2009).

Jerker, D and Svantesson, B, *Private International Law and the Internet* (Wolters Kluwer:2012), 2nd edn.

Jongsma, D, 'Parody after *Deckmyn*—a comparative overview of the approach to parody under copyright law in Belgium, France, Germany and the Netherlands' (2017) 48(6) IIC 652.

Jougleux, P, 'The plurality of legal systems in copyright law: an obstacle to a European codification?', in TE Synodinou (ed), *Codification of European Copyright Law—Challenges and Perspectives* (Wolters Kluwer:2012).

Jütte, BJ, 'The beginning of a (happy?) relationship: copyright and freedom of expression in Europe' (2016) 38(1) EIPR 11.

Jütte, BJ and Maier, H, 'A human right to sample—will the CJEU dance to the BGH-beat?' (2017) 12(9) JIPLP 784.

Kalėda, SL, 'The role of the principle of effective judicial protection in relation to website blocking injunctions' (2017) 8(3) JIPITEC 216.

Karapapa, S, *Private Copying* (Routledge:2012).

Karapapa, S, 'Reconstructing copyright exhaustion in the online world' (2014) 2014/4 IPQ 307.

Karapapa, S, 'The requirement for a "new public" in EU copyright law' (2017) 42(1) EL Rev 63.

Kono, T and Jurčys, P, 'General report' in T Kono (ed), *Intellectual Property and Private International Law* (Hart Publishing:2012).

Koo, J, 'Away we Ziggo: the latest chapter in the EU communication to the public story' (2018) 13(7) JIPLP 542.

Koo, J, 'Enforcing the EU right of communication to the public', in P Torremans (ed), *Research Handbook on Copyright Law* (Edward Elgar:2017), 2nd edn.

Král, R, 'On the choice of methods of transposition of EU Directives' (2016) 41(2) EL Rev 220.

Kuczerawy, A, 'The power of positive thinking—intermediary liability and the effective enjoyment of the right to freedom of expression' (2017) 8(2) JIPITEC 226.

Kulk, S and Zuiderveen Borgesius, F, 'Filtering for copyright enforcement in Europe after the *Sabam* cases' (2012) 34(11) EIPR 791.

Kur, A and Dreier, T, *European Intellectual Property Law—Text, Cases & Materials* (Edward Elgar:2013).

Lehmann, M, 'The EC Directive on the harmonisation of certain aspects of copyright and related rights in the information society—a short comment' (2003) 34(5) IIC 521.

Leistner, M, 'Closing the book on the hyperlinks: brief outline of the CJEU's case law and proposal for European legislative reform' (2017) 39(6) EIPR 327.

Leistner, M, 'Copyright at the interface between EU law and national law: definition of "work" and "right of communication to the public"' (2015) 10(8) JIPLP 626.

Leistner, M, 'Copyright law on the internet in need of reform: hyperlinks, online platforms and aggregators' (2017) 12(2) JIPLP 136.

Leistner, M, 'Structural aspects of secondary (provider) liability in Europe' (2014) 9(1) JIPLP 75.

Lee, YH, 'The persistence of the text: the concept of the work in copyright law—Part 2' (2018) 2018(2) IPQ 107.

Lim Saw, C, 'Linking on the internet and copyright liability: a clarion call for doctrinal clarity and legal certainty' (2018) 49(5) IIC 536.

Linklater, E, '*UsedSoft* and the Big Bang theory: is the e-exhaustion meteor about to strike?' (2014) 5(1) JIPITEC 12.

Liu, D, 'Of originality: originality in English copyright law: past and present' (2014) 36(6) EIPR 376.

Lodder, A and Polter, P, 'ISP blocking and filtering: on the shallow justification in case law regarding effectiveness of measures' (2017) 8(2) EJLT, available at <http://ejlt.org/article/view/517/764> (last accessed 15 August 2018).

Lutzi, T, 'Internet cases in EU private international law—developing a coherent approach' (2017) 66(3) ICLQ 687.

Malovic, N, 'Online copyright enforcement in Sweden: the first blocking injunction' (2017) 28(5) Ent LR 171.

Malovic, N and Haddad, P, 'Swedish court finds that an embedded link to unlicensed content infringes copyright' (2017) 12(2) JIPLP 89.

Marsoof, A, 'The blocking injunction—a critical review of its implementation in the United Kingdom in the context of the European Union' (2015) 46(6) IIC 632.

Martin-Prat, M, 'An introduction—the EU copyright agenda', in IA Stamatoudi (ed), *New Developments in EU and International Copyright Law* (Wolters Kluwer:2016).

Masiyakurima, P, 'Fair dealing defences', in PLC Torremans (ed), *Intellectual Property Law and Human Rights* (Wolters Kluwer:2015), 3rd edn.

Matulionyte, R, 'Enforcing copyright infringements online—in search of balanced private international law rules' (2015) 6(2) JIPITEC 132.

Max Planck Institute for Innovation and Competition, *Position Statement of the Max Planck Institute for Innovation and Competition on the Proposed Modernisation of European Copyright Rules PART G Use of Protected Content on Online Platforms (Article 13 COM(2016) 593)* (2017), available at <https://www.ip.mpg.de/fileadmin/ipmpg/content/stellungnahmen/MPI_Position_Statement_PART_G_incl_Annex-2017_03_01.pdf> (last accessed 15 August 2018).

Mazziotti, G, 'Is geo-blocking a real cause for concern in Europe?' (2016) 38(6) EIPR 365.

McBride, P, 'The "new public" criterion after *Svensson*: the (ir)relevance of website terms and conditions' (2017) 2017(3) IPQ 262.

McDonagh, LT, 'Is the creative use of musical works without a licence acceptable under copyright law?' (2012) 43(4) IIC 401.

Mezei, P, 'Digital first sale doctrine *ante portas*' (2015) 6(2) JIPITEC 23.

Mezei, P, *Copyright Exhaustion—Law and Policy in the United States and the European Union* (CUP:2018).

Monti, M, *A New Strategy for the Single Market at the Service of Europe's Economy and Society. Report to the President of the European Commission José Manuel Barroso* (9 May 2010).

Mylly, T, 'The constitutionalization of the European legal order: impact of human rights on intellectual property in the EU', in C Geiger (ed), *Research Handbook on Human Rights and Intellectual Property* (Edward Elgar:2015).

Mysoor, P, 'Exhaustion, non-exhaustion and implied licence' (2018) 49(6) IIC 656.

Mysoor, P, 'Unpacking the right of communication to the public: a closer look at international and EU copyright law' (2013) 2013(2) IPQ 166.

Nérisson, S, 'Collective management and exclusive rights: friends or foes?', in P Torremans (ed), *Research Handbook on Copyright Law* (Edward Elgar:2017), 2nd edn.

Nordemann, JB, *Liability of Online Service Providers for Copyrighted Content—Regulatory Action Needed?* (2018) Directorate General for Internal Policies—Policy Department A: Economic and Scientific Policy, IP/A/IMCO/2017-08 - PE 614.207.

Nordemann, JB, 'Recent CJEU case law on communication to the public and its application in Germany: a new EU concept of liability' (2018) 13(9) JIPLP 744.

Ohly, A, 'Choice of law in the digital environment—Problems and possible solutions', in J Drexl and A Kur (eds), *Intellectual Property and Private International Law—Heading for the Future* (Hart:2005).

Ohly, A, 'The broad concept of "communication to the public" in recent CJEU judgments and the liability of intermediaries: primary, secondary or unitary liability?' (2018) 13(8) JIPLP 664.

Oprysk, L, Matulevičius, R, and Kelli, A, 'Development of a secondary market for e-books—the case of Amazon' (2017) 8(2) JIPITEC 128.

O'Sullivan, KT, 'Enforcing copyright online: internet service provider obligations and the European Charter of Human Rights' (2014) 36(9) EIPR 577.

Page, W, *Adventures in The Netherlands—Spotify, Piracy and the Dutch experience* (2013), available at <https://www.musicbusinessworldwide.com/files/2014/12/Will-Page-2013-Adventures-in-the-Netherlands-Final.pdf> (last accessed 15 August 2018).

Patry, WF, *Patry on Fair Use* (Thomson Reuters:2018), 2018 edn.

Patry, WF, 'The lack of value in the value gap' (2017) 30(4) Quarterly Copyright (Korea Copyright Commission) 189, available at <http://digital.kyobobook.co.kr/digital/article/articleDetail.ink?selectedLargeCategory=006&barcode=4010026168264> (last accessed 15 August 2018).

Peukert, A, 'Intellectual property as an end in itself?' (2011) 33(2) EIPR 67.

Pihlajarinne, T, 'Should we bury the concept of reproduction—towards principle-based assessment in copyright law?' (2017) 48(8) IIC 953.

Pila, J, 'A constitutionalized doctrine of precedent and the *Marleasing* principle as bases for a European legal methodology' in A Ohly and J Pila (eds), *The Europeanization of Intellectual Property Law—Towards a European Legal Methodology* (OUP:2013).

Pirou, FM, 'The ruling of the Court of Justice in *Soulier* revisited' (2 October 2017) Kluwer Copyright Blog, available at <http://copyrightblog.kluweriplaw.com/2017/10/02/ruling-court-justice-soulier-revisited/#_ftnref1> (last accessed 15 August 2018).

Poort, J, Leenheer, J, Der Ham, J, and Dumitru, C, 'Baywatch: two approaches to measure the effects of blocking access to the Pirate Bay' (2014) 38(4) Telecom Policy 383.

Pryke, M, 'Online copyright infringement—is jurisdiction now simply a matter of accessibility' (2015) 26(4) Ent LR 152.

Psychogiopoulou, E, 'Copyright enforcement, human rights protection and the responsibilities of internet service providers after *Scarlet*' (2012) 34(8) EIPR 552.

Pullen, M, 'The Green Paper on copyright and related rights in the information society (is it all a question of binary numbers?)' (1996) 7(2) Ent L Rev 80.

Quintais, JP, 'Private copying and downloading from unlawful sources' (2015) 46(1) IIC 66.

Quintais, JP, *Copyright in the Age of Online Access—Alternative Compensation Systems in EU Law* (Wolters Kluwer:2017).

Quintais, JP, *Global Online Piracy Study—Legal Background Report* (July 2018), available at <https://www.ivir.nl/publicaties/download/Global-Online-Piracy-Study-Legal-Background-Report.pdf> (last accessed 15 August 2018).

Quintais, JP, *Untangling the Hyperlinking Web: In Search of the Online Right of Communication to the Public* (2018) Amsterdam Law School Research Paper No 2018-16.

Quintais, JP and Rendas, T, 'EU copyright law and the Cloud: *VCAST* and the intersection of private copying and communication to the public' (2018) 13(9) JIPLP 711.

Rahmatian, A, 'European copyright inside or outside the European Union: pluralism of copyright laws and the "Herderian paradox"' (2016) 47(8) IIC 912.

Rahmatian, A, 'Originality in UK copyright law: the old "skill and labour" doctrine under pressure' (2013) 44(1) IIC 4.

Ramalho, A, 'Conceptualising the European Union's competence in copyright—what can the EU do?' (2014) 45(2) IIC 178.

Ramalho, A, 'Copyright law-making in the EU: what lies under the "internal market" mask?' (2014) 9(3) JIPLP 208.

Ramalho, A, *The Competence of the European Union in Copyright Lawmaking—A Normative Perspective of EU Powers for Copyright Harmonization* (Springer:2016).

Rendas, T, 'Copyright protection of designs in the EU: how many originality standards is too many?' (2018) 13(6) JIPLP 439.

Rendas, T, 'Copyright, technology and the CJEU: an empirical study' (2018) 49(2) IIC 153.

Rendas, T, 'How Playboy photos compromised EU copyright law: the *GS Media* judgment' (2017) 20(11) J Internet L 11.

Ricketson, S, 'The boundaries of copyright: its proper limitations and exceptions: international conventions and treaties' (1991) 1991/1 IPQ 56.

Ricketson, S and Ginsburg, JC, *International Copyright and Neighbouring Rights—The Berne Convention and Beyond* (OUP:2006), 2nd edn.

Ringelhann, AP and Mimler, M, 'Digital exploitation of out-of-print books and copyright law: French licensing mechanism for out-of-print books under CJEU scrutiny' (2017) 39(3) EIPR 190.

Riordan, J, *The Liability of Internet Intermediaries* (OUP:2016).

Rizzuto, F, 'The liability of online intermediary service providers for infringements of intellectual property rights' (2012) 18(1) CTLR 4.

Rosati, E, *Originality in EU copyright—Full Harmonization through Case Law* (Edward Elgar:2013).

Rosati, E, 'The Orphan Works Directive, or throwing a stone and hiding the hand' (2013) 8(4) JIPLP 303.

Rosati, E, 'Towards an EU-wide copyright? (Judicial) pride and (legislative) prejudice' (2013) 2013(1) IPQ 47.

Rosati, E, 'Closed subject matter systems are no longer compatible with EU copyright' (2014) 12 GRUR Int 1112.

Rosati, E, 'Copyright in the EU: in search of (in)flexibilities' (2014) 9(7) JIPLP 585.

Rosati, E, 'Struggling to understand how to address a copyright infringement issue? Here's my checklist' (24 November 2014), available at <http://ipkitten.blogspot.com/2014/11/struggling-to-understand-how-to-address.html> (last accessed 15 August 2018).

Rosati, E, 'The right of adaptation has not been generally harmonised at the EU level: true or false?' (1 May 2014) The IPKat, available at <http://ipkitten.blogspot.com/2014/05/the-right-of-adaptation-has-not-been.html> (last accessed 15 August 2018).

Rosati, E, 'Just a laughing matter? Why the decision in *Deckmyn* is broader than parody' (2015) 52(2) CMLRev 511.

Rosati, E, 'Online copyright exhaustion in a post-*Allposters* world' (2015) 10(9) JIPLP 673.

Rosati, E, 'Linking after *GS Media* … in a table' (10 September 2016), The IPKat, available at <http://ipkitten.blogspot.com/2016/09/linking-after-gs-media-in-table.html> (last accessed 15 August 2018).

Rosati, E, 'The CJEU decision in *Soulier*: what does it mean for laws other than the French one on out-of-print books?' (17 November 2016), The IPKat, available at <http://ipkitten.

blogspot.com/2016/11/the-cjeu-decision-in-soulier-what-does.html> (last accessed 15 August 2018).

Rosati, E, 'Why a reform of hosting providers' safe harbour is unnecessary under EU copyright law' (2016) 38(11) EIPR 668.

Rosati, E, 'Am I covered by that UK copyright exception? Here's my checklist' (11 April 2017), available at <http://ipkitten.blogspot.com/2017/04/am-i-covered-by-that-uk-copyright.html> (last accessed 15 August 2018).

Rosati, E, 'French Conseil d'État invalidates decrees implementing law on out-of-commerce works' (8 June 2017), The IPKat, available at <http://ipkitten.blogspot.com/2017/06/french-counseil-detat-invalidates.html> (last accessed 15 August 2018).

Rosati, E, '*GS Media* and its implications for the construction of the right of communication to the public within EU copyright architecture' (2017) 54(4) CML Rev 1221.

Rosati, E, 'Intermediary IP injunctions in the EU and UK experiences: when less (harmonization) is more?' (2017) 12(4) JIPLP 338.

Rosati, E, 'The CJEU *Pirate Bay* judgment and its impact on the liability of online platforms (2017) 39(12) EIPR 737.

Rosati, E, 'The *Monkey Selfie* case and the concept of authorship: an EU perspective' (2017) 12(12) JIPLP 973.

Rosati, E, 'The right of communication to the public … in a chart' (24 July 2017), The IPKat, available at <http://ipkitten.blogspot.com/2017/07/the-right-of-communication-to-public-in.html> (last accessed 15 August 2018).

Rosati, E, 'Respect of family life cannot be abused to trump copyright protection, says AG Szpunar' (6 June 2018) The IPKat, available at <http://ipkitten.blogspot.com/2018/06/respect-of-family-life-cannot-be-abused.html> (last accessed 15 August 2018).

Rosati, E, 'The AG Opinion in *Levola Hengelo*: more questions than answers?' (25 July 2018), The IPKat, available at <http://ipkitten.blogspot.com/2018/07/the-ag-opinion-in-levola-hengelo-more.html> (last accessed 15 August 2018).

Rosati, E, *The Exception for Text and Data Mining (TDM) in the Proposed Directive on Copyright in the Digital Single Market—Technical Aspects* (2018), Briefing requested by the JURI Committee of the European Parliament, available at <http://www.europarl.europa.eu/RegData/etudes/BRIE/2018/604942/IPOL_BRI(2018)604942_EN.pdf> (last accessed 15 August 2018).

Rosati, E, 'When does copyright protection arise in works of applied art and industrial models and designs? A new CJEU reference' (25 January 2018), The IPKat, available at <http://ipkitten.blogspot.com/2018/01/when-does-copyright-protection-arise-in.html> (last accessed 15 August 2018).

Rosati, E, 'Why originality in copyright is not and should not be a meaningless requirement (2018) 13(8) JIPLP 597.

Rosén, J, 'How much communication to the public is 'communication to the public'?', in IA Stamatoudi (ed), *New Developments in EU and International Copyright Law* (Wolters Kluwer:2016).

Ross, A, '*Vcast Ltd v RTI SpA*—a cloudy judgment re network personal video recorders' (2018) 29(3) Ent L Rev 89.

Savič, M, 'The CJEU *Allposters* case: beginning of the end of digital exhaustion?' (2015) 37(6) EIPR 378.

Savič, M, 'The legality of resale of digital content after *UsedSoft* in subsequent German and CJEU case law' (2015) 37(7) EIPR 414.

Savin, A, *EU Internet Law* (Edward Elgar:2017), 2nd edn.

Savola, P, 'Proportionality of website blocking: internet connectivity providers as copyright enforcers' (2014) 5(2) JIPITEC 116.

Savola, P, 'The ultimate copyright shopping opportunity—jurisdiction and choice of law in website blocking injunctions' (2014) 45(3) IIC 287.

Savola, P, 'EU copyright liability for internet linking' (2017) 8(2) JIPITEC 139.

Schaefer, M, 'ISP liability for blocking access to third-party infringing content' (2016) 38(10) EIPR 633.

Schütze, R, *European Constitutional Law* (CUP:2012).

Schütze, R, 'Supremacy without preemption? The very slowly emergent doctrine of preemption' (2006) 43(4) CML Rev 1023.

Schweizer, M, 'The Enforcement Directive permits punitive damages—or does it?' (24 February 2017) The IPKat, available at <http://ipkitten.blogspot.com/2017/02/the-enforcement-directive-permits.html > (last accessed 15 August 2018).

Senftleben, MRF, *Copyright Limitations, and the Three-Step Test: An Analysis of the Three-Step Test and EC Copyright Law* (Kluwer Law International:2004).

Senftleben, MRF, Kerk, M, Buiten, M, and Heine, K, 'New rights or new business models? An inquiry into the future of publishing in the digital era' (2017) 48(5) IIC 538.

Seville, C, 'Copyright in perfumes: smelling a rat' (2007) 66(1) CLJ 49.

Sganga, C, 'The eloquent silence of *Soulier and Doke*' (2017) 12(4) JIPLP 321.

Sganga, C and Scalzini, S, 'From abuse of right to European copyright misuse: a new doctrine for EU copyright law' (2017) 48(4) IIC 405.

Smith, J and Deacon, L, 'Live blocking orders: the next step for the protection of copyright in the online world' (2017) 39(7) EIPR 438.

Smith, J and Newton, H, 'A pause in private copying: judicial review holds the UK private copying exception to be unlawful because there was no evidence to support the decision not to provide compensation to rights holders' (2015) 37(10) EIPR 667.

Spoor, JH, 'The copyright approach to copying on the internet: (over)stretching the reproduction right?', in PB Hugenholtz (ed), *The Future of Copyright in a Digital Environment* (Kluwer Law International:1996).

Stanley, S and Ringelhann, AP, 'Casting doubt on the legality of remote recording services' (2018) 40(5) EIPR 333.

Steyn, E, 'Private copying: unlawful once again' (2015) 21(7) CTLR 212.

Strowel, A, 'Secondary liability for copyright infringement with regard to hyperlinks', in A Strowel (ed), *Peer-to-Peer File Sharing and Secondary Liability in Copyright Law* (Edward Elgar:2009).

Strowel, A, 'Towards a European copyright law: four issues to consider', in I Stamatoudi and P Torremans (eds), *EU Copyright Law—A Commentary* (Edward Elgar:2014).

Synodinou, TE, 'The foundations of the concept of work in European copyright law', in TE Synodinou (ed), *Codification of European Copyright Law—Challenges and Perspectives* (Wolters Kluwer:2012).

Synodinou, TE, 'Decoding the Kodi box: to link or not to link?' (2017) 39(12) EIPR 733.

Torremans, P, 'Jurisdiction in intellectual property cases', in Torremans, P (ed), *Research Handbook on Cross-Border Enforcement of Intellectual Property* (Edward Elgar:2014).

Ubertazzi, B, 'The principle of free movement of goods: Community exhaustion and parallel imports', in I Stamatoudi and P Torremans (eds), *EU Copyright Law—A Commentary* (Edward Elgar:2014).

UK Intellectual Property Office, *Copyright Exception for Parody—Impact Assessment BIS 1057*, 13.12.12, 6, available at <http://webarchive.nationalarchives.gov.uk/20140603102738/http://www.ipo.gov.uk/consult-ia-bis1057.pdf> (last accessed 15 August 2018).

United States Copyright Office, *The Making Available Right in the United States—A Report of the Register of Copyrights* (February 2016), available at <https://www.copyright.gov/docs/making_available/making-available-right.pdf> (last accessed 15 August 2018).

Van Der Ende, M, Hageraats, M, Poort, J, Quintais, J, and Yagafarova, A, *Global Online Piracy Study* (July 2018), available at <https://www.ivir.nl/publicaties/download/Global-Online-Piracy-Study.pdf> (last accessed 15 August 2018).

van Eechoud, M, 'Along the road to uniformity—diverse readings of the Court of Justice judgments on copyright work' (2012) 3(1) JIPITEC 60.

van Eechoud, M, Hungeholtz, PB, van Gompel, S, Guibault, L, and Helberger, N, *Harmonizing European Copyright Law—The Challenges of Better Lawmaking* (Wolters Kluwer:2009).

Vinje, TC, 'Harmonising intellectual property laws in the European Union: past, present and future' (1995) 17(8) EIPR 361.

Vitoria, M and Others, *Laddie, Prescott and Vitoria—The Modern Law of Copyright and Designs* (LexisNexis:2011), 4th edn.

Vitorino, A, *Recommendations Resulting from the Mediation On Private Copying and Reprography Levies* (2013), available at <http://ec.europa.eu/internal_market/copyright/docs/levy_reform/130131_levies-vitorino-recommendations_en.pdf> (last accessed 15 August 2018).

Vivoda, J, 'After Sweden and Germany, *GS Media* finds its application in the Czech Republic' (6 February 2017), The IPKat, available at <http://ipkitten.blogspot.com/2017/02/after-sweden-and-germany-gs-media-finds.html> (last accessed 15 August 2018).

von Lewinski, S, 'International exhaustion of the distribution right under EC copyright law?' (2005) 27(7) EIPR 233.

von Lewinski, S, *International Copyright Law and Policy* (OUP:2008).

Voorhoof, D, 'Freedom of expression and the right to information: Implications for copyright', in C Geiger (ed), *Research Handbook on Human Rights and Intellectual Property* (Edward Elgar:2015).

Vousden, S, '*Infopaq* and the Europeanisation of copyright law' (2010) 1(2) WIPOJ 197.

Walsh, A, 'Parody of intellectual property: prospects for a fair use/dealing defence in the United Kingdom' (2010) 21(11) ICCLR 386.

Walter, MM and von Lewinski, S, *European Copyright Law—A Commentary* (2010:OUP).

Wilman, FG, 'A decade of private enforcement of intellectual property rights under IPR Enforcement Directive 2004/48: where do we stand (and where might we go)?' (2017) 42(4) EL Rev 509.

Wittem Group, The Wittem Project—European Copyright Code (2010), available at <https://www.ivir.nl/publicaties/download/Wittem_European_copyright_code_21_april_2010.pdf> (last accessed 15 August 2018).

World Intellectual Property Organization, *Guide to Copyright and Related Rights Treaties Administered by WIPO and Glossary of Copyright and Related Rights Terms* (2003).

Xalabarder, R, 'The role of the CJEU in harmonizing EU copyright law' (2016) 47(6) IIC 635.

Index

Printed and bound by CPI Group (UK) Ltd, Croydon, CR0 4YY